THE

Lives of the Saints

REV. S. BARING-GOULD

SIXTEEN VOLUMES

VOLUME THE FIFTEENTH

First Edition . . . . . *published 1872*
Second Edition . . . . ,, *1897*
New and Revised Edition, 16 *vols.* ,, *1914*

MADONNA ENTHRONED.

After the Picture by Cima da Conegliano, in the Louvre, Paris.

Dec., Frontispiece.]

THE

Lives of the Saints

BY THE

REV. S. BARING-GOULD, M.A.

With Introduction and Additional Lives of English
Martyrs, Cornish, Scottish, and Welsh Saints,
and a full Index to the Entire Work

New and Revised Edition

ILLUSTRATED BY 473 ENGRAVINGS

VOLUME THE FIFTEENTH

December

EDINBURGH: JOHN GRANT
31 GEORGE IV BRIDGE
1914

Printed by BALLANTYNE, HANSON & Co.
at the Ballantyne Press, Edinburgh

CONTENTS

vii

LIST OF ILLUSTRATIONS

LIVES OF THE SAINTS

December 1.

S. CASTRICIANUS, *B. of Milan ;* A.D. 136.
SS. DIODORUS, *P.M.,* AND MARIANUS, *D.M. at Rome ; circ.* A.D. 283.
S. ANSANUS, *M. at Siena ; circ.* A.D. 303.
S. OLYMPIAS, *M. at Emilia in Umbria ; circ.* A.D. 304.
S. NATALIA, *W. at Byzantium (see* Sept. 8); *circ.* A.D. 305.
S. FLORENTIA, *V. at Comblé in Poitou ;* A.D. 367.
S. ALGERIC, *B. of Verdun ;* A.D. 588.
S. ELIGIUS, *B. of Noyon ;* A.D. 659.

S. FLORENTIA, V.

(A.D. 367.)

[Gallican Martyrologies. Authority:—Lessons in the Poitiers Breviary; historically worthless.]

THE legend told of this saint is that when, in 359, S. Hilary in exile traversed Isauria on his way to attend a council at Seleucia, as he entered the church of a little village, a young girl precipitated herself at his feet, and conjured him to regenerate her and associate her with him in his ministry. He had her baptized, and when he returned to Arles, she followed him. He found it convenient to put her under restraint, and he confided the impetuous enthusiast to S. Triasia, who was living as a solitary at Comblé, near his estate at Celle-l'Evêcout. Her prayers, fasting, and vigils, exhausted her frame, and she died before the prelate, on December 1, 367. The relics were translated from Comblé to Poitiers in the 11th century, they were nearly all scattered by the Huguenots, who pillaged the churches of Poitiers in 1562, but some have been preserved, and are now in the cathedral of Poitiers.

S. ALGERIC, B. OF VERDUN.

(A.D. 588.)

[Roman and Gallican Martyrologies. Authorities :—Greg. Turon. Hist. Franc. lib. ix. c. 10, 12, 13, and a distich of Venantius Fortunatus.]

S. ALGERIC or Ageric, vulgarly called S. Airy, was born at Harville, in the diocese of Verdun, of a humble family. Thierry, king of Austrasia, acted as his godfather. He was sent to Verdun at the age of seven to study for the Church. He was only thirty-three when made bishop of Verdun, in the room of Desiderius, who died in 554. His simplicity, virtue, and charity, are praised by Venantius Fortunatus, who visited him at Verdun on his way home from Rome. He baptized Childebert, son of Sigebert of Austrasia. Bertfried, who revolted against Childebert, took refuge in the chapel of S. Algeric at the feet of the saint; the emissaries of the king pursued him, and in disregard of the remonstrances of the saint, killed Bertfried in the sanctuary.

S. ELIGIUS, B. OF NOYON.

(A.D. 659.)

[Roman and Gallican Martyrologies, Usuardus, &c. Authorities :—A Life by Dado (S. Ouen) bishop of Rouen, d. 683; in Ghasquière, AA. SS. Belgii, iii. p. 198; and Dachery, Spicil. v. p. 156; in Surius altered and curtailed.]

ELIGIUS was born at Châtelat near Limoges. His father's name was Eucherius, his mother's Terrigia. He was placed

early with a goldsmith of Limoges, named Abbo, master of
the mint there, and with him Eligius acquired great skill in
the work of the precious metals, and, perhaps, also in that
enamel work which afterwards made Limoges famous. He
went next to Paris, and was placed with Bobbo, treasurer of
Clothair II. The king wanted a seat, or throne, made of
precious metal, and as he could find no one else capable of
undertaking the task, he confided it to Eligius, giving him at
the same time the metal necessary for making the throne.
Eligius found that he had enough to make two seats. When
they were done he gave one to the king, who admired it,
and ordered payment to be made to the skilful workman.
Then Eligius produced the second throne.[1] The king was
so struck with his honesty, that he immediately advanced
him to be master of the mint, and gave him his entire confidence. The king, anxious to secure Eligius to him more
securely, brought him before some relics and bade him place
his hand on them, and swear to him devout allegiance. The
goldsmith hesitated: he was uncertain how far he could serve
his master with a good conscience. Clothair, instead of
being offended at this hesitation, respected it, and said he
had rather have the word of Eligius than the oath of another
man.

S. Ouen was then at the court of Dagobert; he was a young
noble, a few years the junior of Eligius. Ouen and Eligius
became mutually attached, and confided to each other their
desires and troubles. Eligius hung little packets of relics from
nails in the ceiling all round his bedroom. After having made
his general confession, and imposed on himself a penance,
he was very desirous of knowing if he were really pardoned,
and his penance accepted. One of the little hanging packets

---

[1] " Volebat rex sellam urbane auro gemmisque fabricare—et sellam auream regiæ
dignitati congruam." Mediæval artists rendered this a saddle, and made of Eligius
a farrier. Aimoin speaks of Dagobert using a golden throne, no doubt that fashioned
by Eligius.

began to emit a peculiar odour, and drip with some oily matter, and Eligius accepted this as an omen that he was absolved in heaven.

The affection borne by Clothair II. to Eligius passed to the king's son Dagobert, and this king honoured his master of the mint with his special confidence. He even chose him as his ambassador to the prince of Brittany, apparently Judicael, who had assumed the royal title, and attacked and defeated the Frank soldiers in the plains of Le Mans. Judicael was the father of S. Winoc and S. Judoc, and is also honoured among the saints. Dagobert found the Breton prince a dangerous neighbour, and the commission he gave to Eligius was a delicate one—to enforce on the prince the danger of provoking the powerful Frank monarch, and to establish peace without having recourse to arms. Judicael, according to Fredegar, came to Clichy and did homage to Dagobert.

Eligius returned to Paris, and occupied himself in hammering out gold and jewel-encrusted vessels for his master. As master of the mint he struck coins, some of these remain, bearing his name.[1] His friend S. Ouen gives the following description of his appearance :—" He was tall, with a ruddy face, his hair and beard were naturally curly ; his hands well-made and his fingers long, his face was full of angelic sweetness, and his expression was one of prudence and simplicity. At first he wore habits covered with gold and precious stones, he had also belts sewn with pearls. His dress was of linen encrusted with gold, and the edges of his tunic trimmed with gold embroidery ; indeed, his clothing was very costly, and

---

[1] (1) A gold ½ sou with the head of Dagobert on one side and the legend " Parisina ceve fit " (Parisina civitate fecit), on the other a cross and the legend " Dagobertus rex." Under the arms of the cross " Eligi." (2) Another gold ½ sou, with similar head and cross, and the legends " Parisiis fit " and " Eligius mone " (monetarius). (3) Another coin of same value, with legend " Mon palati " (moneta palatina) and " Scolare T.A." Under the arms of the cross " Eligi." (4) Another of same value, with legend " Parisi civ. . . .", " Dagobertus rex," and " Eligi fit." (5) One struck in 637 or 638 for Clovis II.

some of his dresses were of silk. Such was his exterior in
his first period at court, and he dressed thus to avoid singu-
larity; but under these rich garments he wore a rough sackcloth, and later on, he disposed of all his ornaments to relieve
the distressed, and he might be seen with only a cord round
his waist, and common clothes. Sometimes the king, seeing
him thus divested of his rich clothing, would take off his own
cloak and girdle, and give them to him, saying, ' It is not
suitable that those who live for the world should be richly
clad, and that those who despoil themselves for Christ should
be without glory.' "

Dagobert was ready to grant him any favour he liked to
ask in reason. Eligius requested the king to grant him the
estate of Solignac in Limousin, on which to found a monastery. The situation was delightful, a river swept round the
tongue of land on which the abbey was to rise, hills and
woods surrounded it, and the rocky descent to the river was
rich in spring with golden broom and purple lungwort, and
in autumn with crimson wild vine, yellow maples, and brown
beech. The abbey when completed by Eligius was filled by
a swarm of monks, the numbers grew to a hundred and fifty,
and when S. Ouen lodged there he found that it was unsur-
passed by any monastery in France in its regular observance
of discipline. He gave up his own house in Paris to S.
Aurea, to become a convent for religious women under her
guidance. His strict integrity appeared in the foundation of
this religious house, as in the making of a throne. He had
asked of the king a grant of the land on which the house
stood, and had been accorded it. He had represented it as
occupying so many yards of ground. But when outbuildings
were cleared away, and the land was remeasured, it was
found that his estimate was wrong by a yard or two, and that
there was more ground than he had represented. He at
once stopped the works, and refused to allow them to be

proceeded with till he had stated the fact to the king, and obtained his consent to the appropriation of the additional few yards. After this he rebuilt the dilapidated church of S. Martial. Not long after Paris was in flames, and the conflagration neared the new church. Sparks and smoke were carried over the roof, and at every moment it was thought S. Martial's church would burst into flame. Then Eligius cried out: "Martial! Martial! look well after thy church, for if thou dost not protect it, thou must be assured that Eligius will not take the trouble to rebuild it for thee." The saint took the hint, and saved the church from destruction.

He continued to work at the precious metals, and made shrines for a great many relics, the most famous ones were those for S. Martin and S. Brice. The marble tomb of S. Denys he covered with gold and jewels, he encased the ends of the altar in gold, with gold apples set with jewels, probably pomegranates, with crimson rubies for the seed bursting through the golden pods.

On the death of Acharius, bishop of Noyon, Eligius was elected to succeed him. He and his friend S. Ouen were consecrated the same day, May 14, Rogation Sunday, 640, he to the see of Noyon, including that of Tournai, with jurisdiction over Ghent and Courtrai, and Ouen to the bishopric of Rouen.[1]

As a bishop, Eligius was as conscientious as he had proved himself when a layman. He laboured indefatigably at the conversion of the half-Christian, half heathen Flemings, and at making his clergy lights to the world. S. Ouen has preserved to us a most precious sermon of Eligius, which throws much light on the superstitious practices then in vogue among the people. He warns his people not to regard sneezing as ominous, except, of course, of the coming

[1] "Consecrati sumus *gratis* ab episcopis pariter episcopi ego Rodamo (*sic*), ille Novimo."

on of a heavy cold in the head, nor to pay superstitious
regard to the songs of birds, nor to the days on which they
leave home—such as the first day of the new moon, or the
eclipses ; he forbids the observance of the first of January
with feasting, dancing, and profane ceremonies, or the
festival of S. John the Baptist, and the solstices, with capers,
"carols," and diabolical songs.[1] The observance of the
month of May he specially condemns ; as also the festivals of
moths and mice.[2] The lighting of torches along the side of
a road—not apparently for the sake of giving light, but for
some superstitious reason—was to be avoided. He reprobates
the custom of priests writing passages of Scripture on scraps
of paper to be hung round the neck as charms.[3] Such
charms, says S. Eligius, very sensibly, are not a Christian
remedy, but devil's poison.   The passing of cattle through a
hole made in the earth, or through a hole in a tree, is also to
be renounced ; women must not wear amber round their
necks, or in their zones, with invocation of Minerva.   Only
fools think, says Eligius, that madmen are affected by the
changes of the moon.   Quack doctors and witches are not
to be resorted to in cases of sickness, but the efficacy of
holy unction is to be tried, and that will prove of avail in
recovering the sick of his malady.   Fountains are not to be
held sacred, trees which receive veneration are to be cut
down, and whoever finds little representations of feet hung
up in cross roads is to fling them away.[4]   The sermon goes

[1] "Nullus in festivitate S. Joannis . . . . solstitia, aut vallationes, vel saltationes,
aut caraulus aut cantica diabolica exerceat."
[2] " Dies tinearum vel murum."
[3] An Irishman came to me one day in Yorkshire, and asked me for a " Gospel," *i.e.*,
for a text to be written on a scrap of paper to hang round his child's neck, "as a
preservative against measles and looseness of the bowels." These charms are commonly sought by the Irish of their priests, and are sewn up in little bags. They pay
a fee for them.
[4] " Pedum similitudines, quos per bivia ponunt, fieri vetate, et, ubi inveneritis, igni
cremate." The Council of Auxerre (589) forbade (art. 3) "nec sculptilia aut pede aut
homine lineo fieri præsumat."

on to give very wholesome moral advice, which, however, contains little that is peculiar.[1]

S. Eligius found most paganism hanging about the neighbourhood of Antwerp,[2] and he is said to have converted many Suevi. One would hardly have expected to find Swabians so far north as his diocese.

But if Eligius pursued the conversion of heathen and the perfecting of professed Christians as a duty, he prosecuted the discovery of the bones of martyrs with the zest of pleasure. Noyon flattered itself that it was the scene of the martyrdom of S. Quentin. If Quentin had died there, he must have been buried there. If buried there, he might be found. Eligius determined to discover the bones. Several persons represented to him that if buried, Quentin must have dissolved to dust long ago. But Eligius was above conviction by such arguments as these. He vowed not to eat a morsel till he had found a body which would, at all events, pass for that of S. Quentin. He turned up the earth of the church floor. The sacred precincts resembled a mine. Workmen grubbed here, and grubbed there, in all the most likely places, but found nothing. Eligius had passed three days without food, when at last, in the most unlikely place for a martyr's body to be laid, in the ditch of the church, the labourers came on a tomb of stones, and within it were bones and nails. The enthusiasm of Eligius passed into the wildest transports of exultation, when, on pulling the teeth

---

[1] Except, perhaps, this: "Qui ante legitimas nuptias habere concubinam præsumit, pejus peccat quam qui adulterium committit."

[2] In heathen times phallic worship prevailed in the neighbourhood of Antwerp. A phallus was sculptured over one of the city gates; this has been obliterated only in recent times. Christianity so far sanctioned this heathen superstition as to make the "sacrosanctum præputium" the palladium of Antwerp. In like manner in Elsass in heathen times the club of Hercules received sacred worship. When Elsass was Christianized this was converted into the staff of S. Peter given to S. Maternus. Fragments still receive veneration. The "sacrosanctum præputium" has been made to disappear; it has not, at all events, been presented to the adoration of the faithful since the riots of 1566.

out of the jaw for distribution to other churches, a drop of some slimy matter that looked like blood exhibited itself at the root of one of the fangs. The nails found in the vault had probably belonged to a wooden coffin, but their presence served to convince Eligius that he had the genuine body of the martyr, who, according to legend, was put to death by means of nails driven into his head.[1] After this discovery Eligius set to work to unearth other saints, and was so happy as to discover also S. Piatus, also with nails. He made gold shrines for all these relics, and also for the bodies of SS. Crispin and Crispinian, which he exhumed at Soissons. At Beauvais he discovered miraculously the body of S. Lucian, the companion of S. Quentin, and he made a shrine for him also.

He attended the council of Châlons-sur-Saône in 644 or 650—the date cannot be fixed with certainty; and it was on his return from this council that he took charge of S. Godeberta, as is related in the life of that saint (April 11).

S. Eligius died in 659, on December 1, in the midst of his faithful servants, beloved by his flock.

The relics of S. Eligius are still in the cathedral of Noyon. His head is in the parish church of S. André at Chelles. Other relics, teeth, bits of bone, &c., at S. Barthélemy, Noyon, the cathedral at Bruges, S. Martin at Tournai, S. Pierre at Douai. In the cathedral at Paris an arm.

In art he is represented erroneously as a farrier, with a horse's leg in his hand; the story going that as he was one day shoeing a horse, the animal proved restive, so he took the leg off, shod it, and put it on again, without evil consequences.

---

[1] It is, however, quite possible that this discovery of nails in the vault containing the supposed relics may have originated the fable of the martyrdom by means of nails.

December 2.

SS. Aurelia, Eusebius, Marcellus, and Others, *MM. at Rome;* A.D. 256.

SS. Severus, Securus, Januarius, and Victorinus, *MM. in Africa; circ.* A.D. 300.

S. Bibiana, *V.M. at Rome;* A.D. 363.

S. Chromatius, *B. of Aquileja; circ.* A.D. 409.

S. Peter Chrysologus, *B. of Ravenna;* A.D. 449.

S. Nonnus, *B. of Edessa; circ.* A.D. 468 (*see* S. Pelagia, Oct. 8).

S. Luperius, *B. of Verona;* 6th cent.

S. Trumwin, *B. of the Picts;* A.D. 686.

B. John de Ruysbroeck, *C. at Vauvert, near Brussels;* A.D. 1381.

S. BIBIANA, V.M.

(A.D. 363.)

[Roman Martyrology. Usuardus, Ado, Notker, &c. Authority:—
The Acts, which are wholly untrustworthy.]

. BIBIANA was the daughter of Flavian, prefect of Rome, and his wife Dafrosa. Her sister's name was Demetria. In the reign of Julian the apostate Apronius was appointed governor of Rome, and he began to persecute the Church—not in fact, but in the fabulous acts. As a matter of fact there was no persecution in the reign of Julian, though some Christians did suffer in the army under other accusations. Bibiana was, of course, not in the army, and it is most improbable that any virgin suffered for her faith in the reign of Julian. However, the story goes on to say that Apronius arrested and executed her father, Flavian, and he receives commemoration on December 22. Dafrosa was next decapitated, and is venerated on January 4. Demetria, when brought before the governor, died of excitement, and Bibiana, after having been in vain solicited to evil by an old woman to whom she was confided, was tied to a pillar and scourged to death.

Either there had been such a martyr in an earlier persecution, which is probable, or the romance which passes as her acts had acquired sufficient credence to impose on a pope a century later. For it would appear that Pope Simplicius built a church over her remains, near the Licinian palace. Pope Urban VIII. discovered the bodies of Bibiana, Demetria, and Dafrosa, and placed them in a porphyry shrine under the high altar. The office for S. Bibiana is a semi-double in the Roman Breviary. The pillar at which she was scourged to death is shown at Rome in the church bearing her name.

S. PETER CHRYSOLOGUS, B.

(A.D. 449.)

[Roman Martyrology, Dec. 2 and 4. Authorities :—Mention in Life of S. Germanus of Auxerre, his Epistle to Eutyches, &c.]

S. PETER CHRYSOLOGUS was a native of Imola. He was ordained deacon by his bishop, Cornelius. On the death of John I., bishop of Ravenna, Peter was elected by the clergy and people as his successor.

S. Germanus of Auxerre died at Ravenna, and was buried by S. Peter, who inherited as an inestimable treasure his old rough sackcloth.   Eutyches wrote to the archbishop to complain of his condemnation by Flavian, and Peter sent him a letter in reply which is still preserved. Seventy-six of his sermons are also extant. If they obtained for him his title of "Golden Speaker," the average powers of preaching at the period must have been very leaden. The chapel in which he was accustomed to officiate is still standing, adorned with contemporary mosaics, in the archiepiscopal palace at Ravenna.

S. TRUMWIN, B. OF THE PICTS.

(A.D. 686.)

[The Scottish Menology of Dempster. Authority:—Mention by Bede, H. E. l. iv. c. 12, 26, 28.]

TRUMWIN, a monk of Whitby, was ordained bishop in 681, and sent among the Picts, who were then subject to the Angles. After the battle of Nectanesmere, in which Ecgfrid, king of Northumbria, who had invaded their province, was defeated and slain, the Picts recovered their territory, and Trumwin retired from the monastery of Abercorn, where he had resided, to Whitby, along with a few companions. He died there, and was buried in S. Peter's Church. He was one of the religious who accompanied King Ecgfrid to Lindisfarne to persuade S. Cuthbert to accept the episcopate.

MURDER OF PETER MARTYR. (See April 29th.)

Probably after the Picture by Titian, formerly in the Chapel of
SS. Giovanni e Paolo, at Venice.

Dec., p. 12.]   [Dec. 2.

December 3.

S. Lucius, *K. at Coire in the Grisons.*
SS. Claudius, Hilaria, Jason, and Maurus, *MM. at Rome;*
   circ. A.D. 257.
S. Merocles, *B. of Milan;* A.D. 315.
S. Cassian, *M. at Tangiers;* A.D. 398.
S. Birinus, *B. of Dorchester;* A.D. 650.
S. Attala, *V. at Strassburg;* A.D. 741.
S. Solus, *H. at Solnhoven, near Eichstädt in Bavaria;* A.D. 790.
S. Galgan, *H. at Siena;* A.D. 1181.
S. Francis Xavier, *S.J. at San Can;* A.D. 1552 (*see* Nov. 30).

S. LUCIUS, K.

(DATE UNCERTAIN.)

[Roman Martyrology: "Curiæ in Germania Sancti Lucii Britan-
norum Regis qui primus ex iis regibus Christi fidem suscepit, tempore
Eleutherii Papæ." The Menology of Dempster: "In Scotia baptizatio
Lucii regis per Timotheum S. Pauli discipulum cum Emerita sorore."
The baptism of Lucius properly on May 26, and his death on Dec. 3.
At Mainz, S. Lucius on Dec. 5.]

UCIUS, king of Britain, baptized by Timothy the
disciple of S. Paul, by solemn decree converted
all the heathen temples throughout his realm into
Christian churches, and transformed the sees of
twenty-eight flamens and three archflamens into so many
bishoprics and archbishoprics. According to another version of the story, Lucius sent letters to Pope Eleutherius
(171-186)[1] desiring instructors in the Christian religion,
and was supplied with Faganus and Duvanus, who converted all Britain, and then returned to Rome to give an
account of their success. Lucius died childless at Glou-

[1] Or 179-194.

cester, says Geoffrey of Monmouth, and was buried there in the cathedral. But according to the belief of the Church of Coire in the Grisons, he made a pilgrimage to Rome in company with his sister Emerita, and died at Coire, where he was honourably interred, and where his relics are shown to this day.

Such are the extravagant stories of fiction. It is necessary now to ascertain on what foundation they repose. The story of Lucius, the British king, sending to Eleutherius for missionaries rests *solely* on the later form of the "Catalogus Pontificum Romanorum," which was written about A.D. 530, and which adds to the "Vita Eleutherii" in the earlier catalogue, among other things, that "He (Eleutherius) received an epistle from Lucius, king of Britain, that he might be made a Christian by his command." But this passage was not in the original catalogue, written shortly after A.D. 353, and was manifestly added in the time of Prosper, with the spirit of whose notices of the missions of Germanus and Palladius in 429 and 431 it precisely tallies. Bede (H. E., i. 4, v. 24, and Chron. in an. 180), copies the Roman account, giving however two different dates, and adding the names of the emperors, whom he calls Marcus Antoninus Verus and Lucius Aurelius Commodus. Gildas (A.D. 560), his usual authority for British Church history, knows nothing of Lucius. The earliest British testimony to the story is that of Nennius (9th century), who says, "After the birth of Christ one hundred and sixty-seven years,[1] king Lucius, with all the chiefs of the British people received baptism, a legation having been sent by the emperors of Rome and by Evaristus, the Roman Pope. Lucius was called Lleuer Maur, that is of Great Splendour, on account of the faith which came in his time."

The Roman story is copied—with fewer blunders, but

[1] Other versions 164 and 144. Evaristus was pope about 100-109.

equal exaggerations, and fresh details—by the Liber Landa-vensis (12th century)—" In the year of our Lord 156 Lucius, king of the Britains, sent his legates to Eleutherius, twelfth pope on the apostolic throne, imploring that according to his admonition, he might be made a Christian, &c." William of Malmesbury adds that the Roman missionaries Phagan and Deruvan came to Glastonbury. Geoffrey of Monmouth and Walter Mapes complete the story.

The Welsh Triads have something to say about Lucius. Bran ab Llyr, the father of Caradog, or Caractacus, is said to have been the first to introduce Christianity into Britain. Bran and Caradog were betrayed into the hands of the Romans by Arcgwedd Foeddog, who is supposed to be the Cartismandua of the Roman writer. Bran was detained seven years at Rome a hostage for his son, and by this means obtained an opportunity of embracing Christianity. At the end of the seven years, *i. e.*, in 88, he returned to Britain. But the Welsh tradition does not agree with the Latin historians. Tacitus mentions Caractacus appearing before Claudius with his wife and daughter and brothers, but makes no mention of the father, and Dion Cassius says that the father of Caractacus was Cunobelinus, who died before the war with the Romans commenced. The de-scendants of Bran are styled in the triads, one of the three holy families of Britain, and Eigen, a daughter of Caractacus, is recorded as the first female saint among the Britons. Claudia, the wife of Pudens, is also thought to have been a daughter of Caractacus. Cylliu, son of Caradog or Carac-tacus, is also called a saint; he was the father of Lleurwg, or Lleufer Mawr, the Lucius of ecclesiastical fable. One triad states that he erected the first church at Llandaff, the first in the isle of Britain; and that he gave freedom of country and nation, with privilege of judgment, and surety, to such as were of the faith of Christ. Another triad speaks of him as the founder of the church of Llandaff. And the Silurian Catalogue of Saints further relates that he applied to Rome for spiritual instruction; upon which, four persons, named Dyfan, Ffagan, Medwy, and Elfan, were sent him by Eleutherius. It is not possible to fix the date when these triads were composed. The second is certainly not earlier than the 7th century.

From the Welsh accounts Lucius or Lleurwg appears to have been only a chief of that part of Siluria which was afterwards known by the joint names of Gwent and Morganwg.

The triads make no mention of the mission to Eleutherius. The notice in Achau-y-Saint is too late to deserve regard as independent testimony. Still, putting together the evidence of the triads and of the Roman tradition, it is not impossible that there may have been such an expedition. But it must be remarked that the Roman missionaries supposed to have been sent by the Pope bear unquestionably British names. There are churches of very ancient foundations in Wales dedicated to Lleurwg, Dyfan, Ffagan, and Medwy.

Another legend of foreign growth represents Lucius as baptized by one Marcellus, bishop either of Tongern or of Trèves.[1] There was a Marcellus of Tongern about 250, according to the list drawn up by Hubert of Liége in the 8th century, but it is untrustworthy; and a Marcellus of Trèves, about the same period, probably the same man, if there be any reliance whatever to be placed on these lists. According to another version (Notker, Martyrol.) he was baptized, as already said, by Timothy, whom Dempster makes the disciple of S. Paul. At Coire, the story goes that Lucius having laid aside crown and sceptre, attended by his sister, crossed Gaul, passed through Augsburg, and came to the Alpine valley of the Grisons, and became the apostle of the Rhetian

[1] Gesta Treverorum.

Alps. He preached to the people, who then adored the
Urochs as a deity, and they cast Lucius into a hot spring,
from which, however, he issued unhurt. He then retreated
into a cave, the Luciuslöchlein, near Coire, with Emerita.
She was seized by the pagans and burned to death at Trim-
mis, and Lucius lost his life in the castle of Martiola, where
now stands the cathedral.

The Lucius of Coire is certainly quite another person
from the Lucius of Wales.

S. BIRINUS, B. OF DORCHESTER.

(A.D. 650.)

[Roman Martyrology. Hereford Kalendar, not that of Sarum. Authorities :—Bede, H. E. iii. 7; Roger of Wendover, Florence of Worcester, Henry of Huntingdon, &c.]

BIRINUS, monk of S. Andrew's monastery in Rome, a
child of illustrious parents, though apparently not of Roman
but of Teutonic race,[1] came to England at the instigation of
Pope Honorius, though probably as the result of his own
convictions, for he declared to the Pope that he "would
sow the seed of the holy faith in the inner parts beyond the
dominions of the English, where no other teacher had been
before him." He received episcopal consecration from
Asterius, bishop of Genoa.

A story, not told by Bede, but by later historians, who
incorporated legend in their records, with slightly differing
details, is that Birinus, having celebrated the holy sacrifice
before going on board ship, left behind him his corporal,
which was the gift of Honorius. When he remembered it,

---

[1] Birinus is probably Bjorn or Bærin or Berin, a compound expressive of Bear in
some form, High or Low German.

the ship was already out at sea ; in his sorrow, Birinus threw himself overboard and made for shore, recovered the corporal, and returned over the water to the ship, which remained stationary in spite of an off-shore wind. When the heathen mariners saw that his garments were not wet, they were amazed, and eagerly desired baptism. The ship was driven by the wind and weather to the coast of the Gewisse, or West Saxons, where he landed, 634. The voyage was represented in a window at the abbey church of Dorchester, but nothing remains of it but a few fragments of painted glass.

Finding that all the inhabitants were pagans, he determined to preach the word of God there, before proceeding further.

Next year he was at the court of Cynegils, king of Wessex ; Oswald, the saintly king of Northumbria, was also there, having come to demand of Cynegils the hand of his daughter Cuneberga in marriage. Cynegils was baptized in the presence of Oswald, who stood sponsor to him, and, as Bede says, "by an alliance most pleasing and acceptable to God, first adopted him, thus regenerated, as his son, and then took his daughter in marriage."

The union, according to later Roman usage, would have been regarded as incestuous, and demanded a special and expensive dispensation. The baptism is supposed to be represented on the font in Winchester Cathedral, and Robert of Gloucester thus recounts it in his Chronicle :—

> " Saint Birin the bishop, a holy man was,
> That into this land, through the pope Honorius, sent was
> To turn king of Westsex, Kingils, to Christendom
> And that land of Westsex, and to this land he come.
> S. Birin him to Christendom turnde through GODE's grace
> And as GOD wolde, S. Oswald was in thulke place ;
> And of holy font stone this great king did nome
> And his Godfader was, in his Christendom.

S. Oswald and this other king, through our Lourde's grace
Provided S. Birin to his will, a place
That Dorchester is called, that beside Oxenford is,
As in the east south, and seven mile I wis."

While Oswald remained with Cynegils, they consulted
together concerning the establishment of a bishop's see, and
as the kingdom of Mercia was without a bishop, Dorchester
near Oxford was fixed upon as being convenient for the
two kingdoms. The jurisdiction of the bishop extended
therefore over the modern dioceses of Winchester, Lichfield,
Worcester, Hereford, Bath and Wells, Salisbury, Lincoln,
Ely, Oxford, Gloucester and Bristol, Exeter, Peterborough,
and Chester. This arrangement was evidently but a temporary one, for Cynegils began to rebuild the cathedral at
Winchester, but died before it was completed, in the thirty-
first year of his reign, having enjoyed the happiness of a
long-extended peace. His remains are placed with those of
King Ethelwulf in a mortuary chest in Winchester Cathedral,
on the screen on the north side of the sanctuary.

After the death of Cynegils, his son Kenwalch succeeded.
"He refused to embrace the mysteries of the faith, divorced
his wife, the sister of Penda of Mercia, and married another."
This proceeding called down on him the wrath of the
redoubtable Penda, who attacked, defeated, and drove him
from Wessex. For three years he took refuge with Anna,
the Christian king of the East Angles, and there, considering
the political necessity of the case, or growing tired at once
of the new wife and of the position of a dethroned king, he
returned to the embraces of Penda's daughter and the
Christian Church. He was baptized by Bishop Felix, of East
Anglia, in 646. He was then restored to his kingdom. He
set to work at the completion of the church at Winchester,
and it was consecrated on Christmas Day, 648.

We have no record of the labours of Birinus during the

time he had the spiritual charge of the kingdoms of Wessex and Mercia. History only sums up the events of his life by informing us that he planted Christianity firmly everywhere, and consecrated churches. He gave his spirit to heaven on the 3rd December, having governed his church fourteen years. He was buried at Dorchester, but his body was removed to Winchester by Bishop Hedda, and an entrance to a vault in the cathedral bears his name amongst those of others whose bones repose therein.

S. ATTALA, V. ABSS.

(A.D. 741.)

[French, German, and Benedictine Martyrologies. Authority :— Strassburg Breviary.]

ATTALA, daughter of Adalbert, duke of Elsass, and of Jerlinda his wife, was brought up by her aunt, S. Odilia. She took the vow of virginity, and was placed by her father at the head of the monastery of S. Stephen he had founded at Strassburg. Her virtue, gentleness, prudence, and charity made her to be generally beloved and admired. She governed the sisters as abbess for twenty years, and died in the year 741, aged fifty-four.

S. SOLUS, H.

(A.D. 790.)

[German Martyrologies. Authority :—A Life written by Ermenold, or Ermanric, abbot of Elwangen (d. 866), in Mabillon, Acta SS. O. S. B. sæc. iii. p. 2.]

SOLUS was an Englishman, who followed S. Boniface into Germany, and was ordained priest by him. He sought out a solitary place near the banks of the Altmuhl in Bavaria,

and fashioned for himself there a simple cell. The place
was not unattractive, with the winding river, clear as crystal,
the beautiful, though not lofty hills,[1] with broken limestone
rocks peeping through the brushwood. The Romans had
worked quarries there,[2] and they were not, probably, then
wholly deserted. Solus may have served as missionary to
the rude quarrymen, and mused and wondered over the
fossils he found in the rocks they chipped, fish as distinct as
if killed the other day, and the impress and bones of the
pterodactyl, or flying lizard. No doubt he pointed to them
as proofs of the Deluge.

Solus found that the Altmuhl abounded in trout, and
especially in huge crayfish.

Charlemagne heard of his virtues, and gave him a grant
of the land all round his cell. Willibold, bishop of Eichstädt, not many miles distant, regarded his fellow countryman with great respect, so did also the bishop's brother
Wunebald.

His biographer tells an odd story about him, which he
heard from some old people of the neighbourhood. Solus
was one day travelling with his ass, when he came to a place
where sheep were pasturing without their shepherd, who
had deserted them for a while. Suddenly the ass pricked up
its ears, erected its tail, and dashed out of the road.[3] Solus
looked round, and saw a wolf crouching under a tree, watch-
ing the sheep. Then Solus called to his ass, " In the name
of my Lord Jesus Christ, O jackass, I command you, that
you attack the beast lying under that fruit tree, plotting
destruction to the sheep !"[4] Neddy at once arrested his

---

[1] " Undique alpibus celsis circumseptus est," an exaggeration of Ermenold.

[2] These quarries supply Europe with lithographic stones.

[3] " Cæpit assellus aures vicissim erigere, dein offensis pedibus caput in altum
extendere ; ad extremum elevata cauda declivis per avia currere cæpit."

[4] " In nomine Domini mei Jesu Christi, O asine, præcipio tibi, ut concito cursu
irruas in eam bestiam quæ sub frutice latet, insidiando insciis bidentibus."

precipitate career, dashed up to the startled wolf, and assailed him with hoofs and teeth. The shepherds arrived whilst this strange duel was going on, and watched in amused surprise till the ass stood panting, exultant, and bloody over the corpse of the ravenous beast.

Solus departed to his Lord on the 3rd December, about the year 790. A chapel was built where his oratory had stood, and his body was taken up and enshrined by the authority of Pope Gregory IV., in or about the year 830. Solnhoven became afterwards a monastery subject to Fulda.

December 4.

S. CLEMENT OF ALEXANDRIA, *P.D. at Alexandria; circ.*
A.D. 217.
S. BARBARA, *V.M. at Nicomedia; circ.* A.D. 235.
S. MELETIUS, *B. in Pontus; circ.* A.D. 320.
S. FELIX, *B. of Bologna;* A.D. 429.
S. MARUTHAS, *B. in Mesopotamia; circ.* A.D. 430.
S. THEOPHANES, *M. at Constantinople;* A.D. 780.
S. ANNO, *Abp. of Cologne;* A.D. 1075.
S. OSMUND, *B. of Salisbury;* A.D. 1099.

S. CLEMENT OF ALEXANDRIA.

(ABOUT A.D. 217.)

[Martyrology of Usuardus. Withdrawn from Roman Martyrology
the reasons given in the preface to the Martyrology of 1751. Authorities :—Eusebius, Jerome, and his own writings.]

TITUS FLAVIUS CLEMENS, commonly called
Clement of Alexandria, to distinguish him from
Clement of Rome, was one of the most distinguished Christian fathers of the third century.
The ancients were not agreed as to the place of his birth ;
some placed it at Alexandria, others at Athens, and say that
he only obtained his title from the fact of his having made
a long stay and taught in Alexandria.[1] His parents were
pagans, and he did not become a Christian till he had reached
the ripe age of manhood. On this account he classed himself with those who abandoned the sinful service of paganism
for faith in the Redeemer, and received from Him the forgiveness of their sins.[2] By free inquiry he convinced himself of
the truth of Christianity, after he had acquired an extensive

---

[1] Epiphan. Hær. xxxii. 6.   [2] Pædagog. ii. 8.

knowledge of the system of religion, and of the philosophy of Divine things known at his time in the enlightened world. This free spirit of inquiry, which had conducted him to Christianity, led him, moreover, after he had become a Christian, to seek the society of eminent Christian teachers of different mental tendencies in different countries. He informs us that he had had various distinguished men as his teachers : an Ionian in Greece, one from Cœlo-Syria, one in Magna Græcia (Lower Italy), who came originally from Egypt, an Assyrian in Eastern Asia (doubtless Syria), and one of Jewish descent in Palestine. He finally took up his abode in Egypt, where he met with a great Gnosticus, who had penetrated most profoundly into the spirit of Scripture. This last was doubtless Pantænus. Eusebius not only explains it so, but refers also to a passage in the Hypotyposes of Clement, where he has named him as his instructor.[1] Clement was ordained priest of the church of Alexandria, and was appointed by Demetrius, the bishop, to succeed Pantænus as president of the catechetical school, about A.D. 189. It was from this date that he became famous as a doctor and writer. His vast erudition, his thorough knowledge of Greek literature, his philosophic education, and his glowing eloquence, commanded the respect of the heathen, and drew them to his lectures. The most famous of his pupils were Origen and S. Alexander of Jerusalem.

Clement had occupied his position at Alexandria in the school for twelve years, when, in 202, the persecution broke out under Septimius Severus. He retired from Alexandria, and probably took refuge with his disciple Alexander, then bishop of Flaviades in Cappadocia. When Alexander was appointed coadjutor to Narcissus, bishop of Jerusalem, in 209, he followed him to that city and opened in it a school. In 211 Alexander sent him to Antioch to assist in the

[1] Præp. Evang. vi. 13.

election of a bishop. In a letter he thus describes Clement:—
"This epistle, my brethren, I have sent to you by Clement,
the blessed priest, a man endowed with all virtue, and well
approved, whom you already know, and will learn still more
to know; who, also, coming hither by the providence and
superintendence of the Lord, has confirmed and increased
the Church of God."[1]

This is all we know of the life of this remarkable man.
We do not know when he died, but as S. Jerome says that he
flourished under Septimius Severus and his successor Cara-
calla, he cannot have died later than 217.

We have three works of his, which form, as it were, a connected series: the first, his Exhortation to the Gentiles; the
second, his Pædagogos; and the third, his Stromata. The
Hypotyposes and other works of his pen are lost.

S. BARBARA, V.M.

(A.D. 235.)

[Roman Martyrology. Usuardus, Ado, Notker, &c. All Greek
Menæas and Menologies. Authority:—The fabulous Acts.]

USUARDUS and Ado in their martyrologies make S. Barbara a martyr in Tuscany; Metaphrastes says she suffered at
Heliopolis; Baronius, in the Roman Martyrology, sets her
down as a martyr at Nicomedia. One authority is just as
right as the other, for S. Barbara is a wholly mythical personage.

There was once upon a time a very wealthy and noble
Greek named Dioscorus, an idolater, who had a daughter so
beautiful in face and form that he shut her up in a tower,
very lofty and inaccessible, so that no man might see her,

[1] Euseb. H. E. lvi. c. ii.

and that thus she might be kept out of mischief. According to one account, however, he allowed her to take lessons of masters, of advanced age, or, no doubt, of disagreeable appearance.[1]

At last Dioscorus determined to marry her to a suitable partner, but when he broached the subject, he found his daughter wholly opposed to the scheme. By some means or other the lovely Barbara had imbibed the doctrines of the Gospel, and had resolved to dedicate her virginity to God. Her father was about to go a long journey. Before he departed, she expressed to him her desire to have a bath constructed at the basement of her tower, in which she could disport herself, and while away the tediousness of the long hours of her incarceration. Dioscorus consented, but gave strict orders to the workmen to make two windows to this bath so high in the wall as to be inaccessible to any impudent and forward youth who might desire to look in whilst Barbara was splashing in her bath. The judicious father departed before the bath was completed. Barbara urged on the workman the insufficiency of two windows, and insisted on their making a third. After great hesitation they consented to make a third opening. Barbara drew her finger on the marble rim of the bath, and a cross remained furrowed in the stone. On the return of Dioscorus from his journey, he was surprised and indignant at finding three windows to the bath-room instead of two. Barbara took occasion to preach to him on the mystery of the Trinity, and to illustrate and make it comprehensible by means of the three windows. She also pointed to the miraculous cross she had drawn on the marble, and continued her discourse on the mystery of Redemption.

Dioscorus was furious ; he drew his sword and rushed upon the maiden to put her to death. But suddenly the rock

[1] "On croit qu'Origene fut de ce nombre."—Guérin et Giry. He was unobjectionable on other grounds.

S. BARBARA.

After the Painting by Hans Holbein (the elder).

One of the wings of the Altarpiece of S. Sebastian in the Pinakothek, Munich.

cleft, received her into its bosom, and left Dioscorus striking furiously on its flinty surface.[1]

The excited and astonished parent tore about the mountain looking for his daughter. She had, in the meantime, slipped out of the rock at a distance from the tower. His search was in vain ; at last, however, he lit on two shepherds, and asked them if they had seen his daughter. They had, in fact, caught sight of Barbara emerging from the mountain, and knew where she was lurking. One of the shepherds, being a good man, told a lie, and said that he had not seen her anywhere. The other shepherd, being very wicked, pointed with his finger in the direction in which Dioscorus was to seek her. The father found her, kicked and beat her, and drew her by the hair before the chief magistrate, Marcian, who, when he saw her, was captivated by her appearance, and did his utmost to persuade her to sacrifice to the gods. She refused. He therefore ordered her to be stripped, and beaten, till her back and sides were raw. She was then taken to prison, when Christ appeared to her in a blaze of light and healed all her wounds. Next day she was again brought before the judge, who ordered her sides to be torn with iron combs, and her " venerable head " to be hammered. A girl named Juliana, who witnessed these barbarities, burst out crying. She was therefore arrested and treated in the same manner.

Notwithstanding the hammering on her " venerable head," the blessed martyr Barbara preserved her faculties, and was able to address an eloquent prayer to Heaven. Marcian then ordered the breasts of Barbara to be cut off, and that she should be led naked round the town. The virgin prayed, and Christ at once came from heaven with a gown and put it over her.

[1] So Thecla was received by a rock from pursuit. So the mother of Rabbi Jehuda the Pious was received by a wall at Worms, when a Christian drove his car against her. The recess in the wall is still shown at Worms. So also the mother of Rabbi Raschi (Scholmo ben Isaac) was saved from violence.

Marcian, at a loss what more cruelty to exercise on Barbara, gave sentence that she and Juliana should be executed with the sword.

As they were led to execution Barbara prayed. On reaching the destined place, her father cut off her head, and Juliana suffered likewise. A flash of lightning fell and consumed Dioscorus, another flash reduced Marcian to a smoking ash-heap. Accordingly S. Barbara is held to be the patroness of firearms, and is invoked against the lightning.

Just before her death she prayed that whoever should invoke her aid might receive what they asked, and a voice from heaven replied that so it should be. She is therefore also regarded as a proper saint to call upon at the hour of death; and as a patroness by whose aid one may insure not perishing without the last sacraments. She is accordingly represented not only with the three-windowed tower, but also holding a chalice with the Host above it.

The relics of S. Barbara are very numerous, especially in Germany.

The date of her death is as arbitrary as the fixing of the locality where she suffered. The real locality of her passion was the brain of the inventor of her legend.

S. MELETIUS, B.

(ABOUT A.D. 320.)

[Roman Martyrology. Usuardus, Ado, &c. Authorities :—Eusebius, H. E. lib. vii. c. 32 ; S. Basil, De Spir. Sanc. c. 29.]

MELETIUS, bishop of Pontus, called "Attic Honey," both from his name and his eloquence, was a man of great learning and virtue. In the persecution of Diocletian he took refuge in Palestine and remained there seven years, after which he returned to his diocese.

S. ANNO, ABP. OF COLOGNE.

(A.D. 1075.)

[Roman and German Martyrologies. Authorities :— A Life by a
monk of Siegburg, written in 1109, in Pertz, Mon. sc. xi. p. 465-514.
A valuable vernacular metrical Life by an unknown author, thought by
Lachmann to have been written in 1183, but by Holtzman to have been
composed by Lambert of Hersfeld (or of Aschaffensburg) in 1080. Of
this there are several editions ; the latest and best by K. Roth, " Leben
des heilen Anno, nach der Opitzischen Handschrift herausgegeben,"
München, 1848. Also especial mention of S. Anno in Lambert of
Aschaffensburg's contemporary Chronicle, from which the monk of
Siegburg makes verbatim extracts.]

S. ANNO was the son of Walter, count of Pfullingen and
Engela, of an honourable family, but not either wealthy or
important, and was destined for military service. But his
uncle, a canon of Bamberg, having visited the father of the
boy, persuaded him to let Anno be brought up for the
Church. He carried the lad back with him to Bamberg,
and instructed him in letters and the Latin tongue. He
became master of the school at Bamberg, and having gained
the goodwill of the Emperor Henry III., he was attached to
his person as chaplain. On the death of Hermann II.,
archbishop of Cologne, the emperor appointed Anno to that
important see, investing him with both crosier and ring.
He thought, no doubt, that by thus elevating a man of unim-
portant family and fortune he would secure the allegiance of
one of the most powerful electors of the empire, and attach
him to his crown. The people of Cologne were, however,
by no means pleased at having so insignificant a personage
set above them, and they received him with murmurs and
scoffs. He was consecrated in spite of their discontent, in
the cathedral church, on March 3, 1056. His gratitude was
forgotten in the pride of precedence above the haughty archbishop of Mainz, which was accorded him by Henry III., and

he forgot both gratitude and decency in his violent rebukes administered to the emperor, who went to him for confession before attending a diet of the empire. Anno even beat the emperor with his fists, slapped his face, and refused to allow him to wear his imperial crown next day, till he had disbursed a large sum of money, which Anno scattered amongst the poor.

In 1055 the emperor was in Italy, but was obliged to hasten home on account of an insurrection organized by Godfrey of Lorraine, and threats of war from France. Victor II., whom Henry had elevated to the papacy from the bishopric of Eichstädt, came to Goslar to the emperor in 1056, to the aid of his old master. He arrived to receive his confession, and administer to him the last sacraments. The emperor, in consequence of violent exertions in the chase, had caught a fever, which, working on a mind harassed by the perplexing state of affairs, brought him to the grave. He died, leaving an infant son, Henry, to the care of his wife Agnes of Poitou, and of Pope Victor.

Agnes, left alone at the head of the state, chose Henry, bishop of Augsburg, and Guibert, archbishop of Ravenna, to be her advisers. She was a pious, cultivated woman, but deficient in the energy befitting her station. She sought to rule the turbulent spirits of the age by gentleness and persuasion. One aim of her policy was to keep the haughty archbishops in check by means of the lay princes, and she endeavoured to unite the dukes to the young king by binding them with favours. Anno of Cologne and Siegfried of Mainz, with Eckbert, margrave of Meissen, and Otto, count of Nordheim, determined, if possible, to wrest the government from the hands of Agnes. The two archbishops were jealous of the bishop of Augsburg, a pious man, but proud, and not disposed to bribe them. They trumped up a vile report of criminal attachment between the pure empress and the holy bishop, and agitated men's minds with suspicion, to prepare them for the execution of the bold stroke which they contemplated.

Agnes was celebrating the feast of Pentecost on the island of Kaiserwerth in the Rhine. The conspirators were also there. After the banquet, when the young prince was in high spirits, the archbishop of Cologne invited him to inspect the new and beautiful ship that had brought him down the river. The boy was easily persuaded to enter the ship, when, at a signal, the vessel was cut adrift, and the rowers bowed over their oars, the sail was spread, and the boat shot up the river. The young king, fearing an attempt on his life, sprang overboard, but was saved by Count Eckbert and brought back again into the vessel. The confederates endeavoured to pacify him with flattery and assurances, and brought him safely to Cologne. In the meantime those on the island, seeing the archbishop's vessel breasting the stream, ran to the shore and shouted wrathfully against the confederates, bitterly inveighing against their treachery. The news spread like wild-fire, and the whole of Germany was in agitation. Many nobles demanded of Archbishop Anno that he should restore the king to his rightful guardians, the bishops of Freisingen and Halberstadt loudly and indignantly complained, the people murmured, and Anno saw his former popularity changed into hatred. But he was not disposed to relinquish his hold of the goose that laid golden eggs, and he used his power to bribe those loudest in their complaints into acquiescence in his plans. He made the bishop of Freisingen archbishop of Magdeburg, and he gave the archbishopric of Salzburg to the bishop of Halberstadt. To the bishop of Bamberg, who, after having been loaded with gifts by the empress Agnes, had turned against her, he restored the lordship of Froschheim and thirty-six estates of which he had been deprived by the emperor

Henry III. He stopped the mouth of Duke Ordulf of Saxony with munificent gifts of lands belonging to the emperor. Of course the confederates took good care to reward themselves out of the imperial possessions. To keep up appearances, Anno ruled that the regent and guardian of the young king should be that bishop in whose diocese he happened to reside, but he was fully resolved not to let his charge escape his guardianship, and if allowed to leave Cologne it was only that Henry might pass to the care of the archbishop of Mainz, who was in league with him. But perhaps the most dreadful incident in the whole of this infamous proceeding was the revengeful murder of the bishop of Augsburg, whom Anno and his confederates condemned, on notoriously false charges, to a horrible and shameful death.[1] The broken-hearted empress, bereft of her son, resigned the regency, and retired to an Italian convent. However, Anno soon found out that King Henry hated him and the archbishop of Mainz alike, and that from this cause it was impossible for him to obtain the power he desired. He was therefore obliged to look out for someone who could adapt himself to the position by acquiring the confidence of the youth, without becoming independent of the archbishop. He hoped to have found such a man in Archbishop Albert of Bremen, a prelate of high birth, great accomplishments, and courteous manners. Anno was austere and sanctimonious, and Henry made no secret of his hatred of him. Albert was a gentleman, the brother of the Palatine Frederick of Saxony, was a keen politician, zealous in spreading Christianity among the heathen of Scandinavia, accustomed to, and loving pleasure, was very handsome, pure in morals, fond of splendour, munificent in his charities, a genial friend, but an implacable enemy. He had formed the plan of raising the number of bishoprics under

[1] "Coleis ligneo palo pertusis."

his rule to twelve, and of constituting himself Patriarch of the North. To carry out this scheme it was necessary for him to have a share in the government of the empire, and when Anno of Cologne offered to admit him to the joint guardianship of the young king he embraced the proposal with enthusiasm, and in a very short while had obtained for himself nearly the whole of the power.

Archbishop Albert won the favour of the young king, who was only too glad to escape the cloistral monotony of the palace of Cologne for the splendid luxury of that of Bremen. Archbishop Albert, instead of rebuking the boy for his faults, laughed at them—instead of going counter to his wishes, gave them full rein; and treated with equal indulgence his companion and friend Count Werner, a frivolous and undisciplined youth. Albert, himself loving pomp, gave the king a train of courtiers, and prepared for him magnificent banquets and varied entertainments, the cost of which was defrayed from the funds of the see. In order to protect himself from the envy of powerful vassals of the crown, he had recourse, like Anno, to bribery. For this purpose he gave away the wealthy abbeys. Archbishop Siegfried of Mainz was given, together with other imperial estates, the abbey of Seligenstadt; Archbishop Anno of Cologne, who had already managed to appropriate a ninth part of the imperial treasure, was further enriched by the gift of the abbeys of Malmedy and Cornelis-Münster; Duke Otto of Bavaria received the abbey of Kempten; Duke Ordulph of Saxony was secured by the gift of the castle of Ratzeburg; Count Werner, the king's favourite, received Kirchberg, although it belonged to the abbey of Hersfeld, and Archbishop Albert had no right to dispose of it. The bishop of Speyer was given two abbeys, and all the other bishops and archbishops were given monasteries, lands, and privileges at the expense of the imperial crown. Archbishop Albert of

Bremen, as may be supposed, took care to feather his own nest well. The amount of lands, the number of monastic houses, whose revenues he appropriated was enormous. The empire during the regency of the bishop of Augsburg and the archbishops of Cologne, Mainz, and Bremen, was a great mine which these unscrupulous prelates plundered at will.

Archbishop Anno had used his time of power to enrich his relations and friends : in defiance of the right of election belonging to the chapters, he appointed his brother Wetzel to the archbishopric of Magdeburg, his nephew Burkhard to the bishopric of Hildesheim, and his friends Eilbert and Wilhelm to the bishoprics of Minden and Utrecht. But Albert was too proud to distribute church offices among his relatives, at the cost of the empire. He desired that those whom he benefited should derive their benefits from himself alone. He therefore made to his kinsmen munificent presents in money out of his own possessions. Those lands which the king gave him he gave as feudal tenures to others, or to the diocese, being desirous of making a great show through the number of his vassals. Before he had become governor of the king he had spent his revenues in building churches; now they went in the erection of castles, and in the satisfaction of extravagant caprices. He amused himself by turning barren districts into gardens and vineyards, not for purposes of utility, but to astonish by the exhibition of his power. At the same time he lost all control over himself : when he was angry he struck those who offended him, even priests, till he drew blood; if he felt a charitable impulse, he gave extravagantly : thus, on one occasion, he gave a beggar a hundred pounds of silver.

His extravagance in time exhausted the revenues of his see and of the royal possessions, and he then had recourse to unworthy means of supplying himself with the means necessary for keeping up his usual sumptuousness and lavish expenditure. First he ground down his subjects with taxes, and after that sold bishoprics, abbeys, and every office in Church and State. The proceeds he divided with Count Werner, the king's favourite. At last no single office could be had, whether secular or ecclesiastical, except by purchase. To increase his revenue he tried to obtain from the king the wealthy abbeys of Lorsch and Corbie. He endeavoured by every means in his power to obtain the deposition of the abbot of Lorsch, but the abbot conducted himself with such caution that no occasion could be found against him. Then the king without excuse gave the abbey to the archbisLop; but the retainers of the abbot assembled, armed, in such numbers to oppose his taking possession, that Albert did not venture to enforce his claim. The king nominated the abbot of Corbie to the bishopric of Pola, in Istria, to draw him from his possession; but Duke Otto of Bavaria having discovered that the bishop of Pola was alive, and that the nomination was a trick to get the abbot out of the way in order to install the archbishop of Bremen in his place, protected the abbot. Other abbots were not so fortunate. They were forced to pay large sums to the king and the archbishop to be allowed to retain peaceable possession of their lands and offices. When Bishop Gunther of Bamberg was dead, his steward betook himself to court, and bought the bishopric for himself.

The pride and avarice of the archbishop of Bremen had stirred up against him many enemies, and a conspiracy was formed to oppose and overthrow him by Archbishop Anno of Cologne, Archbishop Siegfried of Mayence, the Dukes Rudolf of Swabia, Otto of Bavaria, and Gottfried of Lorraine. A diet was held at Tribur, and the king was required either to abdicate the throne, or to dismiss the archbishop from his court. The king gave no answer, and Archbishop

Albert advised him to take horse and fly by night with the imperial insignia to Saxony. The confederates were informed of this, and placed guards round the palace; and the king was obliged to disgrace the archbishop. Albert retired humbled and poor to his exhausted see, and was reduced to live on the pittance he could drain from the monasteries of his diocese.

The character of the young emperor had been ruined by his two episcopal governors. Anno had been harsh, conscientious in a way, ascetic in life, and despotic in his rule of the youthful prince. Albert had been the reverse in every particular. The sudden change from the severity with which he had been disciplined by Anno to the unlimited indulgence with which he was treated by Albert was most pernicious. The gravity and study to which he had been inured had been abruptly exchanged for the thoughtless gaiety of a luxurious court, where affairs of State were treated as lightly as a jest.

The unbridled simony of the archbishop knew no scruple as to the means whereby he could obtain benefices of importance for his partizans. He is accused, perhaps unjustly, of having employed for this shameless object the caresses of beautiful courtezans, and even of abbesses and nuns of high birth, to extract from the prince the letters, signatures, and donations requisite for the success of his plans. But as Albert, with all his faults, was of pure morals himself, this charge is perhaps an invention of his enemies. The disorderly life of the king was beyond his control, but it was his fault that this was the case.

The fall of Albert reinstated Anno, who had no sooner resumed the power, than he appointed his nephew Cuno to the archbishopric of Trèves, in defiance of the right of election which had always belonged to the clergy and people of the electorate. As the people of Trèves refused to receive the archbishop thus unconstitutionally forced upon them, Anno sent a body of armed men, and the bishop of Speyer to induct him into the see; but Count Dietrich, marshal or vogt of the diocese, attacked him at Bittburg, cut the retinue to pieces, and plundered the treasure of the archbishop. The bishop of Speyer took refuge in a church behind the altar, where he was caught and cudgelled, stripped of his clothes, and obliged to fly barefooted and half-naked on an old horse. The intrusive archbishop was loaded with chains, brutally maltreated, and then given to some knights to make away with. They threw him down some rocks, but as he still breathed, ran him through with their swords. The murderers were never punished.[1]

In 1065, Henry had been, at Anno's advice, solemnly declared capable of bearing arms. No sooner was his sword girded on, than he drew it jestingly upon Anno—an action at once indicative of dislike and levity.

Anno next committed the grave mistake of forcing on the young prince a wife whom he detested. Bertha, daughter of the Italian margrave of Susa, a noble-spirited woman, who only wanted beauty easily to supplant the mistresses of the young emperor, had been affianced to him in childhood. Anno insisted on their being married, and Henry, as soon as the marriage ceremony was over, deserted her, and refused to live with her.

In the meantime, owing to the dissensions that prevailed throughout the empire, and the humiliation of Albert of Bremen, who for three years was obliged to remain in concealment, the Saxons devastated the archdiocese of Bremen, and the Northern Sclaves in Mecklenburg and Pomerania rose and extirpated Christianity. The vain attempts of Ordulf of Saxony, and, after his death, those of his son Magnus

[1] A full account of this transaction is given by a contemporary, Dietrich, monk of Tholei.—Pertz, Mon Sacr. viii. p. 212.

to oppose the inroads of the Sclaves merely added to the
misery of the Saxons, and embittered their hatred of their
inactive and licentious emperor. Hamburg and Mecklenburg were destroyed by the pagans, who sacrificed John,
bishop of Mecklenburg, to their deities, stoned S. Ansverus,
the abbot of Ratzeburg, and twenty-eight monks to death,
assassinated Gottschalk, the Christian chief of the Obotrites,
at Leuzen, at the foot of the altar, and turned his Danish
wife out naked.

Whilst the north was thus convulsed, the imperial court
presented a continued scene of petty dissension. The
emperor, still influenced by the prejudices of his youth, was
alternately swayed by conflicting passions, but at length,
notwithstanding the opposition of Anno and Bertha, recalled
Albert of Bremen to court in 1069. The fidelity and patience
of the wretched empress merely contributed to increase the
dislike manifested towards her by her husband, and to
strengthen his resolution to free himself from the tie that
bound him to her. Siegfried, archbishop of Mainz, offered
to assist him in procuring a divorce, on condition of receiving
in return the tithes of Thuringia. To these tithes he had
no right, except this : that during the minority of Henry
his predecessor had obtained from the prince a donation of
them. This the Thuringians had steadily and successfully
resisted. The promise of Henry to support the claim embittered the Thuringian nobles against him. In a diet held
at Worms Henry made a public declaration of his uncon-
querable aversion to his unoffending wife, from whom he
demanded a separation. His plan was frustrated by the
arrival of S. Peter Damiani, the legate of Pope Alexander
II., whose eloquence impressed even his versatile mind.

The death of Albert of Bremen, which, fortunately for
the empire, took place in 1070, once more threw the reins
of government for a short period into the hands of Anno.

A synod held by the emperor at Erfurt, in which he imposed the tithes demanded by the archbishop of Mainz on Thuringia, effectually alienated the minds of the Saxon bishops from him, and in 1073 a conspiracy was formed against him by the Saxon and Thuringian nobles, and among the bishops, by Wetzel of Magdeburg, by Bucco of Halberstadt, whose pursuits were rather those of a warrior than a bishop, Anno's nephew, and Henry's most violent opponent, and by Benno of Meissen, a peaceful missionary, a planter of the fruit tree and the vine, besides all the other Saxon bishops, with the exception of those of Bremen, Zeiz, and Osnabrück, who sided with the emperor, and were consequently expelled the country.

But it would carry us too far to follow the miserable discords of that long reign, and relate all the treasons, insurrections, and violences of the German bishops against Henry IV. His fifty years' reign was passed in contest and bloodshed. He fought sixty-two battles, and in each one of those a prelate was among his opponents. The many opposition kings who started up were all supported by the bishops, who even incited his own son to supplant him.

It was in 1104 that Henry, the best loved and youngest son of the old emperor, instigated by Pope and prelates, raised his hand against his father. The touching appeals of the emperor to his son being disregarded, Henry IV. put himself at the head of his troops and marched against him; but the emperor discovering that he was betrayed by his followers, fled in the sorrow of his heart. He had still numerous adherents in the Rhineland, and his son, finding force unavailing, attempted by cunning to oblige him voluntarily to abdicate the throne, and proposed a conference at Coblentz. The emperor came; but struck to the heart at the sight of his ungrateful child, flung himself at his feet, exclaiming: " My son, my son, if I am punished by God for my sins, at least stain not thine honour by sitting in judgment on thy father."

The emperor was shut up in the Castle of Bingen, and was required by the archbishops of Mainz and Cologne, and the bishop of Worms, to surrender the crown jewels. The aged emperor placed the imperial insignia of Charlemagne on his own person, and appearing in state before the bishops, defied them to touch the ornaments worn by the ruler of the world. But to these prelates nothing was sacred : the crown and mantle of Charlemagne were plucked off him, and they hasted to adorn with them the person of his son, then at Mainz. The fallen emperor was given into the hands of Gebhard, bishop of Speyer, who took a fiendish pleasure in humbling and tormenting the prostrate monarch, aged fifty-four. He kept him without sufficient food, so that the old emperor was obliged to sell his boots in order to procure bread. Henry IV. had formerly richly endowed the cathedral of Speyer, and he entreated the haughty prelate to grant him a prebend, to supply his necessities. The meek request was scornfully refused. He was forbidden the use of a bath and of a barber to shave him, and even of a priest to confess him. At length he found means of escaping into Lorraine, where he was offered a refuge by the bishop of Liége and the count of Limburg. His rebel son pursued him, but was defeated on the Meuse. The old king died at Liége, after solemnly pardoning his son, in token of which he sent him his sword and ring. But the animosity of the prelates followed him after death. They forced Bishop Albert of Liége, who had buried him in the church of S. Lambert with imperial honours, to dig him up and lay him in unconsecrated ground, where an aged pilgrim from Jerusalem for several years watched over his tomb. In 1111, his body was brought to Speyer, but the bishop refused to allow Divine service to be performed over it, placed the bones in an unconsecrated chapel, and put to penance those who had taken part in the ceremony.

We have seen a good deal of the doings of Archbishop Anno, but we have not seen all that darkens his character. A saint he has been regarded because he fasted, and prayed, and saw visions, but there was little of sanctity of the truest and noblest description in this ambitious and revengeful prelate. As has been already shown, he left no stone unturned for acquiring wealth, possessions, and power, whilst he was self-constituted guardian of Henry IV. Amongst other abbeys which attracted his rapacity was that of Malmedy; and he obtained it for himself from the king. But the abbot of Stablo (Stavloo) claimed the abbey of Malmedy as belonging to Stablo, as it certainly did, and Abbot Dietrich loudly and vehemently protested at this infringement of his rights. His protests were not listened to, for the young king was wholly in the hands of the archbishop, and Frederick, duke of Nether Lorraine, the protector of Stablo, was either not powerful enough or interested enough in the quarrel to reverse the donation made to S. Anno.

The abbot was invited to the royal court at Tribur, near the Rhine, above Mayence, and when he remonstrated at the separation of Malmedy from Stablo he was arrested. However, he persisted in asserting his right, and was at length liberated. In vain had the abbot expended the treasures of his church in presents to the courtiers and to the king himself; in vain also had he procured a brief from the Pope in his favour: Anno remained in possession, and boldly affirmed that he would not surrender it even were the patron of the house, S. Remacle, still alive. As the abbot had tried every ordinary means to recover his rights to Malmedy, and they had failed, he had recourse to a singular expedient, prompted by despair.

King Henry had summoned a diet at Liége in 1071. The Abbot Dietrich betook himself thither with all his monks in solemn procession, carrying the bones of the blessed Remacle, and these he laid on the table before the king as he sat at banquet with his lords and prelates. Henry was startled, and gave a solemn assurance to the abbot that he would investigate the claims of Stablo at the diet. The abbot urged an immediate examination. Archbishop Anno, who sat at the right hand of the emperor at table, rose, and angrily advised the king not to let himself be turned into ridicule by the monks. The king left the table, unable to proceed with his meal in such close proximity to the august relics of the saint, and the abbot refused to remove the bones from the banquet table till right was done him. In the meantime the crowd that had followed the procession poured into the hall and shouted frantically for justice. A few miraculous cures happening on the spot still further excited the mob. Anno stormed, and swore that the miracles were impostures, but the people would not attend to his words, and when the king saw that the temper of the people would not brook opposition, he promised to confirm the rights of the abbot of Stablo to Malmedy, and threatened Anno with his displeasure if he did not peaceably restore Malmedy to the monks, and assured him, in the event of his neglecting to comply with his orders, that he would wrest the abbey from him by force.

Then the monks returned in triumph to their cloister, bearing the bones of their patron, and the king resumed his seat, and continued his meal.

In 1074, Archbishop Anno celebrated Easter at Cologne, and Bishop Frederick of Münster was his guest. On the day of the bishop's departure, S. Anno sent his servants to the Rhine to prepare a vessel for the accommodation of the bishop. The servants took the ship of a rich merchant, and ordered the sailors to unlade it of all the wares. The sailors refused, and the merchant's son, a bold young man, much esteemed in Cologne for his excellent qualities, called his friends to his assistance and drove off the archbishop's servants and the town constable, who had been summoned to their assistance. The constable called out the mercenaries, and there would have been a bloody skirmish had not the archbishop threatened with his ban whoever broke the peace. S. Anno was far too haughty to bear with equanimity the refusal of the vessel to his servants. Next feast of S. George he ascended the pulpit and rebuked in most violent terms the audacity of the city in refusing him the vessel, and declared that if the citizens did not do penance therefor, they would become the prey of Satan and all his devils. The merchant's son, who was present during the sermon, was highly incensed. He hurried to his friends, stirred up the people, reminded them of the citizens of Worms, who, without being as powerful and wealthy as those of Cologne, had driven away their bishop when he had taken part against the emperor, and urged the good folk of Cologne to do the same. Many young men, apprentices and sons of merchants, joined him, and attacked the archbishop's palace, where, at the moment, S. Anno was banqueting with the bishop of Münster and his friends. The mob broke the windows, penetrated into the courtyard, and threw stones into the hall. The servants of the archbishop were killed or driven back.

Whilst the Cologne mob was storming the palace, the servants of the bishops conveyed the two prelates by a secret passage into the cathedral, and locked and barricaded the doors. A moment after, the mob burst into the palace, and sacked it from the attics to the cellars. Some stove in the barrels and let the rich wine flow away; others carried off all the costly goods they could lay hands on. Such an abundance of wine was let out, that the cellar was flooded, and several men were drowned in it. A servant, mistaken for the archbishop in the scuffle, was murdered; but when it was discovered that the saintly archbishop had taken refuge in the cathedral, the people streamed towards it, surrounded it, and threatened to fire it unless the obnoxious prelate was given up. But the night was far spent, and Anno took advantage of the darkness to disguise himself in a lay dress, and to escape out of the cathedral and take refuge in the house of one of his servants, to whom he had shortly before accorded permission to break a doorway through the city walls from his house, which was built against them. Through the door he fled the town, and escaped his enemies. He met the bishop of Münster and his servants with horses awaiting him, and he escaped to Neuss. In the meantime, the rioters were storming the minster, and breaking open the doors with sledge hammers. The servants within pretended that they were searching for the prelate, but could not find him, and when they felt satisfied that he was safe, they threw open the door, and the mob rushed in to seek him themselves.

After the people had satisfied themselves that the archbishop was not there, they locked the city gates, and sent a deputation to the emperor, who was then quarrelling with Anno, to inform him that they had been forced to maintain the honour of their city against the archbishop, and that they requested Henry to take possession of Cologne.

But the news had spread through all the electorate, and the peasants, who had a great veneration for the sanctity and liberality of their archbishop, rose in his support against the citizens, with whom there had been a long-standing jealousy. S. Anno soon found himself at the head of an army, and he at once marched against his capital. The citizens, alarmed at the promptitude and power of the prelate, sent an embassy to him, asking pardon, and promising amendment. The archbishop answered that he would not withhold forgiveness. He sang a High Mass at S. Gereon's, which was then outside the city walls, and after it ordered as a preliminary that all those who had taken part in the insurrection should be put to penance. They accordingly appeared before him barefoot, in white sheets, and he had the greatest difficulty to restrain the peasants from falling upon them. He then commanded all to appear the next day in S. Peter's church, and hear his ultimate decision. The night he spent in prayer in S. Gereon's church.

The citizens of Cologne were not at ease, for clemency was not a distinguishing feature in his saintly character, and during the night six hundred of the wealthiest burghers fled for protection to the emperor. In the meantime the servants of Anno entered the city, and pillaged the houses and murdered the citizens who resisted them; but this was without Anno's knowledge, he was busy praying among the bones of the Theban martyrs, and knew nothing of what was taking place among his living subjects.

Anno's final judgment, after long prayer, was that the young merchant and many of his companions should have their eyes plucked out, that many others should be publicly whipped, and that others should be expelled the city. All who remained in the city were to take oaths of allegiance to the archbishop.

Although the people of Cologne were certainly guilty of insurrection, yet unquestionably Anno was to blame in forcing them to it, and his savage reprisals led to most disastrous results. The city, which, like Mainz, had been the most populous and wealthiest of the German cities, was suddenly reduced to desolation. The streets were empty, the houses fell into ruin, and the markets were deserted.

With what bloody severity S. Anno administered justice

may be gathered from another instance. A widow complained to him that the magistrates had given wrong judgment against her. The archbishop summoned the magistrates before him to Siegburg, where he held his court, and finding that the widow's appeal was just, he had all the magistrates blinded except one who was his own kinsman. There were seven whose eyes were plucked out ; and by the archbishop's orders stone heads without eyes were built into the walls of their houses as a witness to all the town of his uncompromising love of justice.

He set priests to acts as spies at night, and watch for men who followed women of loose character. These men he seized, shaved their heads, and publicly branded them.

Anno is renowned for several miracles. Perhaps the most interesting of them is the following. He was one day saying Mass, and had just come to the fraction of the Host, when a fly buzzed up, and carried off a particle.[1] The horror of the saint cannot be expressed in words. He grew deadly pale, his blood froze in his veins, his conscience smarted for his incaution, and in an agony of remorse, and a tempest of groans and tears, he prayed that the fly might restore what it had taken. Scarcely had he done praying, when the insect returned, deposited the particle on the paten, then fell over on its back, was convulsed, and died miserably.[2]

He had visions. In the church of S. Gereon lay, somewhat disregarded, the bones of three hundred and sixty martyred Moors. When S. Gereon and the Theban legion had been put to death at Cologne and Xanten, a legion of Moors had been sent to the Rhine to supply their places. But on their arrival, it occurred to the authorities to inquire

[1] "Imago dæmoniorum, musca videlicet spurcissima visu nauseam generans impetu super corpus Domini ruit, ereptamque morsu particulam, cum maximo dolore sacerdotis avolans exportavit."

[2] "Seorsum super altare ruit exanimis, dignam tanti flagitii pœnam luens."

into their religious convictions, and they found to their disgust that the empire had again been put to the expense and trouble of conveying to Germany a band of Christian soldiers. They were accordingly also put to death. The people of Cologne were certainly not kept short of relics; they had the bones of the eleven thousand virgins, and of S. Gereon with his three hundred and ten companions. They might therefore be excused, one would have thought, if they somewhat overlooked the merits of the black martyrs. However, these latter were not disposed to be treated with indifference. One night S. Anno saw himself in vision in the church of S. Gereon, in the midst of a council of negro saints, whom he would probably have mistaken for devils, but for the aureoles about their heads. The martyrs complained of the neglect of the prelates and people of Cologne, and resolved by acclamation to make the present occupant of the see suffer for it. The three hundred and sixty thereupon fell on Anno, pummelled and lashed him, till the breath was all but beaten out of his body. When he woke, aching in all his bones—no doubt with rheumatism—he resolved to give the holy Moors the respect and devotion they demanded. The church of S. Gereon was then circular. He added a nave, and enlarged the crypt, and magnificently enshrined the black saints.

On his way to Salfeld, in Thuringia, riding in his car, he was rapt in vision, and became so big and heavy with the mysteries revealed to him, that his attendants were obliged to yoke sixteen horses to the conveyance to get it along.[1]

Just before his last illness, in vision he saw himself in a magnificent mansion surrounded with thrones, all occupied by the great bishops and saints of the German Church. One throne was vacant, and Anno went forward to take it. Then

[1] "Sülich mancraft ihn unvieng, daz man sescein ros ci demo wagine spien."—Annolied, 41.

up rose Arnold of Worms and forbade him, saying that he was not destined to occupy the seat till he had purged his conscience from the stain that defiled it. Anno looked round, and saw the same prohibition on the faces of Bardus of Mainz, of Boppo and Eberhard of Trèves, and of Cunibert of Cologne. Then the vision faded, and when he woke and considered the matter, it occurred to him that he had nourished a bitter, revengeful temper towards the citizens of Cologne since their outbreak. He resolved to overcome it. He went to Siegburg, and was there laid up with gout in his left foot. The gout spread up his leg. He thought he saw a wicked little black devil at his side pinching his tortured limb, and he screamed for holy water wherewith to drive the demon away. The gout reached his stomach, and he died, forgiving the people of Cologne, and ordering his money to be distributed among the poor.

S. OSMUND, B. OF SALISBURY.

(A.D. 1099.)

[Roman Martyrology. Sarum Kalendar. At Seez on Dec. 5. Canonized by Calixtus III. in 1459. Authority:—William of Malmesbury, De Pontiff. Angl. lib. ii.; "Canonizatio S. Osmundi Sarisburiensis ep.," in Acta SS. Boll. 1 Jan. i. p. 77.]

S. OSMUND was by birth a Norman, Count of Seez, and kinsman of William the Conqueror, with whom he came over to England, and by whom he was created Earl of Dorset and Chancellor of England. In 1077 he was chosen to succeed Hereman as bishop of Salisbury, and he completed the cathedral which Hereman had begun. As a bishop, Osmund appears to have retired much from the world, and to have lived chiefly in the society of the learned canons whom he had drawn together by his liberality. He

S. OSMUND, B. OF SALISBURY.

collected for his church a noble library ; and it is stated, as
a proof of his humility, that he not only copied books himself, but that he also bound them with his own hands. He
placed thirty-six canons in the cathedral, which he dedicated to the Blessed Virgin, in 1092. The church was
struck by lightning and much injured, but he had the satisfaction of repairing it before he died. He is said to have
written a Life of S. Anselm, which is not now extant. Finding that great confusion reigned in England through the
Norman clergy endeavouring to force their continental practices on the English Church, Osmund drew up a ritual for
the church of Sarum, on strictly conservative principles,
retaining old usages, and introducing few novelties A
13th century MS. of this valuable work exists in Salisbury
Cathedral Library. S. Osmund died on the night between
the 3rd and 4th of December, 1099. His bones still lie at
Salisbury, under a plain monument.

December 5.

S. Bassus, *B.M. at Nice;* 3*rd cent.*
S. Crispina, *M. at Thebeste in Africa;* A.D. 304.
SS. Julius, Potamia, and Others, *MM. at Thagara in Africa;* A.D. 304.
S. Dalmatius, *B.M. at Pavia;* A.D. 304.
S. Pelinus, *B.M. of Brindes;* A.D. 362.
S. Sabas, *Ab. at Metalala in Cappadocia;* A.D. 531.
S. Nicetius, *B. of Trèves;* A.D. 566.
ꜱ. John the Wonderworker, *C. at Polybotum in Asia Minor:* 8*th cent.*
S. Gerald, *Abp. of Braga in Portugal;* A.D. 1109.

S. CRISPINA, M.

(A.D. 304.)

[Roman Martyrology. Carthaginian Kalendar. Some copies of Mart. of Jerome, as Crispinus; Usuardus, Ado, &c. Authorities :—S. Augustine on Ps. cxxxvii., and another sermon on Ps. cxx., and the genuine and trustworthy Acts in Ruinart.]

O many of the Acts of Martyrs are forgeries, or have been amplified by later hands, that it is a pleasure to come upon those which are undoubtedly genuine. Such are the Acts of S. Crispina, and they shall be given unaltered, or only slightly abbreviated.

When Diocletian and Maximian were consuls, on the nones of December, at Thebeste, where Anulinus was pro-consul, the clerk of the court said, in the tribunal of justice, "Crispina, of Thagara, who has disregarded the imperial commands, if it please you, shall be heard."

Anulinus the judge said, "Let her be brought in."

Then the blessed Crispina was introduced.

Anulinus the pro-consul said, "Have you heard the

decree ?" The blessed Crispina replied, "I know not what that decree is." Anulinus said, "It is to this effect, that you should sacrifice to all the gods for the welfare of the emperors."

Crispina. "I will never sacrifice, except to the One God and to our Lord Jesus Christ, His Son, who was born and suffered."

Anulinus. "Put away this superstition, and bow to the worship of our gods."

Crispina. "I daily worship my God, and I know no other."

Anulinus. "You are hard and audacious, and will call down on you the severity of the law."

Crispina. "Come what may, I will suffer for my faith."

Anulinus. "You will lose your head if you do not obey the commands of the emperors; all Africa has submitted, and you shall be made to do so."

Crispina. "I will sacrifice to the Lord who made heaven and earth, the sea and all things that are therein, but never shall I be forced to do sacrifice to demons."

Anulinus. "Then those gods will not be accepted by you to whom you are forced to give honour to save your life ?"

Crispina. "True worship does not use compulsion." [1]

Anulinus. "But will you not formally, with bent head, offer a little incense in the sacred temples ?"

Crispina. "I have never done this since my birth, and I will not do so as long as I live."

Anulinus. "Do it, however, just to escape the severity of the laws."

Crispina. "I have no fear for the event. But I fear God, who, if I obeyed, would cast me off as sacrilegious."

---

[1] This noble sentiment thus stands, "Nulla devotio est, quæ opprimi coegit invitos."

Anulinus. "You cannot be sacrilegious if you obey the law."

Crispina. "Would you have me sacrilegious before God, that I might not be so before the emperors? God is great and omnipotent: He made the sea, and the green herbs, and the dry earth. How can I prefer His creatures to Himself?"

Anulinus ordered her hair to be cut off, and her head shaved. As she remained unmoved, he said, "Do you wish to live, or persist in your intention to die, like Maxima, Donatilla, and Secunda,[1] your companions?"

Crispina answered, "If I wished to die, and give over my soul to destruction, I should do to your demons what you require."

Anulinus said, "I will cut off your head if you persist in mocking our venerable deities."

Crispina replied, "I should indeed lose my head if I took to worshipping them."

Anulinus the pro-consul said, "You persist, then, in this opinion?"

Crispina answered, "My God, who is, and was, He ordered me to be born; He gave me salvation by the water of Holy Baptism; He is with me, to support my soul, and stay it from committing sacrilege as you desire."

Anulinus said, "We can endure this impious Crispina no longer."

The acts of the trial were read over, and then Anulinus gave command that Crispina should suffer by the sword.

Crispina exclaimed, "I give praise to Christ, I bless the Lord, who has thus deigned to deliver me out of your hands."

She suffered at Thebeste on the nones of December.

---

[1] In Ado's Martyrology on July 30, but said to have suffered at Tuburbo.

S. SABAS, AB.

(A.D. 531.)

[Roman Martyrology. Greek Menæas and Menologies, Menology
of Basil, Russian Kalendar. Authority:—A Life by Cyril of Scythopolis, written in 557; in Cotelerius, Mon. Eccl. Græcæ, iii. pp. 220-376.]

S. SABAS was born at Mutalasca in Cappadocia, in the year
437. His father, John Conon, and his mother Sophia were
both of illustrious family. John followed the profession of
arms, and being obliged to go with his legion to Alexandria,
and unable to take his child with him, he left the little Sabas
to the care of his brother Hermias. Sabas remained with
his uncle till he was eight, and then, unable to endure the
temper of his aunt, ran away to another uncle, a priest named
Gregory, who lived at Scandos, not far from Mutalasca. This
gave rise to angry recriminations between the brothers, and
contests about the property of the father of Sabas. The boy,
sick at heart at the discord, retired, before he was nine years
old, to the monastery of Flavianum, where he occupied himself in learning the Psalter by heart. One day the baker of
the monastery got wet through in a shower, and he put his
clothes to dry in the oven. The other monks, not knowing
this, lighted the fires to heat the oven, intending to do some
baking. The baker came in and found, to his dismay, that
his clothes had not been removed. However, Sabas daringly
scrambled into the oven, and pulled them out. The monks
admired the pluck of the boy, and in after years, when Sabas
became famous, magnified the incident into a miracle. After
ten years spent in this monastery, Sabas went to that of
Bessarion, governed by S. Elpidius, but was thought too
young to remain in it, and was sent further, to S. Theoctistus.
This abbot sent him on business into Egypt, where he met

his father and mother. They naturally desired him to quit the monastic life, enter the army, and live with them, but he refused, and returned to Palestine.

When Sabas was aged thirty, he retired into a cavern, but appeared every Sabbath [1] and Lord's day at the monastery church to assist at the sacred mysteries.

S. Euthymius chose him as his companion in his yearly retreats into the desert of Ruban. In one of these wanderings in the wilderness, Sabas discovered a cavern in the face of a precipice that overhung the brook Cedron. He reached it with some difficulty, and then hung a cord from the mouth, by which he was enabled to ascend to it and descend from it. He was aged forty when he retired to the cavern, and by the end of five years he saw himself surrounded by seventy disciples, whom he lodged in caves near him. He had much difficulty, however, in obtaining a supply of water, as that of Cedron was not drinkable; but one moonlight night he saw a wild ass pawing the gravelly soil at a distance from the brook, and, when it had made a hole, drinking the water that filtered through the gravel and sand into the place. This was a hint to Sabas, and he opened a well at the spot, and found a sufficiency of potable water. In one of his rambles among the rocks of the desert he came on an ancient sculptured cave-temple, and it struck him that it might serve eventually as a church. His disciples had become a hundred and fifty, and could not be accommodated in the simple oratory he had built on first entering the wilderness. He now built himself a tower above the rock, and pierced a passage, which wound down into the old temple, and he used it as his private chapel, till Sallust, patriarch of Jerusalem, ordained him priest, and consecrated the old

---

[1] Both the Sabbath and the Lord's Day were long observed in the Eastern and Egyptian Churches. The offices of the Latin Church show traces of the ancient observance of the Saturday as a holy day in the West as well.

pagan temple as a church (A.D. 490). Sabas retired from
the throng of monks for long tracts of time, into remote parts
of the desert. On one occasion he tumbled into a pit of
boiling sulphur and gypsum in the volcanic district of the
Dead Sea, and was so severely scalded that he could not get
over it, and his face was for some time disfigured. Once he
resolved boldly to occupy a rock which it was alleged was
haunted. When, however, he came to take up his abode in
it, he found that the rents of the cliff were haunted, not by
devils, but by innumerable ravens and crows, which flew
screaming and croaking round their invaded home. In the
desert he was praying one night, whilst his disciple slept
on the sand. By the moonlight a great lion came up, and
sniffed at the sleeping man. Sabas uttered a loud cry to God
for help, and the king of the beasts ran scared away, without doing any injury to either of the hermits. On another
occasion, Sabas lay down to sleep in a cavern, which was the
lair of a lion. The beast came in full gorged from a meal,
when Sabas was asleep, and taking the old man's habit in his
teeth, dragged Sabas outside. The monk awoke, and making
the sign of the cross, got up, and crept back into the cave,
lay down and went to sleep again. Not long after he found
the lion again pulling at his clothes. Sabas sat up, and said,
" If you do not care to share your lair with me, go and seek
a separate one for yourself, and let me sleep in peace." The
lion left him alone, and departed. Next morning Sabas
abandoned the cavern.

The raven rock so delighted him that he resolved to establish on it a monastery. It was the site of an old Roman
fortress, and still bore the name of Castellum. Among the
ruins was a well-preserved hall, which with little trouble
could be converted into a church. He carried thither a
swarm of brothers from his own monastery, and placed over
them a favourite monk, named Paul. Among his disciples

were Egyptians and Armenians; he made each sing the offices, and celebrate the mysteries, in his own tongue; but he required the Armenians to chant the Trisagion in Greek, because he found that some were disposed to add the paragraph of Peter the Fuller, "Who was crucified for us," as applying to the whole Trinity, and thus to renew the heresy of Sabellius. He built two infirmaries at Castellum, a hospital near Jerusalem, and another at Jericho.

About forty of his disciples had complained to the patriarch Sallust that the long absences of Sabas rendered him incompetent to act as abbot to so large a community, but had been dismissed with reproof. The number of the discontented increased, and during one of the long disappearances of the abbot, sixty of the monks left his laura,[1] and established themselves in the desert of Thecua. On the return of Sabas, he heard, not only of this migration, but also that the malcontents were very badly off. He at once went to them, and, without rebuking them, built them a church, obtained for them a grant of land, and furnished them with food and money.

As Eutychianism was making great inroads among the religious of Palestine, the patriarch constituted him head of all the ascetics or solitaries in the deserts, and Theoctistus he appointed cenobiarch, supreme over all the monasteries.

One day Sabas was walking from Jericho to the Jordan with a young monk, his disciple, when they passed some travellers, amongst whom was a very handsome girl.

"Who was that one-eyed young woman?" asked S. Sabas of his companion.

"She was not one-eyed," said the young ascetic.

"You mistake, surely," persisted the abbot.

"No, father; I know she has two eyes," said the monk,

---

[1] A laura was a monastery of separate cells. Those inhabiting a laura were called 'anchorites;" those in a monastery, "cenobites."

" for I particularly observed them, and very beautiful eyes they are."

" Oh, indeed! you particularly looked into the girl's eyes, did you?" exclaimed Sabas. And he added, " Depart from me, you are not suited to become a monk in my monastery."

Sabas was involved against his will in the troubles about Severus, patriarch of Antioch. Severus had embraced Euty-chianism, and denounced those who held by the Council of Chalcedon as Nestorians. The Emperor Anastasius favoured Eutychianism, and had deposed Macedonius from the patri-archate of Constantinople, and put Timothy in his room (A.D. 511), who sent synodal letters to the bishops of the East. Elias of Jerusalem and Flavian of Antioch refused to approve of the deposition of Macedonius, though they did not denounce Timothy, whom they believed to be orthodox.

The emperor was highly incensed against Elias, who had hovered between condemning and approving the Council of Chalcedon, and shrank from committing himself to a course which would involve him either in heresy or in the hostility of Anastasius. Half measures did not satisfy the emperor.[1] Elias sent S. Sabas with other venerable abbots to Constan-tinople to intercede for him with the emperor.

All the abbots were admitted to the imperial presence except Sabas, whom the guards took to be a beggar, from his ragged appearance. The letter of Elias was read to Anastasius, in which he mentioned Sabas in terms of eu-logy. The emperor asked where he was. He was discovered without, in a corner, repeating psalms. The old man, bent, with habit rudely patched, and ragged white hair, hobbled from behind the purple curtain that hung over the door. The emperor rose to meet him, and then requested the abbots to seat themselves. They all began to clamour for gifts; one wanted a piece of land, another money. Sabas asked

---

[1] See about Flavian and Elias, July 4, pp. 99-105.

for nothing, save that the emperor would leave the Church alone, and not meddle with her bishops. Sabas spent the winter in Constantinople, and returned to the East in May. He visited his native place of Mutalasca on his way, and converted his paternal mansion into a church.

A council was held on his return, at Sidon; Elias of Jerusalem and Flavian of Antioch were present, as well as Severus, whom the emperor had intruded on the see of Flavian. Elias refused to receive the synodal letters of Severus, and the emperor sent Olympius, duke of Palestine, to banish Elias from Jerusalem, and replace him with John, who had promised to anathematize the Council of Chalcedon. Sabas hastened to Jerusalem, and standing on Calvary with other abbots, pronounced anathema against Severus, and those who communicated with him. When John was installed in the patriarchal chair, Sabas so instantly urged him not to denounce the Council of Chalcedon, that he agreed not to do so, and to refuse communion with Severus of Antioch.

On a given day ten thousand monks assembled in the church of S. Stephen, as that of the Resurrection was too small to receive the crowd; and there John, with Sabas, head of the Anchorites on the one hand, and Theodosius, head of the Cenobites on the other, stood in the ambone, and all three pronounced anathema on Nestorius, Eutyches, and Severus.

Elias was visited in his exile by Sabas, who also was present at his death. Anastasius died about the same time, and Justinian, who succeeded him, befriended the orthodox, and eagerly persecuted heretics.

The reign of Justinian was, indeed, a uniform yet various scene of persecution. Heretics were allowed three months in which to feel or feign conviction, and if too honourable to embrace tenets which they could not believe, were cruelly and relentlessly banished and plundered. The churches of the Montanists were given up to flames, and the unhappy heretics, rather than abandon their hysterical ravings, perished in the fires. The Jews, who had been gradually stripped of their immunities, were oppressed by a vexatious law which compelled them to observe the feast of the Passover at the same time as the Christian Easter. The Samaritans of Palestine were a motley race, an ambiguous sect, rejected as Jews by the Pagans, by the Jews as schismatics, and by the Christians as unbelievers. The Emperor Zeno had built a church, and placed a garrison on Mount Gerizim. Under Anastasius, the Samaritans surprised the fort and church; and when the Emperor Justinian showed himself ready to persecute to the death, they rose in revolt, set up a rival emperor, killed a bishop, and cut to pieces several priests. Justinian sent the regular forces of the East against them; twenty thousand were massacred, twenty thousand were sold as slaves, and the remains of that unhappy nation purchased safety by submitting with disgust and disbelief to baptism. It has been computed that one hundred thousand Roman subjects were extirpated in this Samaritan war, in the extension of the kingdom of the Prince of Peace. But, as Procopius observes,—" It is not murder to massacre unbelievers." The devout and orthodox Christians of Scythopolis having caught a Samaritan of rank named Sylvanus, who incautiously ventured himself among Christians, emulated the enthusiasm and zeal of their emperor by burning him alive in their market-place. But Sylvanus was a Roman citizen, and had powerful relations. His son Arsenius went to Constantinople and appealed to the emperor for redress. Then Peter, patriarch of Jerusalem, and other bishops of Palestine, deputed S. Sabas to go to Justinian and obtain immunity for the enthusiasts who had burned Sylvanus, and demand the execution of a few more obnoxious Samaritans, and the relief of the province from certain taxes which could not well be paid on account of the injury done by the Samaritan revolt. S. Sabas was received by the emperor with the highest honour, galleys were sent to meet him, he was presented before the emperor by Hypatius of Ephesus, and Justinian cast himself at the feet of the old hermit to receive his blessing. S. Sabas was so successful in his mission, that he obtained orders from the emperor for the execution both of the unfortunate Arsenius, who had objected to his father's being burned alive, and also of all the chiefs of the Samaritans who had made themselves obnoxious to the bishops of Palestine. The emperor decreed, also, that the Samaritans should be forbidden assembling for religious worship, entering any public office, and enjoying any inheritance from their parents. Arsenius found that his only chance of life was to submit with rage in his heart to the mockery of baptism by the hands of S. Sabas.

Justinian sent for Sabas, before the saint returned to the East, to ask him what he could do for him. "Nothing," replied the holy abbot, " except deliver the Church from the Arians, Nestorians, and Origenists."

Justinian gladly promised to do his best to extirpate them. He hastened to confiscate the goods of the Arian churches.

It is curious to note that this persecuting emperor himself died a heretic. Nicetius, bishop of Trèves, wrote to the emperor when he was dying, "Unless you destroy what you have taught, and exclaim, 'I have erred, I have sinned ; anathema to Nestorius, anathema to Eutyches,' you deliver your soul to the same flames in which they will eternally burn." He died in his heresy.

S. Sabas, on his return, published the letters of the emperor ; the patriarch and other bishops went to Scythopolis, Cæsarea, &c., and proclaimed the decision of Justinian, and saw to the execution of its infamous requirements. Sabas went back to his laura, and died there shortly after.

S. NICETIUS, B. OF TRÈVES.

(A.D. 566.)

[Roman Martyrology. The Martyrologies of Bede and Usuardus on Oct. 1. Authority:—Gregory of Tours, De Vitæ Patrum, c. 17; De Gloria Confessorum, c. 94. His own letters.]

NICETIUS came into the world with a fringe of hair about his head, and it was therefore supposed that he was pre-destined to the religious life. He was educated in a monastery and became its abbot.[1] King Thierry held him in high respect because he boldly rebuked the king for what he did amiss, and on the see of Trèves falling vacant in 527, Thierry had him consecrated to it, with the consent of the clergy and people.

On his way to Trèves, before his consecration, the officers of the king, when camping for the night, turned their horses out into the cornfields of the peasants. Nicetius at once interfered. " Remove your horses from the fields of these poor people," he said, " or I shall excommunicate you all." " Ha !" said the officers, " You are not yet bishop, and you excommunicate us !"

" The king," answered Nicetius, " has drawn me, a poor abbot, from my quiet cloister, to set me over this people, and by God's grace I will do my duty by them and protect them from wrong and robbery." And he went himself into the fields and drove the horses out.

Theodebert succeeded Thierry (A.D. 534), and Nicetius was obliged to show great firmness towards this prince also, to check the violence committed against the weak, and to restrain the licentious nobles of the court. One day that

---

[1] This was his advice to his monks :—" Avoid scurrility and idle talk, for as the body should be kept pure, so should talk be decent. A man may fall in three ways— by what he thinks, by what he says, and by what he does."

Theodebert entered the church at Trèves, a madman began to howl out that Theodebert was an adulterer and a ravager of the poor. The king begged the saint to stop the disturbance. Nicetius answered, "Let the adulterers, murderers, and robbers of thy train, sire, be expelled the church, and then I can cast the devil out of this poor mad fellow."

He preached almost daily to the people, denouncing by name all wrong-doers, especially the nobles and princes who ill-used the poor, utterly indifferent to his own safety, so long as he could save his poor people from oppression. Clothair, who came to the throne in 554, called down the excommunication of the intrepid bishop on his head, and the king revenged himself by sending Nicetius into banishment (A.D. 561). But Clothair died immediately, and the bishop was recalled by Sigebert.

That the morals of the people of Trèves were as bad as bad could be, is evident from the city becoming a prey to a shameful malady, which, indeed, ravaged Gaul in the 6th century, and which made its first appearance in 546. To this Gregory of Tours alludes again and again. It was fatal, and the city suffered terribly. One night it was reported that voices of demons had been heard on the bridge of the Moselle, saying, "What can we do? Maximinus guards one gate, Eucherius the other, and Nicetius keeps watch in the centre. We can prevail no longer." After that the plague ceased, and, it is to be hoped, the morals of Trèves mended.

A dream of S. Nicetius is recorded. He saw a tall tower, with angels guarding it, and an angel stood on it with a book in his hand, and he read out of it as he turned over the pages the names, qualities, and length of reign of all the kings of France, that had been, were, and would be, to the end of the monarchy. And after declaring the name and quality of each king, the other angels cried, Amen.

S. Nicetius attended the Council of Clermont held at the

beginning of the reign of Theodebert, the 5th Council of Orleans, in 549, and the 2nd Council of Paris, in 551.

He wrote to Clodesind, wife of Alboin, king of the Lombards, on the occasion of her sending ambassadors to her brothers the kings of the Franks, exhorting her to labour at the conversion of her husband from Arianism, and bidding her make him observe that miracles were wrought abundantly in Catholic churches, but none in those of the Arians. He also wrote to the Emperor Justinian, as already mentioned in the life of S. Sabas. Nicetius died shortly after writing this letter, and was succeeded by his disciple, S. Magneric.

December 6.

S. Nicolas, *B. of Myra in Lycia; 4th cent.*
S. Asella, *V. at Rome; circ.* A.D. 410.
SS. Dionysia, Majoricus, Dativa, Leontia, Æmilian, Terecius, and Others, *MM. in Africa;* A.D. 484.
S. Gertrude, *W. Abss. of Hamage in Belgium; circ.* A.D. 655.
S. Peter Paschal, *B. of Jaen, M. at Granada;* A.D. 1300.

S. NICOLAS, B. OF MYRA.

(4TH CENTURY.)

[All Oriental Menæas and Menologies. Roman Martyrology, Usuardus, and all Western Martyrologies. The translation of his relics to Bari on May 9. Authorities :—A Life by Metaphrastes, and that in the Legenda Aurea of Jacobus de Voragine.]

NFORTUNATELY we have little or no trust-worthy information concerning the probably most popular saint in Christendom. That he was bishop of Myra in the fourth century, is really all that we know for certain of him. But legend has supplied the deficiency with an abundant supply of material for the construction of an interesting, if fictitious, history of the saint.

He was born at Patara, a town of Lycia, in Asia Minor. Directly he was born he was put in a basin to be washed, but, to the astonishment of the nurses, he stood up in the basin, and remained for two hours in an ecstasy, his hands clasped, and his eyes raised to heaven. Dionysius the Carthusian, not stopping to inquire whether this was true or not, argues from it that Nicolas was endued with reason from the moment of birth. He began to fast from his cradle.

On Wednesdays and Fridays he refused nourishment from
his nurse's breasts, except in the evening, after sundown,
when he sucked vigorously. He lost his parents when
young, and was left with a considerable fortune. One day
he heard that the father of three maidens, being unable to
provide them with a jointure, was going to send them on to
the streets to pick up a disreputable living. Nicolas stole one
evening past the house, and flung a bag of gold through the
window. The father then married honourably the eldest of
his daughters. Soon after, Nicolas threw in a second bag of
gold, to serve as a marriage portion for the second daughter ;
and afterwards a third sum, to assist the third maiden in
finding a husband. But on this last occasion he was observed
by the grateful father, who was on the watch.

The three bags of gold have been converted into three
gold balls, and serve as the emblem of pawnbrokers, who
have chosen S. Nicolas as their patron.

Nicolas was ordained priest, and set off on a voyage to
the Holy Land. On his way, the ship that bore him was
nearly wrecked, but by the prayers of Nicolas the storm was
suppressed, and the waves controlled, so that the vessel
was enabled to reach Alexandria in safety. From that city
he made his way to Jerusalem. On his way back by sea,
the captain endeavoured to put into Alexandria instead of
going to Lycia, but a violent storm prevented him, and he
was obliged to deposit Nicolas at the port at which he
desired to disembark.

About A.D. 325 he was elected bishop of Myra. After
his consecration, a woman brought into the church a child
which had fallen into the fire and was burnt. Nicolas made
the sign of the cross over it, and restored it to health. On
this account he is invoked against fire. His power over
tempests has caused him to be also invoked by sailors. He
is thought to have been a confessor under Licinius. Tra-

dition insists that he was present in the great council of Nicæa, and he is invariably represented among the assembled fathers, in the pictures of the council common in Eastern churches, though he is not mentioned as having been present by a single ancient historian. In that council were read the songs composed by Arius, under the title of Thalia, for the sake of popularizing his speculations with the lower orders. The songs were set to tunes, or written in metres, which had acquired a questionable reputation from their use in the licentious verses of the heathen poet Sotades, ordinarily used in the low revels or dances of Alexandria; and the grave Arius himself is said, in moments of wild excitement, to have danced like an Eastern Dervish, whilst he sang these abstract statements in long straggling lines, of which about twenty are preserved to us. To us the chief surprise is that any enthusiasm should have been excited by sentences such as these,—" God was not always the Father; once He was not the Father; afterwards He became the Father." But, in proportion to the attraction which they possessed for the partisans of Arius, was the dismay they roused in the minds of those by whom the expressions which Arius thus lightly set aside were regarded as the watchwords of the ancient faith. The bishops, on hearing the song, raised their hands in horror, and, after the manner of Orientals, when wishing to express their disgust at blasphemous words, kept their ears fast closed, and their eyes fast shut. It was doubtless at this point that occurred the incident embodied in legend, of the sudden outbreak of fury in Nicolas, bishop of Myra, who is represented in the traditional pictures of the council as dealing a blow with all his force at Arius's jaw. It is this incident, real or imaginary, that gave some colour to the charge of violence brought by Peter Martyr against the Nicene fathers. But the story itself bears witness to the humane spirit which exalts this earliest council above its successors. The legend best known in the West goes on to say that for this intemperate act S. Nicolas was deprived of his mitre and pall, which were only restored to him long afterwards by the intervention of angels—*i. e.* of monks, interceding for the restitution. But in the East, the story assumes a more precise and polemical form. The council, it is said, on the appeal of Arius, imprisoned the bishop of Myra. But in prison, the Redeemer, whose honour he had vindicated, appeared with His Mother; the One restored to him the Gospel, the other the pall, and with these credentials he claimed and obtained his freedom.[1]

He is said to have wrung from Eustathius, governor of Myra, the pardon of three men condemned to death and imprisoned in a tower. He was afterwards represented with this tower at his side, and three little men rising out of it. By degrees the tower was cut down, and the men converted into naked children; and then a new legend was composed to account for the transformed symbol. It was said that an innkeeper, running short of bacon, had cut up three little boys, and pickled them in his salting-tub. S. Nicolas heard that three scholars had gone to the inn, and had disappeared there. He went to the tavern, asked for the pickle-tub, and at his word the remains of the butchered children came together, and the little pickles stood up alive in the tub.

Even in his lifetime he was invoked by sailors. In a tempest he was thus called on, when he appeared, seized the rudder, and guided the ship in safety through the waves.

His tomb at Myra was much resorted to, and it was contrived that an oil should flow from it, which was collected as miraculous. In 1087 some merchants of Bari, in southern Italy, made a descent on Myra, and carried off the relics of the saint, which they deposited in their own city. Since then

---

[1] Stanley, "Lectures on the Eastern Church," lect. iv.

the oil has been made to flow from the bones as effectually as before their translation.

S. Nicolas is represented in art with three children in a pickle-tub at his side, or with three golden balls or purses in his hand.

S. ASELLA, V.

(ABOUT A.D. 410.)

[Roman Martyrology. Authority :—The letters of S. Jerome.]

S. JEROME, when in Rome, undertook to guide in the ascetic life a number of noble Roman ladies, who placed themselves under his direction. Among these were Marcella and her sister Asella. The latter had dedicated her virginity to God at the age of ten. When aged twelve, she shut herself up in a little cell, lay on the earth, ate only bread, and drank nothing but water, would not look at a man, nor speak to her sister. Great lumps grew on her knees, like those on the legs of camels, from continual kneeling on the hard stones. When a religious solemnity drew her to church, she endeavoured to avoid attention. She dressed quietly, was always sad, never smiled, and was deadly pale. She wore sackcloth next her flesh, and lived till she was over fifty, without, we are assured, ever knowing what it was to have a pain in her stomach. She flattered herself that she had never in her whole life spoken to a man. This was the ideal perfection of a woman, for which she had been created, in the eyes of S. Jerome, who also, unquestionably, regarded her name as inappropriate.

SS. DIONYSIA, MAJORICUS, AND OTHERS, MM.

(A.D. 484.)

[Roman Martyrology. Usuardus. Authority:—Victor of Utica, De Pers. Vandal. lib. v.]

In 484 Huneric, the Arian Vandal king of Africa, banished the Catholic bishops. Dionysia, a lady remarkable for her beauty as well as for her piety, was taken up, and scourged in the forum, till her back and sides were raw, and dripped with blood. Majoricus, her son, turned deadly pale, and trembled. Seeing him faint with horror, she turned towards him, and said, " My son, do not forget that you have been baptized in the name of the Holy Trinity into the Catholic Church, our Mother. Let us not lose the garment of our salvation, lest the Master of the Feast find us without the wedding raiment, and cast us forth into outer darkness."

The lad was encouraged by her words to endure martyrdom. His mother embraced his dead body, and buried it in her own house, that she might pray over his tomb. Dativa her sister, her cousin Æmilianus, a physician, Tertius or Terecius, Leontia, and Boniface also were scourged and tortured. A nobleman of Tuburbo, named Severus, was beaten, and then hoisted into the air, then jerked down on the pavement, and pulled up again, the whole weight of his body being supported by ropes round his wrists. He was next dragged over the pavement, along the streets, which were reddened with his blood.

At Cucusa there were many confessors and martyrs. Among them was a lady named Victoria, who was hung over a slow fire. Her husband, who had become an Arian, brought her babes to the place, in hopes that the sight of them might nerve her to abandon her confession of the Consubstantial. But she turned her eyes away from them. She was cast off the rack when the executioner thought her dead, but she eventually recovered.

S. GERTRUDE, W. ABSS.

(ABOUT A.D. 655.)

[Belgian Martyrologies. Authority:—Notices collected in Acta SS. Belgii, ii. p. 427.]

S. GERTRUDE of Hamage, who is not to be mistaken for S. Gertrude of Nivelles, was the daughter of Theobald, Lord of Douai. She married a noble named Rigomer, and had by him several children, of whom Erchinoald, who was mayor of the palace to Queen Bathild, and Sigebert, who married S. Bertha, are those principally known. It is not certain whether Adalbald[1] was son or grandson of S. Gertrude. On the death of her husband, S. Gertrude built an oratory at Hamage, and, after some years, Eusebia, the eldest daughter of S. Adalbald and S. Rictrudis, came to live with her. Gradually a community of religious women formed itself around Gertrude. Adalbald was assassinated in Gascony about 652, and Gertrude died not long after. Her body rested in the monastery of Hamage till 686, when S. Vindician, bishop of Cambrai and Arras, translated it to the new church at Hamage, built by Gertrude II., who had succeeded S. Eusebia.

Feb. 2.

S. PETER PASCHAL, B.M.

(A.D. 1300.)

[Roman Martyrology on 6th Dec., but his festival is observed on Oct. 23. In 1673 Clement X. by brief allowed the Order of Mercy to recite his office as bishop and martyr. He extended the privilege to all the clergy, regular and secular, of the dioceses of Valencia, Granada, Jaen, and Toledo, and had his name inserted in the Roman Martyrology on Oct. 23 and Dec. 6. Authority:—The Acts of Canonization.]

THE ancestors of S. Peter Paschal came from Valencia, and were noted for their charitable benefactions, given for the keeping up of the Convent of the Holy Sepulchre, in the city of Valencia. Five of the family are said to have shed their blood for their religion. The saint was born on December 6th, 1227; he was educated by a priest whom his parents had redeemed from slavery among the Moors. On the conquest of Valencia (1238) from the Moors by the king of Aragon, Peter was made canon of the cathedral, and he went to Paris to complete his studies in that university. On his return to Spain, he entered the Order of Mercy founded by S. Peter Nolasco for the redemption of captives, and received the habit in 1251. After his profession, he went to Barcelona, where he taught theology, till called to be tutor to Don Sanchez, third son of James I. of Aragon, whom he persuaded to enter the same Order as himself, and dedicate himself to the Church. Don Sanchez was appointed archbishop of Toledo, while still a boy in his teens. As he was too young to govern his church, Peter Paschal was given him as his coadjutor, by Urban IV., with the title of Bishop of Granada. He was consecrated in 1262, and governed the archdiocese till 1275, when the youthful archbishop died in battle, fighting the Moors.

He visited Granada, still under the Moors, and consoled the Christians in captivity, and redeemed many from their slavery. In 1269 he was made bishop of Jaen, then under Moorish government. His success in bringing renegades back to Christianity exasperated the Cadi, and he had Peter Paschal imprisoned. A large sum was collected for his ransom, but he expended it on a number of captive women and children, whom he feared the Mussulmans would force into apostacy. A story not without its beauty and meaning is told of the saint at this period. He was saying Mass, and a little boy served at the altar, with book and bell, most properly. When Mass was over, Peter turned to the server, and, thinking he was a Christian child, put him through his catechism. The child repeated it with great quickness and apprehension. But when the catechist asked the boy who was Jesus Christ, he was startled by receiving the answer, "Myself." There can be little doubt that the great truth that mercy shown to the little ones believing in Christ is accepted as done to Christ Himself, was distorted in the mouth of the people into this story.

Whilst in prison he composed a work against Mohammedanism, anything but complimentary to the founder of the religion and to the merits of the Koran. This so incensed the Moors that they clamoured for his execution, and he was sentenced to lose his head. He spent the night before his martyrdom in an agony of fear, but was consoled by a vision, in which Christ appeared to him, and assured him that before His passion, He also had been agonized by natural fear of death.

Peter Paschal suffered on January 6th, 1300, at the age of seventy-three. The Moors, not valuing his relics, readily abandoned them to the eager deputies of the churches of Jaen and Baeza, who quarrelled which should have them. The contest was settled by mutual consent, that they should be placed on the back of a blind mule, and the beast be allowed to take them where it liked. The mule had formerly, no doubt, belonged to some one in Baeza, though of this the deputies of Jaen were not informed, and the animal trotted home with the bones.

December 7.

S. Agatho, *M. at Alexandria;* A.D. 250.
S. Ambrose, *B.D. of Milan;* A.D. 391.
S. Severus, *M. at Tuburbo in Africa;* A.D. 484 (see p. 69).
S. Martin, *Ab. at Saintes;* 5th cent.
S. Gerebald, *B. of Bayeux; circ.* A.D. 620.
S. Fara, *V. at Meaux;* 7th cent.
S. Urbanus, *B. of Chieti in South Italy;* 9th cent.

S. AMBROSE, B.D.

(A.D. 391.)

[In the Roman Martyrology, in Usuardus, on April 4, "Depositio B.
Ambrosii Ep. et Conf." On Dec. 7 in the Roman Mart., "Ordinatio
Amb. Ep. et Conf." Greek Menæa, Menology of Basil, Jerusalem Kalen-
dar of 10th cent., Russian and all other Oriental Kalendars on Dec. 7;
the Neapolitan Kalendar of the 9th cent. also on Nov. 3. Authorities:—
A Life written by Paulinus the Priest (fl. 422), at the request of S. Au-
gustine, in most editions of the works of S. Augustine, and in Surius,
Vit. SS. 4th April; S. Isidore of Seville, "De Viris Illustribus," c. 4;
Ruffinus, H. E. lib. ii.; S. Basil, Ep. 55; Sozomen, H. E. iv.; Socrates,
H. E. vi.; Theodoret, H. E. iv. v.; the Epistles and other writings of
S. Ambrose.]

UXENTIUS of Cappadocia, an Arian, had occupied the see of Milan for twenty years (355—
374); he had been forced on the see by Constantius, after the council held at Milan in 355,
which had ended in the condemnation of S. Athanasius and
the expulsion of S. Dionysius.

It was at the close of 374 that Auxentius died. Valentinian desired the people to choose a successor. The
governor of Liguria was in the act of exhorting the people

S. AMBROSE.   After Cahier.

to observe order, when a child suddenly uttered the words,
"Ambrose Bishop." The people took up the cry; it was
deemed a special case, in which Divine intervention pointed
out the predestined bishop. It mattered not in their view
that Ambrose was not yet baptized. The principle embodied in a Sardican canon, which required a time of pro-
bation before the episcopate, was held not to apply to an
occasion so extraordinary. Ambrose tried various means of
escaping from a burden which he unfeignedly dreaded,
duties for which he, perhaps, felt no particular call. He
attempted to destroy the high opinion which had been formed
of him by a curious expedient. He hastened to his judgment-
hall, and had some criminals brought before him and put on
the rack. The shrieks of the victims he hoped would convince the electors that he was a judge without mercy. But
the people cried, "We take on ourselves the responsibility."
Next he went home and ordered some prostitutes to be
introduced into his house. "We," said the people, "will
bear your sin." Then he attempted flight, and did actually
hide himself for a time, but was given up by the owner of
his place of refuge to the authorities who were busy searching
for him. Finding resistance hopeless, he asked that none
but a Catholic might baptize him. This was readily granted.
Seven days after his baptism he was consecrated, December
7, 374, being thirty-four years old. Whether the form of the
Sardican canon was to some extent complied with by con-
ferring on him, during the week, the inferior orders, has
been doubted. From the Greek historians we should infer
the negative; but Paulinus, his secretary and biographer, is
a much higher authority, and his words are: "It is said that
after his baptism he discharged all ecclesiastical offices,"
before his consecration. In any case, Ambrose might well
say of himself, that he was "snatched from the tribunals to
the episcopate, and had to begin to teach before he had

begun to learn." He set himself to study theology under Simplicianus, a Roman priest.

Ambrose was the son of a prefect of the prætorium in Gaul, also named Ambrose. He had a brother named Satyrus whom he dearly loved, and a sister named Marcellina, considerably his senior. Both are numbered with the saints.[1] Apparently Ambrose was born in Gaul, but it is impossible to say whether the claim made by Trèves to have been his birthplace is well founded, though it is not improbably just. S. Ambrose was born about the year 340. In after years, when he had made himself famous by his eloquence, the legend that a swarm of bees had settled on his cradle as he lay asleep in infancy, told originally of Plato, was transferred to Ambrose, much as legends related of a Norse king reappear as historical anecdotes told of William the Conqueror, and again of Napoleon Bonaparte.[2] The father of S. Ambrose died whilst the saint was very young, and his mother returned with him to Rome. He was brought up carefully by her and by his sister Marcellina. Amicius Probus, prætorian prefect of Italy in 368, chose Ambrose to be his assessor, having noticed his probity and clear intelligence, as he acted for awhile in the capacity of advocate in his court. Afterwards Ambrose was made governor of Liguria and Æmilia, and when Amicius Probus gave him the governorship, it was with words which were afterwards deemed prophetic, " Go thy way, govern not as a judge but as a bishop."

S. Ambrose was no sooner consecrated than he disembarrassed himself from all the ties which could distract his mind from exclusive attention to his new duties. He made

---

[1] S. Satyrus, on Sept. 17 ; S. Marcellina, on July 17.

[2] The tale of an invader slipping on landing in the country he invades, and happily explaining it as stooping to kiss the land he has come to claim, is told of S. Olaf Haraldson, and of William the Conqueror. The story of Abram conveying his wife through the *douane* into Egypt in a box, reappears in the story told by Sanders of Archbishop Cranmer bringing " Black Joan " through the Custom-house at Dover.

over the portion of the family estates which had fallen to
his share to his brother Satyrus, sold much, gave much to
the Church, and devoted himself with conscientious diligence
to his theological studies and episcopal obligations. Soon
after his ordination, he wrote to the Emperor Valentinian to
complain of injustices committed by some of the magistrates.
The emperor replied: " I have long been aware of the
freedom of your speech, yet that did not hinder me from
consenting to your consecration. Continue applying to our
sins the remedies prescribed by the Law of God." S. Basil
wrote to Ambrose to congratulate him, or rather the whole
Church, on his promotion, and urged him to oppose the
Arians, and to fight the good fight of faith.

On the death of Valens in 378, the empire fell to his
nephews Gratian and Valentinian II. The latter was an
infant, Gratian a youth of great energy and abilities. The
feeble Valens had been goaded by the jeers of his people in
the circus to going in person against the invading Goths.
Flattered by his eunuchs into contempt for his barbarous
opponents, he did not wait for the arrival of Gratian,
who was hastening to his assistance, but attacked the
Goths under the walls of Hadrianople, and met with a
crushing defeat, and with death. Gratian, on his way to the
East, knew that he was rushing not only against barbarian
adversaries of redoubtable power, but also into the midst of
theological polemics. He trusted to the shields of his legions
to guard him against the missiles of the former. He appealed to Ambrose to furnish him with a theological maga-
zine which might protect his own bosom from the barbs of
heretical argument. Ambrose at once complied with the
request of the youthful emperor, and wrote a treatise in two
books on the Faith, which he forwarded to him in 379.

He had not been bishop for three years, and yet his
reputation had spread far and wide. Many virgins came to

Milan, and placed themselves under his direction. To them he preached a course of sermons which, at the request of his sister, he collected into a book. Not long after, he wrote a book on Widowhood, on the occasion of a woman who had lost her husband and was tolerably advanced in life marrying again.

The ravages of the Goths in Thrace and Illyria excited his most lively compassion for the sufferers. He melted down the vessels of gold and silver in the churches, and disposed of them for the redemption of the captives, keeping only as many chalices and patens as were necessary. The Arians reproached him, and denounced his conduct as sacrilegious, but Ambrose indignantly vindicated his conduct. The Church, he said, has gold, not to store up, but to use for the necessities of her children.

After the death of Valens, Gratian, following the dictates of a liberal mind, passed a law which accorded permission to all heretics, with the exception of Manichæans, Photinians, and Eunomians, to follow their religion without molestation. But in the month of August next year Gratian was in Milan, and it is much to be feared that Ambrose used his influence with the emperor to obtain a repeal of this rescript, and to exact one to the contrary effect. It is certain that Gratian addressed a letter to Hesperius, prefect of Italy, from Milan on the 3rd of August revoking the liberties accorded to the heretics, and forbidding all, without exception, the exercise of their religion, and the assembling of themselves either in churches or in private houses.

When Gratian was at Sirmium in 378, Palladius and Secundianus, two Illyrian bishops, complained to him that they were denounced and decried as Arians, and entreated him to summon a council to judge their case. The Catholic bishops requested Gratian to hear them and decide whether they were orthodox or not, but the youthful emperor, still in

his teens, was too modest, and probably knew himself to be
too ignorant, to judge subtle questions of theology. S. Ambrose wrote to Gratian to tell him that it was not worth
troubling the whole episcopate about a couple of heretics—
prejudging their case—and that he and the Western Catholic
bishops would speedily confound them. A council was summoned to meet at Aquileja. Ambrose now added three more
books to his work on the Faith, in which he dealt with the
arguments of the Arians, and explained in a Catholic sense
those passages of Scripture which they quoted to sustain
their doctrine.

The Emperor Valentinian I. had been twice married; if
we might trust the ecclesiastical historian, he had taken to
his arms the lovely Justina at the same time that he had a
legitimate wife, Severa. Socrates indeed asserts that he
boldly assumed the right of having two wives, and that he
extended by law to all his subjects the same domestic
privilege which he had assumed for himself. But it is more
probable that he married Justina after having repudiated
Severa. His first wife was the mother of Gratian. Justina
bore him Valentinian II.

After the death of her husband, Justina retired to Sirmium. The bishopric of the capital of Illyria was then
vacant, through the death of the Arian Germinus. Justina
was bent on replacing him by another Arian. It was most
important to obtain an orthodox bishop for this influential
see. Although Ambrose had no jurisdiction whatever in
Illyria, he hastened to Sirmium, and Justina heard to her
dismay that he was in the cathedral enthroned, had summoned the people, and was about to proceed with the
election and consecration of a bishop.

She sent orders that he should be removed from his place.
Ambrose sat immovable on his tribune, and would not stir.
An Arian consecrated virgin went up to him, caught hold of

his garments, and tried to drag him out of his seat. Ambrose took no more notice of her than to say, " It befits neither a woman nor one of your profession to lay hands on a priest. Beware, lest the judgment of God fall on you."

The woman was so frightened that she fell ill and died in the night, and this caused such a scare among the Arians, that they no longer attempted to interfere with the proceedings of Ambrose. The Catholic party elected Anemius, and Ambrose returned to Milan, having earned the hatred of Justina.

The Western Council summoned by Gratian at Aquileja, to hear the case of the Illyrian bishops Palladius and Secundianus, met in 381. It was attended by only about thirty bishops. Palladius remonstrated; he had appealed to the whole Church, had demanded to be heard by a general council; he had calculated on support from some of the Eastern bishops. The bishops called on Palladius to condemn the statements in the letter of Arius to S. Alexander. Like the Eusebians at Nicæa, he had recourse to pitiable evasions: he would call Christ "very Son," "good and powerful," but would not say whether He were created or uncreate. When asked, "Is Christ very God?" he answered, " He is the power of our God." He adduced the texts John xvii. 3, 1 Tim. vi. 15, John xiv. 28. As he would not condemn Arius, he was deposed; he sneered at the proceedings, " Have you begun to play? play on." His companion, Secundianus, who rejected as unscriptural the proposition "the Son is very God," was condemned with him. The debate lasted from daybreak till one o'clock in the afternoon. The bishops wrote to Gratian and to Valentinian II., announcing the decision of the council.

In 382 a council was held at Rome, which S. Ambrose attended. Whilst there, he was invited by a lady of exalted rank to offer the Holy Sacrifice in her house beyond the

Tiber; he visited her for the purpose, and is reported to
have cured a paralysed woman on that occasion. Whilst in
Rome he fell ill, and was attended by his sister Marcellina,
and visited by S. Ascholius of Thessalonica. In the same
year he began his treatise on the Incarnation, which he was
induced to undertake by the following circumstances. Two
chamberlains of Gratian, who were Arians, while Ambrose
was preaching one day, proposed to him a difficulty, and demanded his answer. He promised to give it next day in
the Portian basilica. Accordingly he attended, along with
such of the people as were fond of theological discussions.
But the two chamberlains had not been serious in their
challenge—they had spoken out a difficulty as it rose in their
minds, and were too indifferent to go to the Portian church
to hear it elaborately and ponderously refuted. They had,
in fact, gone out for a drive in the country. Ambrose and
the people waited, but as the chamberlains did not appear,
he mounted the ambone and began an explanation of the
struggle between Cain and Abel, in which he made it abundantly clear that Arians, Apollinarians, and heretics in
general were that wicked one who slew his brother, and that
Christ was the true Abel whom they put to death afresh by
denying His divinity. This led to Gratian proposing to him
a difficulty, which Ambrose resolved; and out of these
circumstances grew his treatise on the Incarnation. Popular
imagination, of course, has made the two chamberlains tumble
out of their chariot and break their necks, but as Ambrose says nothing about this judgment in his treatise when
alluding to them, it is almost certain that nothing of the sort
took place.

Maximus revolted in 383, and Gratian was murdered at
Lyons. The whole of Gaul, and the army which Gratian
had led against Maximus, had gone over to the usurper.
Justina trembled for her son Valentinian, and in her distress

had recourse to Ambrose, and sent him to Trèves to nego-tiate with Maximus. Ambrose remained there the whole of the winter, awaiting the result of a deputation sent by the usurper to Valentinian. Maximus contented himself with the sovereignty of Gaul, Spain, and Britain, and left the child-emperor of Italy to be crushed on a future and more con-venient occasion. During his stay at Trèves, Ambrose refused to communicate with Maximus, the murderer of his sovereign. The interests of his earthly monarch or of the empire would not induce him to sacrifice for an instant those of his Heavenly Master; he would have no fellowship with the man of blood. Ambrose, who had loved Gratian, and directed his studies, and guarded his virtue, mourned for the young sovereign with tears, as for a son.[1]

In the senate-house at Rome stood, in the reign of Gratian, an altar of Victory, which Constantius had removed when he visited Rome,[2] and Julian had restored. Gratian, who showed his Christian zeal by refusing the robe of the Pon-tifex Maximus, which emperors had usually worn, again ordered the removal of the altar. The "great city," which had been "drunken with the blood of the saints," remained at this time, in spite of the energy and stateliness of its church, a stronghold of idolatry. Among its pagan nobles were the virtuous and high-minded Prætextatus, famous for his sarcasm about the Roman episcopate;[3] Flavian, one of the prætorian prefects; and Symmachus, the great orator of the party, who now went to plead for the restoration of the altar. But Damasus the Pope sent a memorial from Christian senators, repudiating all share in the pagan peti-tion, and declaring that they would not come into the senate-house if it were granted. Ambrose took charge of this

---

[1] "Doleo in te, fili Gratiane, suavis mihi valde."—De Ob. Val. 80.
[2] Probably wanting it for Constantinople, where his father had collected a great number of the best statues.　　[3] See S Damasus Dec.

memorial; Gratian refused to admit Symmachus, or to hear his eloquent appeal. This appeal is still extant. Couched in a feeble and apologetic tone, we perceive at once that it is the artful defence of an almost hopeless cause ; it is cautious to timidity ; dexterous, elaborately conciliatory ; moderate, from fear of offending, rather than from tranquil dignity. Ambrose, on the other hand, in the memorial he bore, and of which he was the author, writes with all the fervid and careless energy of one confident in his cause, and who knows that he is appealing to an audience already pledged by their own feelings to his side. He has not to obviate objections, to reconcile difficulties, to sue or propitiate ; his contemptuous and criminating language has only to inflame zeal, to quicken resentment and scorn. But it was not for the statue of Victory alone that the heathen orator appealed. Gratian had confiscated all the property of the temples, and swept away the privileges and immunities of the priesthood, even of the vestal virgins. Symmachus pleaded for toleration in the name of Rome. "Most excellent princes, fathers of your country, respect my years, and permit me still to practise the religion of my ancestors, in which I have grown old. Grant me but the liberty of living according to my ancient usage. This religion has subdued the world to my dominion ; these rites repelled Hannibal from my walls, the Gauls from the Capitol. Have I lived thus long, to be rebuked in my old age for my religion? It is too late ; it would be discreditable to change in my old age. I entreat but peace for the gods of Rome, the tutelary gods of our country. . . . . Heaven is above us all : we cannot all follow the same path : there are many ways by which we arrive at the great secret." [1]

The end of the third century had witnessed the persecution of Diocletian ; the fourth had not elapsed before

[1] "Uno itinere non potest perveniri ad tam grande secretum."

paganism˙ was pleading for toleration in her stronghold. Symmachus remonstrates against the miserable economy of saving the maintenance of the vestal virgins; the disgrace of enriching the imperial treasury by such paltry gains; he protests against the confiscation of all legacies bequeathed to them by the piety of individuals. "Slaves may inherit; the vestal virgins alone, and the ministers of religion, are precluded from this common privilege." The orator concludes by appealing to the deified father of the emperor, who looks down with sorrow from the starry citadel, to see that toleration violated which he had maintained with willing justice. Far different is the tone and manner of Ambrose as he appeals to the young and contracted mind of Gratian to prohibit the fatal concession. He asserts, in plain terms, the unquestionable obligation of a Christian sovereign to permit no part of the public revenue to be devoted to the maintenance of idolatry. "The emperor who shall be guilty of granting such a concession as is demanded will find that the bishops will neither endure nor connive at his sin. If he enter a church, he will either find no priest, or else one who will defy his authority. The Church will indignantly reject the gifts of him who has shared them with Gentile temples. The altar disdains the offerings of him who has made offerings to images."

Symmachus, foiled in his attempt, waited till the death of Gratian, and then made a second application in behalf of the altar of Victory, now to the childish Valentinian. But Ambrose was again prepared to resist him. He reminded Valentinian that no pagan was obliged by a Christian sovereign to join in Christian worship, and that boyish years would not excuse a weak betrayal of Christianity. He dwelt on the moral deadness and impotence of paganism.

"How long did Hannibal insult the gods of Rome? It was the goose and not the deity that saved the Capitol. Did

Jupiter speak in the goose? Where were the gods in all the defeats, some of them but recent, of the pagan emperors? Was not the altar of Victory then standing?" He insults the number, the weaknesses, the marriages of the vestal virgins when grown old. " If the same munificence were shown to Christian virgins, the beggared treasury would be exhausted by the claims." " Are not the baths, the porticoes, the streets still crowded with statues? Must they still keep their place in the great council of the empire? You compel to worship if you restore the altar. And who is this deity? Victory is a gift, and not a power. She depends on the courage of the legions, not on the influence of the religion—a mighty deity, who is bestowed by the numbers of an army, or the doubtful issue of a battle!" Valentinian refused to restore the altar.

The Empress Justina was ungrateful to S. Ambrose for his intercession with Maximus. In Lent of 384 she demanded in her son's name, for Arian worship, first the Portian basilica[1] outside the walls of Milan, and then, in its stead, the new and larger church of the Apostles within the city. As the former had been a basilica, or hall of justice, made over by the State to the Church, Justina thought the State had a right to reclaim the gift, to use it for the religious worship of the emperor. The Arians had been deprived of their churches under the Catholic emperor, Gratian. Under the Arian Valentinian they claimed at least a right to one church in which to perform their devotions. Officers of state came to Ambrose on Friday before Palm Sunday; he answered, " The priest cannot give up the temple." On Saturday the prefect in vain endeavoured to obtain at any rate the Portian church. The people clamoured to Ambrose to resist, and he did so. On Palm Sunday, Ambrose was in the baptistery, explaining the Creed, as was usual on that day, to the competentes, or

[1] Now San Vittore

candidates for the Easter baptism, the ordinary catechumens having left the church. A message informed him that curtains were being put up in the Portian, the ordinary sign of the emperor's claiming any place. "However," Ambrose wrote to his sister, "I remained at my duty, and began to perform Mass."[1] While he was "making the oblation," he heard with grief that Castulus, an Arian priest, was in the grasp of the Catholic population, who were likely to tear him to pieces. He forthwith sent clergy to his rescue, and prayed at the sacrifice that no blood might be shed in the contest. The court, highly incensed at the riot and the ill-treatment of Castulus, demanded a fine of the city for the disturbance, and imprisoned several Catholic tradesmen. Ambrose was urged by counts and tribunes to submit. "If," he firmly answered, "I were asked to yield what was mine, I would not refuse, although what is mine belongs to the poor. But what is God's I cannot surrender. Put me in irons, lead me to death; you cannot better gratify me." "At all events," said the officer, coldly, "control the passions of the excited rabble." He replied, "It is in my power to refrain from exciting them. The hand of God can alone allay them."[2] It was impossible, as they and he knew, to employ force, without a massacre ensuing. Ambrose spent the whole night in the old basilica. Before daybreak he went out, and found the church surrounded by soldiers. He returned to the Portian to save its falling into the hands of the Arians. This was on Wednesday. The soldiers quietly followed, and surrounded the basilica. Ambrose forbade communion with them; but as the guard was made up mostly of Catholic soldiers, the men's religious fears were thus appealed to, and they began to steal into the church. The women screamed and fainted; but the soldiers declared they had come there to pray, and

[1] "Missam facere cœpi." The earliest instance, apparently, of this term.
[2] "Referebam in meo jure esse, ut non excitarem, in Deo manu, uti mitigaret."

not to use violence against anyone. The lessons were from the Book of Job. Ambrose began to preach on Job's trials. He himself, the Catholic flock indiscriminately, were Job on his dunghill. The devil had robbed them of children, and goods, and good name. Ambrose thought it not indecent and disrespectful to the empress-mother to liken her to Job's wife urging him to blaspheme God, to Eve tempting Adam, to Jezebel encouraging the prophets of Baal and persecuting Elijah, to Herodias, the incestuous, seeking the life of the Baptist. Intelligence arrived that the populace were tearing down the hangings of the church on which was the sacred image of the sovereign, which had been suspended in the Portian basilica, as a sign that the church had been taken possession of by the emperor. Ambrose sent some of his priests to allay the tumult, but went not himself. He looked triumphantly around on the soldiers who had entered the church, and had listened without drawing their swords to the insults heaped on the name and character of the empress-regent. "See!" he said, "the Gentiles have entered into the inheritance of the Lord; but the armed Gentiles have become Christians and co-heirs of God. My enemies are now my defenders."

A confidential secretary of the emperor appeared, not to expel or degrade the refractory prelate, but to deprecate his tyranny and complain of his domineering. "Why do ye hesitate to strike down the tyrant?" replied Ambrose; and he added, "Yes, the priest has his dominion—it is in his weakness. When I am weak, then am I strong."

Ambrose spent the night with his priests in chanting psalms in the "little basilica."[1] Next day was Maundy Thursday, the solemn day for absolving penitents. While

[1] An oratory apparently in connection with the great basilica. The old churches were supplied with numerous buildings connected with them—baths, halls, galleries, sleeping-rooms, and rooms for eating in; so that people often spent nights and days in the churches.

Ambrose was preaching on the lesson, which consisted of the Book of Jonah, word came that the soldiers were recalled from their post, and the tradesmen restored to their homes. A scene of tumultuous joy followed; regardless of the sanctity of the spot where they were assembled, the people clapped their hands, and the soldiers rushed to the altar and kissed it.

The imperial authority quailed before the resolute prelate. The court dared not prosecute a struggle which might have jeopardized the life of the emperor. The Catholic rioters, abetted, as was proved, by the soldiers, who were ready to tear an Arian priest to pieces, might not shrink from putting an obnoxious emperor in his minority to death. When Valentinian was urged to confront Ambrose in the church, the timid and prudent youth replied, " His eloquence would compel you yourselves to lay me bound hand and foot before his throne." Ambrose triumphed in the destruction of the old dragon, smitten by God and cast out. But some of the officers of the court were highly incensed at the way in which Ambrose had allowed himself to speak of the emperor and his mother.

" While I live, dost thou thus treat Valentinian with contempt ? " said the eunuch, Calligone. " Verily, I shall strike off thy head." Ambrose replied, " God grant that thou mayest fulfil thy menace; I shall suffer as a bishop, and thou do the job of an eunuch." [1]

But it was intolerable that the free exercise of Arian worship should remain illegal whilst the emperor and his mother professed that form of faith. Justina persuaded Valentinian to repeal the law of Gratian, so far as it affected the Arians, and to allow them full liberty of worship. Benevolus, Prefect of the Memorials, or Secretary of State, refused to draft this law. He was not yet baptized, but he was an ardent

[1] " Tu facies, quod spadones."

controversialist and partisan on the Catholic side.   He was degraded, and retired to Brescia, his native place, where he made the friendship of S. Gaudentius, while Justina found a secretary more complaisant, and the law was promulgated in January, 386.   It granted complete and equal toleration to Catholics and Arians alike, and ordered that such as excited riots, or opposed the execution of this law by overt or covert measures, should be punished with death.

An Arian bishop, who took the name of Auxentius, claimed the throne of Milan.   Ambrose was called on to plead against him in the imperial consistory.   He gave in a written refusal to admit the principle of lay judges in matters of faith, and cited the words of Valentinian I., " It is not for me to judge between bishops."   The present sovereign, he boldly observed, was young and unbaptized ; one day he would see the absurdity of asking a bishop to " place his rights at the feet of laymen."

He took up his abode within the church, which was again filled with a zealous congregation, and guarded, as before, by soldiers who prevented all egress.   To enkindle enthusiasm, he set the people to sing hymns which he had written, full of terse and condensed energy, and to chant the Psalms antiphonally, " after the manner of the East."   He knew "how mighty a strain " was the doxology to Father, Son, and Spirit, which " made all who sang it teachers."   After some days had been thus spent, Ambrose preached, apparently on Palm Sunday, assuring his flock that he would never abandon them ; referring to Elisha in Dothan, and Peter in prison, denouncing Auxentius, and using the lessons of the day— Naboth's history and the entry into Jerusalem—for apposite and telling illustrations.   He quoted the passage about " tribute to Cæsar," and said that in the Church there was but one image, Christ the image of the Father.   There was no question about paying taxes; they were levied, as of course, on Church lands. That the Church had gold to bestow he denied not; Christ's poor were her stipendiaries. He summed up his principles in the words, "The emperor is of the Church, is in the Church, but is not above it."

It appears that the soldiers were withdrawn. After a new struggle, Ambrose had won a new triumph, the imperial power had sustained a new defeat. He was left free to dedicate a church—the Ambrosian; after which the people asked him to place some relics of martyrs in the new church, according to custom. "I will," he said, "if I can find any." The church of Milan, he admitted, was barren of relics; more the need for finding some now. He ordered the people to dig in the earth before the chancel screen of SS. Felix and Nabor. As they approached the place, a madman went into a paroxysm, and it was thought that the devil within him was disturbed by the holy remains. The bones of two men of great stature were found, with much blood.[1] The bodies were disinterred, and conveyed in solemn pomp to the Ambrosian church. There was great exultation. It was concluded that these were the relics of SS. Gervasius and Protasius, martyrs of Milan. A blind butcher, named Severus, recovered, or pretended that he had recovered, his eyesight by the application of a handkerchief which had touched the relics. Other wondrous cures were spoken of in a sermon preached that day by Ambrose; but this was the chief case. The Arians laughingly declared that the whole thing from beginning to end was a fraud; but we have not an account of their reasons for doubting the genuineness of the bones and the miraculous illumination of the butcher.[2] The popular excitement caused by the discovery,

[1] "Invenimus miræ magnitudinis viros duos, ut prisca ætas ferebat."
[2] They asserted that the madmen who cried out and went into convulsions in the presence of the relics had been bribed and educated to play the part. They drowned one of these wretches, but whether from anger at his testimony, or conviction that he was an impostor, we have no means of judging.

and by the reputed miracles, was so great as to stop Justina's attempts to recover the use of a church for the Arians in Milan.

It was not long after this that Augustine and Ambrose met. Augustine was engaged in the struggle against the Manichæan errors which had darkened his soul, and was preparing in a house near Milan for baptism at the ensuing Easter. Ambrose recommended him to read Isaiah. Augustine attended the sermons of the bishop, but, on account of the crowds who sought interviews with Ambrose, he had not the opportunities he desired of holding long conversations with him, and opening to him fully his heart.

On Easter eve, April 25, 387, Augustine, with his friend Alypius and his son Adeodatus, were baptized together by S. Ambrose in the baptistery at Milan.

Justina, having failed to crush S. Ambrose, employed him again in her service. He visited Trèves to ask Maximus for a ratification of the peace, and for the delivery of the remains of Gratian. Maximus treated the archbishop with disrespect, by refusing to see him except in public audience ; and Ambrose, on entering the consistory, declined the proffered kiss of peace, on the ground of this affront to his dignity. After some conversation, Maximus promised to consider Valentinian's request. Ambrose held aloof from the communion of the prince who had slain his master ; he refused also to communicate with Ithacius and the other bishops who had denounced and obtained the execution of Priscillian and those who agreed with him. S. Martin had also refused communion with bishops whose hands were red with the blood of heretics. In consequence of this, Maximus bade Ambrose leave the city. His chief regret was that an old and dying bishop, Hyginus, who had also refused communion with these prelates, was ruthlessly hurried into exile. "When I begged that the old man might not be thrust forth without a cloak and a feather-cushion, I was thrust forth myself." He made his way back to Rome, and wrote on his road a letter to Valentinian to be wary, and on his guard against a man who, under a semblance of peace, disguised a hostile purpose.

The conduct of Ambrose towards the Ithacian bishops was quite in accordance with his views of the sacredness of human life, though opposed to that intolerance which denied heretics the public profession of their religion, the logical sequence of which was persecution with fire and sword. A judge named Studius consulted Ambrose about his religious situation should he be called on to condemn criminals to death. Ambrose told him that it was necessary that capital sentences should be given, and there was no sin in pronouncing them. But he said that most Christian judges when they passed such sentences abstained from communion, and he praised the feeling which dictated this conduct. "You are excusable," he said, "if you communicate, but you are not praiseworthy." Several heathen magistrates were proud never to have stained their axes with human blood, and Christian judges should endeavour to be equally sparing in dealing forth sentence of death. In another letter Ambrose says that he had waxed warm on this subject, since certain bishops—he is alluding to the Ithacians—had dragged criminals before the courts and had obtained their execution. "When the guilty is made to die," he says, "the person of the criminal is destroyed, but not the crime. But when the criminal turns from the error of his ways, then the crime is blotted out, and the person of the criminal is saved." He recommends, however, great caution in bishops interceding for the lives of criminals; vanity and not charity may make them intercessors, and too liberal an extension of pardons to malefactors may encourage crime, and defeat the ends of justice.

Justina, fearing an invasion of Italy by Maximus, fled with her son to Thessalonica, to place herself and him under the protection of Theodosius. Maximus crossed the Alps, and Italy without opposition accepted him as emperor. In the meantime Valentinian was learning orthodoxy from the lips of Theodosius, and Theodosius love from the lips of the sister of Valentinian.

In his zeal for the faith, which was altogether genuine, if "not according to knowledge," glowing from his recent baptism, Theodosius dictated an edict, authorizing the followers of the doctrines held by Damasus of Rome and Peter of Alexandria, to assume the title of Catholics, and "as we judge that all others are extravagant madmen, we brand them with the infamous name of heretics, and declare that their conventicles shall no longer usurp the respectable appellation of churches."

Demophilus, bishop of Constantinople, was offered the alternative of subscription to the creed of Nicæa or banishment. The Arians were deprived of the hundred churches they had filled to overflowing, which were given over to the inconsiderable number of orthodox believers, a number, however, certain to multiply enormously under the quickening sunshine of imperial patronage.

About six weeks afterwards, Theodosius declared his resolution of expelling from all churches of his dominions the bishops and their clergy, who should obstinately refuse to believe, or at least to profess, the doctrine of the Council of Nicæa. On March 10, 388, he forbade heretics inhabiting cities, ordaining clergy, holding assemblies, and even appearing to plead their cause or their wrongs in his presence. He now made war on Maximus, who was defeated in Pannonia and put to death at Aquileja in the summer of 388. Theodosius remained at Milan several months. It was probably in the early part of his stay that, after approaching the altar to present his offering, he did not return, like other laymen, to the nave, but continued standing in the sanctuary. Ambrose asked what he wanted; he replied that he intended to communicate. Ambrose, by his archdeacon, bade the emperor withdraw from a part of the church reserved for the clergy. Theodosius at once acquiesced, explaining that he had been accustomed at Constantinople to remain in the sanctuary, but thanking Ambrose for giving him better instruction. In another case the prelate's admonition was less reasonable and less readily obeyed.

The Christians of Callinicum, in Osroene, had burned the synagogue of the Jews—it was said, at the instigation, if not under the actual sanction of the bishop. The church of the Valentinian Gnostics had likewise been destroyed and plundered by the zeal of some monks. Theodosius commanded the restoration of the synagogue at the expense of the Christians, and fair compensation to the heretical Valentinians for their losses. The pious indignation of Ambrose was not restrained by the remoteness of these transactions from the scene of his own labours or by the undeniable violence of the Christian party. He stood forward, designated, it might seem, by his situation and character as the acknowledged champion of the whole of Christendom, to claim the right and the honour to sack, and burn, and defile the sacred edifices of such as did not adore God after the most perfect way of the Catholic Church. In a letter to the emperor, he boldly vindicated the bishop; he declared himself, so far as his approbation could make him so, an accomplice in the glorious and holy crime. If martyrdom were the consequence, he claimed the honour of that martyrdom; he declared it utterly irreconcilable with Christianity that it should in any way contribute to the restoration of Jewish or heretical worship. If the bishop should comply with the mandate, he would be an apostate, and the emperor would be answerable for his apostacy. The act was but a slight and insufficient retaliation for the deeds of plunder and destruction perpetrated by the Jews and heretics against orthodox Christians. He argued that as Julian had not punished heathens for outraging churches, Theodosius ought not to punish Christians for lawless violence done to a synagogue. He followed up the letter with a sermon addressed to the emperor, when he was in the church. When he came down from the pulpit, Theodosius said, " You have been preaching at me." Ambrose did not deny it. " Well," said the emperor, " I certainly did give rather a severe order, but I have softened it. Those monks commit many outrages!" Ambrose flatly refused to proceed with the eucharistic service until the emperor promised to cancel the obnoxious orders. Theodosius at last gave way, at least in part; the law-breakers should not be punished. He was not so lost to the elementary principles of justice in his fanatical obedience to an imperious bishop as to remit the command that the synagogue should be rebuilt, and that the stolen treasures of the Valentinian "temple" should be restored. Ambrose pertinaciously repeated, " I depend upon you—I depend upon you." " Yes, depend upon me." Then Ambrose went up to the altar. "I would not have done so," he triumphantly adds, " if he had not given me a full promise."

A third application on behalf of the altar of Victory was not so promptly refused by Theodosius as Ambrose probably expected; but after some days his bold and pertinacious exhortations had their effect.

But if these acts of Ambrose might to some appear to savour of the narrowest bigotry, and unwarrantable aggressions on the dignity of the civil magistrate, the Roman world could not withhold its admiration from another act of the Milanese prelate. It could not but hail the appearance of a new moral power, enlisted on the side of humanity and justice; a power which could bow the loftiest, as well as the meanest, under its dominion. For the first time since the establishment of the imperial despotism, the voice of a subject was heard in deliberate, public, and authoritative condemnation of a deed of atrocious tyranny and sanguinary vengeance; for the first time, an emperor of Rome trembled before public opinion, and humbled himself to a contrite confession of guilt and cruelty.

The people of Thessalonica had quarrelled in a disgraceful cause with Botheric, the commander-in-chief of the forces in Illyricum; and having risen in tumult, had murdered him and several other officers. At first, Theodosius had been kindled into fury; Ambrose, apparently, had calmed him; but the high officials of his court, particularly Ruffinus, his chancellor, or "master of the offices," had persuaded him to order a general massacre. The circus, filled with the entire population of the city, was surrounded by troops, and an indiscriminate massacre of all ages and sexes, the guilty and the innocent, revenged the insult on the imperial dignity. Seven thousand lives were sacrificed in this remorseless carnage. The massacre lasted three hours. The most piteous case was that of a father, who offered himself as a substitute for his sons; the soldiers answered that they could only spare one of the youths, because they had to make up their tale of victims. The unhappy man, gazing on both, could not make up his mind to choose one before the other; and the impatient soldiers cut down both.

Such was the tragedy of which Ambrose now heard. Wishing to give Theodosius time to bethink himself, he withdrew for a while from Milan, and wrote to the emperor. The letter expressed the horror of Ambrose and his brother bishops at this inhuman deed, in which he should consider himself an accomplice if he could refrain from expressing his detestation of its guilt; if he should not refuse to communicate with a man stained with the innocent blood, not of one, but of thousands. The deed which had been done had no parallel. The emperor must repent like David. "You are a man, and temptation has come upon you; conquer it. Only penitence can take away sin. No angel or archangel can do it; even the Lord Himself forgives no sinners, save those who repent. I would persuade you, I entreat, exhort, admonish." The devil, he proceeded, had been envious of that kindness of heart, which was the crowning grace of the emperor's character. "I am attached to you, I love you, I pray for you; but I love God better."

Theodosius attempted to enter the church as usual; but Ambrose, who had returned to Milan, met him at the gate, took hold of his purple robe, and asked, "How can you presume to receive the most holy Body of the Lord, and to carry His precious Blood to lips which ordered so much bloodshed?" "David himself committed crimes," said Theodosius. The answer was ready: "You followed him in sin, follow him also in amendment." The emperor, abashed, did not press forward, but retired from the church, and remained excommunicate for eight months.

The feast of the Nativity of Our Lord arrived, and he remained shut up in his palace, and wept. Ruffinus, master of the offices, asked the cause of these tears. "I weep," the emperor answered, "because this day the temple of God is open to slaves and beggars, and I am alone excluded." Ruffinus offered to run and plead with Ambrose for restoration to communion. "You will not succeed," said Theodosius; "his sentence was just, and respect for the imperial power will not lead him to transgress the law of God." Ruffinus persevered. "Then run fast," said Theodosius. And, no longer master of his impatience, he followed his master of the offices at a distance. S. Ambrose saw Ruffinus coming. "You, the adviser of this massacre, are come to excuse it," he said. As Ruffinus urged the case, Ambrose, inflamed with zeal, said, "I tell you, Ruffinus, that I shall stand and withstay his entrance. If he will press in, it shall be over my body."

Ruffinus returned to Theodosius, who was in the middle of the square, and told him what Ambrose had said.

"Nevertheless I will go on," said the emperor, "I will receive the affront I have deserved."

He went on to the church, but instead of entering it, he turned into the audience hall where Ambrose was enthroned, and besought of him absolution.

"What penance have you done for this great crime?" asked the bishop. "It is for you to teach me what to perform," answered the emperor. Ambrose laid on him two obligations: one, to make public penance; the other, to pass a law by which sentence of death was suspended for thirty days, so as to allow time for a remission of the sentence should it have been delivered in a moment of anger, or on imperfect information.[1]

Then Ambrose raised the excommunication, and Theodosius entered the church. The emperor removed his imperial ornaments, and remained prostrate on the pavement, weeping and saying, "My soul cleaveth unto the dust, quicken Thou me according to Thy word." The people wept and prayed with him.

It was probably in allusion to this memorable deed of Ambrose that Chrysostom said, addressing the clergy: "If the unworthy person who comes to communion be a general or a prefect, or even he that wears the diadem, debar him; your commission is greater than his. But if you are afraid,

---

[1] This is told by Ruffinus, H. E. lib. xviii., and by Theodoret, lib. v. c. 18. But the law in the Theodosian Code bears the name of Gratian as well as of Theodosius, and is dated Aug. 18, 382.

refer him to me; I will shed my own blood, sooner than
administer Blood so awful, contrary to what is meet."[1]

A fourth application about the Altar of Victory took place
in the beginning of 392. The deputation could wring
nothing from Valentinian, who gave his answer without
any communication with S. Ambrose. The young western
emperor was now in Gaul. He gave promise of a noble
reign, being just and equitable, tender-hearted, pure in life,[2]
and sedulous in imperial duties. He was but twenty years
old, and he was still unbaptized. He looked forward to
receiving the sacrament of regeneration from Ambrose at
Vienne, to which place he summoned him, partly for this
purpose, chiefly to obtain from him release from the gilded
bondage in which he was held by Arbogastes. Valentinian
anxiously awaited the coming of Ambrose. "Think you
that I shall see my father?" he asked. But in May, 392, he
rashly risked a contest with his powerful general and master.
He received Arbogastes on the throne, and, as the count
approached with some appearance of respect, delivered to
him a paper, which dismissed him from all his employments.
" My authority," replied Arbogastes, contemptuously, "does
not depend on the smiles or frowns of a monarch," and he
cast the paper on the ground. Three days after, on Whit-
sun Eve, May 15, Valentinian was strangled by Arbogastes
in his palace. His body was conveyed with decent pomp
to the sepulchre in Milan; and the archbishop pronounced
a funeral oration to commemorate his virtues and deplore
his misfortunes. He spoke of the murdered prince as one
who had longed for baptism, and *therefore* received its
benefits. He represented him as baptized by Christ Himself, because human offices were wanting. Otherwise,

---

[1] In Matth. Hom. 82.
[2] When he gave a feast, he fasted himself; he declined even to look on a beautiful
actress.

reasoned the loving saint, catechumens dying for Christ could be no true martyrs; "but if they were baptized in their own blood, Valentinian was baptized by his piety and desire." He proceeded, in words which allude to Virgil's lament for Marcellus, to speak of offering the Eucharist for Valentinian's soul. "Give the holy Mysteries to my hands, give the heavenly sacraments. . . . . . Not with flowers will I strew his tomb, but will bedew his spirit with the odour of Christ."

On the murder of Valentinian, Arbogastes the Gaul, whose authority over the troops was without competitor, hesitated to assume the purple, which had never yet been polluted by a barbarian. He placed Eugenius, a rhetorician, on the throne. The elevation of Eugenius was an act of military violence; but the Pagans of the West hailed his accession with the most eager joy and the fondest hopes. Throughout Italy the temples were reopened, the smoke of sacrifice ascended from all quarters, the entrails of victims were explored for signs of victory. The frontiers were guarded by all the terrors of the old religion. The statue of Jupiter the Thunderer, placed on the fortifications amid the Julian Alps, looked defiance on the advances of the Christian emperor. The images of the gods were unrolled on the banners, and Hercules was borne in triumph at the head of the army. Eugenius restored the Altar of Victory in the senate, but hesitated about the temple estates which had been granted away, lest pecuniary loss should stimulate Christian zeal into conspiracy against his throne and life.

Ambrose fled from Milan, for the soldiery boasted that they would stable their horses in the churches, and press the clergy to fill their legions; and Eugenius, the renegade, was coming in state to Milan. From Bologna, whither Ambrose had betaken himself, the saint addressed a letter to Eugenius. "How," he asked, "can you make offerings to Christ? How can priests distribute your offerings? Everything that is done by the Pagans will be imputed to you." At Milan Eugenius made presents to the clergy, but they were indignantly rejected. When he sought admission to the churches he was repulsed.

In the meantime Ambrose in his exile was attending a ceremony for which he exhibited great partiality—the translation of relics. The bodies of Vitalis and Agricola, martyrs of Bologna, were "invented," and then translated. The bodies had been laid among the bones of Jews, but were discovered by means of the nails which transfixed S. Agricola, some crumbling remains of wood which the inventors were pleased to regard as part of the cross of the saint, and some bottles of blood which were miraculously, or suspiciously, preserved with the relics. S. Ambrose was not, however, the inventor of these remains—the discovery was due to the bishop of Bologna—but he assisted at the translation, and carried off some of the wood and nails, which were liberally given to him. At that time the bodies themselves were not parcelled out, so that a martyr might be distributed in particles over the globe.[1]

The battle of Aquileja saw the rout of Arbogastes, and the fall of Paganism, never again to raise its head. Eugenius was put to death, and his children brought up to abhor his memory.

Ambrose received the news in an autograph letter from Theodosius. He carried it to the church, placed it on the altar, and held it in his hand whilst offering the sacrifice. In his answer he advised the emperor to show mercy to the conquered, and especially to such as had fled for sanctuary to Christian churches. Then Ambrose went to Aquileja,

---

[1] A law of Theodosius, in 386, forbids the carrying of bodies from one place to another, and the sale of relics of martyrs. S. Augustine speaks of monks trafficking in relics (De Oper. Monach. c. 28), Paulinus, Vit. Amb. c. 27.

pleaded for the prisoners in person, and obtained their pardon. Theodosius, with courtly politeness, assured Ambrose that he attributed his victory, not to his own superior generalship, but to the efficacy of the prayers of the saint.

On reaching Milan, Theodosius abstained from communion, on account of the blood he had shed in battle, till the arrival of his children, whom he had sent for. These were Honorius and, probably, his sister Placidia, for Arcadius did not leave Constantinople. Theodosius presented them to Ambrose to receive his blessing. As he knew that he had not long to live, his speedy death having been announced to him by S. John of Egypt, but also, more certainly, by a dropsical habit, Theodosius divided his empire between Arcadius and Honorius. To the latter he gave the West, and Ambrose for a guide.

When Rome heard of the triumph of Theodosius, the senate met in solemn debate to consider the rival claims of Jupiter and Christ to the adoration of the Roman people. We have two accounts of this debate—one from the pen of the Christian poet, Prudentius, the other from that of the heathen Zosimus. According to the former, Jupiter was outvoted by a large number of suffrages. The decision was followed by a general desertion of their ancestral deities by the obsequious minority; but according to Zosimus, the senate firmly, but respectfully, declared to Theodosius that they adhered to their ancient deities. Theodosius refused any longer to assign funds from the public revenue to maintain the charge of the idolatrous worship. The senate remonstrated, saying that if it ceased to be supported at the national cost, it would cease to be the national rite. This argument was more likely to confirm than to shake the determination of the Christian emperor. From this time the temples were deserted; the priests and priestesses, deprived of their maintenance, were scattered abroad.

Theodosius died the year after the defeat of Eugenius (395), and S. Ambrose made his funeral oration. Next year Ambrose had the gratification of exhuming and translating the bodies of SS. Nazarius and Celsus.[1] The blood was still fresh, "as if shed yesterday," and the bodies entire. The blood was sopped up in rags and in plaster, and was thus distributed. No one had heard of SS. Nazarius and Celsus till these bodies were found. The story of their invention has an unpleasantly suspicious odour. S. Ambrose was probably imposed upon by some one who had committed a murder, and wished to disguise it by an appeal to the credulity of his times.

In 396 the emperor Honorius gave shows to the people of Milan. The wild beasts ranged round the amphitheatre, and roared and rushed on one another. But this was poor sport to those who desired to see human blood shed; and the people clamoured to have a criminal named Cresconius flung to the beasts. Cresconius had taken refuge in a church. Stilicho, who governed Honorius, sent soldiers to remove the criminal, and he was brought to the amphitheatre amidst the exultant shouts of the bloodthirsty mob. But two leopards let loose on the man, flew at the soldiers who introduced him to the arena, and injured them. Stilicho pretended to believe that this was a punishment for removing the man from sanctuary, and sent Cresconius away. Ambrose was highly incensed at this violation of the privileges of the Church.

There was at Verona a virgin named Indicia, whom Zeno, the bishop, had dedicated to God. She had been some time at Rome with S. Marcellina, but then went back to Verona, where she kept herself in hiding for some months, and the report spread that she had given birth to a baby, which she had killed and hidden. Her brother-in-law, Maximus, in whose house she was living at the time, and who ought to

---

[1] The account has been already given, July 28, p. 593.

have known what went on in it, believed that this was true, and complained to the bishop Syagrius of the scandal to his house and to the Church. The bishop asked for witnesses. Three women had spread the report, and two men said that they had heard it from these women. The men appeared before the bishop, but the women refused to state the grounds for their belief that Indicia had been delivered of a child. Syagrius ordered that the nun should be examined by some matrons. But to this Indicia would not submit. She appealed to S. Ambrose against the indignity. He assembled a council of bishops to discuss this delicate matter. They pronounced the two men of Verona excommunicate for having given ear to the tittle-tattle of the women about the nun. And Maximus, her brother-in-law, was also cast out of the communion of the Church. Ambrose wrote an angry letter to Syagrius, rebuking him severely for having dared to propose such a proceeding as a committee of matrons to visit a nun, and remarked, moreover, that indications of a recent confinement were often deceptive, and that the matrons, misled by appearances, might have given a wrong verdict.

S. Ambrose was next engaged in abating the dissensions of the Church of Vercellæ, which kept that see long vacant. He wrote a long letter on the subject, exhorting the people of Vercellæ to proceed in a right spirit to the election of a bishop. He referred to S. Eusebius of Vercellæ as the first Western prelate who had combined the clerical with the monastic life, and as having "preferred exile to ease," and "raised the standard of confession." He also warned them against two monks who had quitted the monastery near Milan, and were propagating the views of Jovinian that the influx of asceticism, which was deluging the Church, was, in reality, an invasion of Manichæan error. Afterwards he himself visited Vercellæ, and procured the election of the pious Honoratus.

His own noble life was drawing to a close. Stilicho, on hearing that he was taken ill, begged him, by messengers of high rank, to pray that he might yet live for Italy. Ambrose made the memorable reply : "I have not so lived among you as that I should be ashamed to live; yet I fear not to die, for we have a good Lord." From 5 P.M. on Good Friday until shortly after midnight his lips incessantly moved in silent prayer ; and after receiving from Honoratus "the Lord's Body as a good Viaticum," he breathed his last on the 4th of April, 397.

His body reposes in the basilica of San Ambrogio at Milan. He is represented in art with a beehive, and as one of the four Doctors of the Early Church.

S. FARA, V.

(A.D. 657.)

[Roman Martyrology. In some Martyrologies on April 3. "The Deposition of S. Burgundofara." Authorities :—Mention in the Life of S. Columbanus by Jonas (d. 665), and in the Life of S. Eustathius by Jonas; also, "Gesta in cœnobio Ebroicensi in dioecesi Galliæ Meldensi," in Mabillon, Acta SS. O. S. B. ii.]

S. FARA, or Burgundofara, was the sister of S. Faro and S. Cagnoald. Their father was Agneric, a powerful Burgundian noble. He was invested with the title which may be translated "Companion of the King;" and he was attached to Theodebert of Austrasia. When S. Columbanus visited Agneric in 612, the noble brought his little daughter before him, and asked him to bless her. The saint did so, but at the same time dedicated her to the Lord. This little girl is known to us only under the name of Burgundofara, or Fara, in reality a title, for Fara is the same as Bara, or Baroness, and Burgundofara really means "The Burgundian

Baroness." When Fara reached the age of fourteen her father wished to see her married; she, however, fell ill, and was at the point of death. In the meantime the abbot Eustace, the successor of Columbanus at Luxeuil, returning from Italy to give an account to Clothair II. of the mission to his spiritual father with which the king had charged him, passed by the villa of Agneric. At sight of the sick girl he reproached her father with obstructing her desire to enter the religious life, and Agneric agreed, if she recovered, to leave his daughter to follow her will. Eustace procured that recovery. But scarcely had he departed for Soissons when the father, unmindful of his promise, attempted again to constrain his daughter to a marriage, which she resisted.

She then escaped, and took refuge at Soissons in the church of S. Peter. Her father's retainers followed her thither, with orders to bring her away from the sanctuary, and threaten her with death. "Do you believe then," she said to them, "that I fear death? Make the trial upon the pavement of this church. Ah! how happy should I be to give my life in so just a cause to Him who has given His life for me!" She held out until the return of Abbot Eustace, who finally delivered her from her father, and obtained from him a grant of land on which Burgundofara might found the monastery which was called after her, Faremoutier.

Her example drew many followers from among the wives and daughters of the Frank nobility; she had even an Anglo-Saxon princess, Earcongotha, daughter of Earconbert, under her direction. Burgundofara lived about forty years in her abbey, faithfully observing the stern rule of S. Columbanus, and maintaining it steadily against the suggestions of the false brother Agrestin, who attempted to engage her in his revolt against Eustace and the traditions of their common master. "I will have none of thy novelties," she said to him ; "and as for those whose detractor thou art, I know them, I know their virtues, I have received the doctrine of salvation from them, and I know that their instructions have opened the gates of heaven to many. Leave me quickly, and give up thy foolish thoughts."

Some young novices, heartily sick of the life they led in the monastery, made an attempt to escape by night and return to the duties and pleasures of life in the world.[1] Some had descended a ladder, and were outside the detested prison, others were getting out of the window, when a globe of fire shot athwart the heavens, and exploded close to the convent. The blaze, the noise, woke the whole monastery, and the fugitives were prevented from escaping, and severely chastised. Two young nuns found it irksome to have to make confession of their faults three times a day, as enjoined by the rule of S. Columbanus, and ran away. They were pursued and brought back. In the monotony and routine of the convent life they pined and died, and Fara cast out their bodies to lie beyond the hallowed precincts of the monastery. A sister could not satisfy her hunger—she was a growing girl—with the short commons provided in the refectory, and she was wont to steal to the kitchen or larder and get more food. One day she saw a great hog seated at table beside her, consuming her food, and knew that it was the spirit of greediness which she had encouraged and nourished.

S. Fara is invoked for sore eyes.

Some of her relics are in the parish church of Faremoutier, others in that of Champeaux.

---

[1] "De canino more relicta viscerum putrimenta denuo sumere velle."

December 8.

THE IMMACULATE CONCEPTION OF THE VIRGIN MARY.
S. MACARIUS, *M. at Alexandria;* A.D. 250.
S. EUTYCHIANUS, *Pope of Rome;* A.D. 283.
S. EUCHERIUS, *B. of Trèves.*
S. SOPHRONIUS, *B. of Cyprus.*
S. ROMARIC, *Ab. of Luxeuil;* A.D. 653.

THE IMMACULATE CONCEPTION OF THE B.V. MARY.

[Modern Roman Martyrology. Anciently:—"The Conception of the most sacred Virgin Mary, mother of our Lord God Jesus Christ." The Oriental Menæas and Kalendars have "The Conception of Anna," on the 9th Dec. Anglican Reformed Kalendar, "The Conception of the B. V. Mary." According to the statement of the Abbot Engelbert, who wrote in the 13th cent., a certain Abbot Alfinus was commanded by God to introduce the festival of the Immaculate Conception by Anna of the Virgin Mary.[1] This Alfinus was no doubt Helchinius, mentioned in the ancient Breviary of Tours. At first it was left free to the people to observe it or not, as by the Council of Oxford of 1222, but not so a synod of London in 1287. It was again enjoined in a synod of London in 1328. It was ordered by the Council of Sens in 1247, and by the Council of Bayonne in 1300. The festival was introduced at Rome only after Benedict XIII. Sixtus IV. published two constitutions appointing this festival to be observed throughout the Church, and issued an office for it, but without making the festival one of obligation. Pope Clement VIII. elevated it to the rank of semi-double, Clement IX. gave it an octave, and Clement XI. constituted it a major festival "de præcepto" in 1708. The festival was, however, everywhere only that of the "Conception of Mary" till the promulgation of the decree of 1854 by Pius IX., making the Immaculate Conception of Mary an article of faith. The Franciscans of Naples asked permission of Pius VII. to celebrate the Immaculate Conception of S. Mary in the preface of the Mass, and this favour was accorded them by bull, dated May 17,

[1] Pez. Thesaur. Noviss. Anecdot. t. i. p. 705.

TREE OF JESSE.

From the Office for the Immaculate Conception in the Vienna Missal.

1806. Many Spanish and French dioceses and religious Orders asked the same favour, and it was accorded them. On Sept. 20, 1839, the Congregation of Sacred Rites granted the bishop of Ghent permission to add to the Litany of Loreto the invocation, "Queen conceived without sin, pray for us." Gregory XVI., in 1840, received petitions from all the Catholic world requesting him to proclaim the Immaculate Conception as an article of faith. This proclamation was, however, made by Pius IX. in 1854.]

BY the Immaculate Conception of Mary the Virgin is meant that, as Jeremiah and John the Baptist were sanctified from their mothers' wombs, so was she purified from all stain of original sin at her conception; thus of her, far more than of Jeremiah, it might be said, "Before I formed thee in the belly, I knew thee; and before thou camest forth out of the womb I sanctified thee;" [1] or of the Baptist, "He shall be filled with the Holy Ghost, even from his mother's womb." [2]

S. MACARIUS, M.

(A.D. 250.)

[Roman Martyrology. Usuardus. Authority:—S. Dionysius of Alexandria in his Epistle on the Sufferings of the Church in Egypt; preserved by Eusebius, H. E. lib. vi. 41.]

In the persecution of Decius, Macarius, a Libyan by birth, "after much solicitation from the judge to get him to renounce his faith, yet remained inflexible, and was burnt alive."

[1] Jer. i. 5.   [2] Luke i. 15.

S. EUTYCHIANUS, POPE.

(A.D. 283.)

[Roman Martyrology. Usuardus, &c.]

OF Eutychianus, pope of Rome, who succeeded Felix, next to nothing is known. The statement made by Usuardus and the Roman martyrology, that "he with his own hands buried three hundred and forty-two martyrs," is a manifest exaggeration. He is thought to have suffered martyrdom himself, and was laid in the cemetery of S. Calixtus. He was a Tuscan by birth.

S. ROMARIC, AB.

(A.D. 653.)

[Roman, Gallican, and Benedictine Martyrologies. At Toul on Dec. 9. Authority:—A Life by an anonymous monk, according to Mabillon, nearly a contemporary, in Mabillon, Acta SS. O. S. B. t. ii.; also the Lives of S. Eustace of Luxeuil, and of S. Amatus.]

ROMARIC was the son of Romulf, a noble in the Vosges. In the struggle between Theodebert and Theoderic, Brunehild had Romulf put to death, and confiscated his lands. Romaric went to Metz, where Queen Brunehild held her court for Theodebert her grandson. She had by her Aridius, bishop of Lyons, a great favourite, the counsellor, if we may trust Fredegar, of the barbarous murder of S. Desiderius of Cahors. Romaric cast himself at the feet of the bishop, and implored his intercession to obtain the restoration of his estates. Aridius kicked him in the face, and drove him away with blows. Romaric took refuge in the church of S. Martin. Next day came news of the death of Theoderic. Romaric was now safe; but he seems to have been disgusted with the world.

On the death of Theoderic or Thierry, Romaric occupied a high position at the court of Clothair II., then sole master of the three Frank kingdoms. One day S. Amatus of Luxeuil came into the Vosges, and was received by Romaric at his table. During the repast Amatus took up a silver dish, and said: " Thou seest this dish; how many masters, or rather slaves, has it already had, and how many more will it still have? And thou, whether thou wilt or not, thou art its serf: for thou possessest it only to preserve it. But an account will be demanded of thee; for it is written, 'Your silver and gold shall rust, and that rust shall bear witness against you.' I am astonished that a man of great heart, very rich, and intelligent, like yourself, should not remember the words of the Saviour, ' If thou wilt be perfect, go, sell all that thou hast, and give to the poor, and follow Me, and thou shalt have treasure in heaven.' "

Romaric at once resolved on abandoning the world. He distributed his lands to the poor, with the exception of his castle of Habend, freed a number of serfs of both sexes, and went to Luxeuil, taking with him all that remained of his wealth, to become a monk. When he presented himself to the abbot to have his hair cut, according to the rite of admission into the order, several of the serfs whom he had liberated appeared at the monastery for the same purpose. He gladly recognized his old servants, not only as brethren, but as superiors; for he sought the lowest occupations in the monastery, and surpassed all the brethren in care for the cultivation of the gardens, where he learned the psalter by heart as he laboured. After some years' residence there, during which time his friendship with Amatus became intimate and affectionate, the two friends left Luxeuil, where, for some unknown reason, they had incurred the displeasure of the abbot, Eustace. With his permission they went to Habend, and founded there a monastery for women, which has since borne the name of Remiremont. Amatus was charged with the government of the nuns, but soon devolved it on Romaric. In this celebrated abbey, which was immediately put under the rule of S. Columbanus by its two founders, everything was established on a magnificent scale, owing to the influx of nuns, and the liberality of the Austrasian kings. Remiremont soon became for women what Luxeuil already was for men. The number of nuns permitted the *Laus perennis* to be organized by means of seven choirs, who alternately sang the praises of God in seven different churches or chapels. The fervour and regularity of these virgins procured for the site occupied by their community the name of the "Holy Mount," which it retained for some centuries.

Romaric directed it for thirty years. Before entering Luxeuil he had been married, and had three daughters; the two younger took the veil in the monastery of their father. The eldest, who had married without the consent of Romaric, and without a fortune, attempted to reclaim a portion of her paternal inheritance. She sent to her father her first child, a girl, hoping that the heart of Romaric would soften, and that he would bestow on his grandchild what he had refused to his daughter. But his religious prejudices had stiffened into the one prevailing idea of monastic life, and had frozen out all the natural instincts of affection and principles of justice. He kept the child, placed her among the nuns, and she became eventually abbess of Remiremont. Then the mother, having a son, sent him, before he was even baptized, to his grandfather, still in the hope that the little babe would touch his heart, and obtain from the old man a good inheritance. But Romaric acted with him as with his sister; he kept the child from the arms of its mother and the influence of home, to be nursed in the hard discipline of the monastery, and the child became eventually an abbot and a saint.

There were two monasteries at Remiremont, one for women, the other for men, side by side, but with a special superior for each of the communities. Monks and nuns were presumably to one another only as brothers and sisters; but as this affection sometimes warmed beyond such relations, or was thought to do so, the council of Agde, in 506, insisted on their separation. This injunction was, however, everywhere disregarded. The monastery of men, also placed under the rule of Columbanus by its two founders, felt the intolerable burden of their rule, and was ready to listen to Agrestin when he attempted to organize an insurrection against the tradition of Irish monachism. After he had been overcome by Eustace at the council of Mâcon, and repulsed by S. Burgundofara at Faremoutier, he was received by Amatus and Romaric, who were already biassed against the abbot of Luxeuil. The death of Agrestin, and the failure of his scheme, induced Amatus and Romaric to return into communion with Eustace. Amatus died on Sept. 13, 627. At the end of his life Romaric regained his olden courage, and began once more to play a political part in the affairs of his country. He had known, in the palace of the kings of Austrasia, the great and pious Pepin of Landen, whose son, Grimoald, had become all powerful as minister under King Sigibert, and threatened the rights and even the life of Dagobert, the young heir of this prince. Grimoald had the long locks of the prince—tokens of his royal rank—shorn off, and sent the youth to Ireland under the care of Dido, bishop of Poitiers, no doubt with instructions that he should not be suffered to return. Romaric, hearing of the ambition and designs of Grimoald, despite his age and presentiment of approaching death, descended from his mountain, and took his way to the palace, which he had not seen for thirty years, to intimate to the nobles and to Grimoald the peril the country would run should such a course be pursued. He arrived in the middle of the night: Grimoald, on being informed of his approach, went to meet him with blazing pine torches. At the sight of his father's friend, of this old man of God, with his elevated and imposing stature and solemn aspect, he trembled. Then he embraced him with great respect, listened to his warnings with patience, but did not act upon them. Romaric retired laden with presents. Three days after, Romaric, who had returned to the monastery, visiting on his way the cultivated lands which belonged to it, was dead and buried beside Amatus, his friend and master.

A woman, kneeling by the one tomb which enclosed the two bodies, thought that she heard Amatus and Romaric conversing together in their narrow bed, and the contemporary biographer has condescended to record the delusion, or poetic fancy, of the woman.

December 9.

S. Syrus, *B. of Pavia ; 1st cent.(?)* [1]
S. Restitutus, *B.M. at Carthage ; 3rd cent.*
S. Proculus, *B. of Verona ; 3rd cent.*
S. Valeria, *V.M. at Limoges ; 3rd cent.* [2]
SS. Peter, Successus, Bassianus, and Others, *MM. in Africa.*
S. Leocadia, *V.M. at Toledo ;* A.D. 303.
S. Gorgonia, *Matr. at Nazianzen ; circ.* A.D. 371.
S. Cyprian, *Ab. of Perigueux ; circ.* A.D. 581.
S. Budoc, *B. of Dol in Brittany ; 7th cent.*
S. Lesmo, *H. at Glentamire in Scotland.*
B. Peter Fourrier, *P.C. at Gray near Besançon ;* A.D. 1640.

S. LEOCADIA, V.M.

(A.D. 303.)

[Usuardus, Ado, Notker, &c. Roman and Spanish Martyrologies. Authority:—The Acts of the Martyrdom, not ancient.]

 LEOCADIA is not mentioned by Prudentius of Saragossa (d. 405), who celebrated most of the Spanish saints. But it is certain that the fourth council of Toledo (A.D. 633) was held in a church dedicated to this saint ; [3] so that in the seventh century she received veneration. The Acts, which are not very trustworthy, say that she was of noble birth, and a native of Toledo. She was summoned before Dacian, governor of Spain under the emperors Diocletian and Maximian, and

[1] Pretended to have been disciple of the Apostles; probably belongs to the ₄th cent.
[2] A fabulous personage known through the apocryphal Acts of S. Martial.
[3] Built by King Sisebut, who died 615.

was scourged, then sent back to prison and reserved for another trial. Whilst in her dungeon, suffering from the blows she had received, she heard of the martyrdom of S. Eulalia at Merida, and the account of the sufferings she had undergone produced such an effect on her nerves, shaken by the treatment she had herself endured, that she died in prison. She is said to have scratched a cross on the wall of her prison, and to have kissed it before she died. There are three churches in Toledo dedicated to her: one built over her tomb, another occupies the site of the prison and contains the stone on which she scratched a cross, the third stands where was her family mansion. According to an absurd legend, when S. Ildefons of Toledo (d. 667) was praying in the church of S. Leocadia, on her festival, in the presence of King Receswinth, the tomb opened of its own accord, and the martyr, rising from it, took the archbishop by the hand and proclaimed in a loud voice, " O Ildefons, by thee the life of Our Lady has been maintained ! " alluding to his defence of the immaculate virginity of the Virgin Mary against the heretics who argued that she had become a mother by Joseph of " the brethren of the Lord." Whilst she was talking, Ildefons, with a prudent eye to relics, got hold of the king's sword with his disengaged hand, and as the virgin martyr was gracefully retiring back into her grave, he snipped off part of her veil, and this fragment is preserved in the church, and receives the most devout homage to this day.

On another occasion the Blessed Virgin Mary herself appeared to S. Ildefons and presented him with a chasuble, saying, " Receive this offering at my hands, which I have brought thee from my Son's treasury."

The Church of Spain instituted a festival on Jan. 21, in commemoration of this latter marvel.

If actual fraud was not on both occasions resorted to, to

help on the cause of orthodoxy, unscrupulous partisans invented these tales for the purpose of giving support to a controverted dogma.   Relics at Toledo, at Oviedo, Soissons, and S. Ghislain in Flanders; also at Vic-sur-Aisne near Soissons.

S. GORGONIA, MATR.

(A.D. 371.)

[Roman Martyrology.   Greek Menæa on Feb. 23; the Martyrology of the Basilian Monks (Græco-Italian) on Dec. 9.   Authority:—Mention in the writings of her brother, S. Gregory Nazianzen.]

GORGONIA was the only daughter of S. Gregory, bishop of Nazianzus and his wife S. Nonna.   She was apparently their eldest child.   Their two sons were Gregory and Cæsarius. Gregory, the father, belonged to the sect of the Hypsistarians, a curious mixture of heathenism, Judaism, and Christianity. These sectarians venerated light and fire, they observed the Sabbath, and abstained from meats.   But they also believed some of the truths of the Gospel.

Gregory was brought into the Church by his wife Nonna, and then was baptized and consecrated bishop of Nazianzus. Gregory, his son, was born the same year, but Cæsarius was born some years after.   S. Gorgonia was married and lived a most virtuous, devout life, though unbaptized.   She loved psalmody and adorning churches.   She was considerate and generous to the poor, devout in prayer, grave, and dressed quietly.   She was baptized when quite an old woman, along with her husband, her sons, and grandchildren.

Her confidence in God was so great that after a fall which had done her some internal injury, she would not, out of modesty, place herself in the hands of physicians.   She was healed by allowing Nature uninterfered-with to repair what was amiss. Had she committed herself to the surgeons, their bungling and ignorant operations would probably have killed her.

On another occasion when ill, and despaired of by the doctors, she went to church, and placing her head on the altar watered it with her tears, and mingled her tears with the Eucharist which was given her. She returned home perfectly well, to the confusion of the medical practitioners.

S. BUDOC, B. OF DOL.

(7TH CENT.)

[The day of the death of S. Budoc was Dec. 8, but the festival is transferred to Dec. 9, in the diocese of Dol, on account of the 8th being the Feast of the Immaculate Conception. In the diocese of Léon the Feast of S. Budoc was formerly observed on Nov. 18. The Gallican Martyrology of Saussaye on Nov. 19. Authorities :—A Life of the Saint in the Léon and Dol Breviaries, and in Legendaries used by Albert le Grand. Lobineau is angry with Le Grand for his Life, and says it is "remplie de fables," but the "fables" are in the Breviary.[1]]

THE legend of S. Budoc of Dol is one of those delightful tales with which the long winter evenings over the fireside were wiled away in the Middle Ages, and which, from the mouths of minstrels and professional reciters passed into the sanctuary, and losing its poetic form, was read in prose in cathedral and church choirs, as a narrative of facts to be believed. The story ranks with "Pierre de Provence and the Beautiful Maguelonne," "Hirlanda," "Robert the Devil," "The Seven Sons of Aymon," "Genoveva of Brabant," "Cæsar Octavianus," and "Fortunatus and his Wishing Cap."

---

[1] As an amusing instance of critical incapacity, it is worth while quoting M. D. L. Miorcec de Kerdanet, editor of the edition of Albert le Grand published in 1837, "Cette legende n'est point un conte . . . elle a toutes ses preuves dans la tradition et dans les actes des églises de Dol et de Léon."

Once upon a time in the days of old, the count of Goelo, in Brittany, sought in marriage Azenor, daughter of the count of Léon, who lived at Brest. The beautiful Azenor, " tall as a palm, bright as a star," consented to his proposals, and the marriage was solemnized with great pomp, " with sea-fights in the gulf and the port, and all sorts of pastimes to exhibit the public rejoicings, during the fifteen days that the wedding lasted." The count and his wife chose as their residence Castel-Audren, near a large mere full of fish.

They had not been married a year before the mother of Azenor died, and her father married again. The stepmother was, it may be at once conjectured, of the type usual in tales of this sort.[1] The new countess of Léon was filled with envy of the beauty, virtue, and good fame of the countess Azenor, and she resolved to compass her ruin. She began accordingly to instil suspicion of Azenor's chastity into the minds of both her husband and father. The poison of suspicion had its desired effect. The count of Goelo shut up his wife in a tower that commanded the mere, and forbade her to speak to any one. In her tribulation, the maligned countess prayed to the Holy Bridget of Ireland, her patroness. The stepmother, not satisfied with the in-carceration of Azenor, but thirsting for her blood,[2] gave her calumnies further shape and consistency. The count of Goelo assembled all his barons and council to judge his wife, accused of adultery. The unfortunate Azenor was brought into the hall for trial, and " seated on a little stool in the midst of the floor." The heads of the accusation were read out, and she was asked what she had to answer. She sobbed and declared her innocence. But in spite of

---

[1] " Matrem habuit novercam,
Nequitiæ plenam, per quam
Prodiit calumnia."—Proper of Dol.
[2] " Noverca vero, sanguinem innocentis
Azenoris summopere sitiens," &c.—*Ibid.*

there being no evidence for her conviction, she was condemned to be sent back in disgrace to her father at Brest.

The count of Léon tried her, and she was sentenced to death by being put into a barrel and cast into the sea, to be carried wherever the winds and tides listed. The sentence was executed. The barrel floated five months on the ocean, tossed up and down.[1] The barrel swam along the Cornish coast, doubled the Land's End, and drifted towards Ireland. During the five months' voyage, Azenor was supplied with victuals by an angel, who poked them in to her through the bung-hole. Whilst in the barrel, moreover, Azenor became a mother, the angel and S. Bridget assisting her as medical attendant and midwife.[2] As soon as the babe was born she made the sign of the cross on his brow, made him kiss the crucifix, and waited her opportunity for getting him baptized. The child began to talk even in the cask, before they came ashore.[3]

At last the barrel was rolled ashore at Aberffraw, or Youghal harbour, in Ireland, in the county of Cork. An Irish peasant, thinking he had found a barrel of wine, when he saw this cask stranded, after performing capers expressive of his delight, got a gimlet and was proceeding to tap the barrel, that he might sit and drink his full of its contents, when the babe from within shouted, " Don't hurt the cask." " And, pray, may I ask, who may you be there inside ? "

---

[1] " Hoc parato judicio
Mensibus quinque, dolio
Mari mansit devia."—Proper of Dol.

[2] " Azenor filium in dolio peperit."—Lect. Brev. Léon.
" Tandem peperit filium
Azenor, intra dolium
Quâdam ut in regiâ.
Ubi, cum luce splendidâ
Ministrans sancta Brigitta
Dabat necessaria."—Hymn in Léon Breviary.

[3] " Natus vero Budocus matri dixisse perhibetur, Ne timeas mater, quia Dominus nobiscum est."—Lect. Brev. Léon.

inquired the Irishman, withdrawing the gimlet. "I am a child desiring baptism," replied the babe. "Go at once to the abbot of this monastery, to which this land belongs, and bid him come and baptize me."[1] The Irishman tore off to Youghal, and gave the message to the abbot. "You are deceiving me," said the abbot. "And is it likely I should be telling your reverence of my find on the sea shore," answered the man, "if there had been anything better than a baby in the barrel?"

The abbot went down to the shore, stove in the cask, and extracted the countess of Goelo and her son.[2] The child was baptized and named Budoc, and was educated by the abbot of Youghal.

In the mean time the wicked stepmother had fallen very ill, and being at the point of death, confessed that she had fabricated the accusations against Azenor, and that they were wholly destitute of truth. When she had made this confession, she died. The count of Goelo, filled with grief at having sent away his wife on a false charge, started on an extensive and somewhat vague expedition in quest of the barrel. His good luck led him to Ireland, and he disembarked at Youghal, where he was happily reunited to his wife, and made acquaintance with his son. The count then had a stately ship got ready, and prepared to return to

---

[1] " Infans ab intus loquitur :
        Ne dolium lania.
    Piscator, mirans auditu,
    Retulit : Qui est ibi tu?
        Baptizandus sum eja.
    Vade, inquit, quæ vidisti
    Dic abbati det ut Christi
        Mihi baptismalia."—Lect. Brev. Léon.

[2] In the Dominican convent at Youghal was formerly preserved a miraculous image of a mother and child, and the story was told there that a great piece of wood had been washed ashore, and the prior was informed in vision that inside it was a Madonna and child.—"Monasticon Hibernicon" of Archdall, ed. by Dr. Moran, t. i. p. 151. One is led to suspect in the story of Budoc a trace of the myth of Velund in the Wilkina Saga.

Brittany with his wife and child. But unfortunately the sea-voyage had upset his constitution, and he died before he was ready to embark. Azenor, not caring to return to Brittany, dismissed the servants of her husband, and devoted herself to good works, prayer, and the care of her son. Budoc, at an early age, resolved on embracing the religious life, and was invested with the monastic habit by the abbot of Youghal. According to another account, Azenor returned to Brittany and built a convent on the headland of Raz, between Goulien and Lanourec, where she died. Two springs dedicated to S. Azenor are seen at Languengar. Women drink from that of Clesmeur to augment their supply of milk. A young man once took a draught from the holy well, and to his horror found his breasts swell and fill with milk. His tears, his prayers, his burning shame softened the saint, and she kindly suffered the fountains of his bosom to fail.

It is possible that the Azenor of these springs and the ruined convent at Raz may be different from the mother of S. Budoc.

S. Budoc, after the death of his father and mother and that of the abbot, was elected to rule the monastery of Youghal. On the decease of the king of Ireland, the natives raised him to the temporal and spiritual thrones, making him at once sovereign of all Ireland and archbishop of Armagh.[1] For two years Budoc exercised the fatiguing duties of his double rule, and he then convoked the estates of his realm to announce his resignation. But the Irish were wild with despair. They surrounded the palace and watched lest he should attempt to escape. But one night as he was praying in his metropolitan church, an angel bade him go to the sea-shore, take boat, and cross to Brittany.

[1] He is unknown to Irish historians. "Ab Hiberniæ populo Rex et Archiepiscopus desideratissime nominatur, exoptatur, deligitur."—Brev. Léon.

He left his palace, found the guards asleep, or drunk, came to the shore, but found there no boat, only a stone trough. He boldly stepped into this, and it floated him across the sea to Porspoder in the diocese of Léon.[1] The natives drew the stone coffer out of the water, and built a chapel and hermitage for the holy man.

Having spent a year at Porspoder, Budoc, who could not endure the roar of the waves, had his stone box mounted on a cart, and having yoked two oxen to it, resolved to follow the cart, and settle wherever the oxen halted. The cart broke down at Plourin, and there Budoc settled down for a short while. But he could not remain there long. His remonstrances with certain nobles who had acted in a disorderly manner obliged him to depart, and he went to Dol, where he was well received by S. Maglorius, the bishop, who soon after resigned his see in favour of Budoc. The saint ruled the church of Dol about twenty years, and died in the early part of the seventh century.

Probably the only element of truth in this long story is, that he was a hermit at Porspoder, and then at Plourin, and was afterwards made bishop of Dol.

---

[1] "Erat autem illi velut arca lapidea quædam, concava petra, in qua noctu jacere solitus erat, quam, angeli ministro, mari proximam conspexit; cujus suasu, tanquam navi quadam usus, transfretavit."—Brev. Léon. "Habebat quamdam petram viridem, velut arcam . . . et audivit vocem angeli, dicentis : Pone te super petram. Mox obedivit voci angeli, et petra, velut navigium, portavit eum supra mare."— Brev. Dol. The origin of the legend of saints boating in stone troughs, which is not uncommon among Breton saints, probably was this. In ancient Celtic mythology, the dead were supposed to be shipped across the western sea to Glasinis, the Isles of the Blessed, and they were often buried in boats in which to make the necessary voyage. The Christian abbots and bishops were buried in stone coffins, and among the vulgar it was said of them that they shipped to the Blessed Land in boats of stone.

December 10.

SS. EULALIA AND JULIA, VV. MM.

(A.D. 303.)

[Roman and Spanish Martyrologies. Usuardus, &c. Authority:— A hymn of Prudentius (d. circ. 406), and the Acts of later date.]

. EULALIA was only twelve years old when the persecution of the Church under Diocletian broke out in Spain. She belonged to a noble family of Merida. Fired with enthusiasm for her faith she presented herself before the judge, Dacian, and declared herself to be a Christian. Going up to a little idol that stood before an altar in the court, she threw it down, and trampled on the cake that was laid before it, and then spat in the face of the governor. By order of Dacian she was partially stripped and her sides were torn by hooks, then lighted torches were applied to her wounds. Her long hair caught fire, blazed up, and she eagerly inhaled the flame, and, exhausted by her tortures, sank and died. The executioners cast off her body from the rack, and a light snow fell and

veiled it. Prudentius relates that a white dove flew out of
her lips when she expired, but this is an addition of popular
imagination during the century between the martyrdom
and the date of the writing of the hymn.

Her maid Julia is said by the Acts to have suffered with
her.

On February 12 is commemorated S. Eulalia, V.M., at
Barcelona, who is said to have been put to death at the age
of fourteen. The Acts of both saints of the same name are
much alike, even to the falling of the snow to cover the
naked body. There can be little doubt that there was only
one S. Eulalia, the martyr virgin of Merida, and that Barcelona having possessed itself of some relics, true or false, of
the Meridan saint, in time got to believe that Eulalia was a
martyr of Barcelona, and distinct from her of Merida. The
relics of S. Eulalia are at Oviedo.

SS. MENAS, HERMOGENES, AND EUGRA-
PHIUS, MM.

(ABOUT A.D. 308.)

[Modern Roman Martyrology.   Greek Menæas and Menologies.
Authority:—The Acts in Metaphrastes, which are wholly apocryphal.]

MENAS was a senator of Alexandria, and philosopher,
who secretly professed Christ. The emperor Maximinus
heard that he was labouring in private to convert the heathen,
and he sent Hermogenes, an officer in whom he felt confidence, to Alexandria to cut Menas off. On his voyage
Hermogenes saw in a dream three luminous personages, who
assured him he would gain great advantage by his journey.

On reaching Alexandria, Menas was summoned into the
theatre, and asked what he believed. Menas replied in a

long oration which lasted four hours, and the judge and all the people hung breathless on his lips, and quite regretted when he ceased speaking—the most remarkable sermon on record. The substance of it, as given by Metaphrastes, would make a modern audience yawn in ten minutes.

Hermogenes ordered the soles of his feet to be scraped away, his tongue to be torn out, and his eyes to be scooped out. In this condition he was taken back to prison, where he perfectly recovered in a night. This miracle led to the conversion of Hermogenes and a number of soldiers. The emperor Maximinus then came to Alexandria, and tortured Hermogenes and Menas as cruelly as he was able, but found it impossible to do them permanent injury, as they were miraculously healed as fast as he could mangle them. Eugraphius, the servant of Menas, joined himself to his master, and finally all three were executed with the sword.

The Acts are inconceivably silly, and are utterly worthless. They are wholly unhistorical, and it is questionable whether they are founded on any basis of fact.

S. MELCHIADES, POPE.

(A.D. 314.)

[Roman Martyrology. Authorities :—Eusebius, H. E.; S. Optatus, the Epistles of S. Augustine, &c.]

POPE S. MELCHIADES succeeded Eusebius in the chair of S. Peter in 310. Maxentius had promised to restore their churches to the Christians; but though he had written a letter to this effect, and his commander of the prætorian guards had done the same, nothing was done. Melchiades sent these letters by some of his deacons to the prefect of the city, and claimed a fulfilment of the promise; but we are not informed whether his application succeeded. Melchiades was accused afterwards of having employed for this purpose a deacon who had delivered up some Church property during the late persecution, but he denied the charge.

In 313 Constantine wrote to Ursus, chief minister of finance for Africa, to pay a certain sum to the clergy of the Catholic Church in Africa, through Cæcilian, the bishop of Carthage; and the pro-consul was directed to announce to him that all persons engaged in the sacred ministry were to be excused from the burden of taking any public office. The Donatists sought to obtain the same immunity for themselves, and they brought a number of charges against Cæcilian, and claimed that they were the true Catholic Church of Africa. Constantine ordered Cæcilian, with ten bishops of his party and ten Donatist bishops to go to Rome; and he wrote to Melchiades on the subject. At the same time he wrote to three Gallic bishops, Rheticius of Autun, Maternus of Cologne, and Marinus of Arles, as well as to some Italian bishops, desiring them to go to Rome and give the rival bishops of Carthage an impartial hearing.

Fifteen Italian bishops joined the three from Gaul and the bishop of Rome in forming this council, which was held in the month of October. The council decided that the election of Cæcilian was regular, and that none of the charges had been proved against him; it was added, however, that the bishops who had condemned him, and who were now come to accuse him, were not to be excluded from communion. Donatus, alone, as the chief promoter of the schism, was excepted from this charitable decision. Melchiades died on Jan. 10, 314, and was buried in the cemetery of Calixtus.

S. DEINIOL, B. OF BANGOR.

(7TH CENT.)

[Anciently commemorated in Wales.   Alban Butler on Nov. 23.]

DEINIOL WYN, the son of Dunawd Fyr by Dwywe, a daughter of Gwallog ab Llenog, assisted his father in the establishment of the monastery of Bangor Iscoed, in Flintshire.   He is said also to have founded another monastery, called Bangor Deiniol, in Carnarvonshire.   Soon after this latter was raised by Maelgwn Gwynedd to the rank of a bishop's see, and Deiniol became its first bishop.   It is said that he received consecration from S. Dubricius, an event which must have occurred, if true, before 522.   But it is much more probable that he was consecrated by S. David. His father, called Denooth by Bede, was abbot of Bangor Iscoed at the time of the council of the Oak with Augustine (A.D. 600-3).   The poems of Llywarch Hên, a contemporary, prove that Dunawd was engaged in battle with the sons of Urien Rheged, who was living in 560.   Dunawd was therefore not abbot till the end of the sixth century, and his son Deiniol was not bishop till the beginning of the seventh century.   He is said to have been present at the synod of Llanddewi-Brefi, which is thought to have taken place before 569 ; but this synod rests on the authority of Rhyddmarch, and is very doubtful.   Deiniol certainly was not bishop at that time.   Geoffrey of Monmouth says that Deiniol died at the same time as S. David.   He died no doubt about half a century later than S. David.

THE TRANSLATION OF THE HOLY HOUSE
TO LORETO.

(A.D. 1294.)

[Roman Martyrology. Clement VII. allowed the festival of the
Translation of the Holy House to be celebrated at Loreto. Urban VIII.
extended the festival to all the Churches of the Marches in 1632. Innocent XII. approved a special office for the festival in 1669, and in 1724
Benedict XIII. extended the celebration to the States of the Church.
By a decree of Aug. 31, 1669, the Congregation of Sacred Rites added,
with papal confirmation, to the Roman Martyrology the following
notice on Dec. 10: "At Loreto in the Marches the Translation of the
House of S. Mary, Mother of God, in which the Word was incarnate."]

ADAMNAN, who wrote an account of the sacred places in
the seventh century, says that a church occupied, at Nazareth, the site "where formerly had stood the house [1] in which
our Saviour was brought up. This church stands on two
mounds, is supported by two arches. . . . Another church
is erected over the spot where the house had been built in
which the angel Gabriel visited the blessed Mary. This
information I had from the holy Arculphus, who remained
at Nazareth two days and nights."[2] John Phocas, who
visited the Holy Land in the year 1185, gives a minute
description of Nazareth. He says that near the first gate of
the village town is the church of the archangel Gabriel, and
on the left side of the altar is a small cave in which is a
spring: it was there that the Blessed Virgin Mary was wont
to draw water. "The house of Joseph was afterwards transformed into a most beautiful church;[3] on whose left side,
near the altar, there is a cave, its mouth adorned with white
marble slabs. Proceeding from the mouth into the cave,

---

[1] "Ubi quondam fuerat domus."
[2] "De Locis Sacris," ii. 26.
[3] This church was built by Tancred, circ. A.D. 1100, as William of Tyre tells us.

you go down some steps and get a view of what was anciently the house of Joseph, and where the archangel saluted the Virgin on her return from the fountain. On the spot where the salutation took place is a black stone cross on white marble, and above it an altar, and on the right side of the altar is a small cot[1] in which the ever-Virgin Mother had her chamber. But on the left side of (the place of the) Salutation is another small cot without opening for light,[2] in which our Lord Christ is said to have dwelt after his return from Egypt till the beheading of the Baptist."[3]

In 1253 S. Louis visited Nazareth, when he heard Mass in this church. In 1261 the Latin patriarch of Jerusalem, James Pantaleon, was suddenly elevated to the pontificate, under the title of Urban IV. He wrote to S. Louis in 1263: "The Sultan of Babylon has laid sacrilegious and destructive hands on the venerable church at Nazareth where the Virgin was saluted by the angel, and conceived by the Holy Spirit; and has *destroyed it entirely, levelling it to the ground.*"[4]

William of Baldinsel (Otto von Rienhuss) returned from a pilgrimage to the holy places in 1335; and wrote an account of them at the request of Cardinal Talleyrand; he describes the condition of ruin in which the church of the Conception and Annunciation had been left.

"In this spot (*i.e.* the place of the Conception) was a beautiful and large church, but alas! it has been destroyed! a small place in it has, however, been covered over, and is diligently guarded by the Saracens, where, near a certain marble column, they assert that the venerable mysteries of the Conception were consummated; . . . . in this place the infancy of Christ was passed. He was there educated by His parents, increased in age and favour, and was made subject

---

[1] Μικρὸς οἰκίσκος.   [2] Οἰκίσκος ἀφώτιστος.
[3] Compend. Descript. c. 10 in Leo Allat. Σύμμικτά.
[4] Ap. Du Chesne, Hist. Franc. t. v. p. 868.

THE B. VIRGIN AND CHILD.
From the Vienna Missal.

to His parents. A fountain is also shown, where the Child Jesus was wont to bathe, and whence the Mother and Child fetched the water for their human needs."[1]

With this agrees the account of Torsellus Sanutus, who made five pilgrimages to the Holy Land, and wrote his account of the sacred sites in 1306. He says, "At Nazareth is shown the place where the angel Gabriel announced the redemption of the world. In the chapel there were three altars, and the chapel was hewn in stone out of the rock, like the place of the Nativity and of the Resurrection. Indeed, great part of the town was of old hewn out of the rock, as is still evident." "These places," he goes on to say, when speaking of Cana of Galilee, "as others where Christ wrought anything, are underground; and persons descend to them by many steps into a vault, as is the case with both the site of the Nativity and the Annunciation."[2]

And so Sir John Maundeville, whose travels began in 1327:—" This salutacion was don in a place of gret awteer of a fair chirche that was wont to be somtyme; but it is now alle downe : and men hav made a litylle resceyt, be-syde a pylere of that chirche, for to receyve the offrynges of pilgrymes."[3]

Bernhardt von Bredenberg, dean of Mainz, visited Naza-reth about a century later, and gives exactly the same ac-count of the site of the Annunciation, the church all in ruins and only one marble pillar standing, and the rock-hewn chapel with its altar. So also Pierre Belon, who visited Palestine in the middle of the sixteenth century. He says also that the place of the Annunciation was a cave to which the pilgrims descended by steps.

This then remains evident :—

1. That originally a large church stood over the entrance

---

[1] Ap. Canis. Thesaur. Eccl. Mon., ed. Basnage, iv. p. 354.
[2] Ap. Gesta Dei per Francos, p. 253.   [3] C. x. p. 112, ed. Halliwell.

to a cave which was reported to have been the house of Joseph, and the scene of the Annunciation, and the place where Christ spent His boyhood.

2. That this church was ruined by the Saracens in 1261, and that only one marble pillar remained, but that access could still be obtained to the cave.

3. That after 1291, when, according to legend, the Holy House was removed from Nazareth, the situation was exactly the same as before : a ruined church with one pillar standing, and a cave containing an altar of the Annunciation.

Now let us turn to the Roman legend of the Translation.

Flavius Blondus, secretary to Pope Eugenius IV. and the following popes up to Pius II., who died in 1463, is the first writer who mentions the Sanctuary of Our Lady at Loreto in Picino, in his Italia Illustrata.[1] He describes it as richly adorned, but says nothing about the legend of its transportation from Nazareth.

The first writer to give this legend is Baptista Mantuanus, in his history of the church of Loreto, written between the years 1450 and 1480,[2] and his sole authority for the story was a "musty worm-eaten tablet," without date, among numerous other votive paintings and offerings, transcribed by Baptista in 1479. Baptista was General of the Carmelites, and the custody of the Sanctuary of Loreto had just been confided by Sixtus IV. to the Carmelite Order, so that it was to the interest of that Order that this shrine should pretend to possess some special attraction. And the next to mention the marvellous translation is Jerome Angelita,[3] who wrote in the sixteenth century, who also refers as the autho-

---

[1] Opp. ed. Basil, 1559, p. 339.

[2] Redemptoris mundi matris, Eccles. Lauret. Hist. in Opp. Bapt. Mantuani, Antwerp. 1576, t. iv. p. 216, seq.

[3] He was father of John Francis Angelita, historian of Recanati ; his history was published in 1601.

THE TRANSLATION OF THE HOLY HOUSE TO LORETO.

After a curious work by Père Kucher, entitled Atlas Marianus.

Dec., p. 132.]

[Dec. 10.

rity to a picture on the wall of the chapel of Loreto, " painted at the public expense of the people of Recanati."

The story soon elaborated itself in the popular mouth, and was adopted. The complete myth may be found in Rohrbacher, who relates it as follows.

In 1291, on May 10th, angels carried off from Nazareth the Holy House where Mary received the visit of S. Gabriel, where she conceived, and where she dwelt with Joseph, and Christ spent His childhood, and deposited it between Fiume and Tersatz, on the top of a hill, not very far from Trieste. A bishop or priest named Alexander, of a church dedicated to S. George, where not known, announced to the astonished people who visited this newly arrived house that it was the real house of Mary. It contained a crucifix; this he announced was made by S. Luke, and was an exact representation of Christ.[1]

Nicolas Frangipani, governor of Dalmatia, Croatia, and Istria, was then absent following Rudolf of Hapsburg in his wars. But when he received information of the arrival of the house, with the consent of the emperor, he hastened to Fiume to visit and venerate it.

Unfortunately for the story, in May, 1291, Rudolf of Hapsburg was holding a diet at Frankfort, and he was engaged in no war at all at the time, indeed he died that year, on July 15, worn out with age. Moreover, no such person as Nicolas Frangipani is known to history. There was also no one person in the thirteenth century who claimed to be governor of Dalmatia and Croatia, except the Doge of Venice and the King of Hungary. Moreover, Dalmatia and Croatia were then divided under the rule of several Venetian counts, whose names are known, and no Frangipani was among them. Nicolas Frangipani was count of

---

[1] The pilgrimage chapel of Tersatz, or Tersato, contains at present a miraculous portrait of the Virgin by S. Luke.

Segna, near Fiume, in the fifteenth century. So that the legend in Rohrbacher and elsewhere is unfortunate in its chronology. Also, there is absolutely no notice of the Holy House at Tersatz by any Hungarian writer, till quite late. The first to speak of the sanctuary there is Palladius Fuscus of Padua, a writer of the beginning of the sixteenth century, who mentions it in connection with the castle of the Frangipani not far from it, and he only speaks of it as a famous shrine of the Blessed Virgin, famous for miracles, but breathes not a syllable about its having been regarded as the site of a translation of the Holy House.

The legend goes on to relate that Alexander, the bishop or priest of S. George, was sent, with three companions, to the Holy Land to examine Nazareth, and report on the marvel. They did so, and were satisfied that the story was true. As it happens, the year 1291 was that in which it would have been impossible for any Christian to visit Nazareth, as it was then that Palestine lapsed back into the hands of the Saracens.

The story proceeds. From Tersatz the house was translated by angels to Recanati in the Marches of Ancona, but the place was so overrun with banditti, that the angels took it up again and put it down on a hill a mile off. There two brothers, possessors of the land, quarrelled over it, so the angels again removed it, this time to give it a permanent place of rest at Loreto, in 1294.

It was not, however, till Leo X. issued a bull dated August 1, 1518, that this story received authoritative approval by the Holy See. In this bull all four translations are stated as facts, and the whole fable is adopted as true history.

The Holy House of Loreto, which is generally stated to have been built of brick, is in reality built of the red sandstone of Ancona, the same stone that the poorer cottages of the neighbourhood are built of. At Nazareth the stone is grey. A Russian traveller in the eighteenth century, Basil Gregorivich Barsk, in his Travels, gives an account of the House of Loreto, and he believed the story; he thought the walls were of red brick, not noticing that they were of a brick-coloured sandstone; but when he got to Nazareth, he recanted his belief, for he found that no houses there were of brick, but all of the grey limestone of the district. It may be added that the Holy House of Loreto has a fireplace and chimney, and that chimneys are unknown to Eastern houses. Although the story is indisputably a mere idle invention, based on a tablet of unknown, if not questionably honest, origin, and has not the smallest shred of evidence to substantiate it, it cannot be denied that the solemn consecration of this myth, and its insertion in the Roman Martyrology are without their value. As the drunken helot was precious to the Spartans as a warning against intoxication, so may the conspicuous folly of the Loreto House serve as a memorial and caution to all ages of the abyss of blunder into which an uncritical temper may precipitate even the Sacred College of Rites.[1]

---

[1] It may be as well to point out some wilful or unintentional errors made by the Père Caillau, in his "Histoire Critique et religieuse de Notre Dame de Lorette," Paris, 1843; a vain attempt to bolster up this myth. He gives a list of early writers who have spoken of the House at Nazareth as still standing. Of these Eusebius, whom he calls to his aid, does *not* speak of Nazareth. The references to S. Epiphanius and S. Jerome are dishonest : Epiphanius says that Christ was brought up in the house of Joseph, *not* that the house was still standing. S. Jerome says that all that survived in Nazareth was its *name.* Two quotations of Caillau are equally dishonest. S. Paulinus, in his letters to Severus, does not mention Nazareth, and the reference to S. Gregory of Tours is equally worthless when examined to substantiate his pleas, for Nazareth is not mentioned. The reference to S. John Damascene is also false. Caillau makes Nicephorus Callistus a writer of the 12th cent.; he flourished in the middle of the 14th. He certainly does say that S. Helena "found the house where the angelic salutation took place," and to give this testimony more weight, Caillau moves back his authority two centuries. So, again, to help out a hopeless case by trickery, he makes Jerome Angelita give an account of the Translation in 1378, when he really lived in the 16th cent. Any one desiring to see the whole question of the Translation of the Holy House of Loreto carefully and critically examined, and the demolition of the Père Caillau is referred to the "Christian Remembrancer" for April, 1854, and an article by P. De Smedt in Analecta Boll., T. xxv. 1906.

December 11.

SS. Thraso, Pontianus, and Prætextatus, *MM. at Rome;*
    circ. A.D. 293.[1]
SS. Victoricus, Fuscianus, and Gentianus, *MM. at Amiens;*
    circ. A.D. 303.
S. Barsabas, *M. in Persia;* A.D. 342.
S. Damasus, *Pope at Rome;* A.D. 384.
S. Sabinus, *B. of Piacenza;* A.D. 420.
S. Daniel the Stylite, *H. at Constantinople; circ.* A.D. 489.

SS. VICTORICUS, FUSCIANUS, AND GENTIANUS, MM.

(ABOUT A.D. 303.)

[Roman and Gallican Martyrologies. Usuardus, Ado, Notker.
Authorities :—Mention in the Martyrology of Usuardus, and the Acts,
which, however, are late and not worthy of much trust.]

ICTORICUS and Fuscianus, two Christians,
lodged with Gentianus at Amiens, and instructed
him in the Faith. They were arrested. Iron
skewers were driven into their ears, red-hot nails
were struck into their temples, and then their eyes were
plucked out. They were run through with arrows, and as
none of these tortures killed them, they were finally decapitated. No reliance can be placed on this story. They
are also said to have taken up their heads and walked after
their execution. Relics in the cathedral at Amiens, others
at S. Quentin, others at Notre-Dame de Beaugency, in the
diocese of Orléans.

[1] Fabulous personages from the apocryphal Acts of S. Marcellus.

S. DAMASUS, POPE.

(A.D. 384.)

[Roman Martyrology. Usuardus, &c. Authorities :—S. Ambrose, Ep. 30 ; Rufinus, H.E. lib. xi. c. 10 ; Theodoret, lib. ii. c. 22, and lib. v. cc. 9, 10, 11 ; Cassiodorus, Tripart. lib. v. c. 28, lib. viii. c. 10, lib. ix. cc. 2 and 7 ; The Epistles, and Chronicle of S. Jerome, Ammianus Marcellinus, lib. xxvii. c. 3.]

DAMASUS, a Spaniard, son of Antonius, was educated by the sophist Eubulus and the philosopher Libanius. He was a cultivated man, able to speak and write both Latin and Greek. His father, Antonius, had been in succession scribe, lector, deacon, and finally priest of the title of S. Laurence, at Rome, and Damasus served the same church as his father, but, unlike him, was unmarried. When Liberius was banished by Constantius in 355, he was in deacon's orders, and he swore along with the greater part of the Roman clergy to receive no other Pope whilst Liberius lived. He accompanied the banished Pope to Beræa. He remained there with him but for awhile, and then, returning to Rome, in spite of his oath, submitted to the Anti-Pope Felix.

On the death of Liberius, the factions, which had been smouldering in secret, broke out into fierce flame. The partisans of Felix, the reputed Arian, elected Damasus, then a priest, and sixty years old ; those who had held fast to Liberius chose Ursinus.[1] Then ensued riot and bloodshed between the infuriated partisans, in which neither the weakness of woman nor the sanctity of the churches was regarded. S. Jerome says : "But after a short time Ursinus was consecrated by certain bishops, and invaded the Sicinine (church),[2] with his supporters, whereupon the people of the

[1] See the preface to the Libellus precum of Marcellinus and Faustinus, published by Sirmondi (op. i. p. 227).
[2] Probably the church of Santa Maria Maggiore in Rome.

party of Damasus rushed thither, and persons of both sexes were barbarously slaughtered." Ammianus Marcellinus, an impartial heathen, who is careful to show no prejudice in his mention of Christianity, says : "Damasus and Ursinus, being both immoderately eager to obtain the bishopric, formed parties, and carried on the conflict with great asperity, the partisans of each carrying their violence to actual battle, in which men were wounded and killed. And as Juventius (prefect of Rome) was unable to put an end to, or even to soften these disorders, he was at last by their violence compelled to withdraw to the suburbs. Ultimately Damasus got the best of the strife by the strenuous efforts of his partisans. It is certain that on one day as many as one hundred and thirty-seven dead bodies were found in the basilica of Sicinus, which is a Christian church. And the populace who had been thus roused to a state of ferocity, were with great difficulty restored to order.

"I do not deny, when I consider the ostentation that reigns at Rome, that those who desire such rank and power may be justified in labouring with all possible exertion and vehemence to obtain their objects; since after they have succeeded, they will be secure for the future, being enriched by offerings from matrons, riding in carriages, dressing splendidly, and feasting luxuriously, so that their entertainments surpass even royal banquets. And they might be really happy if, despising the vastness of the city, which they excite against themselves by their vices, they were to live in imitation of some of the priests in the provinces, whom the most rigid abstinence in eating and drinking, and plainness of apparel, and eyes always cast down on the ground, recommend to the everlasting Deity and His true worshippers as pure and sober-minded men."[1]

---

[1] "Facite me Romanæ urbis episcopum; et ero protinus Christianus," said Prætextatus, præfect of Rome.

The Preface to the Memorial addressed to Theodosius by Marcellinus and Faustinus, two Luciferian priests who had joined the party of Ursinus, enter into further details. The Preface says that Damasus got together labourers, charioteers, and gladiators to support his cause with their arms. Damasus was proclaimed by the followers of Felix in the church of S. Maria Lucina; Ursinus was elected by the priests, deacons, and faithful, who had adhered to Liberius in his exile, and was consecrated in the basilica of Sicinus, by Paul, bishop of Tibur. Damasus, with a mob of charioteers and a wild rabble, broke into the Julian basilica, and committed great slaughter. Seven days after this horrible scene in the church, Damasus succeeded by bribes and promises in winning over some of the priests from the party of his rival, and by their means seized on the Lateran Church, and was consecrated bishop.

Ursinus was now expelled from Rome by Juventius, prefect of the city, and Julian prefect of the Annona, along with his deacons, Anantius and Lupus, and seven priests who had made themselves conspicuous by their violence were also arrested. But the party of Ursinus flew to the rescue, delivered them from the hands of the officers, and conducted them to the basilica of Sicinus, in which Ursinus had received ordination. Thereupon Damasus gathered his rioters together armed with clubs, axes, and swords, and attacked the church at eight o'clock in the morning of October 28, 366. A furious fight ensued. Damasus succeeded in bursting in the doors of the church. The roof was torn off, and fire was thrown down on the partisans of his rival, and Damasus and his followers massacred a hundred and sixty-seven of their opponents. Not one of his own party fell. The party of Ursinians were obliged to withdraw, vainly petitioning for a synod of bishops to examine into the validity of the two elections. Ursinus returned from exile more than once, but Damasus had the ladies of Rome in his favour;[1] and the council of Valentinian was not inaccessible to bribes. Considering the means by which Damasus obtained the chair of S. Peter, it is not possible to read without a smile the judgment of S. Ambrose, "The holy Damasus was chosen by the judgment of God."[2] Ursinus returned to Rome, with his two deacons, in September, 367, but he was driven out again a couple of months later. His followers retained one church in Rome, and continued to assemble in the catacombs. Damasus appealed to the emperor Valentinian to allow him to dispossess them. Permission was given, and the unfortunate Ursinians were driven out by an armed band. Damasu was triumphant.

But the Ursinians, now turned out of their church, began to assemble outside the city walls in considerable numbers. Damasus would not concede them even this liberty, so implacable was his hostility towards those who had dared to oppose his election. He obtained a rescript from Valentinian, forbidding the schismatics from assembling within twenty miles of Rome.

Damasus was not satisfied with persecuting the party of Ursinus, he attacked also the Luciferians. His clergy broke into the church of that party, seized on Macarius the priest, and dragged him over flint stones till he was mortally injured. He further attacked Eusebius, the Luciferian bishop, but was unable to effect his expulsion.

In 375 Damasus condemned Apollinaris in a council he held at Rome.

Valens perished in the battle of Hadrianople, August 9, 378, and Gratian became sovereign of the whole empire. A synod was held at Rome, attended by a number of Italian

---

[1] He was nicknamed "Matronarum auriscalpius" (Ear-scratcher of the Ladies).
[2] Ep. 17.

bishops, partly to reaffirm the condemnation of Ursinus and partly to hear the justification of Damasus in a matter in which he had been accused by a Jew. The accusation was a disgraceful one—it was of adultery.[1] He was pronounced guiltless, and the Jew was exiled to Spain.

In 380 Priscillian, Instantius, Salvianus, and other Spanish bishops had incurred condemnation for their views, and they with all who thought with them were condemned by a rescript of Gratian to leave their churches and country, and were denied refuge in any portion of the empire. The rescript had been wrung from Gratian by the pertinacity of the cruel and irreligious prelate Ithacius. The three Priscillianists above named went to Rome to entreat the Pope to hear their justification, and obtain a mitigation of the sentence passed on them. But Damasus, with scornful injustice, refused even to allow them to enter his presence. Salvianus died in Rome. Instantius and Priscillian went to Milan, and met with a rebuff from S. Ambrose. S. Jerome, in the meantime, had associated himself with S. Damasus, assisted him with his advice, and composed for him many of his letters.

On the wealth, vices, and pride of the Roman pontiffs we have the testimony of Ammianus Marcellinus. The clergy of Rome were scarcely better than their chief pastors, according to the picture drawn of them by S. Jerome. He sketches the clerical coxcomb of his day in Rome, how his whole care was about his dress, that it was well perfumed ; that his feet were well shod, his hair crisped with curling-pins ; his fingers glittering with rings ; how he walked on tiptoe lest he should splash himself with the wet soil.[2]

Damasus died in 384. He left several poetical epitaphs,

---

[1] Bibliothecarius ; Vit. Damasi.
[2] "Sunt alii, mei ordinis, qui ideo presbyteratum et diaconatum ambiunt ut es licentius videantur."—Ad Eustoch.

and some letters. He was buried in a church he had built, beside his mother and his sister. He rebuilt the church of S. Laurence, in which his father and he had served, and adorned it with sacred pictures, five silver coronas for lights, and patens and chalices of precious metal.

S. DANIEL THE STYLITE, C.

(ABOUT A.D. 489.)

[Roman Martyrology. The Greek Menæas and Menologies and Russian Kalendars on Dec. 11, but the Neapolitan marble Kalendar of the 9th cent. on Dec. 12. Authority :—A Life written in the 6th cent., quoted by S. John Damascene. Theodore the Lector (fl. 527) in his Ecclesiastical History. A Life in Metaphrastes.]

S. DANIEL, "that admirable man," as Theodore the Lector styles him, was one of the first imitators of the extraordinary life of S. Simeon the Stylite. He was born at Maratha, near Samosata. His father's name was Elisha, and his mother's Martha. The latter had long been barren, and Daniel was given her after much praying, and a promise that he should be dedicated from infancy to God. Accordingly, when he was only five years old, the father and mother took him to a monastery, nameless, for he had not yet been baptized, and they wished him to receive his introduction to the Church and to Monachism simultaneously. The abbot bade the child go to the altar and bring from it one of the books that lay upon it. The boy obeyed, and returned with the Prophet Daniel. "That, then," said the abbot, " shall be his name."

As Daniel was too young to become a monk, he was sent back to his parents, and they brought him up till he was aged twelve, when he ran away from home, and presented himself at the gate of a monastery not far from Maratha.

He cast himself at the feet of the abbot, and said, "I am come, my father, to live to Jesus Christ, and to die to the flesh. If my health fails under the process, I will gladly die rather than look back." He was taken in, but not allowed for some time to wear the monastic habit. His parents urged the abbot to expedite the day of his profession, and the abbot yielded to their urgency sooner than he would have otherwise thought of doing, and cut off the young monk's hair, and clothed him with the habit of religion, before his parents' eyes.

The superior was obliged after a time to make a journey to Antioch, and he took Daniel with him. They came to Talada, or Telanissa, not far from where S. Simeon was spending his life on the top of a pillar. Daniel was eager to see the saint, and the abbot took him to the spot. Daniel was allowed to ascend the pillar, and he was received with affection by the Stylite, who blessed him, and spoke to him of the love of God.

Daniel remained in the monastery till the death of his abbot, as a humble monk, but when he was elected by his brethren to be their superior, he ran away, and betook himself to S. Simeon, and spent fifteen days with him. He then set out to visit the holy places, but found that the Samaritans were in arms ; and at the advice of an old man of sanctity, he did not risk his life in attempting to traverse their country, but went instead to Constantinople. This was apparently in 452, in the reign of Marcian, when Anatolius was patriarch. For the first seven days he remained in the out-buildings of the church of S. Michael, on the north of the city ; and afterwards he took up his abode in an old temple at Philamporus, which was popularly supposed to be the haunt of evil spirits, but which was really tenanted by owls, jackals, and other wild creatures. These disturbed his rest for some nights by their noises, but Daniel shut himself up from assault by wolves in a small apartment, the door of which he blocked at night with stones.

Some of the clergy and laymen of the better classes in the neighbourhood complained to Anatolius of the ragged monk who was encouraging superstition among the people by his eccentricities and asceticism. Anatolius, instead of driving him away, visited him, and embraced him, wishing him God-speed. Daniel spent nine years in the old heathen temple, and was believed to have wrought miracles. At the end of that time, the desire came upon him to follow the example of S. Simeon, and take up his abode on the top of a pillar. His desire was greatly enhanced by the following circumstance.

S. Simeon had bidden his disciple Sergius take his habit, or scapular, after his death to the emperor Leo. Sergius went to Constantinople with this valuable bequest. But Leo was either too much engaged with business, or too inappreciative of its value, to see Sergius, and the disciple of the great Stylite wandered about Constantinople with his inestimable and yet unvalued treasure, not knowing what to do with it. By chance he came to Philamporus, and made the acquaintance of Daniel, and they fell to talking of the merits of Simeon. Daniel then confided to Sergius his desire of humbly following the example of Simeon by also ascending a pillar, of which there were plenty to choose among in the old temple. Sergius, delighted to hear this, gave the scapular of the saint to Daniel, who received it with enthusiasm, and thought himself blessed as Elisha when the mantle of Elijah descended on him. Sergius then resolved to tarry at Constantinople, and attend on Daniel as he had on Simeon. None of the pillars of the old temple proved satisfactory, at least in their present situation, and consequently a pillar of a commodious height, and with a sufficiently broad capital, was set up by an admirer of Daniel on a hill in the

Anaplian quarter, on the side of the Bosphorus, towards the Black Sea.

Daniel issued from his cell at night, and before break of day mounted his pillar, where he soon became an object of curiosity and devotion to the sight-seers and pious of Byzantium. Crowds came to see him, and brought lunatics and sick people to be healed by him. Those who were afflicted were hoisted up to the top of the pillar, and then Daniel applied his hands to them, and was so successful as to cure many.

The patriarch Gennadius visited Daniel, ascended the column, and ordained the Stylite priest, after which Daniel celebrated the Divine Mysteries on the top of his pillar. The emperor Leo built him a taller, but more commodious pillar, composed, in fact, of two columns, with a little sentry-box on the top, into which he could retire in storms, and he finally roofed over the top of the column, as Daniel was exposed for a couple of nights to a severe snowstorm.

At the request of Daniel, Leo sent to Antioch for the relics of Simeon Stylites, and they were placed in a chapel at the foot of the column. Several houses were built near, to serve as the cells of the disciples of Daniel, and thence sprung up the afterwards important monastery of S. Daniel.

The winter of 466 was very stormy, and, in the gales, the pillar of Daniel was shaken, and threatened to fall. The emperor Leo rode to see it, and was furious with the builder of the column for not having made the structure stronger; his rage, however, does not seem to have extended to the Almighty for having sent rain and tempest against it. He determined to wreak a terrible vengeance on the builder, whom he could reach, and put him to a miserable death. But Daniel interfered, and with difficulty obtained the life of the unfortunate man. On his way back to Constantinople, as Leo was descending the hill on which the column stood, his horse tripped and fell, the emperor was flung on the road, and his crown was dashed with such force on the ground that the pearls started from their sockets. Leo escaped with only a scratch on his forehead, and attributed his deliverance from broken bones to the merits of S. Daniel. The groom of the stables, trembling for his life, and feeling pretty sure that the emperor would maim or kill him, because of the accident, fled to the pillar of Daniel as to a sanctuary. The groom was an Arian, but in the agony of his fear for his life, he assured the hermit on the pillar that he was quite prepared to believe and confess whatever was orthodox, if he would intercede for him. Daniel consented to these terms, and wrote to Leo to announce the conversion of the groom, and his desire that he might be pardoned for the accident which had befallen the emperor. Leo replied, " The danger in which I was placed was due to none but myself, and was my punishment for having dared get into my saddle in your august presence, instead of humbly walking till out of sight of your pillar. Far from being angry with Jordanus, the groom, I rejoice that the fall of my horse has raised him from his errors."

Leo took all the distinguished personages who visited him to see Daniel, as one of the sights of Constantinople. Gobazes, king of Lazica, in Colchis, having come to the capital, was taken by Leo to see the saint. Gobazes prostrated himself before the pillar, which he adored along with the old man on the top of it, and cried out, " I thank thee, King of Heaven, that in having come to see an earthly monarch, I should have been allowed to behold the celestial life of this man."

Leo had been but a humble tribune in the army, an Illyrian by birth, but he had been raised to the throne by the influence of Aspar, the general of the forces in the East. When the emperor Marcian died, without issue, Aspar coveted the throne for himself; but as he was an Alan by birth, and an Arian by profession, he did not venture to assume it, but nominated to it Leo, whom he hoped to rule, and who, he vainly expected, would be grateful to his patron after his elevation above him.

Leo was orthodox and pious, or superstitious. His wife, the empress Verina, veiled under a form of piety a character the infamy of which afterwards transpired. It was their united desire to have a son, to whom to bequeath the throne. For this they applied to Daniel, and he promised his most fervent prayers. A son was given them in 462, but the prayers of Daniel did not succeed in retaining him to his parents, for he died shortly after his birth.

The empress Eudoxia, daughter of Theodosius II., and widow of Valentinian III., came to Constantinople in 462, and showed the saint no less veneration than did Leo. She begged him to come with her to one of her estates, and set up his pillar, and perch himself on the top of it, in the neighbourhood of her mansion, when she could consult him at leisure. But he declined the offer.

The brother of Verina was Basiliscus, a man avaricious, cruel, and crafty, who withheld his hand from no crime which was likely to advance himself. To him was confided the command of the imperial troops.

War broke out between the emperor and Genseric, king of the Vandals. Genseric plundered Italy, and cast longing eyes on Alexandria and Constantinople. Leo sent a fleet against the Vandals, and in this expedition the incompetence or untrustworthiness of Basiliscus appeared. His troops had already plundered the north coast of Africa, and were threatening Carthage, when Aspar, jealous of his success, advised Basiliscus to rest content with these results, and Basiliscus, bribed, it is said, by Genseric, betrayed his own fleet into the hands of the Vandals. The trusty Ad-

miral, John Dominicus, after a heroic defence, plunged into
the sea to drown his grief and shame. Basiliscus returned
to Constantinople, but instead of being punished, was pardoned at the petition of his sister, and one of the generals,
Marcellinus, who murmured at the betrayal of the fleet, was
put to death. Basiliscus was, however, obliged to retire from
Constantinople, and Aspar was left supreme under the
emperor whom he had made.

When the expedition had started, Leo went to the pillar
of S. Daniel, to implore the prayers of the Stylite, in which
he trusted, and not without reason, rather than in the
talents and probity of Basiliscus. Daniel promised him that
Alexandria should not be taken and burnt by the Vandals,
and his words were fulfilled.

The feeble emperor, in order to obtain some support for
his throne from outside, endeavoured to make an alliance
with the Isaurians, a bold nomad horde of robbers, who had
risen to great power. For this purpose he invited one of
their chiefs to Constantinople, had him baptized, and given
the name of Zeno, married him to his daughter Ariadne,
and made him general of the troops in the East. Zeno's
growing influence and fortune awoke the rivalry of Aspar,
who sought his life. Zeno, warned in time, fled to Antioch,
and Leo, to pacify Aspar, named Patricius, one of his sons,
Cæsar, and designated him his successor. He gave his
daughter Leontia to Patricius, and hoped that he had
secured thereby peace for himself.

But Leo had not taken into consideration the religious
prejudices of the citizens of Byzantium. They saw with
suspicion the elevation of an Arian, rose in tumult against
Aspar, and he and his son fled to Chalcedon. Leo went
obsequiously after him, trembling lest Aspar should take the
head of the army and chastise the insolent citizens. He
promised him his protection, and the security of his offices;

then secretly surrounded him with some assassins, who, by Leo's orders, murdered him and his eldest son in the palace of Chalcedon. The two other sons succeeded in escaping, though severely wounded (A.D. 471). This act of treachery and cruelty created a tumult in Constantinople ; the party of Aspar and the Arians threatened the emperor, who was thrown into great alarm, and hastily recalled Zeno and Basiliscus. Another tumult broke out, when Leo named his son-in-law, the Isaurian Zeno, as Cæsar and his successor. Ariadne, ambitious and crafty, persuaded her father to invest her son Leo, aged four, with the title of Augustus. Zeno, like his father-in-law, held Daniel in high repute, and consulted him before undertaking anything of importance. He was sent into Thrace against the barbarians who ravaged that province. Before leaving, he sought S. Daniel, and the saint promised him, what was almost as much as could be promised to a general of the empire tottering to its fall, that his arms would meet with no disgraceful disaster. In January, 474, Leo lost his life in a riot. With the exception of a few laws, no traces remain of his seventeen years' reign. Of feeble body, and purpose, and mind, his only redeeming quality was his orthodoxy, which was unimpeachable. He was greatly under the influence of S. Daniel, and galloped from his palace to the pillar whenever in perplexity, to seek from that oracle advice and enlightenment. He died at the age of seventy-three, and was surnamed by his flatterers "the Great," a title not ratified to him by posterity. Leo II., son of Zeno and Ariadne, was now emperor, surrounded by the triumvirate of his mother, grandmother, and father. The two ruling women, fearing lest the power should elude their grasp during the regency of a feeble child, carried the young emperor to the hippodrome, placed him on the imperial throne, and Zeno bowed before his son with much humility to receive from his infant hands the crown, and from his lips the titles of Augustus and fellow-emperor. This was the first and only act of imperial authority exercised by the poor child, who soon after disappeared, apparently poisoned by his own father, who desired to reign as sole emperor. Zeno was vain, crafty, and revengeful. His stepmother Verina, his wife Ariadne, were women without womanhood; his son, by a first marriage, Zeno, was hated for his intolerable arrogance and excesses, but fortunately was not long-lived; his two brothers, who lived on his alms, and assisted him with their worthless counsel, were men with as little character and genius as the emperor. Thus the court of Byzantium became a nursery of intrigue and crimes. Verina, who found her son-in-law not wholly sub missive to her will, headed a plot against him, along with her paramour, Patricius, to obtain for herself and him the crown. But she carried on at the same time another intrigue with her brother Basiliscus. When this latter conspiracy was on the eve of breaking out, she divulged it to Zeno, pretended great alarm, and urged him to flight with his wife Ariadne. The cowardly emperor believed her assurances, and escaped from Constantinople, and took refuge in Isauria, his native land. Basiliscus was crowned by Verina : he gave his wife Zenoida the title of Augusta, and his son Marcus he created first Cæsar, and then fellow-emperor.

Zeno did not fly till he had consulted the oracle Daniel, who predicted to him a short exile, and then a return to his imperial throne. Daniel told him that like Nebuchadnezzar he would for a time be condemned to eat the herb of the field, but that after a while God would lift up his head again.

Basiliscus and Zenoida were addicted to Eutychianism, and at their call, Timothy Ailourus, or "The Weasel," bishop of Alexandria, who had been banished his see by the orthodox Leo, returned. Timothy the Weasel obtained from Basiliscus an encyclic letter which branded with anathema the whole proceedings of the council of Chalcedon, and the Tome of S. Leo, as tainted with Nestorianism. Everywhere the Eutychian bishops seized the sees, and expelled the orthodox prelates. Peter the Fuller was reinstalled at Antioch by Timothy himself, and Paul was given the see of Ephesus, from which he had been cast out by Leo. Acacius, bishop of Constantinople, was a man of great ability. He beheld the unwelcome presence and increasing influence of the rival patriarch of Alexandria with jealous suspicion, and refused to admit him to the communion of the Church. Fierce struggles for power distracted Constantinople; questions on abstruse points of theology were argued out with cudgels and daggers, and reciprocal curses. On one side were the Eutychian monks; on the other, Bishop Acacius and a large part of the populace and of the monks of Constantinople, for fierce bands of fanatic monks now appeared on each side. But the most powerful supporter of Acacius was S. Daniel. Each faction sought his aid or countenance. Acacius appealed to Daniel to defend with his tongue the truth of Chalcedon. Basiliscus complained to him of the violence of the patriarch, who was fomenting rebellion among his own soldiers. But Daniel sternly bade the emissary of Basiliscus withdraw. The tyrant had risen against God's truth proclaimed at Chalcedon, and God would revenge the defiance by hurling the upstart from his throne. The messenger, aghast, refused to bear such an answer by word of mouth. Daniel wrote it, sealed it, and bade the messenger convey it thus to the emperor.

But Acacius was not satisfied with such partisanship. He sent twice to implore Daniel to descend from that pillar up which more sober Christians would have been glad to escape to be away from the strife of party war. He consented, and went down; but he had lost the power of walking, and had to be carried. His entry into Constantinople was one of triumph. Basiliscus trembled in his palace, and sent word that he would not meet him. He left the city in terror, and took refuge in his country palace at Hebdemon. Daniel, borne aloft in his chair, pursued the flying monarch to his place of refuge, and his attendant monks clamoured at the door for admission. Basiliscus barricaded himself against invasion. A Goth of his guard looking from the window, saw the hermit borne above the heads of the crowd, and said " Ha ! a new consul." As he fell dead on the spot, probably struck by a stone from the rioters without, Basiliscus grew more frightened. Some of the officers of the emperor deserted him and swelled the crowd. One of the towers of the Hebdemon palace fell with a crash. Daniel bade his attendants take off their shoes and shake the dust from their feet against the anti-Christ, the second Diocletian. And he beat out the dust from his old habit towards the palace, as his defiance.

The mob returned to Constantinople without further violence, and Daniel was carried to the great church, where Acacius received him with demonstrations of lively joy. In the church a snake coiled itself round the feet of the hermit saint, but did him no harm.

Basiliscus, fearing for his throne, sent secretly to Daniel to implore him to visit him privately. The Stylite refused. Then the cowed emperor came himself to the hermit, grovelled at his feet, and implored his forgiveness and protection. Daniel poured forth upon him a torrent of denunciation, and predicted his speedy fall—a prediction certain of accomplishment. A coward, such as Basiliscus had proved himself to be, could not maintain himself long on the throne. Basiliscus, in abject terror at the strength and violence of orthodox zeal which he had provoked, issued a second encyclical letter, in favour of Chalcedon, and reversing what he had declared in his first letter. But his guards were disgusted at his want of spirit. There was not much choice between emperors—the stock seemed throughout rotten, and devoid of regenerative vigour ; but Zeno, with all his faults, was not so dastardly as this Basiliscus. Moreover, Basiliscus had discovered, or suspected, the intrigues of his sister, and had executed her lover, Patricius, whom she had destined to dethrone him.

A fire broke out in Constantinople, and destroyed with the finest quarter of the city the magnificent library containing 120,000 manuscripts. Discontent was general. Zeno placed himself at the head of some provincial troops, and the Isaurian robbers. Basiliscus sent Illus against him, but the army and its commander went over to the enemy, and Constantinople yielded without a struggle to the combined army. Basiliscus fled for sanctuary to the church of S. Irene ; but the refuge of Holy Peace was not for a heretic, said the patriarch, and cast him out, on the promise of Zeno that he would not shed the blood of the usurper. The wretched Basiliscus was taken, with his wife and children, to the castle of Limacus, near Cucusus, and shut up with them in a dungeon without food. They died of starvation, and were found, when the jailer opened the prison, locked in each other's arms (A.D. 477). The brief usurpation of Basiliscus had lasted but two years. Zeno was greeted by the orthodox as their deliverer and saviour. He reversed the decrees of Basiliscus, drove the Eutychians from their churches, and restored them to the Catholics.[1]

Zeno did nothing without consulting Daniel. He was under his influence as completely as was Leo. His want of firmness, his cunning and mistrust, filled his reign with distur-

---

[1] Timotheus Solofaciolus resumed the patriarchate of Alexandria, and endeavoured to reconcile the heretics by Christian gentleness. As he passed along the streets, the heretics cried, "Though we do not communicate with you, yet we love you." This great charity has cost him a place in the Martyrology and Menæa.

bances; and the fourteen years it lasted are as discreditable as any in the history of the Byzantine empire. Zeno, in his effort to pour oil on the troubled waters of religious controversy, issued his unfortunate Henoticon. It was composed, if not by Acacius, at all events under his direction, and almost certainly, also, with the sanction of S. Daniel, whose approval would assuredly have been solicited. The aim of this edict was not the reconciliation of conflicting parties, but the prevention of strife between them becoming more bitter, by requiring both to meet with outward conformity to Christian amity. The immediate effects of the Henoticon in the East seemed to encourage the fond hope of peace. The feud between the rival Churches of Constantinople and Alexandria was for a third time appeased. The three patriarchal sees of Antioch, Alexandria, and Constantinople approved the edict; but it encountered deadly opposition from Rome. Pope Felix III. anathematized all the bishops who had subscribed the edict, and condemned the Henoticon as a seed-plot of impiety.

But our narrative has nothing more to do with the events of ecclesiastical history. Daniel was grown too old to descend again from his pillar; his heart, perhaps, too soft with the light of dawning eternity for him to detect the iniquity that lurked in an attempt to enforce mutual forbearance on controversial points. He lived several years after the restoration of Zeno, and then had a little exhortation written down as his last will, to be bequeathed to his disciples.

It ran thus: "My children and brothers, for you are both—my children, because I am your spiritual father; and my brethren, because God is our common Father—I go my way to our common Father. I love you too much to leave you orphans, grieving at the loss of a father. I leave the care of you to our Heavenly Father, Who created me and you; to Him Who made all things with wisdom; Who bowed the heavens, and came down; Who died, and rose again for us. He will dwell with you, and will keep you from evil. He is Master of all things, as He is Sovereign Wisdom, and He will preserve you according to His will. As a Father, He will correct you with love, if you stray; and He will extend to you the arms of His mercy to bring you back to Him. He will keep peace and union among you, and make you as one before His Father, through that love which made Him die for us. Embrace humility, practise obedience, exercise hospitality, keep the fasts, observe the vigils, love poverty, and above all cherish charity, which is the first and greatest commandment. Keep yourselves firmly attached to all that concerns religion, avoid the tares of heresy, separate not yourselves from the Church—our mother. If you do all these things, you will be perfect."

There is a wonderful simplicity and beauty in this last touching instruction.

The saint, on the top of his pillar, when midnight was past, in the cold of a December morning, before the first streaks of dawn had lighted the south-east, by the glimmer of his lamps, celebrated the Eucharist, with the wintry stars shining crisply out of the dark sky. Three hours after, he was dying. Acacius of Constantinople was dead; his successor, Euphemius, hastened to receive his last sigh. A pious lady named Rhais came with expedition. The saint had promised her that she alone should lay out and prepare his body for burial. She placed it in a coffin of lead, and laid it in a tomb at the foot of the pillar. He died on December 11th, about 489, when he was eighty years old.

December 12.

SS. EPIMACHIUS AND ALEXANDER, MM.

(A.D. 250.)

[Roman Martyrology. Usuardus. By the Greeks, Epimachius on May 22 ; the Menology of Basil on Oct. 30 ; and the Translation of his relics to Constantinople on March 11. Authority :—The Letter of S. Dionysius of Alexandria, a contemporary, preserved by Eusebius, H.E. lib. vi. c. 41. The Acts of S. Epimachius are apocryphal.]

IN the persecution of Decius, Epimachius and Alexander suffered at Alexandria. Dionysius, a contemporary, says of them that after a long imprisonment, and after having suffered terribly from scourges and scrapers, they were burned to death.

SS. AMMONARIUM, V.M., AND OTHERS, MM.

(A.D. 250.)

[Roman Martyrology. Usuardus. By some Greek Kalendars on this day " Ammonatha and Antha." Authority :—The Letter of S. Dionysius in Eusebius, H.E. lib. iv. c. 41.]

FOUR women suffered with Epimachius and Alexander. " Ammonarium, a holy virgin, was ingeniously tortured for

a very long time by the judge, because she plainly declared
that she would not utter any of the expressions (in honour
of the gods) which he dictated ; and having made good her
promise, she was led away.   The others were, the venerable
and aged Mercuria ; Dionysia, also, who was the mother of
many children, but did not love them more than the Lord.
These, after the governor became ashamed to torture them
to no purpose, and thus to be defeated by women, all died
by the sword, without the trial by tortures.   But as to Ammonarium, she, like a chief combatant, received the greatest
tortures of all."   It will be seen that Dionysius, though he
says there were four women who suffered, names only three.
The Greeks call the fourth Antha.   The Western Martyrologies say " a second Ammonarium," through a misunderstanding of Dionysius, as though by twice mentioning Ammonarium he alluded to two of the same name.   But it is clear
that this is not the case.

S. CORENTIN, B. OF QUIMPER.

(A.D. 453.)

[Gallican Martyrologies. Nantes Breviary on Dec. 11.   His name
occurs in the 7th cent. English Litany published by Mabillon in his
Annals. Authorities :—The ancient lections for the festival of the saint
in the breviaries of Quimper, Léon, and Nantes.   A Life composed in
13th century worthless.]

S. CORENTIN, first bishop of Quimper, in Brittany, was a
native of Armorica.   He had a hermitage in the parish of
Plou-Vodiern, at the foot of Mont Saint-Côme, where there
was a little spring of water that filled a basin.   By a special
miracle a fish lived in this basin, which served Corentin
with a meal every day.   He put his hand into the water,
drew out the fish, cut off as much of its flesh as he wanted,

and then threw it back into the spring, where it recovered itself before his next meal. And thus the same fish served him for several years.[1]

There was a lame priest, a hermit, named Primael, who had a chapel near Châteauneuf-de-Faon. Corentin went to visit him. He slept the night at his hermitage, and next morning, Primael went to fetch water from the spring, which was at some distance. As the old man was lame, and the way long, Corentin pitied him, and driving his staff into the ground, brought forth a bubbling fountain at the hermit's door. Two eminent saints[2] visited him one day. Corentin was in despair. He had flour, and could give them pancakes for dinner, but pancakes, before it was understood how to season them with sugar, nutmeg, and lemon, were thought very insipid. He went to his fountain to have a look at his fish. It would be killing the goose that laid the golden eggs, if he broiled for his visitors the entire fish. But, to his great joy, he found the spring full of plump eels. He cooked them for dinner in light wine; and his visitors left, licking their lips, and glorifying God for having given them so dainty a meal.

However, one day King Grallo lost his way when hunting, and arrived hungry at the cell of the saint. Corentin was obliged then to cut a large slice out of the back of his fish. The king's cook, without whom Grallo prudently did not lose himself, scoffed at the small supply, but as he began to fry the slice of fish, it multiplied in the pan sufficiently to satisfy the king and all who came up to the hermitage. Grallo was naturally curious to see the fish itself, and Corentin

---

[1] "Ubi ejus sanctitatem Deus, cujus cum simplicibus sermocinatio est, insigni miraculo declaravit. Ex vicino namque fontis rivulo, quem ipse, circa horam prandii, aquam hausturus, frequentabat, piscis exiliens, sic ei se ipsum ultro commodabat, ut, abscissâ in cibum particulâ, integrum se denuo ad idem munus quotidie depræsentaret."—Lect. Brev. Léon.

[2] A Breton poet says S. Malo and S. Paternus, but the dates will not agree.

S. CORENTIN.   After Cahier.

took him to the fountain, where they found the creature fro-
licking about quite uninjured. An attendant of the king
tried his knife on the fish, and the wound remained un-
healed till Corentin discovered what had been done, restored
the fish to soundness, and bade it depart lest it should get
into mischief again through the concourse of the curious
who would be sure to come to the fountain on hearing of
the miracle. The prose for the feast of S. Corentin in the
Quimper Breviary says that it was the bishop of Léon who
tried his knife on the fish, but the lesson for the festival in
the Léon Breviary repudiates the charge, and lays the blame
on an attendant of the king. Grallo, charmed with the
miracles he had witnessed, presented the forest and the
hunting-lodge of Plou-Vodiern to the saint.

He had several disciples, of whom the most celebrated
was S. Winwaloe, afterwards abbot of Landevenec (March 3).
King Grallo raised Quimper into a bishopric, and S. Corentin was sent by him to Tours for consecration.[1] The saint
was at the Council of Angers in 453, and signed the decrees
as *Chariaton*. He died probably not long after.

A small fragment of bone is the only relic remaining of
this saint. It is preserved at Quimper in the cathedral.

In art, S. Corentin is represented with a fountain or a
bucket at his side, in which is a fish.

S. FINNIAN, B. OF CLONARD.

(A.D. 552.)

[Irish Martyrologies. Also on Feb. 23. Authorities :—A Life in
Colgan on Feb. 23.]

THE early history of this famous saint is so full of
anachronisms that it can scarcely be unravelled. It is

---

[1] It is said to S. Martin, but that saint d'ed in 401.

generally admitted that he was a native of Leinster, and that he was son of Fintan, of the race of Loschain, and that his mother's name was Talech. They are represented as Christians ; and accordingly it is related that, soon after the child was born, they sent him to Roscar to be baptized by Bishop Fortkern. The women who were carrying him were met on the way by S. Abban, who undertook to baptize him, and performed the ceremony at a place where two rivers meet. Finnian was brought up by Bishop Fortkern, but when aged thirty, he went to S. Cayman of Darinis, and then, crossing the sea, visited Killmuinne or Menevia, in Wales, and had interviews with S. David, S. Gildas, S. Cadoc, and others. He is said to have remained in Wales founding churches during thirty years. There is a church called Llan-ffinan in Anglesea, which may perhaps have been founded by him. He must have been in Wales about 520, and certainly did not spend so many as thirty years there. He returned to Ireland, and was given land by Muircdeach, prince of Hykinsellagh. He founded churches, and then a school at Magna, perhaps Hy-barche in Carlow, where he taught during seven years. He removed to Clonard about 530, where he opened a school. His reputation for learning was so great, that crowds of students flocked to his school and monastery, among whom are mentioned the two Kierans, S. Columba of Iona, and S. Columba of Tirdaglas. He is spoken of as being bishop as well as abbot of Clonard, yet he is never called so either in his Acts or in the Irish Kalendars. His usual food was bread and herbs, and his drink water. On festival days he ate fish and drank beer. He slept on the bare ground, and had a stone for his pillow. He was attended in his last illness by S. Columba, son of Crimthan, of Tirdaglas, and died at Clonard in the year 552.

S. BERTOARA, V

(ABOUT A.D. 689.)

[Gallican Martyrologies. Authority :—The Bourges Breviary.]

S. BERTOARA was born of noble parents at Bourges. She was wont to pass her days and nights in prayer. One night she found a poor man, called Meroald, covered with rags, lying in the gutter. He implored her to have him carried to the shrine of the bishop, S. Austregisl (A.D. 624). Bertoara called her servants, and bade them convey the man to the altar, and lay him down there. He was immediately healed.

Bertoara founded a monastery for women at Bourges, under the rule of S. Columbanus. She entered it herself, and died in the community.

S. ADELHAID, EMPSS.

(A.D. 999.)

[Gallican and German Martyrologies. Venerated in the diocese of Strassburg. Authority :—The Life or "Epitaphium" by Odilo, abbot of Clugny, d. 1049, in Pertz, Mon. Script. Germ. iv. p. 635. Also Wittekind, Ditmar of Merseburg, Frodoard, and other chroniclers of the period.]

HUGH of Provence, king of Italy, held his court at Pavia. He reigned at a time when the Papacy had sunk to its lowest abasement. The infamous Marozia was supreme in Rome. She had married Guido of Tuscany. She seized Pope John X., the former paramour of her mother, and cast him into prison, where he died, smothered by her orders. On the death of Stephen VII. this shameless woman placed on the

Papal throne her son, John XI., the offspring of her amours
with Pope Sergius, according to one contemporary account;
her lawful son according to another. But the lofty Marozia,
not content with having been the wife of a marquis, the
wife of a duke of Tuscany; perhaps the mistress of one,
certainly the mother of another Pope, looked still higher in
her lustful ambition: she must wed a monarch. She sent
to offer herself and the city of Rome to the new king of
Italy. Hugh of Provence was not scrupulous in his amours,
lawful or unlawful. Through policy or through passion, he
was always ready to form or to break these tender connections. Yet there was an impediment, a canonical impediment, to this marriage, which even Hugh and Marozia dared
not despise. Guido, the late husband of Marozia, and Hugh
of Provence were sons of the same mother. Even the
Levitical law, which seems to have occurred to some, would
not help them, for Marozia had borne children to Guido.
Hugh struck out a happy expedient, at the same time to get
over this difficulty, to obtain Rome, and to assume to himself
also the duchy of Tuscany. He circulated rumours that the
late duke of Tuscany was not the legitimate son of his
father Adalbert, nor was his brother Lambert, the reigning
duke, legitimate either. On the strength of this, Hugh
treacherously seized on Lambert, put out his eyes, appropriated the duchy of Tuscany, and then rushed to Rome to
take Marozia to his arms. The unhallowed marriage was
celebrated in the castle of S. Angelo, and so this "holy
man," as Luitprand designates him, went to his ruin. Alberic, son of Marozia, was commanded to hold the water for
the king to wash his hands after his meal. Performing his
office awkwardly or reluctantly, he spilt it, and received a
slap in the face for his fault. Alberic called the Romans to
arms to resent this insult, and cast off the burden of maintaining the Burgundian soldiers of Hugh. The castle of S.

Angelo was attacked, Hugh fled precipitately, and Alberic cast his mother into prison. Hugh made no further attempts to regain Rome. He held his court at Pavia. He now declared his marriage with Marozia void, and married Alda, daughter of King Lothair. On her death he wedded Bertha, widow of King Rudolf II. of Burgundy, and daughter of Burkhardt, duke of Swabia, and united the daughter of Rudolf to his son Lothair. This daughter was Adelhaid, and she was aged sixteen when she married the son of the man who had wedded her mother. The marriage was incestuous, but no prelate of the time ventured to remonstrate. Hugh bestowed the great bishoprics according to his caprice. One of his bastards he made bishop of Piacenza, another he made archdeacon of Milan, and attempted the assassination of the archbishop in the hope of forcing his son into the place thus bloodily opened to him. To Manasses, a favourite, archbishop of Arles, he gave the bishoprics of Trent, Verona, and Mantua. His court was a scene of debauch and licence. But Berengar, marquis of Ivrea, who had married the daughter of Boso, brother of King Hugh, rose in revolt. At the head of a large army, which gathered as it swept through Lombardy, Berengar approached Pavia, and wrested from the king his richest possessions. Hugh, in disgust, withdrew, drawing after him his treasures in waggon-loads, and buried his chagrin in the cloisters of S. Peter's, at Arles, where he died the year after, A.D. 941. His son Lothair enjoyed the barren honour of the title of king for three years, and then died in delirium, A.D. 950.

Berengar and his son Adalbert became kings of Italy. Berengar sought to unite the young and beautiful widow of Lothair to his own son Adalbert, and on her refusal treated her with indignity. She was stripped of her jewels and costly raiment, beaten, her hair torn from her head, and she was cast into a fetid dungeon of a castle on the Lake of Como.

From this she escaped, it is said, by the aid of a priest, who bored a hole through the wall of her prison. During her flight she was so closely pursued that, on one occasion, she was obliged to crouch among the standing corn to avoid those who were searching for her. She fell into a marsh, and lay there all night, till rescued by a fisherman in the morning. She took refuge with the bishop of Reggio, a kinsman, who sent her to his brother Atto, who commanded the strong fortress of Canossa. In this she was besieged by Berengar and his son during three years, but the impregnable situation and strong fortifications of Canossa defied all their efforts. Atto held counsel with the young queen, and sent entreaties to Otho, duke of Saxony, then victorious over the Hungarians, to come to her assistance, and accept her hand in return for her deliverance.

The castle was reduced to extremity, and about to capitulate, when the messenger returned with the joyful news that Otho had crossed the Alps, and was coming with forced marches to its relief. But the messenger could not get into the castle, so closely was it surrounded. He therefore tied his communication to an arrow, and launched it into the yard of the citadel. The news filled the gallant defenders with fresh courage. Otho was already at Verona, his son Ludolf had preceded him, and was at Milan when the messenger left. The German army caught the besiegers unawares. Berengar fled, but Adalbert and his two sons were taken and sent as hostages into Germany. Otho married the young widow, who was some twenty years his junior.

Ludolf, his son, quarrelled with his unwished-for stepmother, and dreading the fate of his unfortunate uncle Thankmar, suddenly quitted his father and plotted rebellion with the archbishop of Mainz. Ludolf's sister, the wife of

Conrad of Lorraine, to whom Adelhaid was greatly obnoxious, espoused the cause of her brother, who also found an ally in her husband, whom Otho had offended. For four years Otho was engaged in German wars, civil wars against his sons, and wars against the Hungarians. During three years Berengar and his son ruled the Italians with cruel severity. Ludolf, who had returned to the allegiance of his father, was despatched to Italy with an army to restrain them. After having overcome all resistance, he died, probably of fever. Berengar and Adalbert resumed their tyrannies, and the cry was loud for the interposition of the Germans.

Otho descended the Alps in the winter of 961-2, and was met at Pavia by Pope John XII., who anointed and crowned him as emperor, and Adelhaid as empress. Thenceforth the king of Germany claimed to be the Western emperor. Otho swore to protect the Church of Rome against all her enemies ; and Pope John took the oath of allegiance to him in Rome over the body of S. Peter, only to break it as soon as the back of the emperor was turned.

In the midst of the turmoil of political affairs, Adelhaid disappears from view. We only know of her that she was gentle, pious, and charitable, and that she attended with care to her son Otho. At Rome, in 972, this prince was married to Theophano, daughter of Romanus, emperor of Byzantium. Her extraordinary beauty attracted universal admiration. The trappings of the horse on which she rode were adorned with feathers, her Grecian dress was resplendent with jewels and pearls, and her hair was confined in a golden net. Yet all this splendour was outshone by the beauty of her features and the brilliancy of her eyes.

Otho I. died in 967, and the son of Adelhaid was king.

Otho II. was naturally of an impetuous and passionate temper, but his mother had carefully educated him, and not only had refined his tastes, but had given him a love of letters. His wife Theophano also sympathized in his love of learning.

Adelhaid had borne to Otho I. three sons—Otho II., Henry, and Bruno; and two daughters—Adelhaid, abbess of Essen, and Mathilda, abbess of Quedlinburg. Otho II. was only seventeen when his father died, and for a while his mother acted as regent. But Otho could not agree with his mother; the sudden acquisition of power in his hands proved too great a temptation for him to admit of her authority, or, perhaps, influenced by Theophano, his wife, who was jealous of the interference of her mother-in-law, he speedily broke with Adelhaid, drove her from court, and she was obliged to take refuge with her brother Conrad, king of Burgundy, at Vienne. Otho, however, at the exhortation of S. Majolus, abbot of Clugny, and probably stung by his own conscience, for he was good-hearted, recalled her. She went to meet her son at Pavia, accompanied by S. Majolus, and Otho threw himself on his knees before his mother, and asked her pardon for the wrong he had done her. She knelt before him, they clasped one another in their arms, and wept on each other's necks. After that Otho remained firmly attached to his mother.

Adelhaid took as her director first Adalbert, archbishop of the new see of Magdeburg, founded by her husband, and after his death, Odilo, abbot of Clugny, her biographer. She founded or restored several monasteries and convents in Saxony, Italy, and Burgundy.

She endowed the abbey of Murbach in Elsass, and the priory of S. Peter at Colmar. She founded a monastery at Salz, or Schlehm, in the diocese of Strassburg.

On the death of Otho II., Adelhaid had much to endure from the temper and pride of Theophano, who treated her with discourtesy and unkindness.

In the last year of her life Adelhaid went into Burgundy

to endeavour to compose the discord which had broken out between King Rudolf, her nephew, and his vassals.

Whilst she was at S. Maurice, in the Valais, she heard of the death of Franco, the recently-appointed bishop of Worms, at Rome, where was her grandson, Otho III., and she felt anxious lest the fatal soil or lax morals of Italy should affect the health of either the soul or body of Otho. From S. Maurice she went to Lausanne, and then to Orbe, whence she sent presents to several churches—to S. Benoît on the Loire, to Clugny, and to S. Martin at Tours, for the rebuilding of the abbey church, lately burned down. She saw S. Odilo of Clugny, kissed his habit, and bade him farewell : she should see his face no more.

Then she started for Salz, and falling ill with fever on the way, was conveyed there, and died, after having received the last sacraments with great devotion, on the 16th of December, 999, when aged about fifty-eight. She was buried at Salz.

Some of her relics are contained in a shrine which is preserved at Hanover.

December 13.

S. ANTIOCHUS, *M. in the Isle of Solta; circ.* A.D. 121.
S. LUCY, *V.M. at Syracuse;* A.D. 303.
SS. EUSTRATUS, ORESTES, AND OTHERS, *MM. in Armenia;* A.D. 303.
S. ABRA, *V. at Poitiers; circ.* A.D. 400.
S. AUTBERT, *B. of Cambrai;* A.D. 668.
S. JUDOC, *P.H. in Ponthieu; 7th cent.*
S. ODILIA, *V. in Elsass; 8th cent.*
S. ELIZABETH ROSE, *V. at Villechausson, near Courtenay;* A.D. 1130.
S. JEANNE-FRANÇOISE DE CHANTAL, *W. at Annecy;* A.D. 1641.

S. LUCY, V.M.

(A.D. 303.)

[Roman Martyrology. Usuardus, &c. Anglican Reformed Kalendar. Moscow Menology of 1850, with legend from the Latin Martyrologies. Moscow Kalendar of 1818; the Menology of the Emperor Basil. The 8th cent. Constantinopolitan Kalendar, and the marble engraved 9th cent. Neapolitan Kalendar. Authority:—The fabulous Acts, a Christian romance, possibly based on a few facts.]

. LUCY, it is alleged, was the daughter of a noble and wealthy family in Syracuse. Her father died during her infancy, and she was brought up in the faith of Christ by her mother, Eutychia. While she was still very young, S. Lucy, without the knowledge of her mother, dedicated herself to Christ by a vow of perpetual celibacy. Accordingly, when she was asked in marriage by a noble heathen youth of Syracuse, Eutychia used her influence with her daughter in his favour, seeing that the marriage was an advantageous one, both from the

position and fortune of the suitor, and from the known recti-
tude of his character.

Her mother was thereupon attacked by a bloody flux,
which resisted all medicine, till, at the advice of Lucy, Eutychia visited the tomb of S. Agatha at Catania.

Then Lucy obtained her dower from her mother, and at
once dispersed it among the needy.   Her suitor, highly incensed, denounced her to the governor, Paschasius, who had
her arrested and brought before him.   The Acts contain the
particulars of a long discussion between the judge and the
virgin, which bears a family resemblance to all other such
discussions, and which, if genuine, would oblige the reader
to believe that all early Christian martyrs were imbecile, and
all their judges fools.   But as these discussions are all certainly fictitious, they exhibit nothing but the barrenness of
invention of the minds of the romancers who composed or
amplified these tales of martyrdom.

The judge finally ordered Lucy to be taken from the judgment hall.   A crowd of attendants surrounded her.   Some
pushed at her with their shoulders, some dragged, but though
they streamed with perspiration (*deficiebant sudore*), they
could not make her stir an inch.   Then ropes were
attached to her hands and feet, and the crowd pulled at the
ropes, but also in vain.   Oxen were yoked to the virgin, and
though they strained every nerve, not a jot could she be
stirred.

Paschasius then ordered pitch and faggots to be heaped
round her, oil to be poured upon the pile, and the whole to
be kindled.   But this attempt failed as ignominiously as the
other.   Then, as a last resource, the sword was tried : her
throat was cut, and she bled to death.   With saints as with
witches, when everything else proves ineffectual to hurt
them, cold steel breaks the charm.   But before she died, she
was able to announce that thenceforth Catania would not be

the only Sicilian city privileged with the possession of a virgin martyr, but that Syracuse would divide the honour with the former city.

It is not improbable that a virgin Lucy did suffer at Syracuse, and died by the sword, but the Acts are worthless.

The relics of S. Lucy were translated to Constantinople, and thence to Venice. But Faroald, duke of Spoleto, having seized on Sicily in the seventh century, carried off the relics to Corsino, whence they were taken in 970 to Metz. There is consequently a dispute between Metz and Venice as to which possesses the genuine body of the virgin martyr.

S. Lucy is generally represented with a palm-branch in one hand, and in the other a burning lamp, expressive of her name, which means "light" in Latin. In place of this last emblem she sometimes carries a book, or dish, or shell, on which are two eyes—another, but less evident mode of allusion to her name. A wound in her throat, from which issues rays of light, is another mode of suggesting the same ideas.

S. ABRA, V.

(ABOUT A.D. 400.)

[Gallican Martyrologies. Venerated at Poitiers. Authority :—The Life of S. Hilary of Poitiers by Venantius Fortunatus.]

S. ABRA, the only daughter of S. Hilary of Poitiers, was born to him before he was raised to the bishopric. When S. Hilary was driven from his see, she remained with her mother at Poitiers. The governor of that city had a son who was attached to the young Abra, and declared his passion to her mother. When Hilary heard, in his exile, that a marriage was contrived for his daughter, he was highly incensed. He had conceived the idea of dedicating the

young girl to a virginal life. He therefore wrote her a
vehement letter, urging her on no account to listen to proposals of marriage, and exalting the state of virginity as that
which a Christian maiden ought to cleave to as her highest
privilege.

Abra could not well refuse to follow the determination of
her father, whom she reverenced as an oracle of God.
With the letter he sent her a couple of hymns he had composed, one for the morning, the other for the evening, and
he begged her to sing these daily, in order that she might
have her father constantly in mind. The second of these
hymns has been lost, but the first is preserved, and is sung
by the Church of Poitiers at Lauds on the festival of S.
Hilary.

On the return of the bishop in 360, he found that his
daughter had acquiesced more or less readily in his decision.
But apparently the surrender of the youth she had loved was
not without a struggle which had affected her health. Hilary
found her docile indeed, but languid, probably heart-broken.
She died painlessly in his presence shortly after his return,
and was followed not long after by her mother.

S. AUTBERT, B. OF CAMBRAI.

(A.D. 668.)

[Roman, Gallican, and Belgian Martyrologies. Usuardus, Notker,
&c. Authority :—A Life in Surius, apparently by Fulbert (d. 1029),
who wrote by order of Bishop Gerard of Cambrai.]

On the death of Aldebert, bishop of Cambrai, the people
elected in his room Autbert, of whose early life nothing is
known. He received sacred unction on March 21, 633,
from the hands of Leudegast, metropolitan of Rheims,
assisted by Atholus of Laon, and S. Acharius of Noyon.

His virtues soon made him illustrious, and Dagobert I. was wont to listen with respect to his exhortations, and put them in practice when convenient.

Among those youths who were intrusted to his charge to train for the Church, by parents who were overburdened with younger sons, was one named Landelin, who had no real vocation for the clerical life. He was impatient at the restraints, disgusted with the routine, and indisposed to embrace a life of celibacy. He accordingly ran away from S. Autbert, and as he dared not return to his parents, who were only eager to get rid of him, he joined a party of freebooters, called himself Morosus, and led a life the reverse of that to which he had been constrained in the school of the bishop.

One of his companions died, and after the funeral Morosus or Landelin dreamed that he saw him in the torments of hell, and heard that he was himself to share the fate of his comrade unless he returned to Autbert. He at once deserted his band, and went back to his master, and to the gravity and monotony of his former life. He afterwards became abbot of Crespin, and is numbered with the saints (June 15).

S. Ghislain founded his monastery at Ursidongus about this time. Prejudiced persons endeavoured to dispose Autbert to regard Ghislain with suspicion, but he said, " Let us not judge strangers, let us prove the spirits whether they be of God," and he sent for S. Ghislain. He was so well satisfied with the sincerity and earnestness of the stranger, that he offered to consecrate his church for him. And when the church was completed he went to it with S. Amandus and gave the new building episcopal consecration.

Among those present at the dedication was Madelgar, a noble, who then resolved to devote himself to God. He went shortly after to Cambrai, and received the tonsure from the hands of the bishop ; after which he retired to a monastery he built at Hautmont. His wife, S. Waltrudis, followed his example, and built a religious house at Château-Lieu, now called Mons.

S. Aldegund, the sister of S. Waltrudis, learning that S. Amandus and S. Autbert would be together one day at Haut-mont, presented herself before the two bishops, and implored them to give her the veil. They consented, and she founded Maubeuge.

S. JUDOC, P.H.

(7TH CENT.)

[Gallican and Roman Martyrologies. Authorities :—A Life by an anonymous author of the 8th cent. in Mabillon, Acta SS. O.S.B. sæc. ii. Another Life by the Abbot Florentius, in Surius ; a third Life from the Abbey of S. Meen, published in the 1st vol. of " Mémoires pour servir à l'histoire de Bretagne." A Life in Ordericus Vitalis, l. iii c. 13.]

S. JUDOC, also called Josse, was the son of Hoel III., king of Brittany. He was younger brother of S. Judicael, so that he must have been born about 591. His youth was passed in the monastery of San Maelmon. When S. Judicael resolved on abdicating, that he might retire to a monastery, he asked his brother Judoc to ascend the throne in his room, and look after his children. Judoc asked eight days to con-sider the proposal, and during them fled the monastery, in company with some pilgrims who were passing, and took up his abode with Haymon, count of Ponthieu, who had him ordained to serve as his chaplain. After some years Judoc asked leave to retire from the world, and was given Ray, on the river Authie, where he built a cell and chapel. There he spent eight years, till the curiosity of the people who came to observe him, and obtain miracles from him, drove him thence to Runiac, on the river Canche. The site of his cell there has become the town of Saint Josse.

After thirteen years spent at this place, he went into the forest land, and obtained from Count Haymon a grant of the valley of Pidrague. This was in 671, twenty-nine years after his flight from Brittany. He then set off for Rome, where he was received by Pope Vitalianus, and given many relics.

Judoc died a few years after his return, about 675.[1] His relics are preserved in the parish church of Saint Josse, at the mouth of the Canche, near Montreuil.

S. ODILIA, V.

(ABOUT A.D. 720.)

[Roman Martyrologies. Venerated in the diocese of Strasburg. Authority:—A Life by a writer in the 11th cent. ("Scarcely to be used as authentic."—Potthast) in Mabillon, Acta SS. O.S.B. sæc. iii. p. 2. Also a Life by an almost contemporary writer, of which a fragment has been published by Grandidier, "Hist. de l'église de Strasbourg," i. No. 27.]

THE legend of S. Odilia is as follows ; it must not be regarded as serious history, at least in its details :—

Adalric, duke of Elsass, by his wife Berchsind, maternal aunt of S. Leodegar, became the father of a little girl who was born blind. Disgusted at this, he ordered the child to be exposed or put to death, but the mother committed it to a poor woman, and then, when the child had grown to girl-hood, sent her to the convent of Baume.

There she remained twelve years unbaptized, till a Bavarian bishop, named Erhardt, in obedience to a dream, travelled to Baume to baptize the child.

No sooner was she baptized than her eyes were opened. Her brother Hugo brought her to her father, but the duke

[1] Lobineau, however, says 668 or 669. If the date of the abdication of Judicael could be fixed, that of the death of Judoc could be fixed approximately.

fell on the young man and struck him with his dagger, so that he died. Adalric, horror-struck at what he had done, felt the most poignant repentance, and did all in his power to make amends, by showing love to his daughter. He wished to marry her to the duke of the Allemanni, but Odilia fled from home, and when she was pursued by her father, a rock opened and received her in its bosom and concealed her from pursuit. The scene of this miracle is supposed to be a nook in a spur of the Black Forest Mountains that stretches to Freiburg in Breisgau. The spot is marked by a chapel built over a cave in which flows a spring of pure water. Probably the truth is that this was a cave in which S. Odilia took refuge, and where she remained in concealment for some years. Adalric then gave up his attempt, and promised her a convent and nuns, if she would become abbess. He built her a house at Hohenburg, and she retired to it and spent there the rest of her days. On her death, she was buried there.

Her shrine is an object of much resort by pilgrims, and their offerings are considerable; so much so, that in 1849 the pilgrimage church and the relics of the saint were put up to public auction, as a profitable speculation for the investment of capital, in spite of an energetic remonstrance from the bishop of Strasburg. The convent of Hohenburg, most picturesquely perched on the summit of a rock, is now occupied by Sisters of the Third Order of S. Francis.

S. Odilia is represented in art with a couple of eyes reposing on the pages of a book. She is vested as an abbess, and may thus be distinguished from S. Lucy, who has the same symbol, and is commemorated on the same day. It is possible that some confusion between the saints has given rise to the fable of Odilia's miraculously obtaining sight by baptism. She, like S. Lucy, is invoked in cases of ophthalmia and inflammation of the eyes. The spring in the cave at S. Odilien, near Freiburg, is much resorted to by those suffering with ophthalmia. They wash their eyes in the water.

S. JEANNE FRANCOISE DE CHANTAL, W.

(A.D. 1641.)

[Roman Martyrology. Beatified by Benedict XIV. on Nov. 13, 1751, and canonized on Aug. 17, 1767, by Clement XIII., who appointed that her festival should be observed on Aug. 21, though she died on Dec. 13. Authorities :—The Act of Canonization, her letters and those of S. Francis of Sales. Her Life by Beaufils, 1752 ; another by Henri de Maupas, bishop of Le Puy, 1753 ; another by Marsollier, 1772. There is a modern Life by the Abbé Bougaud, "Histoire de Sainte Chantal et des origines de la Visitation," Paris, 1863.]

JEANNE - FRANÇOISE FRÉMYOT was born at Dijon on January 23, 1572. Her mother died when she was only eighteen months old, but her father, Bénigne Frémyot, saw that she was properly educated. She was zealous in her profession of the Catholic faith. One day, when she was five years old, she heard a Huguenot gentleman deny the Real Presence before her father. The child went up to him and said, "Jesus Christ said that He was in the Holy Sacrament, and one must believe His word, or make Him a liar." The gentleman, amused at the precocity of the child, gave her some sugar-plums, but she flung them into the fire. When old enough to be married, her sister planned a union between her and a Calvinist gentleman, a friend of the brother-in-law of Jeanne, but she concealed from her his religious opinions. Jeanne, however, observed him at the Fête Dieu neither kneel nor remove his hat, as the Blessed Sacrament passed, and she at once broke off the engagement.

She was married at an early age to Christophe de Rabutin, baron of Chantal, and lord of Bourbilly and of Monthelm, whose mother was descended from S. Humbeline, sister of S. Bernard. She at once instituted a daily Mass in

S. JEANNE FRANCOISE DE CHANTAL.

the chapel of her castle, but on Sundays and festivals went to the parish church, though situated at some distance, in order to set an example to the peasants.

In a famine she was very charitable, giving soup and bread to the poor at her gates. Some of the poor made the circuit of the castle and reappeared as beggars. She noticed this, but did not refuse them a second portion. "Have I not to beg and beg of my God repeatedly?" she said.

Her husband was accidentally shot whilst out hunting, and left her a widow, aged twenty-eight, with three children. They had had six, but three were dead.

She went to live with her father-in-law, the old Baron de Chantal, at Monthelm. He was seventy-two, and not only was he ill-tempered, but he had introduced into the castle a lady of doubtful reputation, who had gained complete sway over him, and ruled the entire household. This woman treated the young widow with studied discourtesy.

In 1604 she met S. Francis of Sales, and then began that long and tender intimacy which lasted during the life of the saintly bishop of Geneva, and which was the means of drawing forth a beautiful correspondence which is an unfailing source of delight to pious readers. She chose him as her director, and made her vow of submission to him on September 2, 1604, at Notre Dame de l'Étang, a favourite place of Burgundian pilgrimage. She heard Mass every morning, then directed the education of her children. She made her own bed, and cleaned her own room daily, and dispensed with the assistance of a lady's maid for dressing her hair.

One day S. Francis asked her if she wanted to be married again. She answered that she had no such intention. "Then," said he, looking at her piled-up hair, done elaborately according to the fashion of the day, "down with the pilot signal."

She took the hint, cut her hair shorter, and dressed it more quietly.

She continued her charities as far as her means permitted. One day three tramps asked alms of her. As she had no money in her house, she took off and gave them a valuable ring which had belonged to her husband. The moment her back was turned, the tramps, knowing the value of the ring, decamped as fast as they could, shrewdly suspecting that the Baron de Chantal, if he heard of what had been done, would send after them, and reclaim his son's ring. This he apparently did, but the tramps had concealed themselves, so that they could not be discovered. Miracle-mongers have thereupon concluded that they were the Three Persons of the Trinity, visiting Jeanne as the three angels visited Abraham. There can, however, be very little question that the circumstances of the three strangers were simply as described.

S. Francis of Sales had planned an Order of ladies living together in the practice of active works of charity, without any very distinctive dress, or making profession of asceticism which would be modified in the next generation. This Order he resolved to call that of the Visitation, and he persuaded the Baroness de Chantal to become its first superior. The first congregation was formed at Annecy, under the direct supervision of S. Francis of Sales; and the sisters devoted themselves to nursing the sick in their cottages. The Society throve, and it was resolved to establish a second house at Lyons.

The king had granted letters patent for the foundation of a house of "Sisters of the Presentation" at Lyons, and as this foundation had proved a failure, the archbishop resolved to make use of these letters for the authorization of this new Society. For this purpose the words "of the Presentation" were carefully erased from the parchment containing the royal signature, and " of the Visitation " was substituted.

The substitution was, of course, fraudulent, if well intentioned, and rendered the perpetrator of it, should he be discovered, liable to imprisonment in the Bastille. Consequently it was determined to screen the person who had committed the ingenious, but dishonest alteration, by announcing it to be miraculous, and experts decided that the handwriting was indisputably that of the Almighty.

Madame de Chantal had the grief of learning the death of her son, killed on the island of Rhé in opposing the landing of the English, and of her daughter, Madame de Thorens, married to the brother of S. Francis.   Her father also died ; but perhaps her greatest loss was that of her dear friend and guide, S. Francis.   She saw her Society erected into an acknowledged Order, not, however, like most Orders, under one superior, but with each house subject to the bishop of the diocese in which it was situated.   This was the express stipulation of S. Francis.

She made the acquaintance of S. Vincent of Paul, and the two saints recognized the high gifts possessed by each other.

On the 8th December, 1641, she was attacked by inflammation of the lungs, on her way from Paris, at Moulins, and died on December 13, at eight o'clock in the morning, at the age of seventy.

Her body reposes in the church of the Visitation at Annecy.

December 14.

SS. Hero, Arsenius, and Others, *MM. at Alexandria;* A.D. 250.

SS. Justus and Abundus, *MM.;* A.D. 284.

S. Spiridion, *B.C. in Cyprus;* A.D. 350.

SS. Nicasius, *B.M.,* and Eutropia, *V.M. at Rheims; circ.* A.D. 407.

SS. Guinger or Fingar and Piala, *MM. at Ploudiri in Brittany; 5th cent. (see* March 12).

S. Venantius Fortunatus, *B. of Poitiers;* A.D. 600.

S. Fulquinus, *B. of Therouanne;* A.D. 855.

S. John of the Cross, *C. at Ubeda in Spain;* A.D. 1591 *(see* Nov. 24).

S. SPIRIDION, B.C.

(A.D. 350.)

[Roman Martyrology. Usuardus, by the Greeks on Dec. 12. Authorities :—Ruffinus, Hist. Eccl. lib. i. c. 5 ; Socrates, H. E. lib. i. c. 12 ; Sozomen, H.E. lib. i. c. 11 ; S. Athanas. Apol. 2 ; Photius, Biblioth. sub nom.]

MONG the bishops who assembled at the council of Nicæa, one of the most remarkable was Spiridion, bishop of Trimithus, in the island of Cyprus. He had been a shepherd before he was made bishop ; he remained a shepherd afterwards. Strange tales circulated about him. It was said that one night robbers entered his fold to steal a sheep, when they found themselves arrested by invisible bonds. In the morning when the shepherd-bishop came to let forth his sheep, he found the robbers in his fold. "Take a ram and begone, that your trouble may not be unrepaid," he said. "But I wish you

S. SPIRIDION.   After Cahier.

had asked me for one before you ventured to lay hands on my sheep."

On the death of his wife, his daughter Irene attended him ; but she died also. One day a man asked him to restore a deposit that had been left with Irene. The bishop was in despair ; his daughter had not told him where she had concealed it. He went to her grave, and called her by name. She answered, and asked what he wanted. "Where, my child, have you hidden the deposit confided to you?" She told him where it was buried. He dug on the spot indicated, and was able to give the money back to the depositor.

Two less marvellous but more instructive stories bring out the simplicity of his character. He rebuked a celebrated preacher at Cyprus for altering, in a quotation from the Gospels, the homely word for "bed" into "couch." "What ! are you better than He who said 'bed,' that you are ashamed to use His words?"

On the occasion of a wayworn traveller coming to him in Lent, finding no other food in the house, he presented him with salted pork ; and when the stranger declined, saying that he could not break his Lenten fast, the bishop replied, "So much the more reason have you for eating. To the pure, all things are pure," and began himself to eat the pork.

"A characteristic legend attaches to the account of his journey to the council of Nicæa. It was his usual practice to travel on foot ; but on this occasion, the length of the journey, as well as the dignity of his office, induced him to ride, in company with his deacon, on two mules, a white and a chestnut. One night, on his arrival at a caravanserai, where a cavalcade of orthodox bishops were already assembled, the mules were turned out to pasture, whilst he retired to his devotions. The bishops had conceived an alarm lest the cause of orthodoxy should suffer in the council by the ignorance or awkwardness of the shepherd of Cyprus, when opposed to the subtleness of the Alexandrian heretic. Accordingly, taking advantage of this encounter, they determined to throw a decisive impediment in his way. They cut off the heads of his two mules, and then, as is the custom in oriental travelling, started on their journey before sunrise. Spiridion also rose, but was met by his terrified deacon, announcing the unexpected disaster. On arriving at the spot, the saint bade the deacon attach the heads to the dead bodies. He did so, and at a sign from the bishop, the two mules, with their restored heads, shook themselves as if from a deep sleep, and started to their feet. Spiridion and the deacon mounted, and soon overtook the travellers. As the day broke, the prelates and the deacon were alike astonished at seeing that he, performing the annexation in the dark and in haste, had fixed the heads on the wrong shoulders, so that the white mule had now a chestnut head, and the chestnut mule had the head of its white companion. Thus the miracle was doubly attested, the bishops doubly discomfited, and the simplicity of Spiridion doubly exemplified." [1]

Many more stories might be told of him, but to use the words of an ancient writer who has related some of them, "from the claws you can make out the lion." [2]

A large number of the bishops present at the council of Nicæa were rough, simple, almost illiterate men, holding their faith earnestly and sincerely, but without being able very clearly to explain the grounds of their belief, or to enter into the arguments of the philosophical Arians of the polished Alexandrian Church. A story somewhat variously related is told of an encounter of one of these simple characters, whom later writers identify with Spiridion,

[1] Dean Stanley, "Lectures on the Eastern Church," p. 108. The story he had from oral tradition at Mount Athos and in Corfu. The horses are no doubt the legacy of primitive mythology: the white horse of Day with the dark head of Evening, and the dark horse of Night with the luminous head of Morning.
[2] Photius, Biblioth. 471.

with more philosophical combatants.   As Socrates describes the incident, the disputes were running so high, from the mere pleasure of argument, that there seemed likely to be no end to the controversy, when suddenly a simple-minded layman, who by his sightless eye or limping leg bore witness to his having played the man for Christ in the persecution of Diocletian, stepped amongst them, and said abruptly : " Christ and His Apostles left us, not a system of logic, nor a vain deceit, but a naked truth, to be guarded by faith and good works." The bystanders were struck, the disputants were silenced, and the hubbub of controversy subsided.

Another version of the story, or another story of the same kind, with a somewhat different moral, is told by Sozomen and Ruffinus, and amplified by later writers. A heathen philosopher named Eulogius took occasion from the animosities and heartburnings of those present at Nicæa to proclaim the superiority of paganism, its large toleration, its genial readiness to admit of all kinds of worship ; and to argue against the pretensions of Christianity. An aged bishop who was present, uncouth in appearance, mutilated by the cruelty of persecution, was unable to bear the taunts with which the philosopher assailed a group of Christians, amongst whom he was standing, and he worked his way to the forefront and prepared to meet him in argument. His wild, ragged appearance, and his deformity, provoked a burst of derisive laughter from the crowd, and the Christians were not a little uneasy at seeing their cause undertaken by so unskilled a champion. But he felt himself strong in his own simplicity. " In the name of Jesus Christ," he called to his antagonist, " hear me, philosopher. There is one God, maker of heaven and earth, and of all things visible and invisible, who made all things by the power of His Word, and by the holiness of His Spirit. This Word, by which name we call the Son of God, took compassion on men for their wandering astray, and for their savage condition, and chose to be born of a woman, and to converse with men, and to die for them, and He shall come again to judge every one for the things done in life. These things we believe without curious inquiry. Cease therefore the vain labour of seeking proofs for or against what is established by faith, and the manner in which these things may be or may not be; but, if thou believest, answer at once to me as I put my questions to you."

The philosopher was struck dumb by this new mode of argument. He could only reply that he assented. "Then," answered the old man, "if thou believest this, rise and follow me to the Lord's house, and receive the sign of this faith." The philosopher turned round to his disciples, or to those who had been gathered round him by curiosity. "Hear," he said, "my learned friends. So long as it was a matter of words, I opposed words to words, and whatever was spoken I overthrew by my skill in speaking; but when, in the place of words, power came out of the speaker's lips, words could no longer resist power. If any of you feel as I have felt, let him believe in Christ, and follow this old man through whose mouth God has spoken." Exaggerated or not, this story is a proof of the magnetic power of earnestness and simplicity over argument and speculation. Later historians than Sozomen unhesitatingly identify this uncouth but vehement bishop with Spiridion of Cyprus. Tradition has preserved another incident of his acts at the council. He is said, aware of his incapacity for argument, to have taken a brick into the council, and said to the Arians, "You deny that Three can be One. Look at this brick, composed of the elements of earth and water and fire, and yet it is one." And as he spoke the brick resolved itself into its component parts: the fire flashed out, the water poured down, and the clay remained in his hands. Thus he is represented in the pictures of the Nicene Council in Greek churches.

Spiridion died probably not long after the council. His body rested many years in his native Cyprus, it was thence transferred to Constantinople, and thence, a few years before the fall of the empire, his body was translated to Corfu, where it is still preserved. Twice a year in solemn procession he is carried round the streets of Corfu.

SS. NICASIUS, B.M., AND EUTROPIA, V.M.

(A.D. 407.)

[Roman and Gallican Martyrologies. Usuardus. Authority :—A narrative of the martyrdom in Flodoard (d. 966).]

NICASIUS, bishop of Rheims in 400, built the basilica of Our Lady, now the cathedral, and transferred to it the episcopal throne from that of the church of the Apostles, now called the church of S. Symphorian.

In 407 a flood of Vandals and Alans poured over Gaul, entered Champagne, and besieged Rheims. The inhabitants defended their city with heroism. Their efforts were in vain : the invaders burst through the gates, and clambered the walls, and began a general pillage and massacre. A Vandal cleft the skull of S. Nicasius at the door of his cathedral. Eutropia, the sister of the bishop, was reserved for another fate, but fearing this more than death, she boxed the ears of her captor, kicked and struggled, till he lost his temper, and cut her down. With Nicasius suffered his deacon Florentius, and his lector Jucundus.

The relics of S. Nicasius and his sister were laid in the church of S. Agricola, called afterwards by his name. This church was pulled down in 1793.

In the nave of the cathedral of Rheims is a marble slab marking the spot where stood the ancient gates of the church, and where S. Nicasius suffered martyrdom. Only a few fragments of the bones of the saint are preserved in the cathedral of Rheims, most having been lost at the Revolution.

S. VENANTIUS FORTUNATUS, B.

(ABOUT A.D. 600.)

[Gallican Martyrologies. At Poitiers on this day. At Tours on Dec. 17. Authorities :—Mention by Gregory of Tours, his contemporary, and his own writings.]

VENANTIUS HONORIUS CLEMENTIANUS FORTUNATUS was an Italian, born at Duplabilis, near Treviso, and educated at Ravenna. Having had an inflammation of his eyes cured by the intercession of S. Martin, before 560, in gratitude to the saint he left Italy and came to Gaul, to visit the relics of S. Martin at Tours. From Tours he went to Poitiers, and settled there. His eloquence and learning speedily made him renowned. In 565 he wrote an elegiac poem in honour of the marriage of Brunehild and Sigebert. He was raised to the priesthood at Poitiers, and afterwards became bishop of that place, probably after 594, the year in which Gregory of Tours died, for Gregory, who speaks of Fortunatus with admiration, does not mention that he was bishop. He was alive in 600. He was the author of several poems; the famous hymn, "Vexilla regis prodeunt" (The royal banners forward go), is by Venantius Fortunatus; it was used for the first time at Poitiers, on the arrival of some relics of the true Cross sent to S. Radegund, by the emperor Justin. The bishop of Poitiers, Meroveus, either disapproving of the cultus of relics, or doubting the genuineness of these, refused to honour with his presence their introduction into the city, and, mounting his horse, left the town, and forbade their being brought processionally into Poitiers with hymns and lights. King Sigebert interfered at the request of S. Radegund, and the archbishop of Tours, either more easily convinced of the merit of the relics, or indifferent to the question, and eager only to insure the favour of the king, performed the ceremony with the attendance of the clergy and people of Poitiers, and with daring contempt for the canonical rights of the bishop of the see.

When Meroveus died, an obscure person named Plato succeeded him; but on the death of Plato, the party in favour of relics and asceticism carried the election of Fortunatus. He did not live long after his elevation.

S. FULQUINUS, B. OF THEROUANNE.

(ABOUT A.D. 855.)

[Gallican and Belgian Martyrologies. Authority :—A Life by Fulquinus, abbot of Lobbes in the 10th cent., in Mabillon, Acta SS. O.S.B. sæc. iv. 1.]

S. Fulquinus, or Fulk, was the son of Jerome, related to Charlemagne, of Frank race; his mother, Erkensuitha, was of Gothic origin. He was appointed bishop of Tarvenna among the Morini, a people occupying French Flanders. Tarvenna is now the inconsiderable Therouanne. He was elected by the people, and their choice was confirmed by the bishops and the sovereign, Louis. He translated the relics of S. Omer from Sithieu, and placed those of S. Bertin in security from the Normans, whose incursions troubled his episcopal reign. Nothing else is related of him deserving of notice, except that his favourite horse, which was led before his body at the funeral, was observed to have tears running down its nose ;[1] and after the death of his master, the horse refused to be mounted by anyone else. The stole of the saint, in which he was buried, is of great assistance to women in labour, who are allowed for a consideration to swallow a portion of it.[2] As the consumption of stole in Flanders must be considerable, we are thankful to learn from John of Ypres, abbot of Sithieu, that in his time the stole had multiplied into three, each of which was similarly useful to women in their confinement.

[1] "Hunc tantæ scientiæ equum Fratribus dandum, feretrum præeuntem ferunt lacrimasse."

[2] "De stola ejus, quæ adhuc restat, mulieribus difficultate partus laborantibus per ejus merita salutem sæpe provenisse vidimus, cum . . . . in ingressu ejusdem stolæ partum edentes redderentur sanitati pristinæ."

December 15.

SS. Irenæus, Antonius, and Others, *MM. at Rome;* **A.D.** 257.

S. Christiana, *Ap. of the Iberians; 3rd cent.*

S. Eusebius, *B. of Vercelli; circ.* A.D. 374.

S. Valerian, *B.C. in Africa;* A.D. 457.

S. Maximinus, *Ab. of Miscy; 6th cent.*

S. Adalbero II., *B. of Metz;* A.D. 1005.

S. CHRISTIANA, V.

(3RD CENT.)

[Roman Martyrology. Authorities :—Ruffinus, H. E. i. 10, and Moses of Chorene. · Ruffinus gives as his authority Bacurius, an Iberian petty prince, who joined the Romans, and was made captain of a military force in Palestine, and was afterwards honoured by Theodosius.]

THE Iberians, occupying the country now called Georgia, east of the Euxine, were converted by the instrumentality of a slave girl, known in Georgian Church history by the name of Nonna or Nina, said to have been born at Colastri in Cappadocia, daughter of one Zabulon, and the maternal niece of the bishop of Jerusalem, and to have devoted herself, encouraged by visions, to preaching the Gospel in Iberia, whither she proceeded after a missionary tour in Armenia. According to Western versions of her story, she was taken captive by the Iberians, and set an example among them of such continence, prayer, and self-devotion, that she impressed greatly the imaginations of the barbarians. The king's child, a babe, was ill, and Nana the queen sent it to several women reputed charmers, to bewitch it into health. It was taken among others to the maid ; she laid the child on her horse-cloth bed, and said simply, " Christ, who healed many, heal this babe also," and the boy was restored to his mother whole. Not long after, the queen having fallen sick, sent for the slave woman, but she, being a person of modest and retiring manners, excused herself from going. Then the queen had herself conveyed to where the woman lived, and was laid on her bed, when she also recovered. The queen thanked her for her recovery, but the stranger replied, "This work is not mine, but Christ's, and He is the Son of God, who made the world."

Mirian, the Iberian king, amazed at his wife's restoration, wished to reward the woman, but she refused all his presents, saying that she desired but one thing, his conversion to Christ. Next day the king was out hunting, when a thick fog came on, and he lost his way. In his distress he invoked his gods, but the fog remained as thick as ever. He then called on the captive's God, and a wind sprang up and cleared away the mist. He found his way, and returned rejoicing to his palace, and then sent for the captive woman, and required her to inform him who was the God that she adored. She accordingly instructed him in her faith, and her words were with power. His heart was touched and he believed. He convened the chiefs of his nation, told them the circumstances of the cure of his child and wife, and the dissipation of the fog, and declared his intention to introduce the Christian religion among his subjects. Instructed by the captive, he built a church. Again a miracle was wrought to confirm the faith of the Iberians, for a pillar at the prayer of the captive remained suspended in the air. When the church was built, an embassy was sent to Constantine the Great, requesting him to supply the Iberians with a bishop and regularly consecrated clergy. After witnessing the conversion of the country, and building churches in several parts of it, the saint withdrew to the mountain pass of Bodbe,

in Kakheth, there to await her departure; and receiving the
Holy Sacrament from the bishop of Iberia, gave her last
injunctions and blessing to the king and queen, who had
come to take leave of her, and peacefully fell asleep. Her
relics still rest in the cathedral of Bodbe, or Beda, under a
tomb built in her honour by Bakar, twenty-fifth king of
Georgia, founder of the see and cathedral.[1]

In the Roman Martyrology the captive woman is called
Christiana.

S. EUSEBIUS, B. OF VERCELLI.

(ABOUT A.D. 374.)

[Roman Martyrology on Aug. 1, Dec. 15 and 16. His festival fixed
by Benedict XIII. for Dec. 15. In ancient kalendars on Aug. 1.
Authorities :—Hieron. Script. The letters of S. Ambrose, of Liberius,
Sulpicius Severus. Hilar. Orat. 2. The letters of S. Athanasius, and of
Lucifer, &c.]

EUSEBIUS, bishop of Vercelli, in Northern Italy, was a
native of Sardinia, which may account for the attachment he
afterwards felt for Lucifer of Cagliari. He was ordained
lector at Rome, and then went to Vercelli, where he was
elected to the bishopric; and he is the first bishop of that
see whose name has come down to us. He was the first
prelate of the West who united the monastic to the clerical
life; he lived as a monk himself, and made the clergy of his
city adopt the monastic life of the desert.

Liberius wrote to him at a time of emergency. Constantius was bent on Arianizing the Church. Liberius wrote to
Constantius, inviting him to summon a council at Aquileja ;
but the emperor caused it to assemble at Arles, where the
bishop, Saturninus, was an Arian. The first thing insisted
on by the Arians at the council was, that the bishops should

---

[1] Malan, Hist. of Georgian Church.

renounce the communion of Athanasius. Vincent of Capua, who had represented Pope Sylvester at Nicæa, unhappily yielded, in the vain hope of obtaining peace by sacrificing one man. Liberius wrote to Hosius of Cordova : " I had hoped much from Vincent. Yet he has not only gained nothing, but has himself been led into dissimulation." There was then at Rome the Sardinian bishop, Lucifer of Cagliari, a man of extreme sturdiness and vehemence, who, at his own request, was sent to ask the emperor for another council which should proceed on the basis of the Nicene faith. Liberius recommended him to the good offices of Eusebius of Vercelli, a man whom he knew to be " kindled with the Spirit of God." He wrote Eusebius a second letter after the departure of Lucifer, to urge him most earnestly to contend for the faith, and for the absent Athanasius, whom the Arians were bent upon condemning against all law.

Eusebius received Lucifer with great cordiality, and wrote a reply to Liberius, which drew forth from the Pope a third letter to encourage him in demanding the assembling of a new council. The council was summoned, and met early in 355 at Milan, where Dionysius the metropolitan and his people were Catholic. About three hundred Western bishops were present ; of Easterns only a small number. The emperor Constantius was present, to awe the assembly into submission. Foreseeing how the council would end, Eusebius of Vercelli hesitated to attend, and the council deputed two bishops with a letter to him, requesting his presence, and recommending him to place confidence in the assembly, and to keep the bond of unity unbroken. But this exhortation was saddled with the threat that if he did not yield he should be judged by them. Athanasius was designated in this letter, not as a heretic, but as sacrilegious. This epistle was signed by thirty bishops, amongst whom were Valens of Mursa, Ursacius of Singidon, Epic-

tetus of Centumcellæ, Leontius of Antioch, Acacius of
Cæsarea, and Patrophilus of Scythopolis, all declared Arians.
The emperor also wrote to Eusebius, describing affairs as
settled by the council, and needing only his subscription.
Lucifer and the two other papal legates, Pancratius and
Hilary, also wrote to Eusebius, bidding him resist the
artifices of the Arians.

Eusebius went to Milan, but found himself for ten days
denied entrance to the church where the council was sitting.
He was admitted only when the Arian prelates thought their
plan ripe for execution. A condemnation of S. Athanasius
was produced, and his subscription was demanded. Eusebius refused. He declared that he was not satisfied that all
present were sound in the faith, and qualified to sit as
judges, and he said that he would not sign till all had
solemnly signed the Nicene symbol. Dionysius of Milan at
once prepared to attach his name to the creed, but Valens
of Mursa snatched the pen from his hand. A tumult arose,
in which the people of Milan took part, and the Arian
bishops, fearing the rabble, passed from the church to the
palace. Constantius took his place as president in a hall
of his palace, which was surrounded by his guards. He
declared that he had received a command in a vision to
declare the faith and appease the strife, and he produced a
document which was couched in the form of an Arian
symbol of faith. This document was carried by the bishops
to the church and read aloud to the people; they roared
forth their disapproval of its statements. It was not pressed
further, but every nerve was strained to obtain the condemnation of Athanasius. "I am the accuser of Athanasius,"
said the emperor; "believe on my word that the accusations made against him are well founded." Eusebius and
Lucifer replied that Athanasius could not be condemned
without hearing his exculpation.

The emperor was angry; he insisted on their communi-
cating with the Arian bishops. "That," said they, "is against
the rule of the Church."

"My will is the rule," said Constantius. "Obey, or I
will exile you."

Lucifer, Dionysius, and Eusebius raised their hands to
heaven and boldly declared that the empire belonged not to
him but to God, Who could deprive him of it when He
willed. And they entreated him not to corrupt the discipline of the Church by introducing the element of imperial
force into its decisions. Constantius drew his sword on
the daring prelates, and ordered them to execution. But
changing his mind, he commuted their sentence to banishment. But before the bishops were removed, the deacon
Hilary, legate of the Pope, was stripped and scourged
before their faces.

Dionysius of Milan, Lucifer of Cagliari, Eusebius of Vercelli, Paulinus of Trèves, Exuperantius of Tortona, Maximus
of Naples, and a bishop named Rufinian, stood firm, but
many were cowed into submission.

Dionysius was banished into Cappadocia, Rufinian was
compelled by the young Arian prelate, Epicetus of Centumcellæ, to run before his chariot, until he died by bursting a
blood-vessel. Lucifer was kept in a dark dungeon at Ger-
manicia; and Eusebius was sent to Scythopolis, the see of
Patrophilus, an old Arian. In the council Dionysius had
been sufficiently weak to concede the point of condemning
Athanasius, but he would not join in communion with the
Arians. He had attached his signature to the condemnation,
when Eusebius, with dexterity, smudged it out.

At Scythopolis Eusebius was visited by the deacon Syrus
and the exorcist Victorinus, bringing him letters and presents from his church. This so enraged the Arians, that
they removed him with brutal violence to another prison,

drawing him, half naked, along the ground by the feet. He was dragged up and down a stair, bruising him. The bishop forbade admission to him. This drew forth a written remonstrance from Eusebius, which he found means of passing out of his prison. He implored the person who found his protest not to destroy it, but to give it circulation.

After Patrophilus had kept him shut up four days without food, he sent him back to his former prison, from which he had no authority for removing him. The Catholics hastened to give him food and money. The latter he distributed among the poor. After twenty-five days the Arian bishop sent his men, they broke into his cell, armed with cudgels, beat him, and carried him off to the house of a priest named Tegrinus, where he was locked up, along with some priests and deacons who had been with him. These latter Patrophilus banished on his own authority, and he gave up their houses to the rabble to be pillaged. In the house of Tegrinus, Eusebius was kept for six days without food, and only given something to eat when near his last gasp.

The deacon Syrus had not been arrested with the rest, as he had gone on to the holy places to visit them. On his return, Eusebius committed to him a letter describing the persecutions he endured. Eusebius was afterwards placed in the house of the count Joseph, a converted Jew (July 22), and was there visited by S. Epiphanius. He was after a while removed into Cappadocia, and then to the Thebaid. When the purple fell on the shoulders of Julian, the exiled bishops were recalled, and then Eusebius was permitted to go back to his church, A.D. 362. But on his way he remained at Alexandria to attend a council summoned to settle a schism that was troubling Antioch, and the reconciliation of the bishops who had signed the decrees of the council of Rimini, and repented of having done so. And, lastly, the synod was assembled to meet a new heresy which threatened, on the nature of the Incarnation. The council drew up a synodal letter, which Eusebius, Athanasius, and fourteen African bishops signed. Eusebius added to his signature the statement, that "the Son of God assumed all (our nature) except sin."

Eusebius was commissioned to carry this letter to Antioch. But before the decree could reach Antioch, Lucifer had taken, in conjunction with two other bishops, the unhappy step of consecrating Paulinus to that see, in order to gratify his strong sympathy with the Eustatians. An account of the miserable schism has already been given (S. Meletius, February 12), and need not be gone into at any length here. Eusebius, finding that the precipitate action of Lucifer had made the schism worse instead of healing it, remonstrated with Lucifer, who with that violence and impatience which characterized the man throughout his career, and made him, in spite of his real goodness, a source of mischief, at once broke off communion with Eusebius, with the Alexandrian Church, and with all who counselled moderation. Hence arose the sect of the Luciferians, headed after the death of Lucifer by that Hilary who had been a delegate of Liberius at Milan, and reproducing in great measure the hard austerity of the Novatians and the Donatists.

The counsels of Alexandria were adopted by the vast majority of the faithful. Eusebius visited various Eastern churches before he returned to Italy, and in Italy he found S. Hilary of Poitiers ready to co-operate with him. Rufinus says that he played the part of a healer of strife and of a priest, and that he and S. Hilary were as glorious lights irradiating Illyricum, Italy, and Gaul.

In 364, the emperor Valentinian came to Milan. S. Hilary of Poitiers and S. Eusebius of Vercelli were still there, upholding the Catholic cause against Auxentius, the bishop, who was suspected of Arianism, and keeping the faithful apart from his communion. The emperor, who was a Catholic, was also naturally impatient of religious dissensions, and did not choose to worship in a conventicle, while the actual bishop professed himself to be really orthodox. He therefore put forth an edict that no one should disturb the Church of Milan. This, as Hilary said, was indeed to disturb it; and he denounced Auxentius as, in fact, an Arian. Valentinian ordered a trial; Auxentius professed his belief in Christ's true consubstantial Godhead. Being ordered to make a written statement, he obeyed, and insisted on the authority of the council of Rimini, accused Hilary and Eusebius as contentious men who had been deposed, and spoke of the Son in words which might either mean that He was "a true Son," or "a true God." Valentinian was satisfied; Hilary protested that Auxentius was a trickster, but the emperor, weary of the controversy, ordered him to leave Milan.

Nothing further is heard of S. Eusebius. He most likely retired to Vercelli, which had certainly been deprived of his episcopal supervision for some time; and there he probably died, about 374.

S. VALERIAN, B.

(A.D. 457.)

[Roman Martyrology.   Authority :—Victor of Utica, i. 12.]

GENSERIC, the Vandal king of North Africa, in his persecution of the Catholics, sent a deputy named Proculus into the province of Zeugitana, to force the bishops to surrender their sacred vessels and books. The bishops refused to give them up, and the emissary seized on all the church ornaments he could find, and made shirts of the altar linen.

Valerian, bishop of Abbenza, an old man of over eighty

years, having refused to deliver up the vessels of his church, was driven out of his city, and everyone was forbidden to receive him. He was thus left, almost naked, exposed for long to the sun, and obliged to obtain food where he could, without being able to lodge under any roof.

S. MAXIMINUS, AB. OF MISCY.

(A.D. 520.)

[Roman, Gallican, and Benedictine Martyrologies. Authorities :— A Life by an anonymous writer, ancient, probably of 7th cent. Another Life, metrical, by Bertoald, monk of Miscy, circ. A.D. 840. Both in Mabillon, Acta SS. O.S.B. sæc. i.]

THE abbey of Miscy, or Mici, near Orleans, was founded by Euspicius, archdeacon of Verdun, to whom Clovis granted the land. Euspicius took with him to the new foundation his nephew, Maximinus, who had two brothers, saints—Vino, bishop of Verdun, and Lupus, bishop of Troyes. Maximinus was ordained deacon by Eusebius, bishop of Orleans, and on the death of his uncle succeeded him as abbot of Miscy. He was then ordained priest by Eusebius.

There was a very fine umbrageous tree, under which the abbot loved to sit, at the end of a walk. A steward of Bishop Eusebius, out of spite, cut the tree down, and was punished for doing so by losing his sight. Perhaps the story, as originally told, ran that the steward cut down the tree, blinded by his rage against the abbot, and this in time developed into a marvel. Maximinus is said to have destroyed a huge serpent near the Loire, which infected the people of the neighbourhood with its poisonous breath. This is a picturesque way of saying that he destroyed a huge serpentine temple of Druid worship, like that of Carnac, which was still regarded with superstitious reverence.

Maximinus is called in French *Mesmin.*

December 16.

SS. Ananias, Azarias, and Misael, *CC. at Babylon; circ.* b.c. 580.
SS. Valentine, Concordius, and Others, *MM. at Ravenna; circ.* a.d. 303.
SS. Virgins, *MM. in Africa;* a.d. 482.
S. Ado, *B. of Vienne in Gaul;* a.d. 874.
S. Bean, *B. of Mortlach in Scotland;* a.d. 1012.

SS. VIRGINS, MM.

(A.D. 482.)

[Roman Martyrology. Authority :—Victor of Utica, De Pers. Vandal.]

N the persecution of the Catholics by the Arian Vandal king, Huneric, many consecrated virgins suffered. They were hung up with weights attached to their feet, so that an intense strain at the sockets of their arms caused them acute anguish, under which they fainted. Others were burned with heated plates of metal.

S. ADO, B. OF VIENNE.

(A.D. 874.)

[Roman and Gallican Martyrologies. Authority :—Notices collected by Mabillon in his Acta SS. O.S.B. sæc. iv. 2.]

S. Ado was of honourable family. He was brought up in the abbey of Ferrières, near Sens, under the abbot Lupus Servatus. He took the religious habit, and after some years went to Prum, in the Eifel, where Markward, formerly monk of Ferrières, was abbot.

The brethren were jealous of him, and, on the death of Markward, turned him out of the monastery. He then went to Rome, stayed five years there, and moved after that to Ravenna, where he pretends that he found a copy of the old Roman Martyrology, which had been sent to Aquileja. This he copied and added to, and based on it the Martyrology that now goes by his name. But this was a fraud. He then went to Lyons, and the bishop made him take charge of the church of S. Romanus, near Vienne. When the see of Vienne fell vacant in 860, Ado was elected, and in the following year received the pall from Pope Nicolas I.

Lothair II., king of Lorraine, second son of the Emperor Lothair, had married Theutberga, daughter of Boso, count of Burgundy. Soon after his marriage he dismissed her from his court, through disinclination, or a former attachment. Popular feeling obliged him to restore her for a while to conjugal honours; but he could not endure the yoke. He had fallen in love with Waldrada, niece of the archbishop of Trèves. He lived in open concubinage with her, but he was impatient to seat her beside him on the throne as his legitimate wife.

He accused Theutberga, before his lords and great vassals in court assembled, of having been guilty of incest with her brother, Hubert, abbot of S. Maurice, a churchman of profligate character, who lived in oriental luxury, surrounded by a bevy of beautiful dancing-girls.[1] This most revolting charge was made more loathsome by minute circumstances, contradictory and impossible. On this charge the obsequious nobility, with the consent of the clergy, urged on by Gunther, archbishop of Cologne, to whom the king, it is said, had promised to marry his niece, summoned the unhappy queen

[1] Ep. Benedicti III. 857; and Hincmar, De Divortio Hlotharii et Theutbergæ.

to stand her trial. She demanded the ordeal of hot water ;
her champion passed through unhurt. She was restored as
innocent to her position, but could not regain her husband's
affections, nor command even outward respect.

Gunther now (says the Chronicle of Regino) offered to
manage the matter for the king, if he would promise to marry
his niece. Theotgand, archbishop of Trèves, according to
some accounts an uncle of Waldrada, was anxious to see the
union with his niece legitimatized, and a synod was assembled in the palace of Lothair, in January, 860, at Aix-la-
Chapelle. Adventius of Metz, Franko of Tongern, and
some abbots attended. Theutberga was brought before this
packed assembly, and by threats or fraud a confession was
wrung from the weary woman that "she had a fault on her
conscience, but that it was involuntary. She had been
forced to commit it, and she asked to be allowed to take
the veil."

Another synod was assembled in February at Aix-la-
Chapelle, before which the wretched wife was brought to
confess that she had been guilty of incest. She was condemned to an ecclesiastical penance, and to the seclusion of
a convent. But she fled to Charles the Bald, who had
taken her brother Hubert under his protection, and given
him the abbey of S. Martin of Tours. And Charles the
Bald took up her cause with vigour. He had a reason for
doing so. Theutberga was childless. Waldrada had already
borne children to Lothair. If marriage with his concubine
were permitted to Lothair, Charles would be debarred the
hope of inheriting Lorraine, should Lothair die without legitimate offspring. Charles at once sent S. Ado of Vienne to the
Pope to plead the cause of Theutberga. In 862 another synod
assembled at Aix, in which the king asked to be allowed to
marry Waldrada. He was deeply distressed at the crime
of his wife. For his part, he had lived with women from

childhood, he might even say from infancy, and he assured the bishops that if he was not given a wife, he should not remain without at least one concubine. It was a confession much like that of Philip of Hesse to Luther, Melanchthon, and Bucer. The reformers allowed the landgrave two wives simultaneously.[1] The bishops at Aix sanctioned the re-marriage of the king, on the ground that he was entirely cut off from Theutberga. Two bishops in that assembly refused their sanction. Their names have, unfortunately, not been preserved. After the council had separated, Lothair sent for the niece of Gunther, outraged her, sent her back with contempt, and married Waldrada.[2]

By order of Pope Nicolas I. a synod was convoked to meet at Metz to decide the matter. It assembled on February 5, 863. The papal legates were bribed by Lothair, and the council ratified the decrees of the synods of Aix. With this decree in their hands, the two archbishops Gunther and Theotgand were so imprudent as to proceed in person as the king's ambassadors to Rome. They rushed blindly into the net, and that net closed round them. Nicolas summoned a synod and issued an edict, addressed to Hincmar of Rheims and Wanilo of Rouen. The Pope condemned the guilt of King Lothair, and Gunther and Theotgand as the abettors and accomplices in his guilt. He annulled the acts of the synod of Metz, which he designated "a brothel of adulterers," and excommunicated and deposed Gunther and Theotgand. Ado of Vienne was commissioned, as legate of the Roman see, to bear these letters into France.

[1] The concession of two wives was signed by Luther, Melanchthon, Bucer, Corvinus, Adam F——, Lening, Justus Winther, and Melander. Wittenberg, "Die Mercurii post Fest. S. Nicolai, 1539."

[2] The accounts are not clear. According to one account Waldrada was sister of Gunther. But the story of the king playing on the ambition of both archbishops by promising each to marry his niece if his marriage with Theutberga were dissolved, is not improbable, and explains several difficulties.

We need not follow further the sad and disgraceful story of Theutberga, as Ado has no further connection with it. He spent the rest of his life in restoring discipline in his own diocese, and died on December 16, 874.

S. BEAN, B. OF MORTLACH.

(ABOUT A.D. 1012.)

[Roman Martyrology. Dempster's Scottish Menology. Irish Kalendars.]

FORDUN, in his Scotichronicon, says that S. Bean, first bishop of Mortlach, in Banff, was made bishop by Pope Benedict VIII. Near Mortlach is shown his dwelling. Another S. Bean, bishop, is commemorated on October 26. The Breviary of Aberdeen gives no details of his life. He is probably the same as S. Beoan of Tamlacht-Menan, and is not to be confounded with S. Bean of Mortlach. The Roman Martyrology has made a mistake about the bishop of Mortlach, in placing him at Aberdeen and in Ireland.

December 17.

S. LAZARUS, B.M.

(DOUBTFUL.)

[Roman and Gallican Martyrologies. Usuardus, "Lazarus whom the Lord Jesus is said in the Gospel to have raised from the dead." The Roman Mart., "At Marseilles, S. Lazarus, bishop, who, according to the Gospel, was raised from the dead by the Lord."]

CCORDING to the popular fable, which rests on no foundation of historical evidence, Lazarus, whom Christ raised from the dead, came with his sisters Martha and Mary Magdalen to Marseilles, where Lazarus became first bishop of the see, and suffered martyrdom. The story of the wonderful voyage has already been given in the account of S. Martha (July 29). The fable of the visit of Lazarus, Martha, and the Magdalen to Marseilles rests, probably, on a curious confusion of traditions. Martis, the Phœnician goddess of the moon, and special patroness of sailors, was no doubt anciently venerated at Massilia or Marseilles, and Magdalen is Maguelonne, the great lake, either taking its name from, or giving its name to, the ancient episcopal city of Maguelonne, near Montpellier. The old church is now in the midst of a marsh. According to legend, the three Maries, among them the Magdalen, lie at Les Saintes in the Camargue at the mouth of the Rhone. The name Maguelonne comes from Magh and lun, lon, or lann, and means a dwelling in a field. Mone, in his "Celtische Forschungen," renders it "Feldheim." The name occurs again in the Saintonge.[1]

It is possible that the town of Maguelonne may have been represented as a female; we know that the beautiful Maguelonne appears in the mediæval romance of Pierre de Provence as a native of this region, and the heroines of the romances of the Middle Ages are often ancient divinities re-clothed and given local habitation. At all events the beautiful Maguelonne was a favourite mediæval heroine associated with Provence, and may have originated the story of the Magdalen visiting that district. When once it was believed that Martha and Mary Magdalen had arrived in Provence, it was natural to conjecture that they had brought with them their brother Lazarus. Three salt lakes or meres have been transformed into three saints at the mouth of the Rhone—*les trois Maries*—each mar, mêr, or mere having become a Mary; and therefore it is not impossible that an ancient town may have resolved itself into the Magdalen.

The first bishop of Marseilles known to history is Orestius, A.D. 314, and it is possible that there was a Lazarus, bishop before him, but no evidence has been produced to substantiate the assertion that this bishop was the same as the Lazarus raised by Christ, or that he suffered martyrdom.

The relics, principally a skull, are in the cathedral of Autun.

---

[1] In "Gesta Abbatum Fontanellensium," the abbot Benignus gives to the monastery, among other places, "capitalonum et magalonum quæ sunt in pago Sanctonico," in the fourth year of King Hildebert.

S. OLYMPIAS, W.

(ABOUT A.D. 410.)

[Roman Martyrology. By the Greeks on July 24 and 25. Authorities:
—The letters of S. John Chrysostom to her, and the Life of S. Chrysostom by Palladius.]

S. OLYMPIAS was born about 368, and left an orphan under the care of Procopius, apparently her uncle. She was brought up by Theodosia, sister of S. Amphilochius. At an early age she married Nebridius, treasurer of Theodosius the Great, and sometime præfect of Constantinople; but he died twenty days after the marriage. The emperor then pressed Olympias to marry Elpidius, a noble Spaniard, his near relation; but she declined the honour, having made up her mind to remain single for the rest of her days. She put her fortune in the hands of the præfect of Constantinople, and asked him to act as her guardian till she had reached the age of thirty. She thenceforth led an ascetic life, fasting and keeping vigils, and denying herself the use of a bath, under the impression that dirtiness, not cleanliness, was next to godliness. Her alms were most abundant, and S. Chrysostom had to urge her to greater moderation in the bestowal of her bounties. From not eating sufficient nourishing food she destroyed her health and suffered painful disorders for many years. She was ordained deaconess by Nectarius, patriarch of Constantinople, and she made a vow of perpetual celibacy. S. John Chrysostom, when he was raised to the see of Constantinople, held her in high esteem, and she was one of the last persons to whom he said farewell when he went to his place of exile in 404. After his departure, she had to suffer persecution along with the rest of his party. She was summoned before the præfect, Optatus, who was a heathen, and she assured him that she would not communicate with Arsacius, who had been intruded into the see of S. John.

In the spring of 405, Arsacius forced her to leave the city, but she was recalled at midsummer and fined. Her goods were sold by public auction, her clothes torn off her by the soldiers, and her farms plundered by the mob. Her servants, who had long groaned under the life she had led, and which they regarded as unbecoming her rank, now found courage to tell her their mind to her face.

Atticus, the successor of Arsacius, dispersed the community of nuns she governed. She had still, however, ample means, and she sent money and provisions and medicines to Chrysostom in his place of banishment.

She was alive in 408, when Palladius wrote his Dialogue on the Life of S. John Chrysostom, but she did not probably live much longer.

S. BEGGHA, W.

(7TH CENT.)

[Gallican and Belgian Martyrologies. Authority : — Mention in the Life of S. Gertrude of Nivelles.]

S. BEGGHA, daughter of Pepin, mayor of the palace of Austrasia, was the sister of S. Gertrude. She was married to Ausegisl, son of Arnulf, bishop of Metz, and on his death by violence, she went to Rome, and after having received the benediction of the Pope, returned to her native country laden with relics. She founded a convent at Andenne on the Meuse. She took the veil there, and died toward the end of the seventh century. Some think that she was the foundress of the Order of the Beguines, which survives in Flanders and Brabant.

S. STURMI, AB.

(A.D. 779.)

[Roman and Benedictine and German Martyrologies. Authority :— A Life by his disciple Eigil, abbot of Fulda, between 818 and 822 ; in Pertz, Mon. ii. p. 365. Also in Mabillon, Acta SS. O.S.B. sæc. iii. 2.]

WHEN S. Boniface entered Bavaria, in order to bring the clergy there to obedience and subjection to the Roman see, he was given Sturmi, a youth of noble birth, by his parents, to be educated in the monastic life. Boniface left the boy at Fritzlar in Hesse, under the care of S. Wigbert, the abbot, and he was there ordained priest. Three years later, with the consent of S. Boniface, he and two companions retired for solitude to Hersfeld, then situated in the heart of a forest, "where nothing was visible but earth and sky and huge trees." Sturmi did not, however, approve of the spot, and he told S. Boniface that it was open to several objections. S. Boniface, in his explorations of the neighbourhood of the rivers Fulda and Haune, kept his disciple in memory, and sent for him. Sturmi came to him at Fritzlar, and Boniface told him that he thought he had discovered the most delightful spot possible for the foundation of a monastery ; he described it to him as situated where the Luder enters the river Fulda. On his return to Hersfeld, Sturmi had his ass saddled, and mounting, rode in the direction indicated. He travelled among mountains and hills and valleys, springs and torrents, and at night surrounded himself and his ass with a hedge of stakes, as a protection against wild beasts. He pushed on through forest and hilly country till one day he broke suddenly out of the wood upon the road from Mainz into Thuringia, just where it crosses the river Fulda by a ford. There, to his dismay, he saw a swarm of Slavonians bathing in the river. The sight of their naked bodies, "and their smell,"[1] filled him with terror. The naked bathers, amused at the hermit's consternation, capered round him, and by their interpreter asked whither he was going. He replied that he was exploring the head of the river.

The spot where this meeting took place was where now stands the Frauenbrücke at Fulda.

The good-natured barbarians let the hermit go his way, and they went theirs. Sturmi looked about him, and found a place near the main road, but somewhat back from it, where the Geisela enters the Fulda, above where the path from Lauterbach falls into the high road—a path which the biographer of Sturmi calls the Ortessueca, apparently from its meandering character over an unpopulated district. It was evening when he found the place where he intended to camp. The darkness set in swiftly, and he stood listening in anxiety to hear if any Slav or wolf were ranging near. Then he heard a sound issue from a hollow tree.[2] Was a man or a beast stirring within? With his hatchet he rapped against the trunk, and a man emerged, who told Sturmi that he was the servant of a master named Ork at Wettereibe, and was taking a horse to his master. The man told him that the place where they were spending the night was called Eichloch, and next morning he went on his way to Gersfeld.

---

[1] It is curious to remark even in the eighth century the antipathy of the German for the Slav, manifesting itself in a belief that the latter is naturally endowed with an ill savour, which even water will not remove. But the barbarous Slavs on this occasion set a good example of bathing, which it would have been well if certain ascetic saints had followed. The odour of sanctity would not have been removed from them by an ablution.

[2] "Audit procul sonitum aquæ, quod utrum fera an homo fecisset, ignorabat. Stans silenter, intentis auribus auscultabat: audit iterum sonitum aquæ. Tunc, quia vir Dei clamare noluit, cavam ferro quod manu ferebat pulsavit arborem, intelligens hominem esse, nutu Dei."

Sturmi decided on fixing his habitation where the Grezibach falls into the Fulda. He then went back to Hersfeld, and thence to S. Boniface, who promised to obtain for him and his little community a grant of the land from Carloman. In the ninth year after Sturmi had retired into the wilderness he settled at Eichloch. But those who lived in the neighbourhood resented the presence of the monks, and they retired to Chrichlar till the grant came from the king. Then he founded what was thenceforth to be called the monastery of Fulda, in the " hollow of oaks," A.D. 744.

The monastery grew, and was often visited by S. Boniface, who delighted in retiring to it for study, rest, and devotion. A mountain which he loved to climb, and on which to pray and read in quiet, bears to this day the name of the Bischoffsberg.

Sturmi paid a visit to Rome, and spent a year there to become thoroughly imbued with the monastic spirit, and to learn the way in which the rule of S. Benedict was observed in the monastery of his Order there. On his way home he fell ill at Kitzingen, and was laid up there for a month. When he was well, he went to S. Boniface, and saw him for the last time before that great archbishop went to his martyrdom in Frisia. After the death of Boniface, the body was brought to Fulda, and there buried.

S. Lullus, archbishop of Mainz after S. Boniface, was jealous of the fame of Sturmi, and plotted with two discontented monks of Fulda to work the ruin of the abbot. An order was obtained from Pepin for the banishment of Sturmi; and the abbot of Fulda was sent for two years to an abbey called by his biographer Unnedica, perhaps a monastery in Venice. Lullus then got the abbey given him by Pepin, Eigil says by bribes, and appointed a certain Mark to govern it as prior. This led to discord. The monks would not acknowledge him, and turned him bodily

out of the abbey.   The enraged monks moreover resolved
to leave the monastery, and go altogether to Pepin and ask
for their abbot back again.   Lullus, afraid of the scandal,
endeavoured to compromise matters by letting the monks
choose their own prior.   They elected Preszold, who had
been brought up from childhood by Sturmi.

But Preszold and some of the monks went to Pepin, and
wrung from him a recall of their beloved superior.   Sturmi
was received by his spiritual sons with the utmost joy.   In
the wars of Charlemagne against the Saxons, the monastery
of Fulda ran great risks.   Charlemagne chastised the rebel-
lious Saxons with relentless cruelty, and when they were
completely crushed he sent Sturmi and other Christian
preachers among them to turn them to Christ.   The Saxons
sullenly allowed their idols and temples to be destroyed,
and themselves to be baptized, waiting an auspicious moment
when the conqueror would be elsewhere engaged, and they
could rise again, shake off his hated yoke and the religion
they despised, and reassert their native freedom and liberty
of conscience.   Charles remained for some time encamped
in their midst.   He planted his royal residence at Pader-
born.   But when he was called away to cross the Pyrenees
and drive back the Moors, the Saxons again rose ; and the
bones of S. Boniface had to be removed from Fulda lest
they should suffer profanation.   Charles returned in 778 and
defeated the Saxons again.   He sent for Sturmi to recom-
mence the work of conversion, but the abbot was ill.   Charles
despatched to his relief his court physician, named Wintar,
who gave Sturmi a dose intended to cure him, but which
precipitated his end.   He was not the only man, no doubt,
killed by doctors, but he is the only saint who suffered
martyrdom under the hands of the faculty.   When he felt
himself dying, he had all the bells of the abbey rung, and
the monks assembled to receive his blessing.   He died

forgiving his enemies, including S. Lullus, archbishop of Mainz, and the bungling doctor who had dosed him to death.

S. WILLIAM LONGSWORD, DUKE M.

(A.D. 943.)

[Gallican Martyrologies. Venerated on this day at Rouen. Authorities:—Dudo of S. Quentin (1002), William of Jumièges (1137), Wace (1171), "Chronique des Ducs de Norm.," and "Le Roman de Rou."]

WILLIAM LONGSWORD was the son of Rollo, duke of Normandy, by his mistress Papia. William married the daughter of Robert, count of Vermandois. He succeeded Rollo on the death of the latter in 931. William possessed none of the great qualities of his father. He had been educated by the priests, and was more attached to a monastic life—though not to its morals—than a military career. The Normans, who prized personal courage as the highest of virtues, despised the pacific temper of William, and they reproached him with being more French than Norman, on account of the partiality he showed to his wife's countrymen. This imprudent prince gradually excluded the old warriors of his father from the ducal councils, replacing them by Frenchmen, and the Norman barons began to apprehend that he would despoil them of their lands and privileges. Rioulf, earl of the Cotentin, loudly expressed his displeasure, and became the leader of a formidable party. The confederates mutually guaranteed to each other the secure possession of their properties, and insisted on the duke giving them possession of all the country between the Seine and the Rille, as a protection against his encroachments. This demand William refused, and the confederates took up arms, crossed the Seine, and marched to Rouen. The feeble mind of William was alarmed at this movement, and he consented to yield the land between the rivers, but Rioulf, still more emboldened, insisted on his retiring with his wife to Vermandois, and threatened in the event of his refusal to take Rouen by storm.

The courage of S. William now entirely forsook him ; his popularity was sunk to the lowest ebb, and he was abandoned by all his barons, except three staunch friends of his father, Hanlet, Bernard, and Boto. Boto openly reproved him for his cowardice, and Bernard told him that if he did not defend his inheritance with the sword, he would make a voyage to Norway, and return with a chief worthy of ruling the Normans. At these reproaches the slumbering fire of his ancestors was kindled into flame; accompanied by his three faithful barons and three hundred horsemen, William sallied forth from the gates of his capital, surprised the rebels, who had calculated too securely on the cowardice of their duke, and utterly routed them.

Immediately after this victory, William received intelligence that his mistress, Sprota, whom he had sent to Fécamp during the siege of Rouen, had been delivered of a son, who was afterwards Duke Richard I. These two events occurred in 933.

When Charles the Simple was expelled from the throne of France, the sceptre was seized by Raoul, duke of Burgundy. The usurper died without issue, leaving a brother, Hugh, count of Paris, the most powerful baron of the realm, and called Hugh the Great, on account of the extent of his possessions. He might easily have seized the vacant throne, but knowing the difficulty of retaining it in those turbulent times, he contented himself with securing the peaceable possession of Burgundy. During the captivity of Charles the Simple, his queen had sought refuge in England with their young son Louis, known in history by the title of

" Outremer." This child, then sixteen years old, Hugh
determined to proclaim king of France, and he despatched
the archbishop of Sens to London, to prevail on the queen
to return with the youthful Louis; and this, after some hesitation, she did, though entertaining great fears that treachery
was meditated against the last living scion of the Carolin-
gian race. She was, however, inspired with confidence by
the promises of the duke of Normandy, who offered his
protection, agreeing to do homage to Louis, as Rollo had
done to his father; and she was still more encouraged by
the pardon he extended to her friend Alain, then a refugee
in England, to whom he generously restored the earldom
of Nantes, which had been confiscated on account of the
rebellion of the count.

William Longsword met the queen and her son at Boulogne, where they landed, and he then took the oath of
fealty along with several of the French barons.

The authority of the young king, thus placed on the
throne by an exclusive party, and unsupported by the
national will, was but little respected. He was soon em-
broiled with his principal barons, who razed his castles and
conspired against his crown.

Hugh of Burgundy gave him but doubtful assistance, hus-
banding his resources to retain Burgundy, and seeking to
act as umpire between the sovereign and the discontented
nobles. Louis applied for aid to Otho, emperor of Germany,
who refused to interfere, unless with the approbation of
William Longsword. On which the king of France went to
Rouen, and, after some interviews, a triple alliance was concluded between the three princes. Shortly after this transaction, the duke of Normandy stood godfather to the son of
Louis, born at Laon, in 941, who was named Lothair.

When William returned to Rouen he was received by his
subjects with the loudest demonstrations of joy. The im-

pressions of his early education soon rose again in his mind, now unoccupied with foreign war or civil commotion. He rebuilt the abbey of Jumièges, and expressed a wish to pass the remainder of his days in that sacred asylum, ready, if only the privilege might be accorded him of spending the rest of his days in ease from the burden of state affairs, to separate himself from his wife, for whom he did not care, and from his mistress, to whom he was devoted. The abbot resolutely refused his request; he doubted, perhaps, the rigid abstention of the duke, as monk, from all commerce with Sprota; and William would neither eat nor drink, and fell dangerously ill from exhaustion. When reduced to this state, William summoned his most attached barons, and repeated his desire to be allowed to receive the cowl in the abbey of Jumièges. The barons, however, firmly objected; but, at his request, they acknowledged his bastard, Richard, as his successor, and swore homage and fealty to the young prince.

We now come to those events which led to the death, or, as the martyrologists call it, the martyrdom, of this heroic and pure-living saint.

Herloin, the second of that name, Earl of Ponthieu and Montreuil, was brother-in-law of the duke of Normandy, by his marriage with Alice of Vermandois. Arnulf, the first earl of Flanders, was the bitter enemy of Herloin, and had seized the castle of Montreuil in Picardy, near the river Canche, about eight miles from Boulogne. Unable to recover this fortress from his too powerful adversary with his own forces, Herloin applied for aid to Hugh, count of Paris, who was his over-lord. It was refused, Arnulf being the friend of Hugh, who, however, told Herloin that he would not take offence if he obtained assistance from another quarter. He then sought to interest the king of France in his favour, but with like unsuccess. Thus disappointed, he next solicited the protection of the duke of Normandy, who, compassionating his misfortunes, summoned his barons, and prepared to lay siege to Montreuil.

The Flemings made every preparation to resist the army of William, but the contest was short and decisive. The duke harangued his soldiers, and assigned to the Cotentinois the post of honour, and personally led them to the assault. Eager to merit the praise of their sovereign, they rushed on the enemy with irresistible impetuosity, and quickly obtained possession of the town and castle. William generously offered to restore Montreuil without any indemnification, but Herloin begged him to retain it for himself, saying that he was too feeble to defend it with his own troops. The Norman duke, however, insisted on giving back the place, and promised again to assist his friend, should the Flemings venture to attack him. He then returned to Normandy, and repeated his wish to become a monk, and pass the remainder of his days at Jumièges; but his barons still refused their consent.

The count of Flanders nursed his revenge against William for having aided Herloin in the recovery of the castle of Montreuil; but being aware that he could not prevail by an appeal to arms, he contrived a scheme for his assassination. Arnulf sent deputies to Rouen to solicit a treaty of peace, and requested the duke to meet him at Amiens, there to settle the terms, pretending that he was unable to travel on account of the gout. To these overtures the unsuspicious William consented, and repaired to the appointed place. On his arrival at Amiens he received a message from the perfidious Arnulf, stating that he was at Pequigny, a small town on the river Somme. In the middle of this river there is a small island, and thither the treacherous Fleming decoyed the confiding Norman. The duke landed on it, accompanied by twelve attendants. He was received with every semblance of esteem by the count of Flanders, who personally begged a treaty of perpetual peace, which William granted.   He then made the most solemn protestations of fidelity, and took his leave.

William was about to embark in another boat, when one of the conspirators ran down to the shore, and, pretending that he had some important intelligence to communicate privately, induced the duke to return alone.   No sooner was he separated from his companions than the assassins rushed on their victim, and clove his head in twain, and the duke sank dead on the ground, without uttering a word.

Alain and Berengar of Brittany, who had accompanied William on this fatal journey, saw the murder perpetrated from the bank of the river, where they were awaiting the duke's return.   The murderers escaped to the opposite shore, and fled; but the body of the prince was recovered, taken to Rouen, and buried in the cathedral.

The assassination took place, according to Dudo of S. Quentin, on December 20, 943, but, according to William of Jumièges, on December 17, and according to the second epitaph on the duke's tomb, on December 18.   As December 17 is the day on which he is commemorated at Rouen, it is probable that this was the exact date of the murder.

William Longsword reigned twenty-five years.   In person he was tall and robust.   His countenance was remarkable for mildness of expression—in less courtier-like terms, for feebleness.   Disliking a military career, he yet showed courage when forced to draw the sword.   His piety was sincere, it his morals were not irreproachable.   He kept his promises with inviolable fidelity, excepting his marriage vow.[1]

[1] Duncan, "The Dukes of Normandy," London, 1839.

December 18.

THE EXPECTATION OF THE CONFINEMENT OF OUR LADY.

[Spanish, Gallican, Cistercian, Dominican, Franciscan, and Carmelite Martyrologies.]

N several churches of France and Spain, and in certain monastic Orders, on December 18 is begun the commemoration of the "Expectation of the Confinement of Our Lady," which continues till Christmas. This festival was ordered by the 10th council of Toledo, in 654, in the time of King Rechaswinth, because the feast of the Annunciation falls generally in Lent, when the Church is engaged on other solemnities, and cannot celebrate that mystery with the application it deserves. S. Ildefons confirmed the decree. The day often goes by the name in France of "Notre-Dame de l'O," because on it begins the antiphon, "O Sapientia," the first of the eight Greater Antiphons, all beginning with O.

SS. RUFUS AND ZOSIMUS, MM.

(ABOUT A.D. 107.)

[Roman Martyrology. Usuardus. Authority :—The Epistle of S. Polycarp to the Philippians.]

S. POLYCARP, in his Epistle to the Philippians, mentions Rufus and Zosimus, two martyrs among them, whose example he bids them recall, but he gives no details. With them he joins S. Ignatius, though he was not sure that he was already martyred.

S. MOYSES, M.

(END OF 3RD CENT.)

[Roman Martyrology. Usuardus. Authority :—A letter of S. Cornelius of Rome, in Eusebius, H. E. vi. 43 ; and Ep. 16 of S. Cyprian.]

S. CORNELIUS, in his letter to Fabius of Antioch about Novatus, says that the heretic was excommunicated by " Moyses, the blessed witness who but lately endured a glorious and wonderful martyrdom, and who, whilst yet among the living, seeing the audacity and folly of the man, excluded him from communion."

S. GATIAN, B. OF TOURS.

(ABOUT A.D. 301.)

[Roman and Gallican Martyrologies. Usuardus. Authority :—S. Gregory of Tours, in his "History of the Franks," lib. x. c. 41 ; and De Mirac. lib. i. c. 48.]

S. GREGORY of Tours tells us that S. Gatian was sent to Gaul, and established his see at Tours, when Pope S. Fabian sat in the chair of S. Peter, *i.e.* between 236 and 250. But this did not satisfy the ambition of the Touraingeois. If Bourges, Saintes, Toulouse, Verdun, and other sees could claim as their founders saints consecrated and commissioned by the hands of the Prince of the Apostles himself, why not Tours also? Accordingly a legend was fabricated which gave S. Gatian a like date and spiritual commission. As, however, he is said to have founded several material churches, and consecrated a cemetery for the Christians outside of Tours, the date of his mission is probably not so early as the pontificate of Fabian. The year 301 is the earliest that can be assigned for his death. It is more probable that he immediately preceded S. Lidorius, who occupied the see of Tours before S. Martin, and whose accession was between 337 and 340.

S. BODAGISL, C.

(A.D. 588.)

[Venerated at Metz on this day. Authorities :—Venantius Fortunatus, a contemporary, lib. vii. Carm. 5 ; Gregory of Tours, Hist. Franc. lib. viii. c. 22.]

BODAGISL, who is supposed to have been the father of S. Arnoald, bishop of Metz, was a noble at the court of Austrasia. S. Fortunatus of Poitiers praises his great charity, his gentleness, justice, and integrity in the government of the provinces confided to him. He governed Marseilles, Swabia, and Bavaria. He married S. Oda, of Swabian family; and resided with her at Lay near Nancy. After a while, by mutual consent, he and Oda separated, and he retired into the wilds near Hiliriacum, and built a monastery which took the name of Saint-Martin-aux-Chênes, or of Glandières, and since of Longueville-lès-Saint-Avold. He was accompanied into his retreat by Dignus and Udo, two nobles who endowed the new monastery. S. Oda founded the monastery of Hamage near Huy on the Meuse. Bodagisl died in 588, and was buried in the church of his monastery. He is often called Arnoald, but must be distinguished from the other Arnoald, presumed to be his son.

S. FLANNAN, B. OF KILLALOE.

(7TH CENT.)

[Irish Martyrologies on Aug. 28 or Dec. 18. Authority:—A Life, late, and of no great authority. Written after A.D. 1162.]

S. FLANNAN, son of King Turlough of Thomond, was first bishop of Killaloe, at the close of the seventh or the beginning of the eighth century. Killaloe was endowed with ample revenues by the father of the saint. He is said to have sailed to Rome from Ireland on a stone instead of a ship. When three of Turlough's sons had been killed by his enemies, he implored S. Colman to bless him and his descendants. Colman took seven strides, and then said, "Seven kings shall rise from you who shall rule Ireland." And so it was, for after Turlough came Brian, then his son Donatus O'Brian, then Brian, then Merchterdiach O'Briăn, and all the rest Brians; so called, says the writer, "as the Romans call their emperors Cæsar, and the Greeks Basileus, and the Babylonians Admural, so were they all called Brians."

Flannan was sent to grind corn in the mill one night. The steward forgot to give him a light; after a while he sent a boy to see if he did not want one. The lad peeped

through the keyhole, and saw Flannan grinding by the
light of his own hands, from each finger of which shot
flames. A stork flew at the boy, pecked out and gulped
down his eye. Flannan, on hearing his howl of pain, ran to
the door, made the stork disgorge the eyeball, and put it in
its place again.

S. Beggha.   See p. 207.

December 19.

S. Nemesion, *M. at Alexandria ; circ.* A.D. 250.
S. Prothasia, *V.M. at Senlis ; circ.* A.D. 287.
SS. Darius, Zosimus, Paul, and Secundus, *MM. at Nicæa.*
SS. Meuris and Thea, *MM. at Gaza ; circ.* A.D. 305.
S. Gregory, *B. of Auxerre ; circ.* A.D. 530.
S. Samthana, *Abss. of Clonebrone in Longford ;* 8th cent.

S. NEMESION, M.

(ABOUT A.D. 250.)

[Roman Martyrology. Ado, Usuardus, &c. Authority :—The Letter of S. Dionysius of Alexandria on the persecution in his diocese, in Eusebius, H. E. vi. 41.]

CERTAIN Nemesion," said Dionysius, bishop of Alexandria, in his letter to Fabius of Antioch, "an Egyptian, was accused at first of being a companion of thieves ; but when he had repelled this charge before the centurion as a calumny, devoid of truth, he was charged with being a Christian, and was brought as a prisoner before the governor. He, a most unrighteous judge, inflicted a punishment more than double that awarded to robbers, both scourges and tortures, and then committed him to the flames between thieves, thus honouring the blessed martyr after the example of Christ."

December 20.

SS. AMMON, ZENO, AND OTHERS, *MM. at Alexandria; circ.*
A.D. 250.
S. PHILOGONIUS, *B. of Antioch;* A.D. 323.
SS. EUGENIUS AND MACARIUS, *PP. MM. in Arabia ;* A.D. 362.
S. DOMINIC, *B. of Brescia; circ.* A.D. 600.
S. DOMINIC SYLOS, *Ab. in Spain ;* A.D. 1073.
B. JULIA DELLA RENA, *R. in Tuscany;* A.D. 1369.

SS. AMMON, ZENO, AND OTHERS, MM.

(ABOUT A.D. 250.)

[Roman Martyrology. Usuardus, &c. Authority :—S. Dionysius of
Alexandria in his letter to Fabius of Antioch, in Eusebius, H. E. vi. 41.]

N the persecution of Decius, at Alexandria, there
was a band of soldiers standing round the tribunal
of the governor who was trying and sentencing
the Christians. One unhappy man's constancy
gave way before the tortures which were preparing, and he
showed signs of yielding and denying his faith. Some of
the soldiers who were Christians—Ammon, Zeno, Ptolemy,
Ingenius, and an old soldier named Theophilus—could not
control their distress, and made signs to him to stand firm.
When the judge asked about them, they burst into the ring,
and proclaimed themselves Christians.

" The governor and his associates were greatly intimi-
dated, whilst those who were condemned were most cheerful
at the prospect of what they were to suffer. These, therefore, retired from the tribunals, and rejoiced in their testimony, in which God had enabled them to triumph
gloriously."

S. PHILOGONIUS, B. OF ANTIOCH.

(A.D. 323.)

[Roman Martyrology. By the Greeks on same day. Authority :—
A panegyric on his festival by S. John Chrysostom.]

S. PHILOGONIUS was brought up to the law, and made
himself a name for eloquence and for strict integrity. On
the death of Vitalis, bishop of Antioch, in 318, Philogonius
was chosen to be his successor. When S. Alexander of
Alexandria condemned Arius for his heretical doctrine, he
communicated the judgment to Philogonius ; and when Arius
went into Palestine in 320, he found, as he admits in a
letter to Eusebius of Nicomedia, that Philogonius was much
opposed to him. Philogonius met with trouble under
Maximinus and Licinius. S. Athanasius reckons him among
some of the chief bishops of his day, and S. John Chrysostom extols him as a pattern of Christian greatness and
perfection.

December 21.

S. Thomas, *Ap. M. in India; 1st cent.*
S. Themistocles, *M. in Lycia ; circ.* A.D. 249.
S. Glycerius, *P.M. at Nicomedia;* A.D. 303.
S. Severinus, *B. of Trèves ; 4th cent.*
S. Anastasius, *B.M. of Antioch in Syria;* A.D. 609.

S. THOMAS, AP. M.

(1ST CENT.)

[Roman and all Western Martyrologies. By the Greeks on Oct. 6 ; the Christians of S. Thomas in India on July 1. The Greek Menæas, published by Chifletus and Sirmondi, on June 20, "The Translation to Constantinople of the Tunic of S. Thomas," and those of certain other apostles. The Marble Kalendar of Naples (9th cent.) on Sept. 18, and again on Dec. 21, the Commemoration of S. Thomas the Apostle. The Passion of S. Thomas by all the Greek Menæas and Meno-logies, including that of the Emperor Basil, and that of Constantinople (8th cent.) on Oct. 6. In the Mart. of Bede, Dec. 21, is "Natalis S. Thomæ ; " but in that of Usuardus, "In Mesopotamiæ civitate Edessa translatio corporis S. Thomæ apostoli, qui translatus est ab India, cujus passio ibidem celebrata v. non. Julii" (July 3). So also Wan-delbert, "Translati Thomæ celebrat duodenus honorem, Aurea quo structore Dei cognoscere regnum India promeruit, signis comitata tre-mendis." According to the so-called Martyrology of Jerome, the Trans-lation of relics, on July 3, and the "Natalis" on Dec. 21. In the Greek Church there is a commemoration of S. Thomas on the first Sunday after Easter. On Dec. 21, at S. Denis, near Paris, the special vene-ration of the hand of S. Thomas. In Milan anciently on May 9, the commemoration of S. Thomas, S. John, and S. Andrew.]

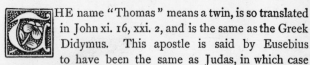HE name "Thomas " means a twin, is so translated in John xi. 16, xxi. 2, and is the same as the Greek Didymus. This apostle is said by Eusebius to have been the same as Judas, in which case he was twin brother of S. James, and one of the Lord's "brethren." The Syriac Acts call him Judas Thomas, or

Judas the Twin. But it is more probable that Judas is the same as Thaddeus. According to another account the apostle Thomas had a twin sister named Lydia. It is possible that his name may have been Judas, as well as that of two other apostles, and that he was generally designated as the Twin for the purpose of distinction.

In the catalogues of the Apostles he is coupled with Matthew, in Matt. x. 3, Mark iii. 18, and Luke vi. 15 ; but with Philip, in Acts i. 13.

The Gospel of S. John is the only one which gives us much information concerning him. When our Lord spoke to His disciples of the dangers and death that awaited him in Judæa, Thomas said to his fellow-disciples, " Let us also go, that we may die with him." During the Last Supper, "Thomas saith unto him, Lord, we know not whither thou goest, and how can we know the way ? " He was absent when Christ appeared after the Resurrection to His apostles ; the others told him what they had seen. He broke forth into an expression of scepticism ; the terms of his exclamation, however, show us what a strong impression had been made on his imagination by the sight of the dead body of Christ as he had seen it prepared for entombment. On the evening of Low Sunday he was with the rest of the apostles, when Jesus stood in the midst, and turning to Thomas bade him reach forth his hand and thrust it into His side, and put his fingers in the print of the nails. The effect on Thomas was immediate. The conviction produced by the removal of his doubt became deeper and stronger than that of any of the other apostles. The words in which he expressed his belief contain a far higher assertion of his Master's Divine nature than is contained in any other expression used by apostolic lips, "My Lord and my God." We only hear twice again in the New Testament of Thomas : once on the Sea of Galilee with the seven disciples, where he is ranked next after Peter, and again in the assemblage of the apostles after the Ascension. Eusebius says that Thomas sent Thaddeus to Edessa, and went himself into Parthia. Sophronius, quoted by S. Jerome, says that he planted the standard of the Cross among Medes, Persians, Hyrcanians, Bactrians, and other neighbouring nations.

The later Greeks make him the apostle of India, following the apocryphal Acts.

According to these Acts, he was appointed to India by the casting of lots. Then he said, "I have not strength for this. I am weak. How can I, a Hebrew, teach the Indians?" But in the night our Lord appeared to him and said, "Fear not, Thomas. My grace will be sufficient for thee." But he would not be persuaded, and said, "Whither Thou wilt, O Lord, but not to India." Whilst he was thus reasoning, a merchant of India, whose name was Habban, came from King Gudnaphar, or Gondophorus, in quest of a skilful carpenter. And our Lord met him in the street and said to him, "Thou wishest to obtain a carpenter. I have a slave for sale, well skilled in carpentering," and He indicated Thomas, and sold him to the merchant for twenty pieces of silver.[1] A regular bill of sale was drawn up, and then Habban went to Thomas and said to him, "Is this your master?" and he pointed to our Lord. Thomas said, "Yes, He is my Master." Then the merchant said, "He has sold you to me outright." And Thomas was silent. And in the morning he arose and prayed, and entreated his Lord, "As Thou wilt, so be it." And he went to Habban, carrying with him the twenty pieces of silver, his price, which the Lord returned to him. Then Thomas sailed with the merchant, and came to the city of Sandaruk.[2] The next episode

[1] It is clear from the Syriac Acts that Thomas is identified with Judas the brother of James, and is thus represented as a skilled carpenter, having been brought up in the house of Joseph to that trade. Further on our Lord says, "I am not Judas, but the brother of Judas" (*i.e.* Thomas).   [2] In the Greek Acts Andropolis.

is very beautiful.   When Habban and his slave came to the
city, they heard the sound of pipes and organs and much
singing, for it was the wedding festival of the king's daughter.
And the merchant and Thomas were invited to the feast.
Thomas would not eat, but he took oil and anointed his
heart and brow with a cross, and placed a wreath of myrtle
on his head, and took a reed branch in his hand.   Now
there was present a flute-girl, a Hebrew maiden, and as she
went round the party in the banquet-hall, she came opposite
Judas (Thomas), but he would not look at her ; he remained
with his eyes cast down ; only when she played on her pipes
he broke forth into a beautiful song : " My Church is the
daughter of light, and the splendour of the king is hers.
Her ways are comely and winning, fair and adorned with
goodly works.   Her garments glow as the flowers, and their
fragrance is sweet.   Her king hath crowned her, and He
feeds all her servants.   Truth is on her head, and her feet
move with joy.   Her beautiful mouth is open, and singeth
songs of praise.   The twelve apostles of the Son, and the
seventy-two, thunder forth His praises in her.   Her tongue
is the veil which the priest lifteth as he entereth the temple.
Her neck is a flight of stairs builded of the chief architect.
Her hands point out the place of life, and with her ten
fingers she opens the gate of heaven.   Her bridal chamber
is lighted with lamps and fragrant with the savour of salvation.   A censer stands in the midst, on which smoke the
grains of hope and faith and charity, gladdening all.   Truth
dwells within, in humility.   Her gates are adorned with
truth ; her groomsmen surround her, and her pure brides-
maids go before her, uttering praise.   The living attend on
her, looking for the coming of the Bridegroom, when they
shall be resplendent with His glory, and shall dwell with
Him in the kingdom that never shall pass away.   And they
shall be in the glory to which the just are gathered ; and

they shall be at the festivity to which some enter ; and they shall put on shining garments, and shall be clothed with the glory of their Lord. And they shall praise the living Father, whose majestic light has covered them, and they shall shine with the splendour of their Lord, of whose food they have partaken, and which never faileth, and have drunk of the life which makes those who drink of it long and thirst for more ; and have glorified the Father, the Lord of all, and the only-begotten Son, who is of Him, and have praised the Spirit, His Wisdom."

"And when he had sung this song," say the Syriac Acts, "all who were beside him were looking on him, and saw that his aspect was changed ; but they could not understand what he said, for he spake in Hebrew. Only the flute-girl had heard everything, for she was a Hebrew, and she was looking at him. And when she left him and played to others, her eyes still sought him, and she loved him as her own countryman ; and in his looks he was more beautiful than all the rest. And when the flute-girl had finished, she sat down before him, and did not turn her eyes from him ; but he did not look up, or at any one, but kept his eyes ever cast on the ground, waiting till he might retire."

In the evening our Lord appeared in the bridal chamber, and exhorted the king's daughter and her bridegroom to mutual continence. And His appearance was so like that of Judas (Thomas) that they thought it was the merchant's slave who spake to them. But in the morning, when the king heard of the impression produced on the hearts of his children by the words of the stranger, he was filled with rage, and went to the inn where the merchant and his slave had spent the night. But they were gone, and they found there the weeping flute-girl, "sitting still and weeping, because Judas-Thomas had not taken her with him. But when they told her what had happened, she was glad,

and said, 'I have found rest here.' And she arose, and
went to the young people, and dwelt with them a long
time."

After a prosperous journey, the merchant and his slave
reached India, and went to salute King Gudnaphar. " The
king ordered Judas into his presence, and said to him,
' What art dost thou practise ?' Judas said to him: 'I
am a carpenter and architect.' He saith to him : 'What
art thou skilled to make?' Judas saith to him : ' In wood
I make yokes and ploughs, and ox goads, and oars for
barges and ferry-boats, and masts for ships ; and in hewn
stone, tombstones and monuments and palaces for kings.'
The king saith to Judas : 'And I want such an artificer.
Wilt thou build me a palace?' Judas saith to him: 'I
will build it and finish it, for I am come to work at building
and carpentering.' "

The king showed him the place where he wished his
palace to be built, and bade the apostle trace its plan on the
ground. " And Judas took a cane and began to measure ;
and he left doors towards the east for light, and windows
towards the west for air ; and he put the bakehouse to the
south, and the water-pipes for the service of the house to the
north. The king saith to him : ' Verily thou art a good
artificer,' and he left him a large sum of money, and departed."

During the absence of the king, Thomas spent all the
money among the poor, and when Gudnaphar returned
from a distant journey he found his treasure dispersed and
no palace built. In a rage he ordered Thomas to be cast
into prison, and that next day he should be flayed alive,
and then burnt. But the king's brother Gad had died :
" And when the soul left him, angels took it and bore it to
heaven, and showed it each place in succession, and asked
it in which it would like to be. Then, when they came to

the palace which Judas had built for the king, his brother saw it, and said to the angels : ' I beg of you, let me dwell in one of the lower chambers of this palace.' The angels say to him : 'Thou canst not dwell in this palace, for it is that which the Christian hath built for thy brother.'" Then the soul of Gad was permitted to return to its body. And the prince, the king's brother, rose up, and told King Gudnaphar that he had seen in heaven a glorious mansion which the carpenter now in prison had built for him.

Then the king released Thomas, and consented to be baptized, he and his brother. "And when they had entered into the bath-house, Judas went in before them. And our Lord appeared unto them, and said to them : ' Peace be with you, my brethren.' And they heard the voice only, but the form they did not see, for they were not as yet baptized. And Judas went up, and stood on the edge of the cistern, and poured oil on their heads, and said :—' Come, holy name of the Messiah ! come, power of grace, which art from on high ! come, perfect mercy ! come, exalted gift ! come, sharer of the blessing ! come, revealer of hidden mysteries ! come, mother of seven houses, whose rest is in the eighth house ! come, messenger of reconciliation, and communicate with the minds of these youths ! come, spirit of holiness, and purify their reins and hearts !' And he baptized them in the name of the Father and of the Son and of the Spirit of Holiness. And when they had come out of the water, a youth appeared holding a lighted taper ; and the light of the lamps waxed dull through its light. And when they had gone forth, he became invisible to them ; and the apostle said : ' We were not able to bear Thy light, because it is too bright for our vision.' And when it dawned, he broke the Eucharist and let them partake of the table of the Messiah ; and they were glad and rejoicing."

The Acts say that S. Thomas suffered under Mazdai,

S. THOMAS. From the Vienna Missal.

probably a Masdæan prince in Persia; and relate that he was stabbed to death on the top of a hill by the soldiers of Mazdai. The Christians of S. Thomas in India pretended that his body lay at Meliapore, and had a chapel over it. John III. of Portugal had this body dug up and transported to Goa. Another body was translated to Edessa, and received veneration there in the time of S. Chrysostom. The Roman Martyrology says: "At Calamina suffered S. Thomas, ... whose relics were first translated to Edessa and then to Ortona." As there is no such place as Calamina, at all events in India, it is ingeniously suggested that Calamina is another name for Meliapore.

Gudnaphar, or Gondophorus, is not a mythical personage. An Aiano Pali inscription has been found at Shâhbâz-Garhi, in the Yusufzai country, on the Punjaub frontier, which is now in the Lahore museum. This inscription bears the name of Gudupharasa, with the year of his reign, and the name of the month, &c. The date of the inscription is Samvat 103, the fourth day of the month Vesâkh (equivalent to A.D. 46), in the 26th year of the king's reign. The inscription itself is simply the record of a votive offering by a Buddhist worshipper, and the greater part of it is illegible.[1] But it seems almost certain that this Gudupharasa is the Gudnaphar or Gondophorus of the Acts.

Relics of the saint are shown at Goa, and at Ortona in Apulia. The hand, before the Revolution, in a reliquary given by John, duke of Berri, third son of King John of France, was shown at Saint Denis. It bore the inscription : "Hic est manus beati Thomæ, Apostoli, quam misit in latus Domini nostri Jesu Christi."

S. Thomas is the patron saint of Portugal and of Parma. In the Greek pictures, S. Thomas is young and beardless; in Western art he is usually bearded. He is represented

---

[1] Trübner's "American and Oriental Literary Record," vol. viii. p. 78.

with a spear or an arrow in one hand, and a book of the gospels in the other. Frequently, however, instead of the spear, he has a builder's rule.

S. ANASTASIUS II., B.M. OF ANTIOCH.

(A.D. 609.)

[Roman Martyrology. Authorities :—The letters of S. Gregory the Great, and Theophanes.]

ANASTASIUS II. was patriarch of Antioch, in Syria, after the death of Anastasius I., in 599. S. Gregory the Great wrote to him in May of that year, on reception of his statement of faith, to say that he was well satisfied with it, and to exhort him, as the first-fruits of his priesthood, to purge the churches under him of simony. Anastasius was killed in a riot of the Jews against the Christians, who had been oppressing them, and had goaded them to violence. The Jews killed several other Christians, whom they regarded as their chief tormentors, and burned their bodies. Phocas sent Bonosus, count of the East, and Cotto, general of the army, to chastise the Jews. Massacre, mutilation, and plunder revenged the murder of Anastasius.

December 22.

S. ISCHYRION, *M. at Alexandria;* A.D. 250.
S. CHÆREMON, *B.M. of Nilopolis in Egypt ;* A.D. 250.
SS. XXX. MARTYRS AT ROME; A.D. 303.
S. ZENO, *M. at Nicomedia;* A.D. 304.
S. FLAVIAN, *M. at Acquapendente in Italy;* A.D. 380.
S. ERNAN, *Mk. of Drumhome in Donegal;* A.D. 640.
S. FELIX II., *B. of Metz;* A.D. 731.

S. ISCHYRION, M.

(A.D. 250.)

[Roman Martyrology. Usuardus, &c. Authority :—The letter of Dionysius of Alexandria to Fabius of Antioch, in Eusebius, H. E. lib. vi. c. 42.]

SCHYRION was hired by one of the rulers (of Alexandria) in the capacity of steward. "This man was ordered by his employer to sacrifice, but as he would not obey, he was abused by him. Persevering in his purpose, he was treated with indignity ; and as he still continued in patient resolution, his employer took a long pole and thrust it through his bowels, and thus slew him " (*i.e.* by impalement).

S. CHÆREMON, B.M.

(A.D. 250.)

[Roman Martyrology. Usuardus, &c. Authority :—Same as for S. Ischyrion, above.]

"WHY should I mention the multitudes who wandered in deserts and mountains," says S. Dionysius in his letter to the bishop of Antioch on the persecution that raged in Alexandria in the reign of Decius, "why mention those that perished by hunger and thirst, by frost and diseases, by robbers and wild beasts? The survivors are the witnesses of their election and their victory. But I will add one fact in illustration. Chæremon was a very aged bishop of Nilopolis. He, fleeing into the Arabian mountains with his partner, did not return again, nor were the brethren able to learn anything more of him, though search has been made for him. They found neither them nor their bodies. But many have been carried off as slaves by the barbarous Saracens from the same mountains. Some have been ransomed, but others remain among them still, unredeemed."

S. FLAVIAN, M.

(A.D. 380.)

[Roman Martyrology. Authority :—The Acts of S. Dafrosa and her daughters SS. Bibiana and Demetria ; not trustworthy.]

FLAVIAN is said to have been prefect of Rome under Constantius. He was deposed by Julian, and his place filled by Apronius ; and Julian gave orders that Flavian should be forced to do sacrifice. As Flavian refused, Apronius had him branded on the brow, like a slave. He then banished him to Acquapendente. He was thus parted from his wife Dafrosa, and his daughters Bibiana and Demetria. He is said to have died whilst praying, at Acquapendente. No reliance can be placed on the Acts, which are eminently unhistorical. Julian would certainly not have had an ex-prefect branded for refusing to sacrifice.

S. ERNAN, MK.

(ABOUT A.D. 640.)

[Irish Martyrologies on Jan. 1. Dempster's Scottish Menology on Jan. 24 and Dec. 22. Adam King's Kalendar on Dec. 22. Aberdeen Breviary Kalendar on Dec. 22. David Camerarius on Dec. 21. Authority :—Adamnan, in his Life of S. Columba, iii. 23.]

S. ERNAN or Ethernan, called also Ferreolus, was of the race of Conall Gulban, and was nephew of S. Columba. With his brother Cobtach he became a monk in Ireland. These brothers were among the twelve followers of S. Columba when he crossed over from Ireland to the work of the conversion of the Scots and Picts.

After many years Ernan returned to Ireland to the monastery of Drumhome in Donegal, which had been founded by S. Columba. Adamnan had seen Ernan, when very old, but speaks of him as having been a strong working man at the time of Columba's death. Adamnan mentions a vision he had on the night of the death of Columba, in his old age.

This Ernan is not to be confounded with Ernan of Rathmew, in Wicklow, who died in 634, and is commemorated on August 18. This latter Ernan was a serving-boy in the monastery of Clonmacnois, when S. Columba visited it about A.D. 590. Ernan tried to touch the hem of his cloak, when S. Columba, perceiving what he was about, took hold of him, and drew him before his face. On the bystanders observing that he ought not to take notice of such a troublesome boy, he desired them to have patience, and giving his blessing to the lad, said to them : "This boy whom you despise now will grow up to be gifted with great wisdom from God."

December 23.

SS. THEODULUS, SATURNINUS, AND OTHERS, *MM. in Crete; circ.*
A.D. 250.
S. VICTORIA, *V.M. at Rome;* A.D. 253.
SS. MIGDONIUS, MARDONIUS, AND OTHERS, *MM. at Nicomedia;*
A.D. 303.
S. SERVULUS, *C. at Rome; circ.* A.D. 590.
S. MAZOTA, *V. in Abernethy; 7th cent.*
S. IVO, *B. of Chartres;* A.D. 1115.
S. THORLAC, *B. of Skalholt;* A.D. 1193.

S. VICTORIA, V.M.

(A.D. 253.)

[Roman Martyrology. Usuardus, Ado, Notker, &c. Authorities :—
The brief Acts in Ado, and a metrical version of the Acts by S. Aldhelm in his book, De Laude Virginitatis. Aldhelm was born about
656, and died in 709.]

 VICTORIA was betrothed to Eugenius, a pagan
of rank and wealth in Rome. Titus Aurelius, a
friend of Eugenius, wanted to marry S. Anatolia,
to whom he was engaged, but she showed such
repugnance towards the marriage state, that Titus Aurelius
went to Victoria, and begged her, as she was a Christian like
Anatolia, to persuade her to be reasonable, and to marry
him.

Victoria readily consented, and went to Anatolia, and
said to her : "Listen to me, my sister : I am a Christian, and
I know that God does not abhor marriage. The prophets
and the patriarchs had wives, and God blessed their posterity. Now listen to me : take your husband ; he is an
upright man, and will not betray that you are a Christian ;

and it is very possible that your connection with him may be the means of his conversion." This advice, so exactly what S. Paul gave,[1] was met with disdain by S. Anatolia. "Oh, Victoria!" said she, "conquer the devil, and be indeed Victoria. God said, when the world was void, Be fruitful, and multiply, and replenish the earth. But now that the earth is populated, and the Son of God has proclaimed, Increase in faith, multiply in charity, and replenish the heavens, carnal unions are vain."

By these and other words Anatolia persuaded Victoria to a life of strict continence. Their bridegrooms carried them off to their estates in the country, and would not let them eat unless they consented to become their wives. Only a little bread was given them in the evening. At last the inveterate resolution of Victoria triumphed; Eugenius abandoned her to the magistrates, and she was decapitated.

If there be any truth in these Acts, it shows that a view of marriage must have obtained a hold in Rome in the middle of the third century which was identical with that afterwards developed by Manes. But it is more probable that the part referring to the opposition of the virgins to their marriage is an invention of a later age.

S. SERVULUS, C.

(ABOUT A.D. 590.)

[Roman Martyrology. Usuardus, &c. Authority:—S. Gregory the Great, Dialog. lib. iv. c. 14, and Hom. 15, in Evangel.]

SERVULUS was a beggar, and had been afflicted with the palsy from his infancy; so that he was never able to stand,

---

[1] 1 Cor. vii. 13, 14.

sit upright, lift his hand to his mouth, nor turn himself from one side to another. His mother and brother carried him into the porch of S. Clement's church at Rome, where he lived on the alms of those that passed by. Whatever he could spare from his own subsistence he distributed among other needy persons. He asked those who passed him on their way to church to read to him portions of the Scriptures, and these he learned by heart. His joy of heart broke out in hymns, which he probably caught from the open door of the church, when the choir sang the praises of God. After some years spent in suffering, his feeble frame sank. As he was dying, he besought the poor and pilgrims to sing by his pallet. He lifted up his feeble voice in concert with theirs. Suddenly he arrested their song; "Hush!" said he, "I hear sweet music from heaven!" And he expired.

S. MAZOTA, V.

(7TH CENT.)

[Aberdeen Breviary, Dec. 23; Dempster on Dec. 22; and the "Elevatio" on Dec. 23. Authority :—The Legend in the Aberdeen Breviary.]

S. MAZOTA, or Mayota, was a holy maid living with S. Brigit in Ireland, not the great S. Brigit, but another, a contemporary of S. Columba. Graverdus, son of Domath, king of the Picts and cousin of S. Brigit, whilst fighting against the Britons, was supernaturally warned to send to Ireland for S. Brigit. The saint obeyed his summons, and brought with her nine virgins, of whom Mazota was one, and settled at Abernethy, where she erected a church to the V. Mary, in which the king and all his family were baptized. Mazota followed S. Brigit in all holy living, and died at Abernethy.

According to the Aberdeen Breviary, Brigit was the great Brigit, and S. Patrick himself consecrated her church. But this is a mistake.

S. IVO, B. OF CHARTRES.

(A.D. 1115.)

[On this day the Gallican Martyrologies. But that of the Regular Canons on May 20. Authorities:—His own letters and those of Urban II.; also Ordericus Vitalis and other chroniclers of the time. There is a Life by Jean Fronteau, canon of S. Geneviève, and chancellor of the University of Paris (died 1662); but it contains nothing that is not to be found in the letters of Ivo, and elsewhere.]

Ivo, bishop of Chartres, was born in 1035, of a distinguished family in Beauvais. In his youth he devoted himself to the study of philosophy and literature. He was at one time in the abbey of Bec, under the eye and instruction of Lanfranc; and he made great progress both in learning and in piety.

In 1078 he became a regular canon in the monastery which Guy, bishop of Beauvais, had just founded in the city of Beauvais, in honour of S. Quentin. When Ivo entered it, he endowed it with a portion of his patrimony.

His merit was speedily recognized, and he was appointed professor of theology and of the Holy Scriptures. In time, he was elected superior of the community, and governed it fourteen years. He ruled it with such discretion that bishops and princes asked him to send canons brought up in his school, to reform old chapters fallen into laxity, or to found new ones.

Geoffry, bishop of Chartres, had been deposed by Hugh of Die, papal legate, for simony, but was reinstated by the Pope, in 1078. In 1081 the legate again deposed him, and

Geoffry went with his uncle, the bishop of Paris, to Rome to complain. Gregory VII. sent for the evidences on which he had been deposed, and to the surprise and vexation of Hugh of Die, the Pope restored him to his office, when he swore on the tomb of the apostles that the charges against him were false. The legate wrote to complain, and, as the event proved, with reason.

In 1091, however, such clear cases of simony, concubinage, adultery, and perjury were proved against Geoffry that Urban II. deposed him not only from the bishopric of Chartres, but from his episcopal orders. Urban then wrote to the clergy and people of Chartres to elect a bishop of a better type, and recommended to them Ivo, provost of S. Quentin, at Beauvais. He wrote to Richarius, archbishop of Sens, to inform him of what he had done, and to request him to favour the election, and consecrate the successor to Geoffry. Ivo was elected in conformity to the wishes of the Pope, was presented before King Philip of France, and received from his hands investiture with staff and ring. Richarius of Sens refused to consecrate. The deposition was illegal and uncanonical, he argued. The case of the morals of the bishop of Chartres ought to have been tried before himself as metropolitan.

Ivo wrote to the Pope, complaining of the burden laid on his shoulders, and asserting that he would never have consented to his election, had not the Church of Chartres assured him that it was the wish of his Holiness. He went to Rome with the deputies of the Church of Chartres, and Urban consecrated him himself, at the close of November, 1091, and sent him back with two letters, one to the people of Chartres, the other to the recalcitrant Richarius. In the latter he said: "We have consecrated Ivo, without prejudice to the obedience he owes to your Church; and we pray you to stifle all resentment, and to receive him with suitable favour, and give him your assistance in the government of his diocese."

Ivo did not take possession of the see of Chartres till the beginning of 1092.

Richarius, irritated at the conduct of Ivo in having gone to Rome and ignored his jurisdiction as primate, wrote him a scornful and angry letter, in which he refused him the title of a bishop, and charged him with usurpation of a diocese already tenanted. Ivo replied, "How can I owe obedience to one who sets himself above the Holy See, and attempts to destroy what it has built up? You forget your own reputation in attempting to re-establish a goat whose filthy conduct, adulteries, and ill reports are in every man's mouth."

Archbishop Richarius summoned a council to meet at Estampes, by the advice of William, bishop of Paris. William was brother of Eustace, count of Boulogne, and uncle of Godfrey de Bouillon. He was chancellor of King Philip; Geoffry of Chartres was his nephew. Richarius attended the council at Estampes with the bishops of Meaux and Troyes, who acted with him. In this council the archbishop accused Ivo of having obtained his ordination at Rome, in prejudice of the royal authority. He demanded the deposition of Ivo, and the reinstatement of Geoffry; but Ivo appealed against the archbishop and the council to Rome, requesting the Pope to send a legate into France to bring the archbishop of Sens and his suffragans into due and becoming obedience.

A matter of another kind now caused Ivo to fall into disgrace with the king. Bertrada, third wife of Fulk, count of Anjou, had succeeded in obtaining the affections of Philip. She had, or affected, scruples of surrendering herself to his arms unless wedded to him.[1] He raked up a relationship which subsisted between himself and his queen, Bertha,

---

[1] She was daughter of Simon de Montfort and Agnes of Evreux.

daughter of the count of Flanders, divorced her, and Bertrada found an equally easy means of shaking off her allegiance to her husband. The king endeavoured to persuade Ivo to consent to their union. Ivo was a noted canonist. He had compiled a volume of canons; and canons, the king thought, could be twisted to sanction or discountenance anything that was wanted. But Ivo stood on moral grounds, and refused to sanction or be present at the proposed marriage. He wrote to Reginald, archbishop of Rheims, on the subject, to dissuade him from sanctioning the union. The letter Ivo wrote to the king is dignified and to the purpose: "I write to you what I said to you to your face, that I will never assist at the solemnity of the marriage, without being assured first that a general council has approved of your divorce, and that you can contract a legitimate marriage with this woman. If I had been called to examine this matter in a place where I could in security deliberate with the bishops, my brethren, on the canons, without the fear of mob interference, I would attend willingly, and I would do my best with the others to do justice. But now that I am summoned to Paris to meet your wife, without knowing if she has any right to that title, my conscience towards God and my reputation as a bishop tell me that I should prefer a millstone round my neck and a plunge into the depths of the sea, to sanctioning such a scandal."

A Norman or a French bishop[1] was tempted by gratitude for actual favours, and by the hope of future advantage, to perform the marriage. The king, to mark his resentment at the conduct of Ivo, declared that his lands were open to the greed of plunderers. Hugh de Puiset, viscount of Chartres, took Ivo and put him in irons. Many of the principal burgesses of Chartres were for calling out the trained bands and the servants of the bishop, and attacking the viscount. Ivo from his prison wrote to conjure them to be quiet; his

[1] Some authorities say Odo, bishop of Bayeux; others, the bishop of Senlis.

cause was committed to the Pope, who would see justice done.

In the year 1094, in September, a council was held at Rheims, by order of King Philip, to approve his marriage. His wife Bertha was dead. He attended in person, with three archbishops—Reginald of Rheims, Richarius of Sens, and Raoul of Tours. The bishops present were William of Paris, Gautier of Meaux, Hugh of Soissons, Elinand of Laon, Radbod of Noyon, Gervinus of Amiens, Hugh of Senlis, and Lambert of Arras. Ivo of Chartres was invited, but would not attend; he knew that it was the purpose of the king or his metropolitan to bring accusations against him, and he appealed to Rome. In his letter to the council he says: "I am accused of perjury, and I have sworn to nobody. I know what violence will be used, to what intimidations I shall be exposed, and that I shall not be allowed in the assembly to speak the truth. No; because I have been the faithful servant of the Holy See, I am accused of perjury and of treason. Permit me to say, accusation of treason should rather be brought against those who have fomented a sore which needs cautery with fire and iron. Had you held firm like me, the grievous sore had by this time been healed."

Gautier, bishop of Meaux, wrote to him to ask whether a man might marry his concubine? The letter was a trap. Bertrada was the concubine of the king, and the queen was dead. Ivo replied that some laws forbade it, and others permitted it. But, he added, as for the marriage of the king with Bertrada, that must absolutely be forbidden. The case was too gross, too notorious to be sanctioned.

Hugh, archbishop of Lyons, legate of Pope Urban, summoned a national council at Autun, in October of the same year, which ventured to anticipate the sentence which could not but be approved and ratified by the Pope. Philip implored delay, his ambassadors appeared at Piacenza, and the Pope consented for a time to suspend the sentence. But the case was too glaring to escape censure, and the monarch too impotent to demand further delay. In the preliminary business of the council of Clermont, despatched with haste, hardly noticed, passed the excommunication of the greatest sovereign in Christendom, at least in rank, except the emperor and ruler of the very country in which the council sat.

In 1096, while Pope Urban was at Montpellier, King Philip endeavoured to obtain for William, brother of Bertrada, the bishopric of Paris, then vacant. William was not of age, and therefore it would require a dispensation to appoint him. Ivo, who saw now an opportunity of pacifying the king without going against his conscience, wrote to Urban in favour of William. He was a clerk at Chartres, and gave promise of being virtuous. Accordingly the Pope consented, and the youthful William was consecrated by Richarius of Sens, whom Urban allowed for the occasion to wear the pall.

Richarius, archbishop of Sens, died in December, 1096, and Daimbert, Vidame[1] of Sens, was elected as his successor. But he remained unconsecrated for fourteen months, because Hugh, archbishop of Lyons, pretended that as primate he must receive the oath of the new archbishop. The clergy of Sens thereupon wrote to S. Ivo of Chartres to request him to ordain Daimbert on the ensuing feast of the Purification; but, on the excuse that he could only consecrate at the Ember seasons, he put off complying with their request till he had corresponded with the archbishop of Lyons.

He wrote to Hugh of Lyons a letter expressive of considerable vexation. The archbishop of Lyons had produced papal letters confirming his primacy over Sens. Ivo wrote: " As to those orders of the Holy See which relate to faith

---

[1] Vidame is one who holds his fief from a bishop instead of from the king.

and morals, we will obey them at any cost. But when they enjoin us to do things which are indifferent, or to go contrary to the usages of our fathers, which is to be obeyed? Your claim to have primacy over the Church of Sens has never been allowed. What if the bishop elect have received investiture from the king's hands? We see in that no ceremony obnoxious to religion. What does it matter if investiture with the temporalities be made by hand, or a nod of the head, or word of mouth, or by gift of crozier? The kings make no pretence to confer spiritual power, but only to consent to the election, and to give to the elect the lands and other goods which the churches have received from their liberality.

" If investitures were forbidden by the eternal law of God, it would not be in the power of superiors to permit them in some cases while forbidding them in others. What then is the result of these inhibitions to receive investiture? Vexation, scandals, discord between the State and the clergy, where concord ought to reign.

" Would that the ministers of the Roman Church applied themselves to heal great evils, instead of straining out gnats while swallowing camels. A fuss is made about trifles, the great scandals and crimes which abound pass unnoticed."

It is a pity that the clear good sense with which Ivo viewed the vexed question of investitures did not prevail among others of his and the preceding generation. The only result of the inhibition against receiving investiture from lay princes issued by Gregory VII. was, he says, that bishops and abbots, instead of occupying themselves with the correction of manners and morals, were engaged in hunting out skilful lawyers and eloquent special pleaders, who could get them out of possible censure for having thus received investiture; and the money which might have gone to the poor, went as bribes into the pockets of lawyers or of those about the Pope.

As might have been expected, this very outspoken letter got Ivo into trouble with the Pope. Hugh of Lyons had, no doubt, sent it on to Urban, and Urban was highly incensed. Ivo was obliged to write to the Pope in justification. He had re-read the letter, he says, and instead of finding anything in it against the Roman Church, he thought there were in it several things in its favour. " For," he added, " I had no other intention than of intimating to you through the archbishop the murmurs which I hear on all sides, in order that the discontent may be remedied. The archbishop, finding in my letter some words he did not like about the primacy of the Church of Lyons, has tried to inflame your anger against me. But I believe there is none on this side of the mountains who has suffered affronts and injustice like me for having been faithful to you, and obeyed your orders. But since my words have irritated you, it is not for me to oppose you; let me resign my bishopric rather than endure your anger, just or unjust. If this satisfaction will content you, I am content. If you want more, add to it. I shall, I doubt not, be more useful to the Church as a private individual than as a bishop. For seven years I have cultivated my vine as best I could, without gathering fruit of it. Set me at liberty in the eighth year. If I may not resign by your permission, I shall be forced to take the step through the hostility of the king, who has taken to him again Bertrada, and through my diocesans, whom neither fear of God nor shame of excommunication can force to give up the sacrileges they commit in the churches, and to do justice.

" But whatever may happen to me, I conjure you by the love of Christ, if the archbishop of Tours, or one of the clergy of Orleans, come to ask you to confirm the young

man chosen to fill that see—do not consent." He describes
him as guilty of crimes such as sullied the old heathen
world. "Some companions of his debauch have made songs
about him, which licentious youths sing in the streets and
squares, and which he has actually not blushed to listen to,
and sing himself. I have sent one of these ballads to the
archbishop of Lyons as a specimen. Do not permit him to
be ordained, if you love your own honour and the welfare of
the Church. The archbishop of Tours crowned the king at
Christmas, against the orders of your legate, and has obtained as a reward the bishopric of Orleans for this young
man, his favourite."

This debauched youth was Archdeacon John. He was
elected on a day of omen, the Feast of the Innocents, 1098,
a day when in every cathedral church in France hideous
and blasphemous buffoonery took place, in the midst of
which a bishop of Fools was chosen.

Ivo, in an agony of righteous wrath and shame, wrote all
he had told the Pope to the archbishop of Lyons, recapitu-
lating what he had said to Urban of the moral character of
John the archdeacon. He added : "Besides, the abbot of
Bourgeuil came at Christmas to court with great confidence,
to receive the bishopric which the pretended queen had
promised him. But because it was found that the friends
of Archdeacon John had heavier money-bags, the abbot was
given the go-by. And when he complained that the king
had made a fool of him, the king replied, 'Wait till I have
made my profit out of this one, then get him deposed, and
I will do what you like.'"

But Urban was too angry to listen to the remonstrances
of Ivo of Chartres ; he confirmed the election. John was
consecrated, and occupied the throne of Orleans for forty
years, from 1096 to 1136, when he resigned it.

In 1099 Urban was still angry with S. Ivo for his letter.

Godfrey, abbot of Vendôme, was at Rome in that year, and endeavoured to soothe the resentment of the Pope. On his way back, he spent five days at Lyons with the archbishop Hugh, and learned to his astonishment that Daimbert of Sens had made peace with this prelate, had submitted to his demands, and had thrown over Ivo of Chartres, and repudiated his letters in his behalf. Godfrey, as a friend of Ivo, did his best under the circumstances to persuade the archbishop of Lyons to renew friendly intercourse with Ivo.

In 1100 two cardinals, John and Benedict, came as legates from Pope Paschal II. into France. John wrote letters to S. Ivo full of praise for his having abstained from communion with the king, contrary to the example of many of the prelates, who had ignored the prohibition of Urban II. and had crowned the king at Pentecost. The legates summoned a council to meet at Poitiers on November 18, and Ivo attended with eighty bishops and abbots. The scandal of the union of Bertrada and Philip was again brought up, and the legates declared their intention of renewing the excommunication pronounced against the king at Clermont, five years before. William IX., count of Poitiers, the most illustrious troubadour of his time,[1] and other nobles and several bishops implored the legates on their knees to defer the sentence, but they were inexorable, whereupon the count and his followers left the church in which the council was being held, with a train of indignant bishops who refused to be present when their monarch was excommunicated, and a great tumult ensued. The legates rose and pronounced the sentence; then a common man who was in the triforium, enraged at the insult offered his sovereign, threw a stone at the legates, but missed them and hit a clerk at their side,

---

[1] He had married the daughter of Fulk of Anjou (whose wife Bertrada had been), but he repudiated her, and married again.

cutting open his head and prostrating him insensible on the pavement. Two abbots, Robert of Arbrissel,[1] and Bernard of S. Cyprian, threw off their cowls and stood defiantly forward to receive stones or blows launched at the representatives of the Pope.

The council passed several canons, one of which was levelled against the claim of laymen to present to livings ; another was perhaps granted out of consideration for S. Ivo : regular canons were permitted to baptize, preach, hear confessions, and bury the dead, but the exercise of these functions was forbidden to monks.

In 1101, whilst the legates were still in France, Ivo wrote to them on the subject of an election which had been made to the vacant see of Beauvais. Stephen, son of William de Garlande, seneschal of France, had been chosen to it. "The Church of Beauvais," wrote Ivo, "is fated to have bad pastors, she has elected only disreputable personages for some time past. Now she has chosen a clerk not in holy orders, ignorant, a gambler, who has been excommunicated from the Church for adultery by the archbishop of Lyons, legate of the Holy See. I warn you to be on your guard. For this intruder will hasten to Rome, or send there, so as to gain the Curia by his promises and bribes, and surprise the Pope by all sorts of artifices. If this attempt of mine to avert a gross scandal should fail, my mouth will be stopped, I shall have nothing to answer to those who speak against the Roman Church."

He wrote also to the Pope : "This Stephen is not yet a subdeacon ; he is illiterate, a gambler, always running after women, excommunicate for adultery." The king and Bertrada favoured him. Stephen went to Rome, and Ivo was guilty on that occasion of the only unworthy act we know

[1] S. Robert of Arbrissel caused great scandal by his double monastery at Fontevrault, which proved not so much a nursery of piety as of babes. See Feb. 25, p. 428.

of him. He gave him the usual formal letter of commendation to the Pope, and united with the Church of Beauvais in requesting his Holiness to grant its request, " so far as the justice and honour of the Holy See permit." How far compulsion was used to extract this from Ivo we do not know. But that he behaved in the matter in a way which was not straightforward, we know from what Paschal II. answered. The Pope refused Stephen, and with great propriety wrote to Ivo to remonstrate with him for having thus openly recommended one whom he secretly disparaged. Ivo replied that he received this reproof with joy ; he added, however, that his second letter was not in contradiction with the former, that between the lines Paschal's sharp eye ought to have detected his covert disapproval ; but he said that the letter was extorted from him by the importunity of Stephen : a poor excuse at the best. "Your Holiness's letter," he concluded, "has clearly let me see how firm you are in the maintenance of justice and in zeal for the house of God ; and I have communicated it to nearly all the churches in the realm."

If Ivo had done wrong, he was not ashamed to publish the reproof he had received, so greatly did his zeal for the Church of God eclipse his care for his own reputation. The conduct of Paschal II. in the matter of the bishopric of Beauvais was in striking contrast to that of Urban II. in that of the bishopric of Orleans.

Ivo wrote at once to the clergy of Beauvais to choose a good pastor, he recommended no one to them by name. The person then elected was Walo, abbot of Saint Quentin, in Beauvais, the monastery which Ivo had so long ruled. Ivo took great interest in the Church of Beauvais, of which he was a child, and he wrote thereupon to Manasses, archbishop of Rheims, to urge him to consecrate Walo before the court could interfere, as he knew it purposed doing.

"You know," he wrote, "that the eighth council approved by the Roman Church forbade kings interfering in the election of bishops; and that the kings of France, Charles and Louis, have granted to the Churches free elections, as they have declared in their capitularies, and have permitted the bishops to decree it in the provincial councils. Do not consider malicious whispers about the servile origin of Walo, for it was honest even if humble, and no man living can prove that it was servile."

Ivo wrote also to Paschal: "The more sane portion of the clergy of Beauvais, at the advice of the nobles and with the consent of the people, have elected Walo as their bishop, a man of exemplary life, instructed in letters, and in church discipline. Some, however, of the party of Stephen who had been rejected, and who were bought by him by presents of rich furs and other like bribes, have refused their consent, though they can bring forward no canonical impediment. They have addressed the king, and have told him that Walo is my disciple, and that if he becomes bishop he will oppose him. The king is, accordingly, prejudiced against him, and will not consent to the election, nor surrender the goods of the Church which he has retained in his hands during the vacancy. The electors would have already appealed to your Holiness, had not the Metropolitan held them back, on the excuse that he wants to bring them to agreement with the other party, but really, I suspect, because he wants to impede the matter, according to the wish of the king."

S. Anselm of Canterbury also wrote to the Pope in favour of Walo, having known, whilst at Bec, the sad condition of degradation into which the Church of Beauvais had fallen.

Walo was consecrated in 1103, but King Philip swore he would not permit him to enjoy the revenues of the see, and retained them in his own hands. Walo went to Rome, and Paschal sent him to Poland as his legate. In the meantime William de Montfort, bishop of Paris, died, and the electors could not agree which of two candidates should fill his place. One, Fulk, the dean, was a man of advanced age. Both parties appealed to Ivo, but he would not interfere unless he were given a safe conduct from the king, so that he might come to Paris and investigate the disputed election on the spot. Fulk went to Rome, and when Paschal saw how incapacitated he was by age for setting a bad example, he consecrated him. Fulk died, after having been bishop about two years, in April, 1104; whereupon the clergy and people of Paris unanimously chose Walo of Beauvais. Walo was then at Rome, returned from his Polish expedition; he obtained from the Pope absolution for King Philip, on certain conditions, and the king thereupon consented to his appointment. Walo on his way to Paris met S. Anselm, at Lyons. Paschal sent Richard, cardinal bishop of Alba, as his legate into France, to publish the absolution of the king; and he summoned a council to meet at Troyes. Ivo wrote to him: "The absolution of the king, if it can be effected to the honour of God and of the Holy See, will rejoice me as much as his excommunication grieved me. If God touches his heart, I am of advice that you should give him absolution solemnly, in presence of as many bishops as may be collected, so that his conversion may be as open as his fault. I desire greatly to attend the council, but I cannot go to Troyes without permission from the king, under whose displeasure I have lain during ten years."

He received permission, and attended the council. The formal absolution of the king and Bertrada was put off to a second council, to be held at Beaugency, on July 30. The king and Bertrada attended this, and on his and Bertrada's swearing on the Gospels to separate and not even to speak to one another again, except before witnesses, the legates

asked the opinion of the bishops present.   Ivo at once
urged his immediate absolution, but several of the bishops
present objected to it on the conditions imposed.   Consequently no absolution was pronounced, and Philip was irritated at the delay.

Paschal then wrote to the bishops of the three provinces of
Rheims, Sens, and Tours, to meet and absolve the king,
and in the event of Richard, his legate, having left France,
he committed the necessary powers to Lambert, bishop of
Arras.

A council accordingly assembled at Paris on December 2,
1104, attended by Daimbert, archbishop of Sens, Raoul of
Tours, Ivo of Chartres, John of Orleans, Walo of Paris,
Lambert of Arras, and four others.   After the letter of the
Pope had been read, John of Orleans and Walo of Paris—
representatives, it would almost seem, of episcopal licence
and episcopal restraint—were sent to the king to request
him to take the required oath.   Philip came barefooted into
the council, and received absolution.   Then, laying his
hand on the Book of the Gospels, he swore to renounce
intercourse with Bertrada.   She took the same oath, and
shared his absolution.[1]

Whilst Richard, legate of the Pope, was in France, the
enemies of S. Ivo took the opportunity of slandering him
as guilty of simony.

Ivo replied: "I have always had this crime in horror
since I was ordained, and since I have been made a bishop
I have cut it off by every effort wherever I met with it.   If
there be some rights which the dean, or precentor, or other
officers exact from the newly-appointed canons, it is in spite
of my opposition.   They defend themselves by the usage of
the Roman Church, in which the chamberlains and ministers of the palace exact various sums from bishops on their

---

[1] The king was then aged fifty-one.

consecration and abbots on their appointment, under pretext of offering or gratuities. It is well known they give nothing gratis, down to the pen and paper on which they write. And I have no answer to make but the words of the Gospel, ' All whatsoever they bid you observe, that observe and do ; but do not ye after their works.' "

Philip I. died on July 29, 1108, at Melun, and was buried at S. Benoît, on the Loire. His son Louis was present at his death and funeral. Louis had incurred the dislike and fear of the nobles, and Ivo of Chartres urged that he should be crowned at once, and at his exhortation, Daimbert of Sens went to Orleans with his suffragans, Walo of Paris, Manasses of Meaux, John of Orleans, Ivo of Chartres, Hugh of Nevers, and Humbold of Auxerre, and crowned him on August 2nd, four days after the death of his father. Scarcely was the ceremony over when the deputies of the Church of Rheims arrived bearing the remonstrance of that Church, and a letter from the Pope forbidding it, on the grounds that the Church of Rheims claimed the prerogative of having the kings of France crowned by it, accorded, it was pretended, by Clovis when baptized by S. Remigius.

To justify the step he had taken, Ivo wrote a circular letter to the Roman Church, and to all who had cognizance of the complaint of the clergy of Rheims, in which he argued that the coronation could not be disputed, by reason, custom, or law. Ivo rejected the claim of Rheims, it had no evidence to its having any just grounds. Moreover, the archbishop then elect was not yet confirmed, and the city of Rheims was under an interdict, so that the coronation could not have taken place there.

The Church of Rheims was, indeed, at this time in a troubled condition. Archbishop Manasses II. had died in 1106, whereupon Raoul le Verd, provost of the cathedral, had been elected by a party of the clergy and people, whilst the other part had chosen Gervaise, the archdeacon, son of Hugh, count of Retel, and each party maintained the validity of its election. Ivo now urged on King Louis to put an end to this confusion, and acting by his advice, Gervaise was driven away, and Raoul enthroned.

The question of Investitures, with which Ivo had dealt so sensibly some years before, was one that now convulsed the West. A very decided line had been taken by Gregory VII. On February 2, 1111, Pope Paschal II. made terms with Henry V. of Germany. He granted the right of investiture to the king, and surrendered all the possessions and royalties which the Church had received of the empire and of the kingdom of Italy from the days of Charlemagne, Louis the Pious, and Henry I.; all the cities, duchies, marquisates, countships, rights of coining money, customs, tolls, advocacies, rights of raising soldiers, courts and castles held of the empire. And the king, on his part, while retaining the right of investing bishops and abbots with their temporalities, resigned the vain and unmeaning sign of conveyance with ring and crook.

This treaty carried dismay among the ranks of those who had hitherto fought the battle of investitures against the crown. The archbishop of Vienne called a council together, which met on September 16, 1112, and which proclaimed that "the investiture of bishoprics, abbeys, and other ecclesiastical benefices from lay hands is a heresy. We condemn, by virtue of the Holy Ghost, the document or privilege extorted by King Henry from Pope Paschal; we declare it null and abominable." And the council proceeded to excommunicate and anathematize the king.

Joceran, archbishop of Lyons, also summoned a council, the same year, to meet at Anse, to consult on this matter, and invited to it the archbishop of Sens and his suffragans. Ivo of Chartres wrote an excuse on their behalf, couched in a strangely hesitating tone. "As to the investitures with which you propose to deal, it is wiser to be silent; by speaking you will be discovering your father's nakedness. What the Pope did, he did under constraint, to prevent the ruin of his people, but his will did not consent. This appears from what he wrote to some of us when he was out of danger. He ordered and forbade then what he had ordered and forbidden before, though at a time of peril he allowed himself to subscribe some detestable writings. If the Pope does not use deserved severity towards the king of Germany, it is because, following the judgment of prudent guides, he exposes himself to the least of many evils. . . . . Let us veil the disgrace of the priesthood, lest we expose ourselves to the mockery of our enemies, and weaken the Church, in our attempts to strengthen her. We think ourselves excusable if we abstain from rending the Pope, and excuse with filial charity what he has accorded to the king of Germany. We even approve of his conduct.

"And now, as to what some speak of as the *heresy* of investiture, let it be remembered that heresy is an error in faith. Faith and error proceed out of the heart, and this investiture which creates such a commotion is a mere manual act of giving and taking. Popes have given investiture with ring and crook. If it had been a heresy, how could they have done that?

"But if any layman should be so great a fool as to suppose that with the pastoral staff he confers a sacrament or the effect of a sacrament, that is another matter—him we judge heretical, not because of the act, but because of the error. If we could give things their proper names, no doubt the investiture by laymen is an abuse, which ought to be done away with, if possible, without troubling peace; but when it becomes a matter of strife, let it be put off, and let us content ourselves with protesting with discretion."

Ivo wrote to Bruno, archbishop of Trèves, in the same sense, but with more freedom. " The crown and the clergy are divided," he said; " let us do what we can to reunite them.   In the state of peril in which we are, one must not be so rigorous, but condescend ; and, as in a storm, throw out some of the lading of the boat to save the rest. Charity stoops to the feeble, and makes herself all in all. Let not private individuals blame the conduct of their pastors if, without prejudice to faith and morals, they do and endure something that is not absolutely perfect, in order to preserve the life of their flock."

Godfrey, abbot of Vendôme, wrote in a very different spirit to Pope Paschal. He declared that investiture was a heresy, and the Pope by permitting it had fallen into heresy. He concluded that a lapse in morals was tolerable in a chief pastor, but not a lapse in faith. In such a case the faithful must rise in judgment against him.

On the 23rd December, 1115, Ivo of Chartres died, after having governed his Church twenty-three years, and was buried at S. Jean en Vallée.

He was a light in a dark age.   His firm, pure, and gentle character inspire the most profound admiration. A man thoroughly conscientious, and not afraid of following the dictates of his conscience, he spoke out bluntly what he felt was true, and ought to be spoken before kings and popes alike, and had to endure the resentment of kings and popes for his plain speaking and determined action. He was entirely without self-seeking, all he cared for was the welfare of the Church.

He was the author of a Pannormia, a collection of canons, and of a larger collection, the Decretum.   Twenty-four sermons of his are extant, and a Chronicle of no great value. His Epistles (288 in all) are his most valuable bequest to posterity, giving us an invaluable picture of the state of the

Church in France at the time in which he lived, a picture by no means pleasant to look upon, it must be admitted.

One feature of this correspondence is the clear good sense which it exhibits. Whether dealing with investitures or with matrimonial difficulties, the judgment of Ivo is rarely at fault. We have seen so much of his letters relating to the ecclesiastical politics of his time, that we may look at a few of his letters on matters of smaller interest.

Ivo was very determined in setting his face against trial by ordeal. Hildebert, bishop of Le Mans, was accused by the king of England of having treacherously surrendered the town, and the bishop wrote to ask if he was to submit to the ordeal of walking barefoot over red-hot ploughshares to prove his innocence. Ivo told him to do no such thing; such ordeal was forbidden by the canons, and was utterly reprehensible. On another occasion he interfered too late. A knight wrote to him to state that he had a suspicion that his wife had been unfaithful to him (he gave his reasons, which were not conclusive), and said that he had made the man whom he suspected walk on red-hot irons, and his feet had been burned. Supposing, therefore, that the guilt of the parties was established, he wished to put away his wife. Ivo told him that his reasons and his evidence of guilt were alike worthless: he should not encourage suspicions, but take his wife's word of honour, and the testimony of her neighbours to her fidelity.

In several cases of difficulty about marriage, he gave clearly the right judgment. He was asked if a daughter promised in marriage when a child by her father, was bound to marry the person chosen when she grew to years of discretion. "Certainly not," answered Ivo. "Nor," he said, in answer to the archdeacon of Paris, "is a Jewess who has married a Christian free to marry another, nor is her husband freed from the tie, even if she relapse into Judaism. Nor can a man who has

promised marriage to a girl, and then finds out that she is a
serf, shake himself free from his engagement. Nor may a
man who, on his bed of sickness, promised his mistress to
marry her should he recover, escape from his obligation to
do so." Hildebert, bishop of Le Mans, had the case brought
before him of a converted Jewess, who, with her new faith,
was desirous of taking to her arms a new Christian husband.
"By no means," ruled Ivo; "she is bound to her Jewish husband till death parts them."

His fearless impatience of abuses appears in many of his
letters. King Louis asked him for a present of costly foreign
furs. It was the custom of the kings to make these demands,
and they were always complied with. On another occasion
the king asked the advancement of a favourite in his church.
Ivo refused the furs and the stall. He wrote to the Pope that
it did not answer, sending ultramontane legates into France;
they stayed too short a time to see what was really wanted,
and, it was said, spent most of their attention on scraping
money together by bribes and other disreputable means.
He forbade relic-hawking priests from preaching. All they
sought was money and trafficking on the ignorance and credulity of the people.

S. THORLAC, B. OF SKALHOLT.

(A.D. 1193.)

[Danish Martyrology published by Olaus Romerus in 1705, on Dec. 23 ; he died on that day. But in Iceland his chief festival was observed on June 29, the day of his election to the bishopric of Skalholt. His canonization and the appointment of his festivals were made by popular suffrage at the Althing, or parliament of Iceland, in 1198. Authorities : —(1) The elder Thorláks Saga, written probably in 1198, when he was canonized. It is referred to by the Pálssaga, written 1216-20. See Biskupa Sögur, formáli, xxxiii.-iv. (2) The younger Thorláks Saga in 1325. There are also two books of miracles by S. Thorlác; the first is that produced by Bishop Paul at the canonization of S. Thorlac, in 1198, collected and written down by him, and read to the Althing; with additions added by him and read to the Althing in 1199. The second was collected after 1200; mention is made in it of Abbot Thorsteinn Turvason, who died in 1224, and Jón Ljótsson, who died in 1224. An appendix to this gives miracles wrought after 1300. (3) Latin fragments of Lives of S. Thorlac used in the lessons for his festival in the Church of Skalholt, in that of Vallanes, in Fljotsdalr, in the Nidaros Breviary, &c. All these Lives and Miracles are printed in Biskupa Sögur, Copenh. 1858, t. i. p. 149-212, 261-404. For critical observations on their dates, see the Formáli.]

S. THORLAC, the most popular of Icelandic saints, was the son of Thorhallr and Halla, and born in 1133. He was educated by Eyjolf the Priest, son of Sæmund the Wise, at Odda. He ever after held his old master in the highest respect, and was wont to quote him as an authority on whom he could rely when making a statement which might be called in question. Thorlac was ordained deacon by Bishop Magnus before he was fifteen.[1] He was ordained priest by Bishop Björn of Holum,[2] when about seventeen or eighteen, and then went to study in Paris and at Lincoln. At the latter place he no doubt made the acquaintance of S. Hugh, who then occupied the see, and the sanctity of that great bishop

---

[1] Magnus Einarsson died in 1148.   [2] Björn Gilsson, 1147-62.

must have had its influence on the character and after life of the Icelander.   He remained six years abroad, and then returned to his native land, filled with that home-sickness which makes the Icelander, however far he may wander, sing, " Iceland is the fairest land on which the sun e'er shines,"[1] and not find exaggeration in the sentiment. His contemporary biographer says that he felt also a great longing to see his mother and sisters.   On reaching Iceland, " his mother clung to him, and followed him wherever he went, and he showed the tenderest love to his sisters, Ragneid, the mother of Paul, who succeeded Thorlac as bishop, and Eyvör." His relations wanted him to take a farm, marry, and settle ; and he was also disposed to do this, for indeed, in Iceland, priests and bishops were all married.   But in the night an old man appeared to him as he slept, and said, " You are meditating taking to you a wife here, but I have another bride in store for you."   We may suspect that Thorlac in a dream saw Hugh of Lincoln, and that the impression he had received in England of clerical celibacy, from the teaching and example of that saint, asserted itself in sleep.   Thorlac abandoned his design, and went to a learned priest named Bjarnhedinn,[2] at Kirkjubæ, and spent six years with him.

A rich farmer at Thykkubæ, named Thorkell, was old, and had no relations, so he left his land " to Christ as his heir," and appointed Thorlac to convert his house into a monastery. Thorlac went thither in 1168, and was " consecrated abbot by Bishop Klængi."   Many placed themselves under his direction, and he imposed on them canonical rule.   His mother Halla went to Thykkubæ with her son, and looked after the monks as her children, cooked their victuals, and mended their clothes.

Bishop Klængi of Skalholt was ill, and obtained permis-

---

[1] " Island er hinn bestr land, sem solar skinar upá."
Ordained priest 1143, died 1173.

sion to have his successor chosen and appointed before his death, to look after the temporal affairs of the see. Three candidates were presented before the Althing, or general parliament of the island, of whom Thorlac was one, and he was chosen in 1174; and went at once to Skalholt.

Klængi lingered on till 1176, confined to his bed. As soon as he was dead, in the summer of 1177, Thorlac sailed to Norway, and was consecrated by Archbishop Eysteinn of Nidaros on July 1, 1178. He returned to Iceland directly after his consecration, and established himself in his see. His ordination had been impeded by Earl Erlingr, who was hostile to the Icelanders.

When first Thorlac woke, he sang aloud the "Credo," the "Paternoster," and the hymn, "Jesu nostra redemptio." Then he meditated a little on the Incarnation and the Redemption. Whilst dressing, he sang the "Prayer of S. Gregory," and after that the 1st Psalm. When clothed, he went to church, and there he sang first the "Gloria Patri," in honour of the Holy Trinity; after that "he praised with song those holy men to whom the church was dedicated in which he then was, and who were the patrons." After that he read the Little Office of Our Lady, and then he prostrated himself before the altar, and prayed for all Christian people; and every day he sang a third of the Psalter. If he were in any perplexity, he sang, "Mitte mihi Domine auxilium de sancto," and when he left the table after a meal, he sang, "Benedicam Dominum in omni tempore." When he went to bed, he sang the Psalm, "Lord, who shall dwell in Thy habitation."

S. Thorlac introduced into the Icelandic Church the observance of the festivals of S. Ambrose, S. Cecilia, and S. Agnes, and the vigils before the festivals of the apostles. He was the first bishop to exercise excommunication in the island, at the instigation of Archbishop Eysteinn. He also

forbade the marriage of priests. But it does not appear that
this command was obeyed, for the priests continued to
marry till long after his time. He forbade also lay presentation to churches, and lay impropriation of ecclesiastical property.

Sigurd Ormsson, a wealthy man, built and adorned a
church at Svinafell, and asked the bishop to consecrate it.
Thorlac refused, unless he endowed it with a farm, and entirely abandoned every claim to presentation to it. Sigurd
refused, and was excommunicated till he submitted.

John Loptsson, nephew of King Magnus Barefeet, one of
the most powerful men in Iceland, one also in deacon's
orders, had the right of patronage to a church at Hofda-
breckja. The church was destroyed by a storm, and he
rebuilt it in the most sumptuous manner. Bishop Thorlac
would not reconsecrate it till John Loptsson had abandoned
his right of presentation. John Loptsson had as his concubine Ragneid, the sister of S. Thorlac.[1] John refused to
surrender his right. The church had been endowed and
founded by his forefathers, and they had always exercised
their right of presentation; and he was backed up by all
the people of position in the island. John charged the
bishop with the exercise of arbitrary authority and the
dealing forth of unjust excommunications, to carry out a
freak of Archbishop Eysteinn. An angry altercation ensued,
but Thorlac was obliged to give way, and abandon his
crusade against lay patronage. Indeed, Eysteinn caused
such hostility to arise against him from the same attempt
in Norway, that he was obliged to leave Nidaros.

[1] " John was a deacon by consecration, and a man of great authority in the
Church. . . . . His wife was Halldora Brand's daughter. Their son was Sæmund.
He was a great woman-lover, and he had many other sons by other women. Paul,
afterwards bishop, and Orm were his sons by Ragneid, sister of Bishop Thorlac.
She and John loved one another from childhood. But she had children by many
men."—Thorlák Saga hinn yngri.

Thorlac, angry at his defeat, excommunicated John Loptsson for adultery. John beset the doors of a church into which the bishop wanted to enter, with armed men. "Why do you impede my entrance?" asked Thorlac. "Because you have forbidden my entrance into the church," answered Loptsson. "You have excluded yourself by your crimes," answered the bishop. "And I am not likely to be brought to repentance by your violence and maliciousness. For God's sake, not constrained by you, I will dismiss your sister."[1] He sent her away.

A priest named Högni, rich, but of low extraction, had two daughters born in wedlock, one of whom was married, the other, named Snælaug, was unwed and at home. She gave birth to a daughter, who was called Gunnlaug, and it was generally understood that a workman of her father's called Gunnar "Cattletyke" was the father. "Högni, her father, was not angry with her for this, nor did he hold her in lower esteem than before this affair. It happened that Snælaug was staying at Saurbæ, and there a priest named Thord, son of Bodvar, fell in love with her; his mind was set on the woman, and he and his father went to Bæ and asked for her to be the wife of Thord. An agreement was struck, and Thord took to him Snælaug, and they loved one another much, and had a son together. Now, it fell out that a man named Hreinn had been foster-son to Högni when Snælaug had her bastard. He went abroad after that, and now the news came that he was dead in Norway. And when the tidings reached Högni and Snælaug, she admitted that he had been the father of her daughter Gunnlaug. When this was known, the bishop Thorlac forbade all inter-

---

[1] S. Paul of Skalholt was aged forty when consecrated in 1195, so that the connection with Ragneid must have been of long standing. Thorlac not only paid no attention to this scandal, but he actually feasted in the house of John Loptsson, where his sister was kept as a mistress, till the personal quarrel broke out between him and Loptsson, when he took advantage of it to excommunicate the adulterer.

course between Thord and Snælaug.[1] But because they loved one another dearly, they paid little attention to what he said. After that he again forbade them, and excommunicated them. The bishop went himself at the Althing to the Lawhill, and pronounced the divorce of Thord and Snælaug, and their child a bastard born in incest. The reason of this was, that Thord the priest and the deceased Hreinn were related in the fourth degree, within which marriage was prohibited without special dispensation.[2] At the same time, S. Thorlac deposed Högni for having allowed such a union to take place. Eyjolf, the other son-in-law of Högni, also incurred his displeasure. He had become possessed of a property which had been held by Steinn, a priest. Steinn was dead, having left two daughters, who had inherited his lands, and they had either sold it or come to some arrangement with Eyjolf as tenant. Thorlac claimed the farm for the Church, on what plea does not transpire, probably because the priest had died intestate, and therefore the Church, not his daughters, should inherit.

Eyjolf, who was excommunicated by S. Thorlac as guilty of sacrilege in seizing on ecclesiastical property, summoned his servants, armed them, waylaid the bishop, and demanded compensation for two of his maids who had been seduced by two of S. Thorlac's clergy. A certain Thorleif Beiskald interfered and patched up a reconciliation. Each priest was to pay five hundred ells of brown vadmal for the seduction.

Thord and his wife tried by all means in their power to induce the bishop to relax his inhibition of their open union, but in vain. They therefore resolved to obtain restoration

[1] See also Sturlunga Saga, lib. iii. 3.

[2] At present, by applying to Rome and paying for a dispensation, marriages are permitted within much nearer degrees. The current Almanach de Gotha gives instances of noble Roman Catholic families in which uncles have married nieces, with dispensation from the Pope.

to communion by converting it into a clandestine union. Thord, it was arranged before the bishop, should remain at his cure of Gard, and Snælaug should return to her father at Bæ. However, they visited each other as often as possible, and she bore him three sons.

Högni, the father of Snælaug, had also a difference with S. Thorlac. He had been to Norway, and had brought home a shipload of timber. He set to work, built at Bæ a handsome church, furnished it with all its necessary equip ments, and then asked the bishop to consecrate it. But Thorlac refused, unless the presentation to it were made over into his hands and those of his successors in the see of Skalholt. Högni would not allow this, and the church re- mained unconsecrated.

Rather than yield his rights of patron, Högni declared he would use his church as a stable.

Högni awaited an occasion when the bishop was on his way from Reykholt to Saurbæ, when he and Eyjolf waylaid him as he was passing a ford in the Grimsá, and insisted on his going at once to Bæ. There the bishop found all the chief men of Reykholtsdale assembled, prepared to support the rights of the patron, and Thorlac was obliged sulkily to give way, consecrate the church, and say mass in it. After that he was dismissed with rich presents, and with mutual but insincere professions of amity.

When old, Thorlac was desirous of resigning his bishopric and retiring to the monastery of Thykkubæ; but before he could carry his project into execution, he fell mortally ill on his visitation tour through the valleys opening into the Bor- garfjord. Feeling that his end was approaching, he bade his friends farewell, and gave his ring to Pául, the bastard of his sister by John Loptsson. After he had received ex- treme unction he renewed and confirmed all the excom- munications he had pronounced, lest in the last agony the solicitation of his friends, or a milder spirit of forgiveness, should overcome his failing resolution. He died in his sixtieth year, after having been bishop fifteen years, on December 23, 1193.

In 1198 he was canonized by vote of the senate of the island, and the days of his election and death appointed as festivals to be observed in his honour perpetually.

His relics received veneration throughout the Middle Ages till the Reformation, when they were buried, except the skull, which is still shown in Skalholt cathedral. The skull, however, proves, on examination, to be a cocoa-nut.

December 24.

SS. XL. Virgins, *MM. at Antioch;* A.D. 250.
S. Gregory, *M. at Spoleto;* A.D. 303.
S. Euthymius, *M. at Nicomedia;* A.D. 304.
S. Delphinus, *B. of Bordeaux;* A.D. 404.
S. Tarsilla, *V. at Rome;* 6th cent.
S. Levan, *B.C. at Tréguier in Brittany;* 6th cent.
SS. Irmina and Adela, *VV. at Trèves;* 8th cent.

S. GREGORY OF SPOLETO, M.

(A.D. 303.)

[Roman Martyrology. Usuardus, &c. At Cologne on Dec. 23. Authority :—A Passion in Surius, late and fabulous.]

THE legend of S. Gregory—it must not be regarded as in any way historical—relates that Maximian appointed Flaccus, governor of Umbria, to root out the Christians. Flaccus came to Spoleto and summoned all the inhabitants together by the town crier into the forum. Then he said to Tircanus, chief magistrate of Spoleto, " Have all these deserted the immortal gods ? " " By no means," answered Tircanus. "They all worship Jove, Minerva, and Æsculapius. There is, however, in this city a man called Gregory, who threw down the images of the gods." Then Flaccus ordered forty soldiers to invest his house and secure him. Gregory was brought before Flaccus and Tircanus, and when asked to adore the gods, affirmed that Jove, Minerva, and Æsculapius were demons. Thereupon his ears were boxed and he was bidden not to blaspheme. He was put in an iron pot over a fire. An earthquake upset the pot before Gregory was quite roasted, and threw down a quarter of the city, burying four hundred and fifty idolaters under the ruins. Then Gregory was laden with chains and sent to prison. Next day his bare knees were beaten with spiked iron scourges, and his sides were scorched with flaming torches. His tortures were at last put an end to by decapitation in the amphitheatre.

The relics of S. Gregory of Spoleto are preserved in Cologne Cathedral. Other relics are at Spoleto.

S. DELPHINUS, B. OF BORDEAUX.

(A.D. 404.)

[Roman and Gallican Martyrologies. Authorities :—A letter of S. Ambrose, and several letters of S. Paulinus.]

DELPHINUS, bishop of Bordeaux, attended the council of Saragossa, held in 380, along with Phœbadius of Agen, and Idacius of Merida. The canons passed are remarkable for the practical good sense exhibited by those who drew them up. They forbid clergy deserting their charges for the sake of embracing the monastic life; and the veiling of nuns earlier than the age of forty. The council passed judgment on the Priscillianist Instantius, and on Hymus of Cordova, who had received the heretics to communion. Priscillianism was a form of Gnosticism or Manichæism; it placed flesh and spirit in antagonism, in irreconcilable opposition. The sect lingered on in Spain, spread into Provence, and broke out later in Albigensianism. Like all Manichæan sects, it had a double aspect, one ascetic and pure, the other licentious. Some, living to the spirit, mortified the deeds of the body, others, living in the spirit, thought that the deeds done in the body in no way stained the soul. With this heresy were mixed up mysticism and hysterical devotion: in their paroxysms of religious exaltation they threw off their clothes and prayed and capered in nudity, like the Anabaptists of the sixteenth century and the Shakers of the present day, the spiritual descendants of these early heretics.

Idacius of Merida, in his wrath against the Priscillianists, appealed to the secular arm, and by a rescript of Gratian they were expelled their churches and the country. Instantius, Salvian, and Priscillian went to Rome to justify themselves and obtain a repeal of this judgment. On their way they passed through the diocese of S. Delphinus. He refused to receive them.

S. Paulinus of Nola was baptized by S. Delphinus in 392, and that great saint ever after reverenced the bishop of Bordeaux as his spiritual father, and kept up with him a correspondence on matters relating to the practice of perfection.

S. TARSILLA, V.

(6TH CENT.)

[Roman Martyrology. Authority :—S. Gregory the Great, Dialog. iv. 16, and Hom. 38 in Evang.]

S. GREGORY THE GREAT had three aunts, sisters of his father, Gordian the senator. They lived a retired religious life in their father's house. Their names were Tarsilla (or Thrasilla), Æmiliana, and Gordiana. The two elder renounced the world and took a vow of celibacy the same day. Gordiana joined them in their vow, but was not prepared to live the life of abject self-humiliation and self-torture which the two elder undertook. She was disposed to be moderate in her diet, but not to starve herself; not to braid her hair and anoint herself with spikenard, but also

not to abandon the bath altogether. However, she did not
withdraw from their company, though she found it irksome
to her, but bore with patience what she regarded as their
eccentricities. She was apparently very young when her
two elder sisters induced her to vow celibacy. When she
was old enough to understand what it meant, she regretted
the step, and after the death of her sisters relieved her of
restraint, she married her guardian. Tarsilla is said by S.
Gregory to have been favoured with a vision of her uncle,
Pope S. Felix, who showed her a throne in heaven, and told
her it was prepared for her. She fell ill with fever, and
when dying, cried to the assistants, " Depart ! make room !
Jesus is coming ! " S. Gregory assures us, with great satisfaction, that after death the skin of his aunt's knees was
found as hard as the hide of a camel, through her continual
kneeling.

A few days after her death, which took place on December the 24th, she appeared to her sister Æmiliana, and
invited her to celebrate the feast of the Epiphany with her in
eternal bliss. Æmiliana fell sick, and died on the 8th of
January, on which day she is mentioned in the Roman
Martyrology. Gordiana is unnoticed in the Martyrology ;
S. Gregory indeed hints that his youngest aunt went to per-
dition.

S. LEVAN, B.C.

(6TH CENT.)

[By the Bollandists on Oct. 17. "Memorials of British Piety, or a
British Martyrology," on Dec. 24. The day on which he is commemorated in Brittany is Sept. 12.]

ACCORDING to tradition in Brittany, S. Levan or Levian
was a native of Britain, no doubt of Cornwall, where there is
a church dedicated to him. He is said to have vowed him-

self to God at an early age, within the walls of a monastery. He was constituted abbot. As many other British saints in the sixth century migrated to Armorica, Levan was seized with the same impulse, and crossed to Brittany, where he was consecrated regionary bishop; he had his cell at Trédarzec, near Tréguier. Before 1793 he was commemorated merely as an abbot and confessor. His relics were translated to Paris along with those of S. Leuthiern in 965. He is invoked in Brittany in behalf of deformed children.

SS. IRMINA AND ADELA, VV.

(ABOUT A.D. 707.)

[Venerated at Trèves on this day. In Gallican and German Martyrologies generally Irmina alone. Authority :—A Life by John Trithemius, abbot of Spanheim, d. 1516; too late to be of any value.]

S. IRMINA and her sister S. Adela were daughters of Dagobert II., King of the Franks. He turned the royal barn in the neighbourhood of Trèves into a convent for his daughters, and it thence took the name of Horreum or Oehren. The story of Irmina is sufficiently tragical. She was engaged in early youth to a Count Hermann, and was passionately attached to him. The day of the marriage was fixed. It was to take place at Trèves, and she took her way thither with a retinue. There was in her train a young man named Edgar, who had fallen frantically in love with his mistress, and his heart was consumed with jealousy and despair as the day approached when she was to become the bride of Count Hermann. When Irmina and her attendants reached Trèves, on the eve of the marriage, Edgar went to the count, and told him in confidence that there was a foreign merchant near the town who had rare jewels for sale, and offered to lead Hermann to him, so that he might purchase ornaments from him without Irmina suspecting what was in store for her, and he could place them upon her at the wedding. The count fell into the trap, and accompanied the young man out of the town, across the Mosel bridge, and to the top of the rock where now stands the Mariensäule. There Edgar suddenly clasped his rival in his arms, and flung himself with the count over the edge of the precipice. The wedding day came, but no bridegroom was to be seen. It was only after some days that the body of the count was found fast locked in the arms of the dead servant of Irmina. Dagobert then allowed his daughter to take the veil, 676, and founded the convent at Trèves for her. Adela, her sister, took the veil with her. Irmina, according to all accounts, was born in 662, and therefore was only fourteen when this tragedy took place.

Hontheim has published the diploma of Dagobert II. for the founding of the convent, and it was dedicated by Bishop Modoald. Not a trace of the convent remains, but marble pillars and ruined walls existed when Hontheim wrote his History of Trèves.

December 25.

THE NATIVITY OF OUR LORD JESUS CHRIST.
S. EUGENIA, *V.M. at Alexandria;* A.D. 258.
SS. MARTYRS AT NICOMEDIA ; A.D. 303.
S. ANASTASIA, *M. in the Isle of Palmaria;* A.D. 304.
S. ADALSENDIS, *V. at Marchiennes near Namur; circ.* A.D. 678
B. PETER THE VENERABLE, *Ab. of Cluny;* A.D. 1156.
S. FULK, *B. of Toulouse;* A.D. 1231.

THE NATIVITY OF OUR LORD.

[Roman and all Western Martyrologies. Also the Eastern Menæas.
The Carthaginian Kalendar of the 5th cent., and the ancient Roman
Kalendar of the middle of the 4th cent., published by Bucherius.]

ILL the year 325 we have only uncertain traces of
the observance of this festival; but in the middle of
the fourth century, under Pope Liberius, we hear
of it as generally observed in the Roman Church,
and throughout the West. The celebration of the Feast of
the Nativity spread from the West to the East, and S. John
Chrysostom used his utmost endeavour to promote this introduction. Already, in 386, S. John Chrysostom says that the
festival was observed in Antioch. The festival is ordered to
be observed with reverence and dignity by the councils of
Agde in 504 (can. 64), of Orleans in 511 (can. 24), and of
Epaone in 517 (can. 35). Before this, the commemoration
of the Nativity was united with that of the Epiphany, which
is far the more ancient festival of the two.

At Rome is shown, in the church of Santa Maria Maggiore,
in the Sixtine Chapel, the cradle of Bethlehem, encrusted
with silver, and enriched with ornaments, given it by Philip
III. of Spain.

THE NATIVITY. From the Vienna Missal.

There were shepherds abiding in the field, keeping watch over their
flock by night. And lo! the Angel of the Lord came upon them, and
the glory of the Lord shone round about them.—S. LUKE.

The napkins wherewith the Infant Saviour was wrapped, were anciently exhibited in Constantinople, but were translated to Paris in the thirteenth century, and placed by S. Louis in the Sainte Chapelle.

Beside the cradle in which our Lord, it is alleged, was rocked, is the stone manger of the grotto of Bethlehem. One of the stones of this manger is shown in the basilica of S. Maria Maggiore on the Esquiline, in the altar of the crypt of the chapel of the B. Sacrament.

Some of the napkins of Christ are also exposed to the adoration of Catholics in the same chapel. The cloak with which S. Joseph covered the crib, to protect the Child from the cold, is in the church of S. Anastasia at Rome. The basilica of Santa Croce in Gerusalemme at Rome has also the felicity of possessing the first cuttings of His infant hair.

The church of Courtrai in Belgium also pretends to possess three hairs from our Lord's head, but pulled out when He was older. The cathedral of Aix-la-Chapelle also affects to be possessed of some of the napkins.

On December 25th the Greeks also commemorate the Adoration of the Magi.

SS. MARTYRS AT NICOMEDIA.

(A.D. 303.)

[Roman Martyrology.]

THE Roman Martyrology says on this day: "At Nicomedia, the passion of several thousand martyrs, who were assembled on the day of the nativity of their Lord, to celebrate the solemnity. The emperor Diocletian commanded the doors of the church to be closed, and firewood was heaped

up around the church for consuming it. Then he had a tripod
with incense placed at the entrance, and it was proclaimed
with a loud voice by a herald that those who desired to save
themselves from being burned to death might come forth and
offer incense to Jupiter. Thereupon all replied with one voice
that they had rather die for Jesus Christ than commit this
sacrilege. The fire was then applied, and all were consumed,
so that they had the good fortune to be borne to heaven on
the very day on which our Saviour was born on earth for the
salvation of the world." As the feast of Christ's nativity
was certainly not observed at Nicomedia on December 25th,
at the time of the persecution of Diocletian, and not till
long after, we may dismiss these martyrs to the realm of
mythology.

S. ANASTASIA, M.

(A.D. 304.)

[Roman Martyrology. Usuardus. By the Greeks on Dec. 22.
Authority :—The apocryphal Acts, undeserving of confidence, in Metaphrastes. Also the equally untrustworthy Acts of S. Chrysogonus.]

S. ANASTASIA the younger, to distinguish her from the
saint of the same name who is commemorated on October
28th, was the daughter of a heathen father and a Christian
mother. She was married to a Roman nobleman called Publius, who was a pagan, and strongly prejudiced against
Christianity. Anastasia devoted her time and means to the
relief of the martyrs in prison, during the persecution of
Diocletian. Her husband then forbade her leaving the
house. She wrote letters to S. Chrysogonus, and received
replies from him. The letters are extant, but they are not
genuine, they are fabrications by the authors of the Acts of
S. Chrysogonus and S. Anastasia. Publius was sent by the

emperor on an embassy to Persia, and died on his way, to the great satisfaction of his wife.

She at once recommenced her attendance on the martyrs. She was arrested at Aquileja, and brought before Florus, prefect of Illyria. In prison she was visited by S. Theodota, afterwards a martyr (August 2nd).

S. Anastasia was put in a ship along with a Christian named Eutychianus, and a hundred and twenty pagans, condemned to death. The vessel was conveyed out to sea, scuttled, and those on board were left to perish.

The water was already flowing in at the holes, when S. Theodota appeared, seized the helm, and guided the ship to the shore. This miracle caused the conversion of the hundred and twenty idolaters, and three days after they suffered martyrdom.

Anastasia was conveyed to the island of Palmaria with two hundred men and seventy women condemned to death for believing in Christ. She was there stretched to posts stuck in the earth, her hands and feet extended like a S. Andrew's cross, and a fire was lighted about her which speedily consumed her. The rest of the company suffered various kinds of martyrdom.

Her relics were conveyed to Constantinople under the patriarch Gennadius, and placed in the basilica of the Resurrection. This church at Constantinople was dedicated to the Anastasis or Resurrection, as the great metropolitan church was dedicated to S. Sophia, the Eternal Wisdom. Popular ignorance made of Sophia a female saint and martyr, and so also the Anastasis became a saint and martyr.

The name of Anastasia occurs in the Canon of the Mass, but probably not the name of this most mythical martyr, but of Anastasia the elder.

S. ADALSENDIS, V.

(ABOUT A.D. 678)

[Gallican, Belgian, and Benedictine Martyrologies. Authority :— Mention in the Lives of S. Rictrudis and S. Clotsendis.]

S. ADALSENDIS was daughter of S. Adalbald and S. Rictrudis. She was the youngest of their daughters, and after the murder of her father, she followed her mother into the convent of Marchiennes in Hainault. "She who entered last of her sisters in at the gate of temporal life, entered first of them by the gate of death to life eternal." She died on Christmas Day. Her mother restrained her tears for her till the Feast of the Innocents, lest her sorrow should mar the glad solemnity of the Nativity.

B. PETER THE VENERABLE, AB.

(A.D. 1156.)

[Benedictine and Gallican Martyrologies. Authorities :—His own letters and those of S. Bernard and Innocent II.]

PONTIUS, abbot of Cluny, had been elected when young, his character having given great hopes of his proving an active ruler. But by degrees pride overmastered him, and when he appeared in 1116 at the Lateran Council, he arrogated to himself the haughty title of Abbot of Abbots. John of Gaeta, chancellor of the Roman Church, then sarcastically inquired whether Monte Cassino or Cluny was the cradle and head of the Benedictine Order. General discontent against the rule of Pontius prevailed among the Cluniacs, and its mutterings reached the ears of Callixtus II. Pontius then, in a fit of irritation, went to Rome, and insisted on resigning his office into the hands of the Pope, who, with a formal ex-hibition of reluctance, accepted it, and Pontius departed for Jerusalem. The Pope informed the monks of Cluny of what had taken place, and they elected another abbot, Hugh, prior of Marcigny, but a man so old that he died three months after. Another chapter was held, in August, 1122, and Peter Maurice was elected abbot. His nomination was confirmed by the Pope, and he received abbatial benediction from the hands of the bishop of Besançon.

Peter belonged to a noble family of Auvergne. He had been offered in childhood by his parents to the abbot, S. Hugh of Cluny (d. 1109). He had been prior of Vezelai, and was about thirty years old when elected to the govern-ment of the abbey of Cluny, which he governed nearly thirty-five years. He is known by the title of Peter the Venerable, and is one of the most attractive figures which monastic and mediæval history presents to us.

Peter Maurice had scarcely been three years in the enjoy-ment of his preferment, when Pontius, the former abbot, having got tired of the East, and regretting his precipitation in resigning the abbacy, returned to Europe, and built a monastery at Treviso in Italy. But that did not satisfy him, his envious eyes were turned on Peter and Cluny. He left Treviso and came into Aquitain, accoutred with all the in-signia of holy asceticism likely to attract the admiration of the vulgar and superstitious. He wore bands of iron round his arms, eating into his flesh; a sackcloth shirt; scourged himself till blood was drawn, scarcely ate, and worked miracles.

He gradually approached the neighbourhood of Cluny, and took the opportunity, when he had learned by spies that Peter was absent, of swooping down on the vacant nest with a train of monks, and, if we may believe his adversaries, of women, drove out the prior Bernard, and resumed his abbatial chair. Those monks who favoured Peter were driven out or fled. The rest took oaths of obedience to him. He now cast aside the mask of asceticism, called the neighbouring knights and robbers to his aid, enrolled them in an army of occupation, and gave up the villages on the abbey lands which would not acknowledge him to their mercy. The estates of the abbey were ravaged with fire and sword, not, doubtless, at his instigation, but by the lawless robbers whom he had called to his aid, and whom he could not control with the abbatial staff. The prior Bernard and some of the monks threw themselves into castles and walled towns, and summoned the vassals of the abbey to their aid. The summer of 1125 was spent in warfare between the levies of the rival abbots. Pope Honorius II. heard of this disorder, and his legate, Peter de Fontibus, with the archbishop of Lyons, pronounced anathema against Pontius and his adherents; and Honorius summoned both parties before the apostolic throne. Peter the Venerable hastened to Rome, and met Pontius there. And now a curious complication arose.

Pontius was excommunicated for having possessed himself of Cluny and certain estates of the Order. An excommunicate man cannot appear before the papal consistory to argue his cause. He is out of the Church, and therefore cannot plead as a member of it.

Yet he was again summoned before the Pope, and when he would present himself was repulsed. It was explained to him that he must surrender Cluny and all he had secured before the ban was taken off, and he could enter the court and be heard. He lost his temper: "No one has power thus to cast me out of the Church, save Peter in heaven!" he incautiously exclaimed. This dangerous sentiment was speedily wafted to the Pope's ear, and exasperated him to the last degree. Pontius was a heretic, he defied the authority of the apostolic throne. Honorius bade the monks who were with Pontius state their case. They appeared, beating their breasts, with bare feet, and many prostrations, and were absolved. They then stated their case, and were answered by Prior Matthew of S. Martin des Champs, who appeared for Peter the Venerable. There could be no doubt that the judgment would be adverse to the usurper, but it was so overwhelming as to petrify his party. Pontius, usurper, sacrilegious man, schismatic, and excommunicate, was deposed for ever from every ecclesiastical dignity and sacred function; Cluny was to be restored to its rightful abbot forthwith. But Pontius was not allowed to escape and revisit the East; by the Pope's orders he was cast into a dungeon, where he conveniently died on the 28th December following. Matthew of S. Martin des Champs was rewarded with the cardinal bishopric of Alba.

A miserable jealousy had sprung up between the monks of Citeaux and those of Cluny. The monks of Citeaux accused those of Cluny of relaxation of their rule. Those of Cluny replied that the rule of Citeaux was unpractical in its severity, at all events for all monks.

A cousin of S. Bernard, named Robert, was a bone of contention between the two Reforms. Robert had been offered by his parents to Cluny, but he had gone to Clairvaux after a while to his relative. Finding the discipline intolerable for his constitution, he went back to the milder monastic atmosphere of Cluny; on an appeal to Rome, the Pope ordered Robert to remain at Cluny. But to S. Bernard this was an apostacy of his cousin, scarcely less heinous than if he had married and eaten beef. He wrote him a violent letter, declaring the papal rescript null and void, and assuring the youth of damnation through an eternity of flames and gnawing worms unless he cast aside the weeds of Cluny and returned to the habit of Citeaux.

Peter the Venerable, with that gentle forbearance and love of peace which make him stand out conspicuous in his generation, when each man sought his own, or the things of his Order, not the things of Jesus Christ, sent Robert to his cousin at Clairvaux. But the monks of Cluny could not see this tame surrender, as they regarded it, without murmurs, and William, abbot of S. Thierry, near Rheims, wrote a sharp letter to S. Bernard, remonstrating with him for stirring up strife between two Orders which ought to live together in the Church in unity.

S. Bernard answered by sending a string of accusations. The Cluniacs had dishes of great variety at their table, and a great many kinds of fish to make up for not being allowed meat. These dishes have sauces flavoured with pot-herbs and spices. A variety of wines stand in their cellars. Monks shammed illness that they might eat meat in the infirmary, and those who were sick were allowed a stick to support their tottering steps. The material for the habits was of the best. "You say that religion is a matter of the heart, and not of the habit. That may be true, but this daintiness of habit shows the softness of the heart." According to S. Bernard, the Kingdom of God, one would suppose, did consist in meat and drink rather than in righteousness, peace, and joy in the Holy Ghost.

Peter the Venerable wrote an answer to the charges and invectives of S. Bernard, couched in the gentlest of tones, the answer of a man who stood above such petty disputes about trifles in the serene atmosphere of gospel charity.

"You allow fugitives to return more often than the three times prescribed by the Rule," was one of Bernard's charges. "We place no limits to the mercy oi God," was Peter's answer.

"You allow furs to be worn, and furs are not mentioned in the Rule," urged Bernard. "The brothers are allowed to

clothe themselves according to the season," answered Peter.
Other accusations were more difficult to answer, as that the
Cluniacs had given up manual labour in the fields, and
possessed castles and estates, and serfs, male and female,
and had lawsuits and contests by arms about their lands.
Peter the Venerable wound up with a remarkable general
reply. There are two sorts of commandments of God, he
said ;—that of Charity, which is perpetually binding and im-
mutable, and the precepts which vary with the times and
mode of life, and which change subject to the directions of
Charity. Charity is supreme. She may permit at one time
what was forbidden or tolerated at another ; and Charity is
the law overriding all monastic regulations, which sits and
rules in the heart of every true monastic superior. And
then he gently added that surely it would be more charitable,
more in accordance with the love of God, if the Cistercians
allowed the brethren some of those little relaxations which
are needed by those infirm or sickly, and without which
their health must fail.

In 1138 died William de Sabran, bishop of Langres, and
Hugh, son of the duke of Burgundy, wished to appoint to
the vacant see a monk of Cluny, who was probably recommended to him by Peter the Venerable. But S. Bernard
coveted the see for one of his Clairvaux monks. The archbishop of Lyons and the dean of Langres went to Rome to
ask of the Pope permission for the chapter of Langres to
elect a bishop. S. Bernard was then at Rome, and he
opposed them with vehemence, and endeavoured to force an
oath on the archbishop that he would only consecrate and
confirm a nominee of his own. The archbishop gave an
equivocal answer and hastened home. Bernard returned to
Clairvaux, which was situated in the diocese of Langres,
and found that the chapter was about to elect the monk of
Cluny. Bernard interfered, and appealed against them to

Rome. The abbot of Cluny, and the son of the duke of Burgundy, also wrote to Rome along with the chapter. But the monk was consecrated by the archbishop of Lyons, assisted by the bishops of Autun and Mâcon, before Bernard's appeal was answered. His indignation and violence now knew no bounds. He raked together false charges against the unfortunate bishop elect on the merest hearsay, which Peter the Venerable indignantly repudiated, but which Bernard, when convicted of false accusations, never had the honesty to withdraw.

The Pope was too dependent on S. Bernard's authority and influence at that time to be able to resist his imperious dictation: the Cluniac monk was dismissed, his consecration pronounced void, and a monk chosen by Bernard, his own cousin, the prior of Clairvaux, was forced on the reluctant chapter and diocese by his domineering will.

Abelard appealed to Rome against his condemnation by the council of Sens, in which he had been vehemently denounced by Bernard, and ignorantly condemned by men who did not understand his logic. An appeal from Bernard to Rome was an appeal from Bernard to himself. Pope Innocent II. was too deeply indebted to him not to confirm his sentence. Absent, unheard, unconvicted, Abelard was condemned by the supreme pontiff. The condemnation was uttered almost before the charge was fully known. The decree of Innocent reproved all public disputations on the mysteries of religion. Abelard was condemned to silence; his disciples to excommunication.

Abelard had set out on his journey to Rome; he was stopped by severe illness, and found hospitable reception in the abbey of Cluny.

Peter the Venerable did more than protect the outcast to the close of his life. He did not relax his labours of tender charity till he had accomplished an outward reconciliation

between the persecuted Abelard and the victorious Bernard
It was but a hollow outward reconciliation. The reconciliation of minds was psychologically impossible. Abelard published an apology—if apology it might be called—which
accused his adversary of ignorance or of malice. Ignorance
there certainly was in Bernard, he had not the mental capacity to understand the arguments of Abelard, and his conduct
bore at all events the outward aspect of vindictiveness.
Among the most distinguished prelates there were many
who sympathized, if not with the speculations, at least with
the sufferings of Abelard. Bernard wrote to all whom he
suspected of tenderness towards the old, broken-down, and
hunted philosopher, to goad them into hostility. "Though a
Baptist without in his austerities," he wrote to Cardinal Ivo,
"Abelard is a Herod within." Still, for the last two years
of his life, Abelard found peace, honour, seclusion, in the
abbey of Cluny, under the protection of the dove-like Peter.
He died at the age of sixty-three. Peter had written
to the Pope, entreating that the failing old man might be left
at peace to die in that nest. "Pray allow the last days of his
life and old age—not many, I suspect—to be passed in your
Cluny, and let not the impatience of certain ones prevail to
obtain his expulsion from the house in which as a sparrow,
from the nest in which as a dove, it delights the old man to
find his home."

He was allowed to remain there; and when he died, Peter
the Venerable, with delicate kindness, at once communicated
the tidings to the still faithful Heloisa. His language may be
contrasted with that of S. Bernard. "I never saw his equal
for humility of manners and habits. S. Germain was not
more modest, nor S. Martin more poor. He allowed no
moment to escape unoccupied by prayer, reading, writing, or
dictation. The heavenly visitor surprised him in the midst
of these holy works."

In 1143 Peter of Cluny wrote again to S. Bernard on the differences between the two Reforms, so that apparently S. Bernard had again been attacking the Cluniacs. He says in this letter that he loves both Bernard and the Cistercians, and that his charity must be very warm since it has stood the shock both of the strife about tithes, and of that concerning the bishopric of Langres. The question of tithes was the claim of the Cluniacs to demand a tax from a Cistercian monastery situated on their lands, which was indignantly resented, and led to appeal and counter appeal. At the end of the letter, Peter says that he sends S. Bernard a version of the Koran of Mohammed. This version Peter had made for him in Spain by Robert, archdeacon of Pampeluna, an Englishman, and a certain Hermann of Dalmatia, who was in Spain, studying astronomy. He paid them handsomely for the work.

Innocent II. died September 23rd, 1143, and was succeeded by Guido di Castello, cardinal of S. Mario, the scholar of Abelard. He was elected, as he says in a letter he wrote at once to Peter the Venerable, the third day after the death of Innocent, by the cardinal priests and deacons assembled in the Lateran basilica, with the bishops and subdeacons, and with the acclamations of the Roman people.

He took the name of Cœlestine II. Peter the Venerable had his letter read in full chapter; it was written at Rome on November 16th, and received at Cluny on November 29th.

Cœlestine died after a pontificate of less than six months, and was succeeded by Lucius II., who wrote to Peter the Venerable to send him thirteen of his monks whom he wished to establish in Rome in the monastery of S. Sabas.

In 1146 the urgent preaching of Bernard against the infidels, and his efforts to rouse the interests of the Christian princes in a new crusade, led to the disastrous result of rousing the people in France and Germany to massacre the Jews, the nearest infidels at hand on whose bodies to exhibit their enthusiasm for the Cross and hatred of misbelief.

S. Bernard did his utmost to stop the massacre. Peter of Cluny wrote to King Louis VII. to arrest the butchery. He urged the king to restrain the Jews from grinding down the poor by usury, and from being accomplices to burglars, who broke into churches and dwellings, stole chalices and other objects of precious metal, and carried them to the Jews, who bought them, and melted them up at once. But Peter of Cluny was not above the prejudices of his age. If he did not countenance the massacre, he did countenance the plunder of the Jews.

Peter the Venerable wrote a controversial letter on the errors of Peter de Brueys, who had been burned alive by a mob, zealous for the Catholic faith, but whose sect survived. Almost all we know of this obscure heretic is from the letter of the abbot of Cluny. Peter de Brueys is said to have been a clerk; he preached in the South of France during about twenty years. From the epistle of Peter the Venerable, we learn that the heretic denied infant baptism, respect for churches, the worship of the cross, transubstantiation, prayers for the dead, and fasting. "The people," wrote Peter the Venerable, "are re-baptized, altars thrown down, crosses burned, meat publicly eaten on the day of the Lord's Passion, priests scourged, monks imprisoned, or compelled by terror or torture to marry."

It is clear that Peter de Brueys was influenced by Manichæan tenets, such as had produced in an earlier age the Priscillianist heresy, and was shortly to develop rapidly into Albigensianism.

Peter the Venerable went to Rome in 1150, and after spending five months there, returned to Cluny, where he found deputies from the monasteries of his Order in Spain,

England, France, Italy, and Germany. He received a letter
from S. Bernard, but was unable to answer it at once on
his return, on account of the pressure of business which his
absence had occasioned. When he answered S. Bernard, it
was to give him an account of his reception by Eugenius III.
Eugenius was a Cistercian, whose sole recommendation to
the electors was that he was a friend of Bernard. "In elect-
ing you," said Bernard, "they made me Pope, not you."
With his characteristic gentleness and love of peace, Peter
wrote to S. Bernard in the most kindly tone, giving a glowing description of the Pope, who, he said, had shown him
the utmost honour and friendship.

In 1140, Roger, king of Sicily, had lost his eldest son,
Roger, duke of Apulia, after having lost three other sons.
In 1150 he had his only remaining son, William, prince of
Capua, crowned king of Sicily. Peter of Cluny wrote to the
king a kindly letter of sympathy on his bereavements. He
then added that he regretted the disunion which existed
between him and the king of Germany, and offered himself
as mediator. He also urged him to chastise the Greeks for
their ill-treatment of pilgrims to the Holy Land.

Peter the Venerable was the last man of celebrity among
the abbots of Cluny. The Reform fell into obscurity, and
was supplanted by the Cistercian Reform, which inherited its
popularity and, in time, its laxity.

S. FULK, B. OF TOULOUSE.

(A.D. 1231.)

[Gallican Martyrologies. Venerated on this day at Marseilles and Toulouse. Authorities :—Various notices of his Life, collected in "Hist. Littéraire de la France," xviii. p. 586 *seq.*, and Fauriel, "Hist. de la Poésie Provençale," ii. p. 69 *seq.*]

FULK was born at Marseilles between 1160 and 1170. His father was a merchant of Venice, who had retired from business to Marseilles, and who died, leaving Fulk a considerable fortune. The old biographer of the troubadour relates his entry into life in sufficiently remarkable terms, which, if vague, indicate from the beginning the character of the young man, ready to do his utmost to push his way in the world. "Folquet," says he, "showed himself greedy of honour and renown, and began to attend on powerful barons, going, coming, and plotting with them."

When Richard Cœur-de-Lion was on his way to Syria, he made some stay at Marseilles before going on to Genoa, where he was to embark. Fulk insinuated himself into his good graces. His power as a singer and poet, the tender, passionate, and sensual pictures he drew of love, charmed the hot-blooded prince. Fulk was already in favour with Alphonso II., king of Aragon, Alphonso VII., king of Castille, and Raymond V., count of Toulouse. But he chiefly attached himself to Barral de Beaux, seigneur of Marseilles, with whose wife he was enamoured; and he resided in the court of this nobleman, enjoying his hospitality and making love to his wife.

Fulk was married, but his wife was sorely neglected. Azalaïs de Roche Martine, wife of Barral de Beaux, was the subject of his tenderest lays.

Provençal traditions diverge as to the result of his suit of this lady. According to one account, he could "jamais trouver merci, ni obtenir aucun bien en droit d'amour" from the object of his passion; and, in disgust, he turned to make love to Laura de Saint Jorlan, sister of de Beaux, a lady remarkable for her beauty and grace. But the other account is that he made love to both ladies at once, and that Azalaïs cast him off because she found that his fickle heart was already turning to the fresher charms of Laura, and that she could not retain him, though she had accorded him every favour. Anyhow, he made his rejection by Azalaïs the subject of poetical laments, and prosecuted with vigour his siege of the heart and virtue of his patron's sister. And then he pursued with the same ardour the conquest of Eudoxia, wife of William, count of Montpellier.

Azalaïs died, and shortly after her, died also Barral de Beaux, her husband. Richard Cœur-de-Lion was already dead, so were his patrons, Alphonso of Aragon, and Raymond of Toulouse. His youth was past, his locks were tinged with grey, the fires of amorous passion began to grow cold. His ambition was unsated with the conquest of a name as a sweet singer, and some triumphs in love. He determined to push his fortunes in another career.

He retired from the world, made his profession in the monastery of Toronet in Provence, of the Order of Citeaux, and was elected abbot in 1200.

Five years later he was appointed to the episcopal see of Toulouse, which he occupied till 1231, the year of his death.

He was bishop during the war against the Albigenses, and against his own flock he exercised the ferocity of a wolf rather than the tenderness of a shepherd. "There is no act of treachery or cruelty throughout the war, in which the bishop of Toulouse was not the most forward, sanguinary, unscrupulous."[1]

The historian of his life, in the "Histoire Littéraire de la France," says of him: "After having given half of his life to gallantry, he gave up, without restraint, the remainder of his life to the cause of tyranny, murder, and spoliation, and unhappily he profited by it. . . . Loving women passionately, a ferocious apostle of the Inquisition, he did not give up the composition of verses which bore the impress of his successive passions."

In Toulouse he organized a strong confraternity to root out with armed force the heretics, usurers, and Jews. They attacked, and in their religious zeal pillaged and demolished houses, and enriched themselves with the spoil. Raymond, count of Toulouse, was in arms against Simon de Montfort, who invaded Provence under the banner of the Cross to carve out for himself and his needy followers a principality. Fulk hastened to his camp to bless his undertaking and to exult at the chastisement of the heretics as it took place before his eyes, under the remorseless sword of the crusader. We need not follow the details of this hideous and wicked war, and see the bishop steep in blood and infamy his sacred office. He was at the fourth council of the Lateran, 1215, to goad on the wavering Innocent III. to the destruction of the count of Toulouse, whom Fulk hated with deadly animosity.

The bishop and Guy de Montfort together plundered Toulouse. The people rose in revolt and expelled them. De Montfort again forced his way within the walls, and was again repelled, after having set the city on fire in many places. Then Bishop Fulk offered mediation. "I swear by God and the holy Virgin, and the body of the Redeemer, by my whole Order, the abbot, and other dignitaries, that I

[1] Milman, "Latin Christianity," b. ix. c. 8.

give you good counsel, better have I never given. If the count inflict on you the least wrong, bring your complaints before me, and God and I will see you righted." The citizens, trusting the word of their bishop, consented to give hostages of good conduct and restore the prisoners they had taken, and even to surrender their arms. No sooner were they in his power than De Montfort extorted from the citizens 30,000 marks of silver, demolished the walls of the city, and systematically plundered it house by house.

After the treaty by which Raymond VII., count of Toulouse, surrendered his principality, he remained with the barren dignity of sovereign, but without a voice in the fate of a large though concealed part of his subjects. Bishop Fulk of Toulouse, as far as actual power, was master of the land, and he held it crushed into subjection and misery by means of his council, the Inquisition. Heresy could no longer hold itself erect, and be professed without fear by the nobles of the land. The Inquisition of Toulouse under Fulk "drew up a code of procedure, a Christian code, of which the base was a system of delation, at which the worst of the pagan emperors might have shuddered as iniquitous; in which the sole act deserving of mercy might seem to be the Judas-like betrayal of the dearest and most familiar friend, of the kinsman, the parent, the child."[1]

Fauriel says of Fulk's poetic abilities: "Among the best troubadours, there is perhaps not one who surpasses Fulk of Marseilles in delicacy of spirit, in elegance, and artifice of diction. But one already perceives through this elegance and artifice, the signs of the decadence of Provençal poetry."

[1] Milman, b. xi. c. 1; the forms of procedure in Martene and Durand, Thesaurus Anecdot. T. V. "Their authenticity is beyond dispute. Nothing that the sternest or most passionate historian has revealed, nothing that the most impressive romance writer could have imagined, can surpass the cold systematic treachery and cruelty of these, so called, judicial formularies."

Fulk died on the festival of the Nativity of Him who came to bring "peace on earth, and good-will to men." He is placed by Dante in Paradise.[1]   The poet was surely not quite right when he makes the minstrel bishop say of himself in life, " I did bear impression of this heaven, that now bears mine."

[1] Cant. ix.

S. John the Divine.   See p. 307.

December 26.

S. Stephen, *D.M. at Jerusalem;* A.D. 33.
S. Dionysius, *Pope at Rome;* A.D. 269.
S. Marinus, *M. at Rome;* A.D. 283.
S. Zeno, *B. of Majuma;* 4*th cent.*
S. Zosimus, *Pope at Rome;* A.D. 418.
S. Jarlath, *B. of Tuam in Ireland; circ.* A.D. 560.
S. Ildefonsus, *B. of Toledo;* A.D. 667.

S. STEPHEN, D.M.

(A.D. 33.)

[Roman and all Western Martyrologies. Not the old Roman Kalendar of the middle of the 4th cent., but the Carthaginian Kalendar of the 5th cent. In the Glagolitic Kalendar of the 11th cent. on Sept. 15; also in the Moscow Kalendar, and the great Russian Menology published at Moscow, 1850; also the Greek Menæas. A commemoration of S. Stephen in the Greek Menæa of the Milan Library, and that published by Sismondi, on Nov. 19; in the same Menæas on Dec. 11, "in Constantianis;" on Jan. 11, "in Placidianis," in the same. On Dec. 27 all Eastern Menæas and Menologies. On Aug. 2 the translation of the relics of S. Stephen.]

N the Apostolic Constitutions, a work of the end of the 2nd or 3rd century, the festival of S. Stephen is mentioned, but not that of the Nativity, for the commemoration of the birth of Christ was of later institution. But S. Gregory of Nyssa, in the 4th century, united this feast with that of the Nativity. "See, beloved! we celebrate one festival after another. Yesterday the Lord of the Universe feasted us, and to-day the follower of Christ feeds us. How so? Christ put on for us manhood, Stephen put it off for Christ. Christ, for

S. STEPHEN CARRYING THE STONES OF HIS MARTYRDOM.

After the Painting by Martin Schoengauer.

Dec., p. 296.]

[Dec. 26.

us, came down into the valley of life, Stephen for Christ departed out of it. Christ was wrapped for us in napkins, and Stephen for Christ was covered with stones." There is a fragment of Asterius on this festival. Eusebius also mentions it. It is curious that there should be no commemoration of S. Stephen in the old Roman Kalendar, published by Bucherius, which belongs to the middle of the 4th century, but which does give the Feast of the Nativity. The festival of the Nativity was conveyed from the West to the East, and that of S. Stephen followed the reverse course. In the sacramentary of S. Leo we find this festival. Its extension in the Western Church was probably due to the discovery of the relics of S. Stephen in 415, after which, but not before, do we meet with the commemoration in the West. It appears in the Kalendar of Ptolemy Sylvius, written in 448. S. Stephen was the chief of the seven deacons appointed by the apostles to assist them in the daily ministrations, and to attend to the relief of the widows. His Greek name, signifying a wreath, indicates his Hellenistic origin. His importance is stamped on the narrative by a reiteration of emphatic phrases. He was "full of faith and of the Holy Ghost,"[1] "full of faith, and power,"[2] his "wisdom and spirit" manifested by his speech were irresistible.[3] He is said to have performed great wonders and miracles.

He was arrested at the instigation of the Hellenistic Jews and brought before the Sanhedrim.[4] His eloquent speech cut his hearers to the heart, and he was cast out of the court and stoned to death.[5] In the midst of his passion, he saw heaven opened and our Lord standing at the right hand of the Father, risen, as it were, out of His seat, to welcome His first martyr.[6] The person who took the lead in his death was Saul of Tarsus, and the answer to the prayer of Stephen

[1] Acts vi. 5.
[2] Acts vi. 8.
[3] Acts vi. 10.
[4] Acts vi. 12.
[5] Acts vii. 58.
[6] Acts vii. 55.

for his murderers was the conversion of Saul the Persecutor into Paul the Apostle. According to the earliest traditions, the martyrdom took place outside the Damascus gate of Jerusalem, that very gate through which Saul was one day to pass to his miraculous conversion. But the later tradition is that the site of the death was outside the gate now called the Gate of S. Stephen.

The narrative of the discovery of the relics of S. Stephen in 415, by Lucian, priest of Capharmajala, and John, patriarch of Jerusalem, is a sad story of fraud for the attainment of what was deemed a pious end. It is not necessary to tell here the humiliating tale. It is given by Marcellinus, chancellor of Justinian, in his Chronicle (379-534).

Part of these pretended relics were carried by Orosus (A.D. 418) to the island of Minorca, where they are still preserved and venerated. Another portion of the relics was conveyed to Uzala, in Africa. But most of the bones were preserved in a church dedicated to him in 422 in Jerusalem. At Ancona, in Italy, is shown one of the stones, reddened with his blood, which struck him on the head. At Longpont, near Paris, is a bone of the protomartyr. At Metz, a stone reddened with his blood, and a bottle containing his blood. At Halberstadt, some of his blood and two joints of his fingers. Some bones also at Metz. Some bones at S. Etienne, the Birmingham of France. Others in the cathedral at Vienna.

S. Stephen, from having been stoned to death, is the patron of stone-cutters. In accordance with the words of Scripture in detailing his martyrdom, " they saw his face as it had been the face of an angel," [1] S. Stephen is always young and beardless, both in Eastern and Western art, with the exception of Spain, which represents him with a beard and with the lineaments of a man of thirty. He usually

[1] Acts vi. 15.

heads the class of deacons, and sometimes the whole body of martyrs. He wears the dalmatic, &c. of a deacon, though this is, of course, an anachronism; he bears the palm and a book of the Gospels; a stone, or several stones, are on his head, in his lap, in his hand, or on his book; when this, his peculiar emblem, is omitted, it is difficult to distinguish him from S. Vincent (January 22).

S. Stephen's Day was in the south of France called "Straw Day," from the benediction of the straw, which some rituals then appointed. Hence, in Germany, it was "Hafer-Weyhe," with the same meaning. In the North of England it is known as "Wrenning Day," from the custom of stoning a wren to death, a cruel commemoration of S. Stephen's martyrdom. In the South, the pigeon matches usually there celebrated are a relic of the old rite. In Denmark it was sometimes called "Second Christmas Day."

S. DIONYSIUS, POPE.

(A.D. 269.)

[Roman Martyrology. Authorities:—S. Athan. de Sent. Dionysi. Euseb. H. E. lib. vii. c. 26; and the Liber Pontific.]

DIONYSIUS, probably a Calabrian, succeeded S. Sixtus on the throne of S. Peter. Pope Damasus was able to ascertain nothing more of his origin than that he was a monk before he was made Pope. He subdivided the parishes of Rome, and constituted parishes outside its walls. He denounced S. Dionysius of Alexandria, a prelate of the highest sanctity and orthodoxy, on account of some doubtful expressions, as a heretic, and as the forerunner of the arch-heretic, Arius.

Dionysius replied to the Pope in a long letter, in which he explained his views; and as Dionysius of Rome did not proceed to excommunication, he was probably satisfied with them. In 269 the fathers of the second council of Antioch expressed their veneration for his memory and orthodoxy.

Paul of Samosata, bishop of Antioch, condemned by a synod for heretical opinions, and for introducing the pomp of pagan ceremonial into Christian worship, had staked his lot on the fortunes of Zenobia.

On the fall of that princess, the bishops appealed to the pagan emperor, Aurelian, to expel the heretic from his see. Aurelian did not altogether refuse to interfere in this unprecedented case, but, with laudable impartiality, declined to allow the case to be examined by the declared enemies of Paul in the East, and referred him for trial to the bishops of Rome and Italy. A subtle Greek heresy could only be adjudicated on by Greeks, or by Latins perfect masters of Greek ; and Dionysius, by birth and education, was qualified for this task. He passed sentence of excommunication on Paul.

S. MARINUS, M.

(A.D. 283.)

[Roman Martyrology. Usuardus, Ado, Notker, Wandelbert, &c. Authority :—The fabulous Acts in Vincent of Beauvais, Spec. Hist. lib. xiii. caps. 38-40.]

S. Marinus is said to have been a senator of Rome, arrested by the prefect Marcian, under the emperor Numerian. He was placed on the rack, and torn with hooks like a slave. He was afterwards cast on a gridiron, that he might be fried, but the fire went out, and a dew fell over him, and soothed his tortured limbs. He was next exposed to wild beasts, but they would not touch him. He was led a second time before the altars of the gods, and the idols fell, and were broken. He was then decapitated. There is no evidence that Numerian persecuted. The story of Marinus manifestly belongs to the region of romance.

S. ZOSIMUS, POPE.

(A.D. 418.)

[Roman Martyrology.]

ZOSIMUS was a Greek, son of a certain Abraham. He was called to the helm of the Church on the death of Innocent I., in the reign of Arcadius and Honorius.

One of the first acts of Zosimus was to annul the decisions of his predecessor, Innocent, on the Pelagian heresy, and to absolve the men whom Innocent, if he had not branded with an anathema, had declared deserving to be cut off from the communion of the faithful.

Pelagius had drawn up an elaborate creed, which he purposed to submit to Innocent; it touched but briefly on the freedom of the will and the necessity of Divine grace, and entered minutely with orthodox zeal into the subtle questions of the Divinity of Christ and the nature of the Godhead.

Coelestius, the friend and fellow-apostle with Pelagius of man's freedom of determination against the fatalism which Augustine was introducing into Western theology, had been cast out of Constantinople by the patriarch Acacius. He went to Rome, and threw himself at the feet of Zosimus, and bade him hear the case, and adjudicate on his views with impartiality.

A solemn hearing was appointed in the basilica of S. Clement. Coelestius was heard with patience, even with favour; and Zosimus drew up a letter to the African bishops, who had condemned the teaching of Cœlestius and Pelagius, in which he proclaimed Cœlestius orthodox, in full communion with the Catholic Church and the see of Rome, condemned the decision of the council of Carthage, and threatened the chief opponents of Pelagianism, Heros and Lazarus, with excommunication and deposition. A letter had arrived at Rome from Praylus, bishop of Jerusalem, written in favour of Pelagius. Zosimus not only had this read out before the council in S. Clement's, but also sent a second letter to the African Church, in which he again unhesitatingly asserted the complete exculpation of Pelagius and Cœlestius, and denounced the bishops assembled at Carthage as guilty of error, drawn into it by miserable delators of their brethren.

On the reception of these letters, the second of which was written in September, 417, the African bishops met in synod in Carthage, and sent a synodal letter to Pope Zosimus, declaring that "the sentence against Pelagius and Cœlestius, passed by Pope Innocent, ought to continue in force till both Pelagius and Cœlestius had explicitly recognized the doctrine that we must in all our actions be sustained by the grace of God, by Jesus Christ, and that, not only for obtaining the knowledge, but also the practice of righteousness, so that, without it, we can neither have, nor think, nor say, nor do anything truly holy and pious."

The Africans sent this letter by the deacon Marcellinus, and Pope Zosimus answered in a letter, dated March 21, 418, in which he asserted that he had thoroughly examined the question of Pelagianism, and with his letter he sent all the documents on the matter to the Africans, that they might review their opposition, and recant. The close of the epistle of Zosimus, however, manifested a certain amount of hesitation in the mind of the Pope. A suspicion seems to have entered it, provoked by the earnest remonstrances and argu-

ments of S. Augustine, that he had been on the wrong path.
He consented to stay all further proceedings in the affair of
Cœlestius.

It was time for the Pope to retrace his precipitate course.
Augustine and the African bishops had called to their aid a
more powerful ally than even the bishop of Rome. While
the Pope was still maintaining the orthodoxy of Pelagius, or
had begun to waver, an imperial edict was issued from the
court of Ravenna, peremptorily deciding on this abstruse
question of theology. The law was dated April 30, 418, and
in May a council of about two hundred African bishops
assembled at Carthage to renew emphatically the condemnation of the doctrine of Pelagius and Cœlestius. By the law
of Honorius it became a crime against the State to be visited
with civil penalties, to assert that Adam was born liable to
death. Pelagius and Cœlestius were condemned by name,
and, without hearing or appeal, to banishment from Rome.
Informers were invited or commanded to apprehend, to
drag before the tribunals, and to accuse the maintainers of
the freedom of the human will, and its power to impel man
to live a moral life, unfatally constrained by grace. Confiscation of goods and perpetual exile were to be the lot of the
accomplices and followers of the heresiarchs. Augustine had
triumphed, by calling to his aid the sword of the State to
control those whom he could not convince with pen or
tongue.

Zosimus was frightened. He hastily called Cœlestius to
reappear before him, and restate his case. But the proscribed
fugitive, under the ban of the law, expelled from Rome, could
not reappear. He fled, and Zosimus precipitately hasted to
undo what he had done, and place himself in sympathy with
the emperor. He condemned and anathematized the doctrines of Pelagius and Cœlestius, which he had recently declared orthodox, and excommunicated the heretics. Nor

was this all. He sent an encyclical letter to the bishops of Christendom, requiring them to sign an anathema against Pelagius and his disciples. Eighteen bishops alone, of those who received this letter, refused to condemn their fellow-Christians unheard. They turned against Zosimus his own language to the African bishops, in which he had accused their precipitancy and injustice in condemning these very men without process or trial, and appealed to the hearing of a general council. Among these bishops was Julian of Eclana.[1]

Zosimus, indignant at this appeal, flung his anathema at Julian and the other recalcitrants. Julian's demand, however, met at first with some favour with the emperor. But Augustine left no stone unturned to prevent the assembly of a council, of the judgment of which he was doubtful. If we may trust Julian, he did not disdain to use bribery to excite those who had the ear of the feeble Honorius to dissuade him from this perilous attempt.

Before the case of Pelagianism was settled, another cause of misunderstanding arose between the African Church and the See of Rome. Apiarius, an African priest, had been degraded and excommunicated by his bishop, Urbanus of Sicca. He then went to Rome, and complained to the Pope, who took up his cause with much warmth, and peremptorily demanded his restoration. The African prelates were indignant at this interference, as it was a direct infringement of a canon they had passed in the May council, 418, forbidding a priest or deacon to appeal beyond the sea against his bishop. Zosimus thereupon sent three legates to Africa, and Archbishop Aurelius of Carthage assembled a synod to receive them. The legates of Zosimus announced

---

[1] He was the son of a bishop, a great friend of Augustine. He married, after he was in Orders, the daughter of the bishop of Beneventum, and S. Paulinus of Nola wrote their Epithalamium.

that they purposed excommunicating Urbanus of Sicca, unless he at once restored Apiarius.

The Pope also complained of the African bishops forbidding appeals to Rome, and quoted through his legates certain canons of Sardica, which he pretended had been passed at Nicæa. The bishops assembled could not find the canons in their copies of the decrees of Nicæa, and were perplexed. They wrote to Rome to state their difficulty, requesting the Pope to examine the copies of the canons of Nicæa at Rome, and they wrote to Antioch, Alexandria, and Constantinople, to obtain copies of the Greek version of the canons. In the meantime, in deference to the Pope, Apiarius was, on his own petition, so far restored that his rank of priest was allowed him, but he was forbidden to officiate in the Church of Sicca.

The answer of the African bishops did not reach Rome till Zosimus was dead.

S. JARLATH, B. OF TUAM.

(ABOUT A.D. 560.)

[Irish Martyrologies; also on June 6. Authority:—A Life in Colgan on Feb. 11, on which day S. Jarlath of Armagh was commemorated.]

S. JARLATH was the son of Lugh, of the noble house of Conmacnie, in Galway, now the barony of Downamore. He was born about the beginning of the sixth century or the end of the fifth. He founded a monastery at Cluainfois, the site of which cannot now be identified. Among his disciples was Colman, son of Lenine, who died about 601. By the advice, apparently, of S. Brendan of Clonfert, Jarlath moved to Tuam, was consecrated bishop, and made that the seat of his bishopric. Some curious prophecies of his relative to his successors in the see have been handed down; but they are probably not by Jarlath. The date of his death is not known with anything approaching to certainty. He was buried at Tuam, not in the cathedral, but in the chapel called Scrin or Shrine.

S. ILDEFONSUS, B. OF TOLEDO.

(A.D. 667.)

[Roman Martyrology Jan. 23; his Life having been omitted on that day, is given here.]

S. Ildefonsus, or Hildephonsus, was abbot of Agali, in Spain. He embraced the religious life at an early age, and founded a convent for virgins with his patrimony. On the death of Eugenius II., bishop of Toledo, he was compulsorily elevated to that see, A.D. 658, and occupied it during nine years and two months. He died on January 23, 667, and was buried in the church of S. Leocadia, at the feet of his predecessor. He left several works, but of them only one, on the virginity of our Lady, has been preserved. This was written in opposition to those who taught that the B. Virgin was the real wife of S. Joseph, and bore him children after the birth of our Lord. An absurd legend is told of him in reference to this treatise, given already in this volume.

He wrote epitaphs and epigrams, and continued the catalogue of illustrious men made by S. Isidore of Seville.

A second treatise on the virginity of the Virgin Mary, and some sermons attributed to him, have been rejected by scholars, as not his.

Relics at Toledo.

S. JOHN THE DIVINE.

December 27.

S. JOHN THE DIVINE, *Ap. at Ephesus; circ.* A.D. 101.
S. MAXIMUS, *B. of Alexandria;* A.D. 281.
SS. THEODORE, *C.,* AND THEOPHANES, *B.C. at Constantinople and Nicæa;* 9*th cent.*

S. JOHN THE DIVINE, AP.

(ABOUT A.D. 101.)

[Roman Martyrology, and all Western and Eastern Kalendars. In ancient Kalendars not as "Natalis," but as "Transitus" or "Assumptio S. Johannis Evangelistæ." The Carthaginian Kalendar of the 5th cent. In the "Missale Gothicum" with the commemoration of S. James, his brother, on the following day. By the Greeks on May 8, not on Dec. 27. In the prologue to the Menology of Moscow is added, "On the same day the collection of sacred dust, *i.e.* of manna flowing from his tomb." This miracle, or rather myth, is celebrated also on May 8 by the Copts. June 20, the Translation of the Tunic of S. John to Constantinople. A memorial of S. John also on July 10 in some Greek Menæas. The dedication of the church of S. John the Evangelist at Constantinople, near St. Sophia, on Aug. 2. The Translation of the Apostle John on Sept. 26. In all Latin Martyrologies "S. John before the Latin Gate" on May 6.]

 . JOHN the Divine was the son of Zebedee, and his mother's name was Salome.[1] They lived on the shores of the sea of Galilee. The brother of S. John, probably considerably older, was S. James. The mention of the "hired servants,"[2] and of S. John's "own home,"[3] implies that the condition of Salome and her children was not one of great poverty.

[1] Matt. iv. 21, xxvii 56; Mark xv. 40, xvi. 1.   [2] Mark i. 20.
[3] John xix. 27.

SS. John and James followed the Baptist when he preached repentance in the wilderness of Jordan. There can be little doubt that the two disciples, whom S. John does not name (i. 35), who looked on Jesus "as he walked," when the Baptist exclaimed with prophetic perception, "Behold the Lamb of God!" were Andrew and John. They followed and asked the Lord where He dwelt. He bade them come and see, and they abode with him all day. Of the subject of conversation that took place in this interview no record has come to us, but it was probably the starting-point of the entire devotion of heart and soul which lasted through the life of the Beloved Apostle.

John apparently followed his new Master to Galilee, and was with him at the marriage feast of Cana, journeyed with Him to Capernaum, and thenceforth never left Him, save when sent on the missionary expedition with another, invested with the power of healing. He, James, and Peter, came within the innermost circle of their Lord's friends, and these three were suffered to remain with Christ when all the rest of the apostles were kept at a distance.[1] Peter, James, and John were with Christ in the Garden of Gethsemane. The mother of James and John, knowing our Lord's love for the brethren, made special request for them, that they might sit, one on His right hand, the other on His left, in His kingdom.[2] There must have been much impetuosity in the character of the brothers, for they obtained the nickname of Boanerges, Sons of Thunder.[3] It is not necessary to dwell on the familiar history of the Last Supper and the Passion. To John was committed by our Lord the highest of privileges, the care of His mother. John and Peter were the first to receive the news from the Magdalene of the Resurrection, and they hastened at once to the sepulchre,

[1] Mark, v. 37; Matt. xvii. 1, xxvi. 37. [2] Matt. xx. 21.
[3] Mark, iii. 17.

S. JOHN THE DIVINE.
From the Vienna Missal.

and there when Peter was restrained by awe, John impetuously "came first to the sepulchre."

In the interval between the Resurrection and the Ascension, John and Peter were together on the Sea of Galilee,[1] having returned to their old calling, and old familiar haunts.

When Christ appeared on the shore in the dusk of morning, John was the first to recognize Him. The last words of the Gospel reveal the attachment which existed between the two apostles. It was not enough for Peter to know his own fate, he must learn also something of the future that awaited his friend.[2] The Acts show us them still united, entering together as worshippers into the Temple,[3] and protesting together against the threats of the Sanhedrim.[4] They were fellow-workers together in the first step of Church expansion. The apostle whose wrath had been kindled at the unbelief of the Samaritans, was the first to receive these Samaritans as brethren.[5]

He probably remained at Jerusalem till the death of the Virgin, though tradition of no great antiquity or weight asserts that he took her to Ephesus. When he went to Ephesus is uncertain. He was at Jerusalem fifteen years after S. Paul's first visit there.[6] There is no trace of his presence there when S. Paul was at Jerusalem for the last time.

Tradition, more or less trustworthy, completes the history. Irenæus says that S. John did not settle at Ephesus till after the death of SS. Peter and Paul, and this is probable. He certainly was not there when S. Timothy was appointed bishop of that place. S. Jerome says that he supervised and governed all the Churches in Asia. He probably took up his abode finally in Ephesus in 97. In the persecution of Domitian he was taken to Rome, and was placed in a

---

[1] John xxi. 1.   [2] John xxi. 21.   [3] Acts iii. 1.
[4] Acts iv. 13.   [5] Acts viii. 14.   [6] Acts xv. 6.

cauldron of boiling oil, outside the Latin gate, without
the boiling fluid doing him any injury.[1] He was sent to
labour at the mines in Patmos. At the accession of Nerva
he was set free, and returned to Ephesus, and there it is
thought that he wrote his gospel. Of his zeal and love combined we have examples in Eusebius, who tells, on the
authority of Irenæus, that S. John once fled out of a bath on
hearing that Cerinthus was in it, lest, as he asserted, the roof
should fall in, and crush the heretic. On the other hand, he
showed the love that was in him. He commended a young
man in whom he was interested to a bishop, and bade him
keep his trust well. Some years after he learned that the
young man had become a robber. S. John, though very old,
pursued him among the mountain fastnesses, and by his
tenderness recovered him.

In his old age, when unable to do more, he was carried
into the assembly of the Church at Ephesus, and his sole exhortation was, " Little children, love one another."

The date of his death cannot be fixed with anything like
precision, but it is certain that he lived to a very advanced
age. He is represented holding a chalice from which issues
a dragon, as he is supposed to have been given poison,
which was, however, innocuous. Also his symbol is an
eagle.

[1] Eusebius makes no mention of this. The legend of the boiling oil occurs in
Tertullian and in S. Jerome.

S. JOHN THE EVANGELIST.

December 28.

The Holy Innocents, *MM. at Bethlehem.*
S. Troas, *M. at Neocæsarea;* A.D. 250.
SS. Indus, *M.,* Domna, Agape, and Theophila, *VV.MM. at Nicomedia;* A.D. 303.
S. Antony, *Mk. at Lerins; circ.* A.D. 523.
S. Convoyon, *Ab. of Rhedon in Brittany; circ.* A.D. 868.

THE HOLY INNOCENTS, MM.

[Roman Martyrology and all Western Martyrologies. Also in all Greek Menæas and Menologies.]

THE commemoration of the Holy Innocents seems to have been instituted very early. It is mentioned by S. Irenæus,[1] S. Cyprian,[2] S. Gregory Nazianzen,[3] and S. Chrysostom.[4] Origen, or whoever was the author of the third homily, "de diversis," says, that "their memorial has continually been observed, according to their deserving, in the Church, and that the first martyrs went forth from Bethlehem, where Christ was born."

But the observance of this day was in the earliest time bound up with that of the Epiphany. Pope Leo I., in almost all his sermons on the Epiphany, refers to the Innocents. But in his Sacramentary, the Mass of the Children of Bethlehem follows immediately after that of S. John, under the title "In natali Innocentium." It is, however, questionable if we have this Sacramentary in its most ancient form. The two hymns in the Roman Breviary for this day are centos from the hymn of Prudentius on the Epiphany.

[1] Adv. Hæres. l. iii. c. 38. [2] Epist. 56. [3] Serm. 38, In Nativ.
[4] Homil. ix. In Matth.

Hrabanus Maurus composed a hymn for the festival. According to the Responsoriale of S. Gregory the Great, this day was observed with mourning, the "Te Deum" was omitted from the office, and the "Gloria in excelsis," the "Alleluia," and "Ite, missa est," were not used in the mass. Amalarius attributes this regulation to the composer of the Antiphonary, for he says : "The author of this office would have us sympathize with the feelings of the pious women who wept and sorrowed at the death of their innocent children."[1] Micrologus gives another reason : "With right are the sufferings of the Holy Innocents attended with less festivity than the celebration of other saints, for, though they were crowned with martyrdom, they went at once, not into Paradise, but into Limbo."

In Rome meat was forbidden on this day.[2] The colours for the vestments on the feast of the Holy Innocents are to this day purple, as in Lent and Advent, except when the day coincides with the Sunday after Christmas, when the red of martyrdom overrides the purple of mourning.

Skulls of the Holy Innocents were among the relics shown at Paris, in Notre Dame, at S. Denis, and in the church of the Augustines at Limoges.

The council of Cognac, in 1260, forbids dancing in churches on the feast of the Innocents. It was observed in the Middle Ages as the feast of Fools, when a child, or sometimes a clown, was elected bishop, and profane mockery of religious rites usurped the place of sacred services in the churches.

The heathen Saturnalia took place on December 17th, and no doubt held a strong place in the habits and affections of the people of the empire. In the Saturnalia the slaves took the place of the masters, and acted without restraint. The festival of the Sigillaria was afterwards combined with

---

[1] Eccl. Offic, lib. i. c. 41.   [2] Ord. Roman. Benedicti, Can. N. 26.

MASSACRE OF THE INNOCENTS.
After the Picture by Guido in the Museum, Bologna.

that of the Saturnalia, and so the mad frolic was extended to a week. Lucian makes Saturn say during the Saturnalia, "During my reign of a week, no one may attend to his business, but only to drinking, singing, playing, making imaginary kings, placing servants at table with their masters, &c."

Cedrenus says that in the tenth century, Theophylact, patriarch of Constantinople, introduced this festival into the Church.[1] In cathedral churches in France and Italy, a bishop and archbishop of fools were elected, and the election was confirmed with much buffoonery, which was a caricature of ordination. After which the prelates were vested, and gave solemn benediction to the people, holding pastoral staff or archiepiscopal crozier. But in exempt churches (*i.e.* churches depending immediately on the Holy See), a pope of fools was chosen, amidst similar buffoonery.

These pontiffs were assisted by the clergy. Priests and clerks performed all manner of impieties during the divine service, some masked, or with their faces painted, others dressed as women. Priests and clerks danced in the choir, and sang obscene songs. The deacons and subdeacons ate cakes and sausages at the altar, played cards and dice on it, and made offensive odours issue from the censer.

After the mass was ended, everyone ran, jumped, and danced about the church; some stripped themselves naked, and were drawn about the streets in a manure cart, and pelted the people with dung. At intervals the cart stopped and those within evoked laughter by their indecent postures.

Beleth, doctor of theology of Paris, in 1182, wrote that the feast of Fools and Subdeacons was celebrated by some on the Circumcision, by others on the Epiphany. He adds

---

[1] Balsamon complained more than two hundred years after, in his commentary on the 62nd Canon of the Council "In Trullo," of the abominations committed in the church of Constantinople, on the feast of the Epiphany.

that during Christmas four dances took place in the churches —one of the deacons, another of the priests, a third of the choir-boys, and the fourth of the subdeacons. In some churches, he says, at this time the bishops or archbishops join in the revel, and play dice, ball, tennis, and other games; that they dance and make merriment for their clergy in their cathedrals, and in the monasteries before the monks; and that this diversion was called the Liberty of December.

A circular letter written by the university of Paris to the bishops of France in 1444, states that whilst divine service was proceeding, the ecclesiastics of the churches attended, dressed with masks, or disguised as women, elected a bishop or archbishop of fools, made him give benediction to those who sang the lessons of matins, and to the people; that they danced in the choir and sang indecent songs, ate meat at the altar whilst the celebrant was proceeding with mass, and burned their old shoes in the censers, with which they incensed the Host and the book of the Gospels.

In a MS. of the cathedral of Sens, the Office of Fools is preserved as said in that church. It is unnecessary to enter into further particulars of this infamous custom.[1]

S. CONVOYON, AB.

(A.D. 868.)

[On this day in the Gallican Martyrologies, and in the Benedictine Martyrology, but at Quimper on Jan. 5. Authority:—A very curious Life, which has lost its beginning, by a disciple of the saint; also a brief Life written in the 11th cent. Both in Mabillon, Acta SS. O.S.B. sæc. iv. pt. 2.]

S. CONVOYON, first abbot of Rhedon, was born of noble parents at Comblessac, near S. Malo, and was brought up at Vannes under Reginald, the bishop, who ordained

[1] See for full particulars Du Tilliot, " Mémoires pour servir à l'Histoire de la Fête des Foux," Lausanne, 1741.

him deacon, and afterwards priest. Five clerks placed themselves under his direction—Condeloc, born of a Sunday, baptized of a Sunday, ordained priest of a Sunday, and said afterwards to have died of a Sunday; Lohemel, a lawyer, said never to have lost a suit; Gwenkals, the White-Heart, as his name signifies, and two others of less note. These five went to a forest near the river Vilaine, and established themselves at Rhedon. This foundation is placed in 832. The lord of that district was called Rathwyl : he favoured the new monastery in every way, and gave a son to be educated in it. When he was ill and thought himself dying, he had himself carried to the monastery, and his hair cut off after the monastic pattern. He recovered, and returned to his castle to arrange his affairs and then came back to Rhedon and died there, 835.[1] But S. Convoyon met with some difficulty in getting a confirmation of the grants made him. In 832 he went to the castle of Joac in Limousin, to meet Louis the Pious, and entreat his consent to the conveyance to his monastery in perpetuity of the land that had been given him by Rathwyl. But Ricovinus, count of Nantes, and Rainar, bishop of Vannes, opposed this so strenuously, that Louis refused, and Convoyon was driven with contumely from the presence of the king.

Convoyon, unabashed, took the occasion of Louis passing through Tours on his way back from Aquitaine, to make another attempt. He took with him a disciple named Cwmdeluc, and travelled in the suite of some Breton nobles who were going to meet the king on affairs of their own. Convoyon took with him a considerable amount of wax, obtained from his bees at Rhedon, and which he intended to

---

[1] He gave his wooden house to the monastery. "Dederat domum suam ex tabellis ligneis fabricatam pro anima sua sanctis monachis : et idcirco transmissus fuit monachus ut eam colligeret, et cum plaustris ac bobus ad monasterium deferret."

present to Louis. But he was refused admission. He accordingly bade Cwmdeluc go into the market and sell the wax.

The unfortunate monk met there with an adventure. A woman of somewhat disreputable character no sooner saw him in the market, than she exclaimed, in the spirit of mischief, "My dearest friend! Here you are again! What an age it is since we met! Do you not remember how we were brought up together in one house and family, and how often my mother scrubbed your head, and how we used to sleep in one little crib together? Come home with me."[1] No wonder that at this address, the poor monk turned first crimson and then all colours.[2] She caught him by the arm, and attempted to drag him home, the market women taking her part, when suddenly a swarm of monks rushed out of the adjoining monastery of S. Martin and carried off the trembling Cwmdeluc from the hands of the women.

Some little time after the return of Convoyon, Nominoe, governor of Brittany, visited Rhedon and encouraged Convoyon to make another attempt. He was going to send a deputation to the king at Thionville, and Convoyon was at liberty to go with it. In the meantime he gave to the abbot Ros, the tongue of land between the rivers Vilaine and Oulte. The bishop Rainar, who was now reconciled with Convoyon, was present and signed the act of donation. Worworet, a nobleman present, also witnessed the transaction. This Worworet was sent on the deputation to the emperor Louis, and the abbot of Rhedon accompanied him. At court, Hermor, bishop of Aleth, and Felix, bishop of Quimper, urged his cause, and Louis acceded to their request, and confirmed the grants of land made to Convoyon, November 27, 834.

---

[1] "Unde venis, amice carissime? ubi per tot annos latuisti? indica mihi. Recordare quoniam nutriti sumus in una domo et in una familia. Frequenter namque abluit genitrix mea caput tuum, et sæpe in uno stratu jacuimus."

[2] "Cumque ille sanctus hæc verba diabolica audisset, statim erubuit, et vultus ejus in diversis coloribus mutatus est."

The disciple of Convoyon who wrote his Life has left us a pleasing and life-like set of portraits of the principal monks of his monastery. There was Brother Conleduc, who kept the garden, and who, in despair one day at seeing his cabbages covered with caterpillars, cried out, " O worms! what is to be done? I cannot call together a legion of gardeners to pick you off my plants. I must call God to my aid." Whereupon the caterpillars fled precipitately from the garden. There was Fritwen, who had come for a little while, but whose sweetness and piety so won on all the community that they could not bear to let him go back to his hermitage, and so to please them he stayed till he died of cancer. Fritwen healed the biographer, when a boy, of toothache. The writer says that his cheek was swollen, and his tooth had been so troublesome that he could neither eat nor sleep, but when Fritwen stroked it, the pain went away. There was also Doethen, who wanted to run away and return to the world, but was arrested by a paralytic stroke. There were others whom the biographer of Convoyon delighted to recall.

The monastery of Rhedon was built, and its church erected, but it was without one very important adjunct. There was no saintly corpse under its altar to act as palladium to the monastery and work miracles to attract pilgrims to it. To remedy this deficiency, Convoyon went to Angers with two of his monks, Hildemar and Lonkemel, and lodged with a certain pious man named Hildwald. Their host asked them the object of their visit and stay in Angers.

After some hesitation, and after exacting a promise of secrecy, Convoyon told him that they had come on a body-snatching expedition, and asked him to advise them what relics to secure. He told them that Angers enjoyed the possession of the bones of S. Apothemius, a bishop, of whom indeed nothing certain was known except that he was a saint. He lay in a stone coffin with a heavy lid to it.

Hildwald added that several monks and envoys of other churches had tried to steal the body, but had not been successful.

Convoyon and his monks waited three days, and one dark night, armed with crowbars, they went to the cathedral, got in, heaved up the coffin lid, after singing "praises and hymns," and got the bones out, and then made off with them as fast as they could. On reaching Langon, they sent word of their success to the monks of Rhedon, and the reception of the relics was conducted with great dignity and pomp. Miracles were at once wrought, and established the popularity of S. Apothemius.

The peace of the monastery was troubled about this time. Some lawless nobles threatened Convoyon, and attempted to extort money from him. One insisted on his giving him five pieces of gold for the purchase of a sword : he could not furnish the money, and the young noble went away muttering threats. He was killed shortly after in war, and his threats were never put in execution. One day the abbot was visiting one of his estates, when a noble named Ristweten demanded of him money for the purchase of a horse he coveted, and Convoyon was obliged to borrow the money to let him have it.

Rainar, bishop of Vannes, died in 837, and the see was filled in 841 by Susannus, who obtained it by simony. Convoyon was filled with indignation at the prevalence of simony in the Church of Brittany, and he urged Nominoe to summon a council of the bishops and abbots to consider how this might be remedied. In this council the canons against simony were read ; the bishops declared that they did not sell Holy Orders, and that they exacted no fees from those whom they ordained, but admitted that those whom they called to the diaconate and priesthood were wont to make them presents, which they accepted. The most ener-

getic to maintain this right was Susannus. It was decided
that a deputation should be sent to Rome, consisting of
Susannus of Vannes and Felix of Quimper, and that Convoyon should go with them, the bearer of a gold crown in-
laid with jewels, which Nominoe sent to the Pope. The
question to be submitted to the Pope was, whether a bishop
convicted of simony, might do penance without losing his
office, or whether he ought to be deposed. Other questions
were asked. It would appear from them that the monks of
Rhedon claimed the right of appointing clergy to several
churches independent of the jurisdiction of the bishops,
that the custom of examining the Sortes Sacræ still prevailed
at the consecration of bishops, and that Nominoe meddled
in the concerns of the Church in a manner which the
bishops considered unjustifiable. Nominoe wrote also to
Pope Leo IV. to ask him to accept the presents he sent
him, and to sanction a design he had formed for establish-
ing the independence of Brittany, which was oppressed by
the French. Leo IV. assembled the bishops at Rome and
heard the deputation. Susannus and Felix were asked if
they received presents when they gave ordination. They
replied that if they had done so, it was through ignorance.
An archbishop present, named Arsenius, said, "This reply
does not suffice—a priest should not ignore his duties."
The Pope added, "This is in conformity with the Gospel.
Our Lord said, 'If the salt hath lost its savour, wherewith
shall it be seasoned?' The canons enjoin that any bishop,
priest, or deacon who has been ordained for money, must
be deposed along with him who ordained him."

Leo IV. replied to the letter of the Breton bishops that a
bishop could not be deposed except in an assembly of
twelve bishops; but if there were not so many to be collected, the evidence must be substantiated by seventy-two
witnesses.

What the answer of Leo to Nominoe was, is not certain. The Nantes Chronicle asserts that the Pope gave him the title and dignity of duke, with permission to wear a gold coronet. He sent him as a present the body of S. Marcellinus, Pope and martyr, which Convoyon took back with him and deposited in his church at Rhedon. Nominoe revolted against Charles the Bald. He penetrated into Poitou, and ravaged the country with sword and flame. He, however, respected the abbey of S. Florent, but to insult Charles he obliged the monks to place a statue of himself on their tower with the face turned defiantly towards France. No sooner was Nominoe gone than the monks sent to Charles to inform him of the insult. He ordered them to throw down the statue of the rebel, and in its place erect a white stone figure, of ludicrous appearance and mocking countenance, turned towards Brittany. Nominoe appeared to revenge this insult, before Charles appeared for the defence of the monks, and S. Florent was burned to the ground. Nominoe carried off the spoils to enrich the abbey of Rhedon. The successes of Nominoe and his son Erispoe obliged Charles the Bald to come to terms with the latter, and permit him to assume the insignia of royalty, and hold Rennes, Nantes, and all Brittany.

Convoyon's abbey at Rhedon, situated on a tidal river, was so exposed to the ravages of the Normans, that he was obliged to retire further inland with his monks to an asylum prepared for him by Erispoe in one of his castles, at Plelan. There Convoyan died and was buried, about A.D. 868, but the body was afterwards removed to Rhedon. All the relics were dispersed in the Revolution, when the monastery was sacked by an apostate monk of Rhedon, at the head of a party of Sans-culottes.

VIRGIN AND INFANT CHRIST.
From the Vienna Missal.

Dec., p. 320.]

December 29.

S. David, *K. Prophet at Jerusalem; circ.* B.C. 1015.
S. Trophimus, *B. of Arles; 1st cent.*
S. Crescens, *B. of Vienne; 1st cent.*
S. Marcellus, *Ab. at Constantinople;* A.D. 488.
S. Ebrulfus, *Ab. at Ouche in France;* A.D. 596.
S. Thomas à Becket, *Abp. M. at Canterbury;* A.D. 1170.

S. TROPHIMUS, B.

(1ST CENT.)

[Roman and Gallican Martyrologies. Usuardus, Ado, Notker, &c. By the Greeks on April 14 and 15, along with Aristarchus and Pudens. In some Menæas on July 31, in all along with SS. Peter and Paul on Oct. 29. Authorities :—Acts xx. 4, xxi. 27-29 ; 2 Tim. iv. 12, 20.]

TROPHIMUS and Tychicus, two natives of Asia Minor, accompanied S. Paul on his third missionary expedition. Both of them attended S. Paul from Macedonia on his return journey, as far as Asia Minor, where Tychicus remained ; but Trophimus proceeded with the apostle to Jerusalem. There he was the innocent cause of the tumult in which S. Paul was apprehended. From the account we have given us of this tumult, we learn that Trophimus was an Ephesian and a Gentile. We hear no more of Trophimus for a long time ; but in the last letter written by S. Paul, shortly before his martyrdom, from Rome, he mentions both Trophimus and Tychicus : the latter he had sent to Ephesus, of which place he, probably, like Trophimus, was a native ; Trophimus had been left at Miletus, sick. From this we may conclude that the apostle had been shortly before in the Levant, and that Trophimus had accompanied him. Trophimus is probably one of the two brethren who, with Titus, conveyed the Second Epistle to the Corinthians to its destination. He was evidently closely attached to the apostle, and thoroughly in his confidence.

The first bishop of Arles was a Trophimus, and it pleases the members of that Church to suppose him to have been this favourite disciple of S. Paul. But this is quite conjectural, and very improbable. He is also spoken of as one of the six companions of S. Dionysius of Paris, by S. Gregory of Tours, who represents that saint as having preached in Gaul in the middle of the third century. In the time of Decius, Martian, bishop of Arles, favoured the Novatian heresy. Martian probably was bishop in 252, and we may put S. Trophimus at 250. In 417 Pope Zosimus wrote letters in favour of Patroclus, bishop of Arles, to the bishops of Gaul, and in one of these he mentions S. Trophimus as having been sent by the Holy See into Gaul, and as having been the source of true faith there. Had he considered him as the disciple of S. Paul, and sent by him and S. Peter, he would probably have said so. The first instance of Trophimus of Arles being identified with Trophimus disciple of S. Paul, is by the bishops of the province of Arles in 450. The tradition or conceit began then to be received, and when their deputation waited on S. Leo in that year, they represented Trophimus, the founder of the see of Arles, as having been sent into Gaul by S. Peter. On the other hand, Pseudo Hippolytus says that Trophimus suffered martyrdom along with S. Paul. But he also makes him one of the seventy disciples, which could not have been. No Gentile was of the seventy. The Greeks regard him as having suffered martyrdom with SS. Peter and Paul, and commemorate their passion on the same day, October 29.

The Roman Martyrology asserts the identity of Trophimus of Arles with Trophimus disciple of S. Paul.

S. CRESCENS, B.

(IST CENT.)

[Roman and Gallican Martyrologies. By the Greeks on July 30. Authority :—2 Tim. iv. 10.]

CRESCENS, an assistant and companion of S. Paul, is said to have been one of the seventy disciples, but this is most questionable. We may be sure that those seventy were Hebrews. In the Second Epistle to Timothy S. Paul says that Crescens is gone into Galatia. The Greeks, following Pseudo Hippolytus and Pseudo Dorotheus, make him bishop of Chalcedon, in Galatia.[1]

The reading Γαλλίαν instead of Γαλατίαν in 2 Tim. iv. 10, has led to error. Gaul has been understood as the place whither Crescens was sent, and not the small Asiatic province of Galatia; and so he has been made by the French first bishop of Vienne, and by the Germans first bishop of Mainz. Papebroch makes him found both Churches. There may have been a Crescens at each Church, but certainly not the same. The first bishop of Vienne of whom we know the name on historical grounds is Verus, in 314. Yet, that Vienne had a Church in 150 we know from the testimony of the letter about S. Pothinus and the martyrs of Lyons, given by Eusebius. The Roman Martyrology unhesitatingly asserts that "Crescens, disciple of S. Paul, was first bishop of Vienne."

[1] There does not appear to have been any such city in Galatia, that in Bithynia, where the fourth General Council was held, being alone noted by geographers. Nor does any name like it appear in the list of the sees in Galatia Prima and Secunda, under the metropoles Ancyra and Pessinus. The nearest is Calumene.

S. EBRULFUS, AB.

(A.D. 596.)

[Roman, Gallican, and Benedictine Martyrologies. Authority:—
A Life by an anonymous writer in Mabillon, Acta SS. O.S.B. sæc. i. ;
Ordericus Vitalis, Hist. Eccl. Norm. lib. vi. c. 9.]

S. EBRULFUS, or, as he is called in France, S. Evroul, was
born of honourable parents at Bayeux. He went to the
court of Clothair, and married a wife of rank equal to his
own. But he soon wearied of life in the world, and persuaded his wife to let him go into a monastery, and live as a
monk, and to enter herself into a convent. He probably
learned the rudiments of the religious life in the abbey of
the Deux Jumeaux, founded by S. Martin of Vertou (*see*
October 24). After a while he left the monastery with three
companions and went to Montfort—now S. Evroult de Montfort, north of Gacé. They were too much interrupted there
to obtain the peace they desired, and therefore buried themselves in the forest of Ouche and there established themselves. By degrees others placed themselves under the rule
of the saint, and the solitude became populated by monks.
Ebrulfus was visited there by King Childebert, who richly
endowed the monastery. His queen also built a church
there, dedicated to our Lady, now called Notre-Dame-du-
Bois, and placed a marble altar in it, probably an old
sarcophagus. One day the devil was caught by S. Ebrulf
at Echaufour, " who threw him into a fiery oven heated in
readiness for baking bread, and closed it with an iron plug
that he chanced to find. The women who had brought
their loaves to be baked, seeing what was done, said, ' What,
sir, shall we do with our loaves?' To which he replied,
'God is able to bake your loaves without corporeal fire ;

clear the hearth before the oven, and lay your loaves in
order, and you will find them bake without fire.'" And it
was so.

S. THOMAS À BECKET, ABP. M.

(A.D. 1170.)

[Roman Martyrology. Sarum, York, and Hereford Kalendars. On
July 7, the Translation of S. Thomas. Canonized by Pope Alexander
III. in 1173. Authorities :—(1) A Life by John of Salisbury, afterwards bishop of Chartres, an intimate friend of Becket. His short
work is rather a character than a detailed Life of the archbishop. (2) A
Life by Herbert de Bosham, secretary of Becket ; this work was written
in 1185. (3) A volume of letters by Herbert de Bosham, written in
the course of the quarrel of Becket with the king. (4) A Life by
Edward Grim, a monk who went to Canterbury to see Becket after his
return from exile ; he was present at the murder, and received a severe
wound in the arm while attempting to protect the archbishop. (5) A
Passion by Benedict, abbot of Peterborough. (6) A Life by Alan,
abbot of Tewkesbury, embodies that of John of Salisbury. He was
monk of Canterbury and prior in 1179. In 1186 he was made abbot of
Tewkesbury, and died in 1202. (7) A Life by Roger of Pontigny,
attendant on Becket during the two years he passed in that monastery.
(8) An anonymous author, " de plurium narratione collecta . . . .
quam scribi fecit D. Petrus Rogerii," circ. 1370 ; this is called the Quad-
rilogus, being compiled from four earlier writers. (9) A Life by Wil
liam Fitz-Stephen, a clerk of Becket's, who attended his master through
a great part of his public life. (10) A Metrical Life by Guernes du
Pont de S. Maxence in Picardy, written in 1175. (11) A Life by Henry,
abbot of Croyland, assisted by Roger, a monk of Croyland, written in
1220. (12) An anonymous Life by an eye-witness of many of the
events he describes, preserved in Lambeth Library. (13) Another
anonymous Life in the British Museum, written in 1200. (14) A Life
by Grandison, bishop of Exeter, 1327-69, is too late to be of any value.
(15) The Letters of S. Thomas. All the most important materials for
the Life of Becket are being published by Mr. J. Craigie Robertson in
his " Materials for the History of Thomas Becket, Archbishop of Canterbury," in the Rolls series of "Chronicles of Britain." The Letters,
translated into English, have been published by Dr. Giles, in his "Life
and Letters of Thomas à Becket," London, 1846. The Latin originals

were also published by Dr. Giles, but very inaccurately. Additional information or legend about S. Thomas may be gleaned from the chroniclers Hoveden, Radulf de Diceto, John of Brompton, &c.]

" Among the towns, cities, and villages of England, London is the largest and the principal," writes a contemporary of Becket.[1] "When the kingdom fell into the hands of the Normans, large numbers flocked thither out of Rouen and Caen, which are the principal cities of Normandy, choosing to become citizens of London, because it was larger and better stored with merchandise in which they used to traffic. Among these was one Gilbert, surnamed Becket, born at Rouen, and distinguished among his citizens for the respectability of his birth, the energy of his character, and the easy independence of his fortune. His family was creditable, but belonged to the class of citizens. He was industrious in commerce, and managed his household in a creditable manner, and suitably to his station in life; whilst among his fellow-citizens he was known for a worthy man, and without reproach. His wife was Rose [Rohesia], a lady of Caen, also of respectable civic family, fair in person, and fairer still in conduct, an able mistress over her household, and, saving her duty to God, an obedient and loving wife."

" This was the manner of S. Thomas's birth," says Fitz-Stephen, another contemporary. " His father was Gilbert, sheriff of London, and his mother's name was Matilda. Both were citizens of the middle class, who neither made money by usury nor practised any trade, but lived respectably on their income." Herbert de Bosham describes him as " born in the flesh of one Gilbert, and his mother's name was Matilda."

But popular poetry, after the sanctification of Becket, delighted in adorning the early history of the saint with romance. It invented, or rather interwove with the pedigree of the martyr, one of those romantic traditions which grew

[1] Anon. Lambeth.

out of the wild adventures of the Crusades, and which occur in various forms in the ballads of all nations.

The father of Becket, so runs the tale, was a gallant soldier of the Cross in Palestine. He was there taken captive, and inspired the daughter of his master with an ardent attachment. Through her means he made his escape, but the enamoured princess could not endure life without him. She, too, fled, and made her way to Europe. She had learned but two words of the Frank tongue, "Gilbert" and "London." With these two magic sounds on her lips she reached London; and as she wandered through the streets, constantly repeating the name of Gilbert, she was met by Becket's faithful servant. Becket, as a good Christian, seems to have entertained scruples about an honourable union with the faithful, but misbelieving maiden. The case was submitted to the highest authority, and argued before the bishop of London. The issue was the baptism of the princess, by the name of Matilda (that of the empress-queen), and their marriage was solemnized in S. Paul's, with the utmost publicity and splendour.

It is enough to say of this wondrous tale, that not one of the seven or eight contemporary biographers of Becket mentions it, and that the Lambeth anonymous writer distinctly says that the wife of Gilbert was of a burgher family in Caen,[1] and Fitz-Stephen, an officer in the chancery court of S. Thomas, and dean of his chapel, confirms this by saying that both his parents were of the middle class, and William, sub-prior of Canterbury, says that he was "the illustrious son of middle-class parents."

The father of the saint was no knight errant, but a sober Rouen citizen, who settled in London for its commercial advantages. His mother was no Saracen maiden of princely

---

[1] He says her name was Rohesia; one of the sisters of Thomas à Becket was also called Rohesia.

rank, but the daughter of an honest burgher of Caen. His Norman descent is still further confirmed by his claim of relationship, or connection at least, as of common Norman descent, with Archbishop Theobald. The saint, in one of his epistles, speaks of his parents as of citizen stock, and he says that his father's fortune was injured by fires and other casualties.

John of Salisbury says that the future archbishop learned from his mother "the fear of the Lord, and the reverence due to Christ's mother, the holy Virgin Mary, whom, next to her Divine Son, he adopted as his patroness, frequently invoking her name, and placing all his trust in her."

The fond parent of Thomas à Becket used to connect her little boy in a singular and whimsical manner with her deeds of charity. She weighed him at stated times, placing in the opposite scale bread, meat, and clothing, until they equalled the weight of the child, when she made distribution thereof to the poor.

Rohesia, or Matilda Becket, died when Thomas was twenty-one years old, and he was left to the charge of his father only. He was then committed to the charge of Robert, prior of Merton, to be educated for religion. When older, he went to Paris, and studied there. On his return, he began to take part in the affairs of the city of London, and was made clerk and accountant to the sheriffs. But a serious accident befell Becket in the early part of his life, which had well nigh cut short his career. There was a knight named Richard de Aquila, who used to lodge in the house of Gilbert when he was in London. This man, being much addicted to hunting and hawking, became a great favourite with Thomas, then a lad. It happened that during one of the half-yearly vacations, when Thomas was home from school, he accompanied his father's guest on one of his hawking expeditions. They were both on horseback, the knight in advance of his companion. They arrived at a narrow bridge, fit only for foot-passengers, and leading across a mill-dam. The mill was at work below, and the current was running strongly in the direction of the wheel. The knight spurred his horse over the bridge, and reached the other side in safety. Thomas did not meet with the same good luck; he and his horse were precipitated into the mill-stream. The falcon, which Thomas was carrying on his wrist, shared the same fate, and the lad, not content with saving himself, was eager to save the bird, and was thus swept imperceptibly almost under the wheel of the mill. A cry for help was raised, and death seemed inevitable, when the water was let off the wheel, and the mill suddenly stopped. The miller had seen the fall into the water, and had taken immediate measures to prevent an accident which he foresaw. He came out at once, and pulled the boy out of the stream.

Among those who lodged in Gilbert à Becket's house were Archdeacon Baldwin and Master Eustace, from Boulogne, acquaintances of Archbishop Theobald. These men soon perceived the talents of the young man, and introduced him to the notice of the archbishop, and Gilbert took occasion to remind the prelate that they were both of the same Norman origin, and descended from a common ancestor, a knight named Thierci. Becket was at once on the high road of advancement. His extraordinary abilities were cultivated by the wise patronage of the primate. Once he accompanied that prelate to Rome; and on more than one other occasion visited that great centre of Christian affairs. He was permitted to reside for a certain time at each of the great schools for the study of canon law, Bologna and Auxerre. But he was not without enemies.

Roger du Pont l'Evêque, a favourite of the archbishop, looked on the young man with hostility, bred of jealousy. He vented his spleen against him by nicknaming him Baile-

hache, after the name of the man in whose company he had
first appeared at the court of the archbishop. The enmity of
this man caused him to be twice removed from the palace;
but on both these occasions he took refuge with Walter,
archdeacon of Canterbury, brother of the primate. By his
intercession Becket was replaced in the palace, and restored
to favour. When Walter was removed to the see of Rochester
(A.D. 1148), the hostile Roger succeeded to the archdeaconry
of Canterbury.

In 1154, Roger du Pont l'Evêque was appointed to the
archbishopric of York, and the archdeaconry of Canterbury
was given to Becket, then aged thirty-six. He was already
incumbent of S. Mary-le-Strand, and rector of Otford. The
archdeaconry of Canterbury was the richest ecclesiastical
prize in the kingdom next to the archbishopric. From this
time he ruled without rival in the favour of the aged Theobald. Preferments were heaped upon him by his patron with
lavish bounty. He was given a prebendal stall in S. Paul's,
London, another in Lincoln, and he held several livings.
And yet, till made archdeacon, he was not in deacon's
orders.[1] In after years, when in exile, he was reproached
with his ingratitude to the king who had raised him from
poverty. "Poverty!" he rejoined. "Even then I held the
archdeaconry of Canterbury, the provostship of Beverley, a
great many churches, and several prebends."[2]

The trial and triumph of Becket's abilities was a negotia-
tion of the utmost difficulty with the court of Rome. The
first object was to obtain legatine power for Archbishop
Theobald, and to withdraw it from the bishop of Winchester;
the second tended more than almost all measures to secure
the throne of England to the house of Plantagenet. Archbishop Theobald had inclined to the cause of Matilda and

---

[1] After giving a list of his benefices, Fitz-Stephen adds, "In process of time the
archbishop ordained him deacon, and made him archdeacon of Canterbury."

[2] "Plurimæ ecclesiæ, præbendæ nonnullæ," Ep. 130.

her son: he had refused to officiate at the coronation of Eustace, son of King Stephen. Becket not merely obtained from Eugenius III. the full papal approbation of this refusal, but a condemnation of Stephen (whose title had before been sanctioned by Eugenius himself) as a perjured usurper. But on the accession of Henry II., the archbishop began to tremble at his own work; serious apprehensions arose as to the disposition of the young king towards the Church.   The Churchmen feared the possibility of Henry combining with the nobles against the spiritual power.   They no doubt suspected that the augmentation of their privileges, which had been favoured by the necessities or fears of Stephen, might be checked by a union of the king with their natural enemies, the barons.

It was notorious at the court of Henry II. that many members of the young king's family entertained views hostile to the encroachments of the Church, and we shall find in the sequel that these men goaded on the king to the contest which took place between him and the clergy.   The archbishop was therefore anxious to place near the person of the king, one on whom he could rely to counteract these threatening tendencies and influences.   He had discerned not merely unrivalled abilities, but, with prophetic sagacity, his archdeacon's devoted churchmanship.   Through the recommendation of the primate, Becket was raised to the dignity of chancellor, an office which made him the second civil power in the realm, inasmuch as his seal was necessary to countersign all royal mandates.   Nor was it without great ecclesiastical influence, for the chancellor had the appointment of all the royal chaplains, and the custody of the vacant bishoprics, abbacies, and benefices. "The king's chancellor," says Fitz-Stephen, "if he pleases, always dies an archbishop or a bishop."

This office was bestowed on Becket in 1155, when he was

about thirty-eight. "Thomas," says Herbert de Bosham, "now as it were laid aside the deacon, and took on him the duties of the chancellor, which he discharged with zeal and ability." Roger of Pontigny tells us that "it is difficult to describe the way in which he filled both the characters, that of the clerk and of the courtier, for in the outset he was so assailed by the jealousy of rivals and by tales of scandal unblushingly circulated about him, that he complained of them to the archbishop and his private friends, and declared that if possible he would have withdrawn himself altogether from the court."

But this must have been a passing fit of impatience; we hear no more of it, and the distaste for court life probably disappeared as rapidly as it had risen, for the new life had much to recommend it to one who was not destitute of ambition. The king delighted in his company, and gave up all matters of state to his guidance. Thus whilst Henry occupied his time in youthful sports, Thomas was discharging all the royal duties with vigour and activity; at one time he was marching in complete armour, at the head of the chivalry of the kingdom; at another, he was administering justice to the people. It was only in name that he differed from the king himself, for everything was at his disposal; the nobles and magistrates were all under his orders; and it became manifest to all men, that in order to obtain a point with the king, it was absolutely necessary first to gain the ear of the chancellor. Such was the attachment which Henry conceived for his chancellor, that he blindly fancied him devoted to his service in every particular. He did not recollect that Thomas à Becket had already sworn fidelity to another Master, whose servant he more especially was; the stamp of the Church was set on him, and this no civil honours could efface. Though he might "lay aside the deacon and assume the chancellor for a while," yet nothing could divert him from the tendency of his early education.

In the beginning of the reign of Henry, the guidance of a wise head is manifest. Even if we attribute the initiative to the king, yet it is certain that Becket had the execution of what was done. A new and pure coinage was introduced. To revive the vigour of the laws, the judicial and executive offices of the crown were filled, and at their head were placed, as grand justiciaries, the earl of Leicester and Richard de Lacy, men of high character and ability.

All the foreign mercenaries, whom Stephen and others had established in England, were bidden depart the kingdom on a certain day, on pain of death. William of Ypres was deprived of the earldom of Kent, and banished with the rest. The king then proceeded to destroy the castles which had been built during the reign of his predecessor, sparing only a few which were advantageously placed for the defence of the realm. He resumed all the crown lands which Stephen or the empress had been induced to alienate ; the earl of Nottingham, who had poisoned Ranulf of Chester a few years before, fled the kingdom in fear. William of Albemarle, who had long ruled in Yorkshire like a king, was obliged to place the strong castle of Scarborough in the king's hands, together with the estate he had of late acquired from the crown. Henry of Blois, bishop of Winchester, brother of Stephen, in distrust and alarm, secretly withdrew from the kingdom, upon which his strongholds were at once destroyed by the king. It was by the advice of the bishop of Winchester that Theobald of Canterbury had obtained the appointment of chancellor for Thomas, and it is therefore hardly possible to believe that Becket had anything to do with his humiliation. Indeed, throughout, the king's line of conduct seems to have been marked by his own independent mind. He was resolved to establish the prerogatives of the crown, reduce the independence of the nobles, and establish everywhere justice. From the first he saw, there can be no doubt, that he must come into collision with the power which threatened the crown almost as much as the barons, and which by its privilege of the clergy interfered with the execution of impartial justice. But he used Becket as his tool to destroy the gross secular abuses in the realm, and waited his time to strike at the encroachments of the ecclesiastical power. Whether from the initiative of the king, or of the chancellor, the most admirable reforms were introduced, and prosperity dawned on England, sorely wasted by its late troubles. "It seemed," says Fitz-Stephen, "as if the country were enjoying a second spring. The Holy Church was honoured and respected; every vacant bishopric and abbacy was given to some deserving person, without simony. The king, by the favour of Him who is King of kings, succeeded in all he undertook. The realm of England became richer and richer, and copious blessings flowed from the horn of plenty. The hills were cultivated, the valleys teemed with corn, the fields were full of cattle and the folds of sheep."

"The countenance of Thomas was mild and beautiful; he was tall of stature, had a nose elevated and slightly aquiline. In his senses and physical perceptions he was most acute; his language was refined and eloquent, his intellect subtle, and his mind cast in a noble mould. His aspirations after virtue were of a lofty kind, whilst his conduct, amiable towards all men, exhibited singular sympathy towards the poor and oppressed, whilst to the proud he was hostile and unbending. Ever ready to promote the advancement of his friends, he was liberal to all men, of a lively and witty disposition, cautious alike of being deceived and of deceiving others. He distinguished himself for his prudence at an early age, even whilst he was a child of this world, he who was afterwards to become a child of light."

He is said to have resided for some time at West Tarring, in Sussex, and in the rectory garden is an ancient fig-tree which tradition says he brought from Italy and planted there.

The species of fig tree which grows so plentifully in Sussex is believed to have been propagated from this tree.

Of Becket's chancellorship, which lasted seven years, many anecdotes have been preserved, principally by his secretary, Fitz-Stephen. He took the provostship of Beverley, and at least one prebendal stall at Hastings, the governorship of Eye, and of the Tower of London, and of the Castle of Berkhamstead. How many livings he held has not been computed.

Fitz-Stephen tells us that "he generally amused himself, not incessantly, but occasionally, with hawks, falcons, or hunting dogs, or in a game of chess :—

' Where front to front the mimic warriors close,
To check the progress of their mimic foes.'

"The house and table of the chancellor were open to all of every rank who sought the royal court and needed hospitality. He never dined without the society of earls and barons, whom he had invited. He ordered his hall to be strewn every day with fresh straw and hay in winter, and with green leaves in summer, that the numerous knights for whom the benches were insufficient, might find the floor clean and neat for them to sit down on, and that their rich clothes and beautiful tunics might not be soiled and injured. His board shone with vessels of gold and silver, and abounded with costly dishes and precious beverages, so that whatever objects of food and drink were recommended by their rarity, were purchased by his officers at exorbitant prices. But amid all this he was himself singularly frugal. His confessor, Robert, canon of Merton, assured me that from the time of his becoming chancellor, he did not give way to licentious habits, though he was much tempted thereto by the king.[1] When one of his clerks, Richard of Ambly,

[1] The words of Fitz-Stephen seem to suggest that he had not been of a moral character before he became chancellor.

carried off the wife of a friend, pretending that her husband who was in foreign parts was dead, the chancellor dismissed the clerk from his house and friendship, and put him in the Tower of London, where he was long detained loaded with irons."

William of Canterbury tells us that the chancellor was one day with the king at Stafford, and that the citizen in whose house he lodged, suspected him of being on terms of too close intimacy with a distinguished lady of the court. He had the curiosity to enter the chancellor's bedroom at night, to ascertain whether he slept there. The bed, indeed, gave tokens of having been unoccupied, but Thomas à Becket was not in the lady's chamber, but asleep on his floor.

"The nobles of England and of the neighbouring kingdoms sent their sons to serve in the chancellor's house. When they had received from him the proper nurture and instruction, he bestowed on them the belt of knighthood, and sent them home with honour to their parents and relations, whilst he retained some of them in his service. The king himself, his master, committed his son and heir to his charge, and the chancellor placed the young prince in the midst of the sons of the nobility who were of the same age, where he received due attention from them all, and had masters and proper servants as his rank required. Numbers of noblemen and knights did homage to the chancellor, and all of them were readily received by him, always saving their allegiance to the king, and as being now his vassals, were promoted under his patronage. There never passed a day in which he did not make large presents of horses, birds, clothes, gold and silver plate, or money."[1]

" He was followed by so large a retinue of soldiers and persons of all ranks that the royal palace seemed empty in comparison;"[2] and " the king himself was left almost alone,

[1] Fitz-Stephen.   [2] Roger of Pontigny.

and sometimes complained to the chancellor that his court was drained." [1]

John of Salisbury admits that he greedily strove to gain the favour of the populace, and was both vain and proud ; that he conducted himself towards women with a warmth of expression which was, perhaps, equivocal, but he strenuously declares that he remained chaste.[2] When business was over the king and his chancellor used to play together, like school-boys, in the hall or in the church.

One bleak winter day the king and the chancellor were riding together through a street in London. Henry saw an old beggar in rags coming towards them.

"Do you see that man?" he asked of Becket.

"Yes," replied the chancellor.

"How poor and infirm he seems," said the king ; "and he is almost naked. It were an act of charity to provide him with a thick, warm cloak."

"It were so," answered the chancellor. "And your majesty should remember to relieve the old man."

The king accosted the beggar in a mild tone, and asked him if he would like to have a warm cloak. The poor man, not knowing who they were, thought he was being mocked. Then the king said to the chancellor, "You shall have the credit of doing this great act of charity," and laying hands on his rich cloak of scarlet and minever, he endeavoured to drag it off. Becket strove to retain it. The retinue of knights and nobles rode hastily up to see what the struggle was about. But neither could speak, each had his hands fully occupied, and they had much ado to keep from falling off their horses. At last the button of the cloak gave way, and it remained in the king's hands. He gave it to the beggar,

[1] Ed. Grim.

[2] "Erat supra modum captator auræ popularis . . . . etsi superbus esset, et vanus, et interdum insipienter amantium et verba proferret, admirandus tamen et imitandus erat in corporis castitate."

and told the story to his attendants, who burst into loud laughter, to the anger and humiliation of S. Thomas.

Sometimes the king, on his return from hunting, would ride into the hall where his chancellor was dining; call for a cup of wine from the high table, and depart; at other times he would dismount, jump over the table, and seat himself beside Becket, and fall to at his viands with the proverbial appetite of a hunter.

One is inclined to wonder whence came all the wealth so lavishly displayed. It is true that Becket enjoyed the revenues of several benefices, the religious duties of which he never executed, but they were insufficient to keep up the royal magnificence in which he lived. It must be remembered, however, that all grants and royal favours passed through his hands, and that he was guardian of all escheated baronies and of all vacant benefices. No very exact account was kept of what he did with all the moneys that came into his hands from these sources, and he took good care to secure a general quittance from the chief justiciary of the realm before he vacated his chancellorship to take the archbishopric.

We ask, knowing the after history of Becket, whether, as chancellor, he set his face as a flint against interference with the immunities of the clergy. And we find, on the contrary, that, acting on his advice, the king levied a tax for his war in France on the clergy. The personal service of the king's vassals was commuted for a scutage or rate levied on every knight's fee, and this tax was exacted also from the Church.

John of Salisbury, his friend and panegyrist, says he did so, forced by necessity, and that he afterwards bitterly rued it, and took his after exile as the punishment for his guilty compliance. "If with Saul he persecuted the Church, with Paul he is prepared to die for the Church." But probably the worst effect of this compliance with the king's first attempt

to extend even justice over all, and touch the sacred pockets
of the ecclesiastics, to extract something for the preservation
of the commonwealth, whose protection they enjoyed without hitherto contributing towards its expenses—was that
the king was lured on to the delusion that Becket was ready
to go forward with him in the execution of his complete
scheme of reformation, and to support him in his attempt to
bring the Church under control. Hitherto the whole burden
of taxation had fallen on the laity. The clergy were exempt.
The Church possessed a large share of the land of England,
and all that land was untaxed, so that the burden fell with
double oppression on the lay landowners.

One day, when Becket was recovering from an illness at
Rouen, the prior of Leicester came to see him, on his way
from the court of the king, who was then in Gascony. He
said roughly to Becket, "How is this? You, an ecclesiastic,
are dressed as a man who goes out hawking, with a cape with
sleeves! Although but one person, you are archdeacon of
Canterbury, dean of Hastings, provost of Beverley, canon of
this place, and canon of that, proctor to the archbishop, and,
it is whispered, likely to become archbishop yourself."
Becket said, "There are three poor priests in England,
any one of whom I would rather see raised to that dignity.
And, moreover, so well do I know the king, that I should
either lose his favour, or that of God, were I made archbishop." This shows that Becket had mapped out his own
course in his own mind. Not one of the three poor priests,
he knew well enough, was likely to get the archbishopric,
which was certain to be his, could he but keep up the farce
till the death of Theobald.

Henry II. had married Eleanor of Guienne, the divorced
wife of the king of France, and laid claim to the county
of Toulouse, as part of his wife's inheritance. But Raymond
of S. Gilles, who held the county by conveyance from the

father of Queen Eleanor, and, moreover, as the dower of his own wife, sister of the French king, refused to give it up. Louis sustained the cause of his brother-in-law, and Henry prepared for war. As the territory in dispute was far distant, the king, by the advice of his chancellor, resolved to accept from each of his vassals a sum of money in lieu of personal service. The amount so obtained enabled him to enlist a vast body of mercenaries, with which, augmented by his chief barons and their immediate retainers, he took the field.

In his suite appeared the young king of Scotland, a prince of Wales, and the chancellor Becket, leading 700 men-at-arms, paid by himself. In the south, Henry was joined by Raymond-Berenger, king of Aragon, and other allies, with considerable forces. The advance of the formidable host upon Toulouse caused the count urgently to implore the aid of the king of France; and Louis, without waiting to collect his forces, threw himself into the menaced city with a small troop. Upon this, Henry, with a politic respect for his over-lord, immediately gave up the siege, in spite of the counsel of his chancellor. Satisfied with the conquests he had already made, the king returned to Normandy, leaving Becket, with the constable, in command of the force which remained.

Fitz-Stephen says: " If Becket's advice had been listened to, they would have taken, not the town only, but also the king of France, so numerous was the army of the English king. But the king listened to the counsel of others, and from some foolish superstition and respect towards the king of France, who was his over-lord, he hesitated to attack the town, though the chancellor asserted that the king of France had forfeited his right as over-lord by appearing in arms against Henry in defiance of treaty. Not long after, the troops that had been summoned by the king of France entered the city; and the king of England, with the Scottish king and all his army, retired without having accomplished their purpose. However, they took the town of Cahors, and several castles in the neighbourhood of Toulouse, which either belonged to the count of Toulouse and his vassals, or had previously been taken by him from partisans of the king of England. The barons refused to take charge of these castles after the king's departure; so the chancellor, with his retainers, and Henry of Essex, alone remained. He put himself after that in full armour at the head of a stout band of his men, and stormed three other castles, which were strongly fortified, and appeared impregnable. He then passed the Garonne with his troops, in pursuit of the enemy, and after he had confirmed the whole province in its allegiance to the king, he returned crowned with honour.

"Afterwards, the chancellor, in the war between the French king and his own master, the king of England, when the armies were assembled in March, on the frontier between Gisors, Trie, and Courcelles, maintained, besides 700 knights of his own household, 1,200 other knights' mercenaries, and 4,000 private soldiers for the space of forty days. To every knight was assigned three shillings a day of the chancellor's money towards their horses and esquires, and the knights themselves all dined at the chancellor's table. One day, though he was a clerk, he charged with lance in rest, and horse at full speed, against Engelram de Trie, a valiant French knight, who was advancing towards him, and having unhorsed the rider, caried off his horse in triumph. Indeed, the chancellor's knights were everywhere foremost in the whole English army, doing more valiant deeds than any others, and everywhere distinguishing themselves, for he was always himself at their head, encouraging them, and pointing out the path to glory. He sounded the signal for advance or retreat on one of those slender trumpets which were peculiar to his band, but which were well known to all the rest of the army round."

An occasion now arose for Becket's abilities to be called into action on a matter of importance to his royal master. It was judged expedient by the king and his councillors to strengthen the throne by an alliance between Prince Henry and the Princess Margaret, daughter of the French king. The chancellor was sent to demand the hand of the young princess. Fitz-Stephen gives a curious picture of the prodigality and display of Becket in this embassy to the French court : " He had with him 200 men on horseback of his own household—soldiers, clerks, butlers, serving-men, knights, and sons of the nobility, who were performing military service to him, and all equipped with arms. They and their whole train shone in new holiday clothes, each according to his rank. He had also four-and-twenty changes of garments, almost all of which were to be given away, and left in foreign parts—elegant tartans, frieze and foreign skins, cloaks and carpets, such as those with which the bed and chamber of a bishop are adorned. He had also with him dogs and birds of all kinds, such as kings and wealthy men keep. There were in his train eight carriages, each drawn by five horses, in size and strength like chargers. Each horse had his proper groom, in a new vesture, walking by the side of the carriage, and the carriage had its driver and its guard. Two carriages were filled with beer in iron-bound casks, to be given to the French, who admire that sort of liquor, for it is a wholesome drink, bright and clear, of a vinous colour and superior taste. One carriage served as the chancellor's chapel, one as his chamber, and another as his kitchen. Others carried different sorts of meat and drink ; some cushions, bags containing night-clothes, bundles, and baggage. He had twelve sumpter horses, and eight coffers to carry his plate of gold and silver cups, pitchers, basins, salts, spoons, knives, and other utensils. There were coffers for containing the chancellor's money, together with his clothes and a few books. One sumpter horse, that went before the others, contained the sacred vessels of the chapel, the books and ornaments of the altar. Each of the sumpter horses was attended by a suitable groom, trained to his duties. Moreover, each carriage had a large dog tied to it, either above or below, fierce and terrible. There was also a long-tailed ape on the back of each horse. On entering the French villages and castles, first went the footmen, about two hundred and fifty in number, marching six or ten abreast, and singing after the fashion of their country. After an interval, followed the dogs in couples, and harriers fastened by thongs, with their keepers and attendants. At a little distance followed the sumpter horses, with their grooms riding them, their knees planted on the haunches of the horses. The French ran out of their houses, at the noise of their passing, and said, 'What a man the king of England must be, if his chancellor travels in such style!' After these came the squires, carrying the shields of the knights, and leading their chargers; then came other squires, then young men, then the falconers with the birds on their wrists, and, after them, the butlers, masters, and attendants of the chancellor's house, then the knights and clerks, all riding two-and-two together, and lastly came the chancellor, with some of his personal friends about him."

The king of France, having lost his queen, married within three weeks of her death Adelaide de Blois, a niece of King Stephen. Such a marriage was scarcely decent. Louis of France had married the mother of Henry, who was now to be united to his daughter by Constance of Castile. He had been divorced from Eleanor on the plea of consanguinity. The blood relationship between the children to be affianced was not very close, and Becket easily obtained a papal dispensation to allow of the marriage, but of its indecency there can be no question. As soon as the marriage had taken place, Henry II. at once obtained the dower of the princess from the Templars, who were the guardians of it. The French monarch, exasperated, instantly renewed hostilities, but peace was soon again brought about by the exertions of the legate of Alexander III.

On April 18, 1161, the aged Archbishop Theobald of Canterbury was laid in his grave. Henry did not at once nominate his successor; no one doubted who was to become primate of England, it had been openly discussed before, and Thomas expected to be offered it. In the beginning of the year 1162 the chancellor was sent to England from Normandy, where the court then was, to prepare for the crowning of the young prince Henry as his father's successor. Shortly after the king sent the *congé d'élire* by Richard de Lucy, grand justiciary of the realm, and three bishops, to the monks of Canterbury, bidding them elect an archbishop and primate of the Church of England.

The letter giving liberty to elect was read to the prior and chapter by Richard de Lucy, and then the monks retired—invoked the Holy Spirit to guide them to make a right choice, and then humbly invited Richard de Lucy to let them know whom the king recommended. Thomas à Becket, chancellor of England, was designated by Henry for the vacant primatial throne. Some of the monks hesitated, they had never before elected one who was not a monk, but the king's wish was equivalent to a command, and they swallowed their scruples and chose Becket as required.[1]

The deputation from the king then went to London, the election met there with some opposition from Gilbert Foliot, bishop of Hereford, who, perhaps, coveted the archbishopric

[1] Grim says that the election was "extorted" from them by Henry. From Foliot we learn that the commissioners of the king were armed with penalties should the monks prove refractory.

for himself. But his resistance was powerless, it merely took the form of grumbling, and he did not dare to oppose the royal pleasure by overt act. For he was threatened in the event of his objecting with banishment, not only of himself, but of all his relations.[1] Thomas à Becket made the usual protest that he did not desire the vacant throne, and shrunk from the duties involved by accepting, and perhaps with some transient sincerity, for he saw clearly that he would not maintain the favour of the king if he asserted the rights, or rather, claims of the Church to freedom from taxa· tion, and clerical independence of the secular courts.

Thomas à Becket was consecrated by Henry, bishop of Winchester, on May 27, 1162, in the cathedral of Canterbury. He had been ordained priest a few days before.

The general opinion of the appointment was not altogether favourable. It was complained that the election was un-canonical, as the monks of Christ Church had been obliged by the king to elect his nominee, and their free choice had been interfered with. Others said, "How shall a man who has not put his hand to the oar, now assume the helm?" and "Here is a man who in his very dress has cast aside what is befitting a clerk, a man who has delighted in the luxury of a court, and whose conversation has been wholly secular, a man whose ambition has been set to gain this place, now made archbishop. He ought to be ashamed to accept the office."

Herbert de Bosham tells us that Becket did warn the king beforehand that he would not serve him blindly, as head of the English Church. "If you do as you say, my lord, your mind will very soon be estranged from me, and you will hate me then as much as you love me now, for you assume an authority in Church matters which I should not consent to, and there will be plenty of persons to stir up strife between us."

[1] "Exilio crudeliter addicti sumus, nec solum persona nostra, sed et domus patris mei, et conjuncta nobis affinitas, et cognatio tota-" Ep. 194.

For some time after Becket was made archbishop he did not greatly change his mode of life. His table groaned under gold and silver plate, and was furnished with fastidious delicacy, and his retinue and his own dress were as magnificent as when he was chancellor. John of Salisbury, who was afterwards the biographer of the saint, wrote to him in 1165, two years after his consecration, urging him to disengage his mind from the worldly interests which seemed entirely to engross it, and to adopt a more devotional habit of mind and life. "Far better confer on serious subjects with some serious person, and warm the feelings by his example, than dwell on and discuss the subtle controversies of secular literature." The letter was a serious call to the archbishop to commune with his own heart, and to cleanse and discipline a too luxurious and worldly life.

John, bishop of Poitiers, also later wrote a letter to Becket to remonstrate with him on his magnificent style of living. "I have often warned you, and must again press you to get rid of your superfluous incumbrances, and to consider the badness of the times"—and this was written when Thomas was an exile in France.

His biographers, indeed, speak of his wearing a hair shirt, and of his denying himself in food, and drinking water in which fennel had been boiled, of baring his back to the scourge, and sleeping on the floor, but it would appear that these practices grew up later, after he had gone to Pontigny. Indeed, he did not so much as affect to wear an ecclesiastical costume even in choir, till rebuked by one of the monks of Canterbury, and finding that it had become a matter of general complaint.

One of the first acts of Becket on becoming archbishop was to resign the chancellorship, as incompatible with the office and spiritual duties of a bishop. This act of surrender is greatly to his credit. There seems to have been no desire

on the king's part to lose his chancellor, he had hoped that
Becket would have combined both offices, and held simultaneously the highest civil, as well as the highest ecclesiastical, dignity in the kingdom.

The king was vexed at this unexpected surrender, and he
then called on Becket to resign the archdeaconry of Canterbury also, and this the archbishop reluctantly consented to
do. The alienation was, however, slight, and when the king
landed at Southampton, on Christmas Day, seven months
after the election of his favourite to the archbishopric, Becket
met him, and the prelate and his sovereign, forgetful of everything but their former friendship, rushed into each others'
arms, and strove to out-do one another in professions of
regard. They passed the whole day riding together, apart
from the court, talking over the events which had happened
since they had parted.[1]

Becket attended the council of Tours in May, 1163, pre-
sided over by Pope Alexander III., at the head of all the
bishops of England, except those who were excused by age
or infirmity. So great was his reputation, that the Pope
sent out all the cardinals, except those in attendance on his
own person, to escort the primate of England into the city.

That strife which was to cost Becket his life, broke out
next year, if not with full violence, at least with threatenings
of becoming deadly.

Both the king and the archbishop were prepared for
aggressions. The first public collision was a dispute concerning the customary payment to the sheriffs of the counties
of a tax of two shillings for every hide of land. The king
determined to transfer the payment to his own exchequer.
He summoned an assembly at Woodstock, and declared his
intentions. All were mute but Becket ; the archbishop op-

---

[1] This is one account, that of Herbert de Bosham ; but Diceto says the king
showed coolness towards him. De Bosham is most likely to be correct.

posed the enrolment of the decree, on the ground that the tax was voluntary, not of right. " If the sheriffs conduct themselves peaceably towards the people, we shall continue to pay to them, as before ; but if not, no one can compel us." " By God's eyes," said Henry, his usual oath, " it shall be enrolled ! " " By those same eyes," replied the prelate, " none of the men on my estate shall pay it so long as I live ! "

On Becket's part, almost the first act of his primacy was to vindicate all the rights, and to resume all the property, which had been usurped, or which he asserted had been usurped, from his see. During the turbulent times just gone by, there would hardly have been rigid respect for the inviolability of sacred property. The title of the Church was held to be indefeasible. Whatever had once belonged to the Church might be recovered at any time ; and the ecclesiastical courts claimed the sole right of adjudication in such cases. Unfortunately, also, as we can now ascertain by the deeds which have been preserved, many of these claims were based on forged charters or grants of land. In these cases the primate was at once plaintiff, judge, and carrier into execution of his own judgments. The lord of the manor of Eynsford, in Kent, who held from the king, claimed the right of presentation to that benefice. Becket asserted the prerogative of the see of Canterbury. On the forcible ejectment of his nominee by the lord, William of Eynsford, Becket proceeded at once to a sentence of excommunication, without regard to Eynsford's feudal superior, the king. The primate next demanded the castle of Tunbridge from the head of the powerful family of De Clare ; though it had been held by De Clare, and it was asserted, received in exchange for a Norman castle, since the time of William the Conqueror.

The custody of Rochester castle was another subject of

contention. Becket claimed this by virtue of a grant of William the Conqueror.

The king was almost forced by a succession of ecclesiastical scandals, and the escape of the guilty, to insist on the clerks in his realm being brought under obedience to the laws. Crimes of great atrocity, it is said, of great frequency, crimes such as robbery and murder, for which secular persons were hanged by scores and without mercy, were committed with impunity, or with punishment altogether inadequate to the offence, by the clergy; and the sacred name of clerk exempted not only bishops, abbots, and priests, but those of the lowest ecclesiastical rank from the civil power. It was the inalienable right of the clerk to be tried only in an ecclesiastical court. The Church accordingly swarmed with " acephalous " clerks, without title, duty, or settled abode, who led a roving, disreputable life, and were ready for any violence ; " tonsured demons, workmen of the devil, clerks in name only, but belonging to Satan's portion." [1] The only punishment that could be inflicted by ecclesiastical tribunals was deprivation, degradation from orders, and relegation to a monastery. But as the king argued, those who cared least for the loss of orders were those whom a regard for their orders could not restrain from crime. The enormity of the evil is acknowledged by Becket's most ardent partisans. So long as the laity were allowed to compound for murder by paying a fine, as required by the laws of the Confessor, they could not complain of the ecclesiastical treatment of criminous clerks. But in Henry I.'s reign capital punishment for lay murder was introduced, and the contrast between the severity with which lay crimes were punished, and the immunity of ecclesiastical offenders, became conspicuous.

It was admitted that no less than a hundred of the clergy

[1] Fitz-Stephen

had their hands stained with blood. Philip de Brois, canon of Hereford, was charged with having murdered a knight, and was allowed to go free by the bishop of Lincoln, in whose court he was tried, on paying a fine to the relatives of the man he had killed. The sheriff of Bedford was not satisfied with this justice, and in the court of Dunstable, whilst De Brois was present, called him a murderer. On this the canon burst into opprobrious language. He was summoned for so doing before the archbishop, and his benefice sequestrated for a year. A clerk in Worcestershire had debauched a young lady, and murdered her father. The king wanted to have him tried in the lay-courts. The archbishop refused to allow it, and condemned the man to confinement in a monastery. Another clerk had stolen a silver goblet. Again an attempt was made to bring this criminal before the secular judge. Becket interfered, and " he was deprived of his orders, and branded into the bargain, to please the king." [1] The dean of Scarborough had circulated scandalous stories about the wife of a citizen of that town, and refused to desist unless paid twenty-two marks. The burgess grudgingly disbursed, but complained to the king. The dean appeared before Henry, and was given over to the ecclesiastical court, which simply made the dean refund the money. " What, then," exclaimed Richard de Lucy, grand justiciary, " is not justice to be executed?" "The man is a clerk," was the reply vouchsafed him. " Then I will have nothing to do with such a miscarriage of justice," said De Lucy, and he complained to the king. This had occurred whilst Theobald was archbishop; but it was not forgotten by Henry.

Osbert, archdeacon of York, shortly before King Henry's accession, had been charged with administering poison in the eucharistic cup to his archbishop, William; and King Stephen, notwithstanding the strenuous opposition of Archbishop Theobald and his brethren, had insisted on having

[1] Fitz-Stephen.

the charge heard in a secular court. But Stephen was succeeded by Henry before the trial took place, and the bishops
withdrew the case into the ecclesiastical courts, when the
accused appealed to Rome, took oath that he was innocent,
and got off scot free. The king was highly incensed at this,
and did not forget it.

The king, determined to bring these great questions to
issue, summoned a Parliament at Westminster. He began
the proceedings by enlarging on the abuses of the archi-
diaconal courts. The archdeacons kept the most watchful
and inquisitorial superintendence over the laity; but every
offence was easily commuted by a pecuniary fine, which fell
to them. The king complained that they levied a revenue
equal to his own from the sins of the people, yet that the
public morals were only more deeply and irretrievably de-
praved. He then demanded that all clerks accused of
heinous crimes should be immediately degraded and handed
over to the officers of justice, to be dealt with according to
law; for their guilt, instead of deserving a lighter punishment, was doubly guilty. "I also demand, that whilst the
ceremony of stripping them of their orders is performed,
some of my officials shall be present to seize the culprit, lest
he find opportunity of escape."

Becket insisted on delay till the next morning, in order
that he might consult his suffragan bishops. This the king
refused; the bishops withdrew to confer on their answer.
They were disposed to yield, partly because they felt the
justice of the claim, partly because they did not wish to
offend the king. But Becket was resolute. When one
listens to his speech, the feeling is one of stupefaction. To
screen the violators of maidens, adulterers, murderers, slan-
derers, and robbers, is a holy and dignified cause; to yield
them up is base and wicked. The bishops are thus addressed for counselling such a cause : "Fools ! how can
you thus yield to the wickedness of the times, urging you to

open guilt! to the sacrifice of Christ's Church! God can ameliorate the condition of His Church without our deteriorating ourselves. Can the gain of the Church be made by the crimes of its teachers? Let us shed our blood for the liberties of the Church!" Thus, it appeared, notorious guilt and crime on the part of the teachers of the Church consisted in surrendering criminous clerks, convicted of gross atrocities, to civil and impartial justice, not in the wicked deeds themselves, which then deeply stained the clergy.

Becket's resolution prevailed. The king demanded whether the bishops would observe the "customs of the realm." "Saving my order," replied the archbishop. That order was still to be exempt from all jurisdiction but its own. So answered all the bishops except Hilary of Chichester, who made the declaration without reserve. The king left the assembly in a rage, without completing any of the matters for which the council had been summoned. The day closed in, and the prelates returned to their quarters. On their way the archbishop rebuked the bishop of Chichester for his base submission. Next morning the king required the archbishop to surrender the custody of the royal castles and manors which he had received as chancellor, and which he had not given up, and he deprived him at the same time of the charge of the prince, his son. The bishops entreated Becket to withdraw or change the offensive expression. At first he answered that should an angel from heaven give him such counsel, he would hold him accursed. At length, however, he gave way, persuaded, as Edward Grim tells us, by the papal almoner, who was bribed by English gold. He went to Oxford, and made the concession, promising to assent to the royal constitutions without any reservation of the rights of his own order.

The king, in order to ratify with the utmost solemnity the concession extorted from Becket and the bishops, summoned a great council of the realm to Clarendon, to meet in January, 1164. Clarendon was a royal palace between three and five miles from Salisbury. The two archbishops and eleven bishops, and between thirty and forty of the highest nobles, with numbers of inferior barons, were present. The ancient laws of England in reference to ecclesiastical immunities were rehearsed before the council. Among these were laws forbidding ecclesiastical courts deciding questions concerning advowsons and the presentation to livings, forbidding appeals to the Pope, and excommunications launched against tenants in chief without the king's licence; ordering clerks accused of criminal offences to be tried in the king's courts. These ancient laws were uncodified. "It is my wish," said the king, "that the royal constitutions of my ancestors be reduced to writing, and signed and sealed by the archbishop and all present, to prevent future misunderstandings." "I declare," said the archbishop, "before Almighty God, that no seal of mine shall ever be affixed to constitutions such as these." This sudden announcement threw the assembly into confusion. The king broke out into one of his ungovernable fits of passion. William, earl of Leicester, and Reginald of Cornwall expostulated with the archbishop. Richard of Hastings, grand provincial of the Templars, urged him to yield. The archbishop of York and the bishop of Chichester favoured the motion of the king, the former perhaps still actuated by that animosity towards Becket which he had manifested towards him when both were together in the service of Theobald of Canterbury. Becket wavered, and then exclaimed : "It is God's will that I should perjure myself; for the present I submit and incur perjury, to repent of it hereafter as I best may."[1]

[1] Gilberti Fol. Ep. 194.

He took the oath of obedience, which had been already sworn to by all the lay barons. He was followed by the rest of the bishops, reluctantly, according to one account, and compelled on one side by their dread of the lay barons, on the other by the example and authority of the primate; but, according to Becket's biographers, eagerly and of their own accord.

The famous Constitutions of Clarendon were feudal in their form and spirit. All bishops' fiefs were granted by the crown, and the clergy were subjected equally with the laity to the common laws of the land. Clerks accused of crimes were to be summoned before the king's courts, and the clerks found guilty were not to be screened by the Church from suffering condign punishment. Appeals were to lie from the archdeacon to the bishop, from the bishop to the archbishop; and, on failure of justice, in the last resort to the king, who would see to the case being fairly reheard in the archbishop's court, and justice done.

As Becket left the council his cross-bearers remarked that "the Government seemed disposed to upset everything: Christ was not safe, nor His sanctuary, from these devilish machinations. The pillars of the Church were shaking, and whilst the shepherd fled, the flock fell victims." The archbishop appeared in low spirits, and rode apart. At length Herbert de Bosham approached him and said, "My lord, why are you dejected?"

"Alas!" answered Becket, "the Church of England is reduced to bondage through my sins. I was a proud, vain man, a breeder of birds, and was suddenly elevated to feed men. I was a patron of stage-players and a follower of hounds, and I have become a shepherd of souls. I neglected my own vineyard, and am set to care for many others. My past life was alien from the path of salvation, and now I reap its fruits. God has forsaken me, and deems me unworthy to hold the hallowed see in which I have been placed," and he burst into tears.

The immunity which Becket claimed for criminal clerks extended also to those who injured clerks. Such were also tried in ecclesiastical courts, and the utmost that the Church could do to them was to cut them off from communion. Curiously enough, that liberty which Becket claimed for criminals in orders and for offenders against the clergy, and which he achieved at last, was the means of saving his murderers from suffering condign punishment.

But Becket did not consider this point. It must have escaped his notice. Richard, his successor on the throne of S. Augustine, saw the mistake Becket had made, and strove for the alteration of the law. "I should be content," he says, "with the sentence of excommunication, if it had the effect of striking terror into evil doers; but, through our sins, it has become ineffective and despised. The slayers of a clerk or a bishop are sent to Rome by way of penance; they enjoy themselves by the way, and return with the Pope's full pardon, and with increased boldness for the commission of crime. The king claims the right of punishing such offences; but we clergy *damnably* reserve it to ourselves, and we deserve the consequences of our ambition in usurping a jurisdiction with which we have no rightful concern."

A few days after the council had dissolved, Becket sent to Alexander III., who was at Sens, an account of what had taken place, and a request to be released of his oath. This was readily accorded him. On his receipt of the answer from the Pope, Becket went to Woodstock, where the king was, and asked to be admitted into his presence; but he was repulsed from the gates by the attendants. He went on to Aldington in Kent, where he had a manor, and there secretly at night attempted to cross into France in a small

boat. The wind was contrary, and he was obliged to
return and creep stealthily back to his house at Aldington.
The servants had dispersed on the disappearance of their
master, and only one clerk and his servant remained in the
house. In the evening, after supper, the clerk said to his
man, "Go and shut the outer door of the court, and let us
go to bed." The servant lighted a candle and opened the
door to go out, when, to his astonishment, he saw the archbishop alone, crouching in a corner. Thinking he saw a
ghost, he ran back to his master in dismay. Becket, however, followed him, and explained the circumstances of his
return. The object of his attempted flight is not very clear,
unless it were that he shrank from the conflict which he now
saw was inevitable. But it was in direct violation of the
Constitutions of Clarendon, to which he had sworn adhesion
and had appended his seal, one of which forbade a bishop
crossing the sea without leave from the king. It was evident that Henry had to do with a man who would not be
bound by his most solemn oaths. No treaty could be made
when one party claimed the power of retracting, and might
at any time be released from his covenant.

Before the close of the year Becket was cited to appear
before a council of the realm at Northampton. The archbishop could not hope for support from the bishops. Gilbert of London and Roger of York were his deadly foes.
The bishops of Salisbury and Chichester were arrayed on
the king's side. Bartholomew of Exeter, Roger of Worcester, and Robert of Lincoln were anxious to observe a
politic neutrality.

Becket himself attributed the chief guilt of his persecution
to the bishops, since, "if they were not so tamely acquiescent,
the king might have been quiescent."

The assembly of Northampton opened on October 6, 1164.
Becket had been cited to answer a charge of withholding

justice from John the Marshal, employed in the king's exchequer, who claimed the estate of Pagaham from the see of Canterbury. Twice had Becket been summoned to appear in the king's court to answer for this denial of justice ; once he had refused to appear, the second time he did not appear in person. In fact, though he was determined not to sanction the Constitutions of Clarendon, under which John the Marshal had appealed to the royal court against the ecclesiastical court,[1] he had sworn in full council to abide by these constitutions, and he had openly disregarded them. Becket equivocated. He pretended that John the Marshal had sworn, not on the Gospels, but on the Tropologium, a book of ecclesiastical music. The archbishop was charged with treason for disregarding the king's court. Becket made his defence. It turned on quibbles. He did not state his real objection—that he would not acknowledge the right of the crown to receive an appeal from his own court. The judgment of all present, based on the constitutions passed at Clarendon, was that the archbishop had failed in his respect to the king's majesty, and that his defence was inadmissible. He was therefore condemned to have his movable goods confiscated, subject to the king's mercy.

There rose now a difficulty as to who should pronounce the judgment, the lay barons wishing to impose the unpleasant duty on the bishops, and the latter retorting that the judgment was not an ecclesiastical one. It ended in the sentence being read by Henry, bishop of Winchester. The archbishop bowed to the decision in silence, and all the bishops, except Gilbert Foliot, of London, who refused, pledged their security for its being submitted to. The same

---

[1] The hardship to John the Marshal was, that he had to argue his claim for a manor in the court of the archbishop who had wrested the manor from him, and could not therefore expect justice in a prejudiced court.

day another charge was brought against him, of having received three hundred pounds from the wardenship of the castles of Eye and Berkhamstead. To this he replied that the money had been spent on the repair of the palace in London. "That," said Henry, "was done without my authority or sanction." The archbishop then offered to pay the three hundred pounds. Next day another claim was advanced for five hundred marks which had been lent him by the king during the war at Toulouse, and for five hundred more borrowed of a Jew on the king's security. Becket replied that the money had been given, not lent him ; but he said that he would refund it. He was then required to give an account of what he had done with all the money that had come into his hands whilst chancellor. In answer he produced his acquittance obtained on his election from the grand justiciary, De Lucy. The king declared that the justiciary had exceeded his power in granting such an acquittance till the accounts of receipts and expenditure had been gone into formally. It was clear now that the king was bent on the ruin of Becket, and that there were no means in the hands of Becket of avoiding condemnation. He had apparently not kept accounts, and had received the money as it came in, and spent it profusely, not estimating very carefully how much went on matters concerning the king and the State, and how much went on keeping up the lavish splendour of his own house. He struggled, however, against condemnation by advancing the plausible grounds that this demand for accounts had been sprung on him, and he was unprepared at the moment with the papers requisite for meeting it.

In his extreme exigency the primate consulted separately with the bishops. Their advice was different according to their characters and their sentiments towards him. "Would to God that you were not the archbishop, but plain Thomas

à Becket !" said Hilary of Chichester. "The king is reported to have said that either he or you must reign. England cannot contain you both. Throw yourself on his
mercy."

"Remember from what the king raised you," said Gilbert
of London. "If you persist in your opposition you will ruin
the Church. Rather surrender your see."

"No," said Henry of Winchester. "Let nothing be said
of resigning his see at the beck and call of a temporal sovereign. That would indeed bring ruin on the Church."

"This man's life is in danger," said Robert of Lincoln,
"and if put to death he will of course lose his bishopric
along with his head—better lose one than both. What
good a bishop can be without a head I cannot see."

"The times are bad," remarked Bartholomew of Exeter.
"Use dissimulation till the storm is weathered. Better let
one individual be jeopardized than the whole Church
suffer."

"I give no opinion," observed the cautious Roger of
Worcester, "lest I get into trouble myself."

The next day was Sunday ; the archbishop did not leave
his lodgings. On Monday the agitation of his spirits had
brought on an attack of a disorder to which he was subject,
and he could not appear. The king thought he was pretending sickness, and sent to him. The royal messengers
found the archbishop in bed. On the morrow he had determined on his conduct. At one time he had seriously
meditated on a more humiliating course : he proposed to
seek the royal presence barefooted, with the cross in his
hands, to throw himself at the king's feet, appealing to his
old affections, and imploring him not to vex the Church.
But Becket yielded to haughtier counsels, more congenial to
his unbending character. He began by the significant act
of celebrating out of due order the office of S. Stephen, the

first martyr, with the introit, "Princes did speak against me." It was remembered that this was the hundredth anniversary of the landing of the Conqueror, and some signal event was anticipated. After Mass Becket took a portion of the Host, and, vested pontifically, save that he had put off his pall and mitre, he grasped his archiepiscopal crozier and went direct to the king's residence. The cross seemed, as it were, the banner of the Church going forth to defy the royal sceptre.[1] He met the bishops before the opening of the assembly. "My brethren," said he, "during two days you have been sitting upon me as judges, you who ought to have been my supporters. You are ready now, I doubt not, to act the same part in a criminal suit. But now I forbid you, on your obedience, from so doing. And should the secular power lay hands on me, I enjoin you, on your obedience, to launch excommunications in my behalf. Moreover, I appeal to Rome, the refuge of the helpless." Gilbert of London protested, and the others withdrew to communicate with the king. Only Henry of Winchester and Joscelin of Salisbury remained by the primate. He then proceeded on his course. His heart failed him now. "I wish," he sighed, "that I had adhered to my first intention of going before the king with the weapons, more suitable to a bishop, of entreaty and humility." But some of his clerks remonstrated against this temporary weakness, and he pursued his course. Holding his crozier, and armed with the Host, he entered the hall where the bishops and others were awaiting the king. "What means this new fashion of the archbishop bearing his own cross?" asked the archdeacon of Lisieux. "Suffer me to carry it, my lord," said the bishop of Hereford. "No, my son," answered Becket; "I bear the banner under which I purpose fighting." "He always was a fool,"

---

[1] "Tanquam in prælio Domini, signifer Domini, vexillum Domini erigens."—De Bosham.

said the bishop of London, " and a fool he will remain to the end of the chapter." The bishops made room for him. Gilbert of London tried to pluck the crozier out of his hands. Becket held it fast. " My lord archbishop," said Gilbert, " how if the king draw the sword against this uplifted cross? then we shall have king and archbishop in unseemly and unequal conflict."

The bishops were summoned into the king's presence. Becket sat alone in the outer hall. The archbishop of York swept by in disdainful pomp, with his crozier borne before him, in defiance of a mandate which forbade him to have his cross in the province of Canterbury. Like hostile spears, cross confronted cross,[1] badges of unrelenting hosti lity and stubborn defiance.

During this interval, De Bosham, the archbishop's reader, put the question, " If they should lay their impious hand on thee, art thou prepared to fulminate excommunication against them?" Fitz-Stephen, who sat at his feet, said in a loud, clear voice, "That be far from thee; so did not the apostles and martyrs of God; they prayed for their persecutors and forgave them!" " A little later," says the faithful Fitz-Stephen of himself, "when one of the king's ushers would not allow me to speak to the archbishop, I made a sign to him, and drew his attention to the Saviour on the cross." Many years afterwards, when both of them were in exile together at S. Benoît, on the Loire, the archbishop reminded Fitz-Stephen of this little circumstance.

The bishops, admitted to the king's presence, announced the appeal of the archbishop to the Pope, and his inhibition to his suffragans to sit in judgment in a secular court on their metropolitan. This appeal was again a direct violation of one of the Constitutions of Clarendon, sworn to by Becket in an oath still held valid by the king and his

[1] "Quasi pila minantia pilis," quotes Fitz-Stephen.

barons. The king appealed to the council. Some seized the occasion of boldly declaring that the king had brought this trouble upon him by advancing to a giddy eminence a low-born man. All agreed that Becket was guilty of perjury and treason. Some barons came out to attempt a compromise. Becket replied: "I have appealed from the judgment of the bishops, who dealt too harshly with me in the instance of neglect of court. I forbid their proceeding any further in judgment on me. I appeal from their sentence, and place myself under the protection of the sovereign Pontiff." The die was cast, there was now no retreat. The barons withdrew, muttering alarming hints of how refractory prelates might be dealt with.[1] The king now endeavoured to force the bishops to join the assembly of nobles and barons in passing sentence on the archbishop. They were thrown into confusion, and pleaded the prohibition of the primate. Roger of York left the council-chamber, calling to his clerks, "Let us be off and not wait to see how his lordship of Canterbury will be dealt with." "No," replied one of his clerks, "I shall remain. He cannot suffer in a better cause."

Bartholomew of Exeter threw himself at the feet of Becket and implored him to have some consideration for them. The king was determined to treat them as traitors if they refused to condemn the archbishop. "Run away, then," said Becket, contemptuously. "All your thoughts are on your personal safety, none on the cause of God and the Church."

Joscelin of Salisbury and William of Norwich, who had hitherto supported Becket, now implored him to give way. While they were thus urging him the other bishops had come to an agreement with the king to appeal to the Pope against the prohibition of Becket, and they assured the king that

[1] "Stigandum . . . . nigranti injectum puteo, perpetuo carceri damnavit. Godfredus comes Andegaviæ eunuchatorum ante se in pelvi afferri membra fecit."— Fitz-Stephen.

they were certain to gain their cause, as Becket was clearly forsworn in doing that which he had sworn at Clarendon not to do. They now came out into the hall where Becket sat, and Hilary addressed him in words of cutting bitterness: " My lord, at Clarendon, when we were all assembled, and the constitutions of the realm were rehearsed, and we were required to promise obedience, they were placed before us in writing, and we pledged our assent to them, and so did you ; we signed our names, but your name headed the signatures. The king then demanded an oath of us, and our seals. We replied that our oaths, as priests, to observe his laws in good faith, without dishonesty, ought to be sufficient. The king acquiesced in this. And now, my lord, you forbid us to take part in the proceedings of the king's courts, which, nevertheless, we are bound to do by the laws which we and you swore at Clarendon to obey. We therefore hold you to be a perjured man, and we can no longer obey an archbishop stained with perjury. We appeal to the Pope, and cite you to answer in his presence."

" If we fell at Clarendon," answered Becket, gloomily, " we should pluck up courage now. Unlawful oaths are not binding on the conscience."

The bishops withdrew, and Robert, earl of Leicester, and Reginald, earl of Cornwall, approached to signify to the archbishop the sentence of the court. " Hear, my lord, the judgment of the court——"

" I will not listen to it," interrupted Becket. " I was delivered over to the Church by King Henry, ' free from responsibility for the past.' I am not bound to plead in the case of maladministration of moneys as chancellor. I will not listen to the judgment."

The two earls said they would return to the king and consult him, and requested the archbishop to await their return.

" Am I a prisoner, then ? " he asked.

" By S. Lazarus, no," answered the earl of Leicester.

" Then hear me once more," said the archbishop. " I decline to receive judgment from the king or you. The Pope alone, under God, is my judge. I summon the bishops, who have obeyed the king rather than God, before his tribunal, and so, protected by the Apostolic See, I leave this court ! "

He rose and walked slowly down the hall, amidst the hootings and groans of the crowds, and loud epithets of " Traitor ! " and " Perjured ! " In the court below was a heap of wood, and he stumbled against one of the logs and nearly fell. At this there rose a fresh roar of execrations, and Randolf de Broc threw straws at him. " Were it not for my order," exclaimed Becket, at the taunt of sneaking away like a traitor, " my sword would answer that foul speech." He turned on an officer of the court who insulted him and called him " kinsman of a gallows-bird," for he had had a relative hung. Anselm, the king's illegitimate brother, met him. " Bastard, Catamite ! " were the words which Becket flung at him as he passed.

He mounted his horse, which had been waiting for him at the gate. But the outer gate was locked and had no key in it. One of his attendants, however, spied a bunch of keys hanging in a corner, took them down, and was fortunate enough to open the gate at the first trial.

In the meantime the king, hearing the noise, hastily sent a herald to make proclamation that the archbishop was to be left unmolested. Outside was a rabble of poor. Becket invited them to dine with him, and attended by this swarm of rude protectors, he made his way to his lodgings.

In the night Becket fled from Northampton, attended by only two monks and a servant. The weather was wet and stormy, but next morning they reached Lincoln. There he disguised himself as a monk, dropped down the Witham to a hermitage in the Fens belonging to the Cistercians of Sempringham; thence, by cross-roads, and chiefly by night, he found his way to Eastry, about five miles from Deal, a manor belonging to Christ Church in Canterbury. There he remained a week. On All Souls' Day he went on board a boat, just before morning, and by evening reached the coast of Flanders. To avoid observation he landed on the open shore near Gravelines. His large, loose shoes made it difficult to wade through the sand without falling. He sat down in despair. After some delay a sorry nag was hired for a shilling, without saddle, and with only a wisp of hay for a bridle. But he soon got weary of such riding, and was fain to walk, deeming it "easier and more respectable" so to do. He had many adventures by the way. He was once nearly betrayed by gazing with brightening eyes on a falcon upon a young squire's wrist; his fright punished him for this relapse into his secular vanities. The host of a small inn recognized him from his lofty look and the whiteness of his hands, and the way in which he, like a great man, distributed morsels from his plate to the children of the house. As he walked wearily, a good woman pitied him and offered him a stick which was sooty and greasy, for it had been used in her chimney for smoking fish. Becket thanked her, and used the staff.

At length he arrived within an hour's row by canal of Clair-Marais, near S. Omer. It was Friday. "My lord," said one of his attendants, who looked forward with dismay to the sorry fare of the abbey in which they were to reside, "we have gone through hardships; may we not have a dispensation to eat meat?"

"To-day is Friday," answered the archbishop.

"But there may be a scarcity of fish in the abbey," rejoined the clerk. "That must be as God wills," answered Becket.

At S. Omer he was joined by Herbert de Bosham, who had been left behind to collect what money he could at Canterbury; he brought but 100 marks and some plate.

He had an interview there with the grand justiciary, De Lucy, on his way from Compostella. De Lucy told Becket not to reckon on his support. " You owe me homage," said Becket, " and must not speak to me in this style." " I return the homage," answered De Lucy. " It is mine by right, and not yours by loan," replied the archbishop, haughtily.

In the first access of indignation at Becket's flight, the king had sent orders for strict watch to be kept in the ports of the kingdom, especially Dover. The next measure was to pre-occupy the minds of the count of Flanders, the king of France, and the Pope against his fugitive subject. Henry could not but foresee how formidable an ally the exile might become to his rivals and enemies, how dangerous to his extensive but ill-consolidated foreign dominions. He sent at once ambassadors to the king of France, and to Pope Alexander III., then at Sens.

The rank of his ambassadors implied the importance of their mission. They were the archbishop of York, the bishops of London, Exeter, Chichester, and Worcester, the earl of Arundel, and three other distinguished nobles. The same day that Becket passed to Gravelines, they crossed from Dover to Calais.

The ambassadors were coldly received by Louis VII., who had motives of his own for hating Henry. They obtained nothing from him. On the contrary, he wrote a strong letter urging Becket's cause to the Pope. At Sens their reception, if less openly unfavourable, was equally unsuccessful. Alexander was in a position of extraordinary difficulty; on one side were gratitude to King Henry for his pious support, and the fear of estranging so powerful a sovereign, on whose unrivalled wealth he reckoned as the main strength of his cause; on the other, it was his interest to support the privileges of the Church.

Becket's messengers, before the reception of Henry's ambassadors, were admitted by Alexander to a private interview. The account of Becket's "fight with beasts" at Northampton, had drawn tears from the Pontiff's eyes. "Your master," said Alexander, "although he is living in the flesh, may claim the privilege of martyrdom." The ambassadors of Henry were received in state in the open consistory. Foliot of London began with his usual ability; his warmth at length betrayed him into the Scriptural citation, "The wicked fleeth when no man pursueth." "Forbear," said the Pope. "I will forbear him," answered Foliot. "It is for thine own sake, not for his, that I bid thee thus forbear," said the Pope, sternly. "I see plainly that thou hatest and persecutest an innocent man."

This argument was taken up by Hilary of Chichester, who had an overweening confidence in his own eloquence. But a fatal blunder in Latin elicited from the Italian followers of the Pope a burst of merriment—"Oportuebat" was too bad for Italian ears. "So you have got badly into *port* at last," said one; and the abashed prelate was unable to proceed with his address. The archbishop of York next spoke with prudent brevity. He was followed by the bishop of Exeter. And then the earl of Arundel asked to be heard in his native tongue. "My lord," he said, "we who do not know Latin have not understood a word of all that the bishops have said." His speech was mild, grave, and conciliatory, and therefore the most embarrassing to the Pontiff. He and the bishops entreated that legates invested with full powers might be sent to England to decide the points in dispute. Alexander agreed to send legates, but would not invest them with full powers. He mistrusted the venality of his cardinals. "To hear appeals ourselves is a privilege we will never consent to surrender," he said.

The ambassadors retreated in haste; their commission had been limited to a few days. The bishops hastened home with precipitation, hearing that certain knights of the neighbourhood, affecting great enthusiasm for the cause of Becket, were waiting to plunder their baggage and persons on the way.

Far different was the progress of the exiled primate. As he entered France he was met by the king's brothers, and offered ample funds for the maintenance of himself and household from the royal treasury. He was received by the king of France at Soissons, and at the head of a splendid retinue of 300 horsemen entered Sens in triumph. The Pope at once granted him the honour of a public audience; he placed Becket on his right hand, and would not allow him to rise to speak. Becket, after a recital of his persecution, spread before the Pope the Constitutions of Clarendon. They were read, and the consistory raised their hands in pious horror, and exclaimed against the interference with ecclesiastical immunities. On further examination the Pope acknowledged that six of them were less evil than the rest; on the remaining ten he pronounced his unqualified condemnation. He rebuked the weakness of Becket in swearing to these articles, and had only praise to bestow on him for his subsequent violation of his oath. Next day, by what seems to be a skilful mode of getting rid of certain objections which had been raised concerning his election, or with desire of ridding himself of an office which would be barren of profit and conducive to much inconvenience, he tendered the resignation of his archiepiscopate to the Pope. He had already been offered brilliant advancement in France. But the Pontiff could not afford to lose a firm supporter of ecclesiastical immunities in England. The conduct of the other English bishops showed that they were indifferent to their preservation, and he restored to Becket his archiepiscopal ring, thus satisfying his primacy. He assured Becket of his protection, and committed him to the hospitable care of the abbot of Pontigny. "You have long lived in ease and opulence," he said; "now learn the lessons of poverty from the poor."

In his seclusion of Pontigny Becket cultivated holiness by putting on the coarse Cistercian dress, and living on the hard and scanty Cistercian fare. Outwardly, he still maintained something of his old magnificence; this called for the remonstrance of some of his friends. But it was whispered by his admirers, with pious exultation, that he wore sackcloth next his skin, and was overrun with lice. The sackcloth was changed but once every forty days, " pur vers et pur suur." [1] At night he lay on the floor, and every evening was scourged by his chaplain. His health suffered. Wild dreams—so reports one of his attendants—haunted his broken slumbers, of cardinals plucking out his eyes and assassins cleaving his tonsured crown.

Henry, on receiving the report of his ambassadors, gave rein to his wrath; he sequestrated the estates of the archbishopric, and forbade the payment of Peter's Pence to the Pope who supported his contumacious subject. He went further, in a fit of that indiscriminating and intemperate rage which sometimes overcame him and led him into fatal mistakes. In the depth of winter he banished all Becket's relatives. Four hundred persons, it is said, of both sexes, of every age, even infants at the breast, were driven out of England with inhuman precipitation. The monasteries of Flanders and of France received the exiles. But their presence served to excite general indignation against the king who had ordered their expatriation.

For two years Becket sought rest in fasting and prayers, and found it not. In his bosom rankled a bitter sense of

[1] Guerner de Pont S. Maxence.

the wrong done him, and impatience to revenge it on the sovereign who had once been his friend, but was now his deadliest enemy. Henry was in France. Becket was suffering from a swollen cheek and toothache. This, though it may have increased his merits, did not mollify his temper.[1] He became more and more irritated against Henry, and his attendants did not fail to fall in with his humour, and urge him to an extreme course. Three times, by letter, did the exile cite his sovereign, in the tone of a superior, to submit to his censure. In the first message the haughty meaning was veiled in blandest words, and sent by a Cistercian of demeanour gentle as his name, Urban. The king returned a short and bitter answer. The second time Becket wrote in severer language, but yet in the spirit, it is said, of compassion and leniency. The king deigned no reply. His third messenger was a tattered barefoot friar. To him Becket, it might seem, with studied insult, not only intrusted a letter to the king threatening him with Divine vengeance, but authorized the friar to speak in his name. With such a messenger the message was not likely to lose in asperity. The king returned an answer even more contemptuous than the address.[2]

Alexander III. had strongly urged moderation on Becket till Easter. Alexander was settling himself in Rome, and his fears of the anti-Pope, Paschal, getting the support of Henry, made him anxious to avoid exasperating the angry monarch. The letter of the Pope had made Easter the limit of forbearance. The wrathful archbishop, chafing under his toothache and his wrongs, spent the holy passiontide in drawing up lists of proscription of those who had in any way incurred his condemnation, that he might cast them out of the Church and cut them off from the fountains of

---

[1] Edward Grim says he was relieved at last by the extraction of two teeth.

[2] "Quin potius dura propinquantes, dura pro duris, immo multo plus duriora prioribus, reportaverunt."—De Bosham.

salvation. The sentence was deferred at the earnest request of some, or it would have been launched at Easter. But on the Sunday after Ascension Day,[1] the archbishop read from the pulpit of the abbey church of Vezelay, to a mixed congregation, the long list of those whom he delivered over to damnation. The bishop of Salisbury he suspended for having inducted John of Oxford into the deanery of Salisbury without the consent of one or two canons of that church, who were with him in exile. He hardly refrained from excommunicating the king by name, being held back by compunction on hearing that Henry was seriously ill. John of Oxford, the archdeacon of Poitiers; Richard de Lucy, and John of Baliol, the authors of the Constitutions of Clarendon, for having dared to recollect and record the traditional laws of England which warred against ecclesiastical privileges; Ranulf de Broc, Hugh de Clare, and many others who had usurped the estates of the see of Canterbury, fell under his condemnation. The whole congregation, we are told, stood aghast.

The sentence of excommunication Becket announced to the Pope and to the bishops of England. He commanded Gilbert of London and his other suffragans to publish the edict in their dioceses. The bishops met, and sent a letter to Becket, couched in terms of caustic irony. " Whatever disturbances your unexpected departure to so great a distance has produced among us, we had hoped, by God's grace and your humble-mindedness, might have been settled.

" It was consolatory to us to hear from all sides that in your exile you indulged in no vain imaginations, but bore with modesty the indigence to which you are reduced by your own acts. It was told us that you were devoted to study and prayer, and that you strove to redeem by fasting and vigils and penance the time you have squandered, and were

---

[1] So the letter of John of Salisbury to Bishop Bartholomew of Exeter.

carving the road to perfection. But now we hear that you have sent the king a denunciatory letter, without affixing to it the ordinary salutations, and that you threaten him with an interdict. Should this sentence so bitterly denounced be as rigidly executed, the hope of tranquillity will be gone, and all that will remain will be irreconcilable hatred. The king raised you to your present elevation against the advice of his mother, and the voice of the whole kingdom; the Church also, as far as she was able, mourned and murmured at it. What will be said of the way in which you repay his favours? Spare your good fame, and respect your honour. Remember that the king was appointed by God, and that he provides for the peace of his subjects. It is to preserve this peace to the Church and people committed to his care that he requires the dignities granted to his ancestors to be confirmed to himself. By what justice, by what law or canon can you assail him with an interdict, and (God forbid the deed!) hew him off by the spiritual axe from Christian unity? It is praiseworthy not to be carried away by passion. You have also condemned, without inquiry, the bishop of Salisbury and his dean, following the heat of your passion rather than the cool course of justice. This is a novelty indeed, not, as we believe, contained in the canons, to condemn a man first and then hear his cause." The letter concluded with a notice of appeal to the Pope.

When Henry heard that his officers had been excommunicated, and that he himself was threatened, his wrath drove him almost mad. No one dared to name Becket in his presence. The ports were guarded against the threatened interdict, and an oath was exacted of all adults by the sheriffs that they would respect no ecclesiastical censure from the archbishop. Henry's passion betrayed him again into an act which strengthened his adversary's hold on the popular sentiment. He threatened the Cistercian Order with confiscation if they harboured the traitor. The abbot

of Pontigny did not dare to risk the vengeance of the
king on the abbeys of his Order in England, and Becket
withdrew to Sens.   From thence he indited an angry
letter to the bishop of London.   "You complain that the
bishop of Salisbury has been inhibited, without citation,
without hearing, without judgment.   Remember the fate
of Ucalegon.   He trembled when his neighbour's house
was on fire."

Gilbert, bishop of London, who had been placed in charge
of the confiscated revenues of the see of Canterbury, had
paid them into the royal chancery.   "The goods of the
Church, the patrimony of the crucified Saviour," wrote
Becket, "I claim of you.   Pay them back to me within forty
days, without excuse, and without delay."

Gilbert answered his letter by a lengthy remonstrance,
couched in solemn, almost pathetic tones :

"With the promise fresh on your lips that you would
not leave the kingdom without the king's consent, you
attempted to fly the realm.   The words of a priest should
always be the companions of truth.   You say it is an
unheard of thing that an archbishop should be cited in
the king's court to render an account of former money
transactions, but you forget that it was an unheard-of thing
to translate suddenly a man from one day following dogs and
hawks, to bending next day before the altar, and ministering
sacred things before all the bishops of the realm.   You fled
at night in disguise, as if your life were in danger, out of the
kingdom, though no one was pursuing you ; and now you
call on us to encounter death for the sake of Christ's Church.
Truly, if we consider the treasures in store for us in heaven,
we shall not regard the things of earth.   For tongue cannot
tell, nor intellect comprehend, the joys of the heavenly city.
And, indeed, our momentary tribulations here will work out
for us an exceeding weight of glory.   But all this I have long
cherished in my bosom, all this has been the subject of my

aspirations. This head, which still rests on my shoulders, would long ago have fallen by the sword of the executioner, if it could have ensured the favour of God upon my earthly pilgrimage. But it is the cause, and not the stroke, that makes the martyr. To suffer persecution for holiness is glorious, but obstinacy and perverseness are ignominious. You bent the knee at Clarendon, you ran away at Northampton; and now with some effrontery you, from a place of security, urge us to rush upon certain death. The sword hangs over us from which you escaped. It would appear that your revenues are so dear to you that you would freely spill our blood to recover them. Yet even the Jews spurned the money Judas brought back, because it was the price of blood. Blessed be God, this is no question of schism of faith, no question about the sacraments, or about morals. Our faith thrives with the king, the bishops, and the people. All the articles of the Creed are adhered to by the clergy of the realm. And if in morals we sometimes go astray, yet no one defends his evil doings, but all hope by repentance to be washed clean. The whole strife is about certain laws of the ancestors of the king, sanctioned by long usage, which he wishes to be observed towards himself. The tree long planted, and with widespread roots, cannot be plucked up in a day. May it please you to remember that our Lord bade His disciples imitate the example of a child, who, though wronged, is not angry, and soon forgets an injury, and compensates for all by the innocence and happiness of its life."

The bishops sent a lengthy epistle to the Pope, who was now at Rome, though not safe there, threatened by the redoubtable emperor, Frederick Barbarossa. John of Oxford, dean of Salisbury, who had been excommunicated by Becket, was the bearer of the letter. Becket also wrote to the Pope to counteract the influence of the dean of Salisbury. He described the king as a malignant tyrant; he represented Christ as crucified afresh in the person of himself, and he deprecated the sending of legates to try his case. Whilst John of Oxford was in Rome, Frederick Barbarossa was collecting the mighty army which swept, during the next year, through Italy, made him master of Rome, and witnessed his coronation and the enthronement of the anti-Pope. Pope Alexander could not afford to quarrel with Henry of England. He confirmed John of Oxford in the deanery of Salisbury, but wrote to Becket to apologize for so doing. He was obliged to do so, he said, through fear of offending the English king. Vast sums of English money were at this time pouring into Italy, to be expended in the support of Alexander against the emperor Frederick. The king of Sicily, the Frangipani, and the family of Peter Leonis were retained in their fidelity to the Pope by this means. Henry bribed the cardinals, and all who had access to the ear of the Pope. Becket complained piteously that Henry had boasted of having found everything venal in Rome.

In December, 1166, the Pope conceded what the king and the English bishops had long demanded. He appointed William of Pavia, cardinal of S. Peter's, and Otho, cardinal of S. Nicolas, to be his legates in France, to decide the cause of Becket, and, in the meantime, suspended all Becket's acts, by papal authority. At the same time Alexander III. wrote to the archbishop to entreat him to be more moderate, and, if necessary, to use dissimulation,[1] on account of the difficulties of the times.

John of Oxford hastened back to England with the joyful tidings. Becket and his friends were in despair. They could only hope, if not pray, for the death of the feeble Pope. "The Pope has strangled the Church!" exclaimed the archbishop. He had no confidence in the integrity of the

[1] "Si non omnia secundum beneplacitum succedant, ad præsens dissimulet."

judges. " The one," he wrote, " is weak and versatile, the other, treacherous and crafty."

But the departure of the cardinal legates from Rome was delayed with prudent design till the crisis for the Pope was past. They did not arrive in France till the autumn of 1167, when already plague had ravaged the army of Frederick, and Frederick himself was in full flight with the wreck from Rome. The Pope was now no longer in danger, and his need for temporizing was at an end.

But Becket had resolved already to dispute the authority of at least one of his judges. William of Pavia, he was satisfied, would not favour him. He wrote a letter to him so full of violence that John of Salisbury urgently entreated him, and at last persuaded him, to burn it. He wrote a second ; it was almost as insolent and intemperate. At last he was persuaded to assume a milder tone. To Cardinal Otho, on the other hand, his language bordered on adulation.

In the meantime his warmest and best friend, John of Salisbury, had been indefatigable in his entreaties to the archbishop to be more moderate in his conduct, not to give way to the vehemence of his disposition, and to withdraw the sentences of excommunication he had showered in such abundance. He wrote sorrowfully to his friends, the archbishop of Constance and the archdeacon Reginald, that all his efforts had ended in disappointment.

The legates visited Becket at Sens, and then met King Henry at Rouen. After long negotiations, purposely protracted to gain time, a meeting was agreed upon, to be held on the borders of French and English territory, between Gisors and Trie.

Becket was annoyed at being summoned at a time when he was unable to gather an imposing suite of horsemen. Louis of France and Henry of England came to the appointed place on the appointed day, November 23, 1167. The night before the interview took place, the archbishop dreamed that he was offered poison in a golden cup. "The dream was verified," says Herbert de Bosham, "for Cardinal William of Pavia was a man of elegant speech, and smooth and persuasive words. He seemed to be actuated by a love of peace; but when his words were considered, they were found to be fraught with danger to the liberties of the Church." The cardinals urgently entreated Becket to come to terms with the king, and return to his Church, and say nothing more about the constitutions. "The king will, no doubt, tacitly withdraw them. Of this we have a precedent in the case of a bishop who bestows holy orders on a clerk; he does not mention the obligation to celibacy, yet the clerk is bound to observe it." Becket replied that, "As to the constitutions, he would rather bow his neck to the executioner than swear to obey them." The appeal of the bishops was next gone into. Becket inveighed against their obsequiousness to the crown. He declared that he would submit to no judgment but that of the Pope in person.

The king went to Argences near Caen, and the cardinals followed him, and were present when he held there a gathering of the Norman and English prelates. He was getting impatient of delay, and suspected that the cardinal legates would play him false in the end. He treated them with discourtesy. He went out hawking when they expected to meet him; and when they did meet, he said, rudely, in an undertone, which they could not fail to hear, "Would to God I might never clap eyes on a cardinal again."

When all were assembled, the king of England said that he claimed 44,000 marks of silver on account of revenues committed to Becket when he was chancellor, and of which the archbishop refused to give account. "His lordship of Canterbury," said the bishop of London, "thinks that consecration cancels debts as baptism blots out sin."

When the assembly broke up, Henry with tears entreated the cardinals to rid him of the troublesome churchman. The tears of William of Pavia flowed in sympathy, but Otho could hardly suppress his laughter.

The legates gave no definite answer, but it was arranged that envoys should be sent to the Pope for instructions. Becket wrote at the same time to Alexander. William of Pavia gave notice that, till next S. Martin's Day, Becket must abstain from all excommunications and from laying an interdict on the realm. The Pope, anxious to protract the case so as not to offend Henry by approving of the conduct of Becket, nor to throw over Becket, who was contending for the liberties of the Church, confirmed this inhibition. Becket was moved to bitterness of spirit by this hesitation. His thunders were restrained for another twelvemonth. He complained to Alexander that every deputation from the king won fresh concessions. The Pope was at Benevento; he could not remain in safety in Rome, and he still needed the support of Henry, for Frederick Barbarossa was still a danger. He was endeavouring to detach the king of Sicily from his alliance with the Pope. Alexander wrote soothing letters to Becket to explain that the concessions he made were temporary, and would be withdrawn when the difficulties in which he was placed diminished. " Temporary ! " wrote Becket back, in a letter full of indignation. "And this at a time when the Church of England is tottering. This fatal dispensation will be a precedent for ages. But for me and my fellow exiles, all the authority of Rome had ceased for ever in England. There had been none to maintain the Pope's authority against that of the king."

Great efforts were made now on all sides to bring about a reconciliation. Mediators were appointed, and passed between the king and the archbishop. Becket proposed to swear obedience to the customs and constitutions of the realm, " saving the honour of God," instead of the obnoxious qualification, "saving my order." But the mediators insisted on his throwing himself unreservedly on the mercy of the king, without reservation. Becket at length, and with great repugnance, yielded. He left them with the impression that he had promised to do so; and a meeting between him and the king was appointed to be held on the ensuing feast of the Epiphany (1169) at Montmirail. The king of France was to be present, who was then on terms of friendship with the king of England.

On his way to Montmirail, De Bosham whispered in his ear a caution not to show weakness as he had at Clarendon. The warning was not thrown away. In reply he gave De Bosham an expressive look. Becket then threw himself at the feet of the king. Henry raised him, and the archbishop began to entreat the king to show mercy to the English Church. Everyone listened for the important words to which this address was a preamble. "On the subject that divides us, my lord king," said Becket, "I throw myself on your mercy and on your pleasure, here in the presence of our lord the king of France and the archbishops, princes, and others standing round." He paused, and then added distinctly, "Saving the honour of my God."

At this unexpected breach of his agreement, the mediators, even his own most ardent admirers, stood aghast. The king burst into a paroxysm of fury, and poured forth a torrent of abuse, reproaching the archbishop for pride, vanity, and obstinacy. Then turning to the king of France, he said, " Take notice, my lord, whatever his lordship of Canterbury disapproves, he will say is contrary to God's honour, and so he will be always tripping me up. But that I may not be thought to despise God's honour, I will make this proposal. There have been kings of England of greater or less power than myself. There have been good and holy

archbishops of Canterbury before him. Now let him be-
have towards me as the most holy of his predecessors have
behaved towards the least of mine, and I am satisfied."

All present exclaimed, "Enough condescension for the
king." Louis of France said, "My lord archbishop, do you
wish to be more than a saint?" Becket remained unmoved.
"True," he said, "there have been holier archbishops before
me, and they extirpated some abuses. If they had rooted
all out, I should not be exposed to this fiery trial."

The mediators drew him aside and urged, "Give the
king due honour, and suppress the offensive phrase. Now
or never must a reconciliation be made." The papal envoys, the bishops, certain abbots and the nobles present, in
vain endeavoured to move him. Night came on, and the
king withdrew one way, and the archbishop another. As
Becket rode away, his intimate friend, John, bishop of
Poitiers, reproached him with bringing destruction on the
Church. The archbishop replied, "Nay brother, take care
that the Church be not destroyed by you, for by me, by
God's grace, she shall never suffer." Robert de Haughton,
one of the clerks of the archbishop, was riding before him.
His horse stumbled. "Come up," said the rider, "saving
the honour of God and my Order." The archbishop heard
the remark, and his brow contracted, but he said nothing.

At Chartres, where Louis was sleeping as well as Becket,
the French king refrained from calling at the lodgings of the
archbishop, as a mark of his disapproval, and Becket left
for Sens next day without having seen him. But the populace, who had heard that Becket had defied kings, little as
they understood what the question mooted was, sided with
the prelate, and received him with shouts of applause as
he rode into Sens.

But the peace between the two kings was of brief duration.
Some acts of Henry towards the Bretons and Poitevins

excited the wrath of Louis, and led him to break off his alliance with the king of England.

As Becket had left Montmirail, he had caught the scoff of a baron, " England and France are both now closed to the impracticable man." He was sitting at Sens a few days after the meeting, discussing his prospects with his clerks. Some of them remarked on France being no longer safe for him, and asked whither he would go. Becket replied, " Though both England and France be closed to me, I am not undone. One thing I am determined not to do—I will not apply to those Roman robbers who have no interest save in plundering the needy. I will go to Burgundy." At that moment an officer of the king of France entered, and required Becket to attend him to the king, who was then in Sens. " It is to receive notice of banishment," said one of the clerks. " Do not forbode ill," said the archbishop ; " you are not a prophet, nor of the sons of the prophets."

When they came to the king's lodgings, Louis threw himself on his knees before the archbishop, and exclaimed, " Forgive me, forgive me ! You are the only wise man among us."

The envoys of the Pope had received a double set of letters to be used as circumstances indicated. They now served on Henry letters from the sovereign Pontiff, threatening him with the vengeance of the Holy Father if he did not come to terms with Becket.

" And now," says Herbert de Bosham, " the archbishop neither could nor would have patience any longer. He would not spare those whom even the apostolic Pope had by his paramount authority absolved. He smote them with the sword of God's word, and bound them by a sentence of anathema, and sent letters of excommunication to the proper persons. This sentence was passed on clerks and laymen of the court, on some for having received farms belonging to his see from the king, during his exile, on others for having violently possessed themselves of ecclesiastical property."

On Palm Sunday the thunders were launched. Gilbert Foliot, bishop of London, Joscelin of Salisbury, the archdeacon of Salisbury, Richard de Lucy, grand justiciary, and many others, were named. He announced this excommunication to the archbishop of Rouen, and reminded him that whoever presumed to give meat or drink, or a friendly salutation to one of these on whom the ban had fallen, subjected himself likewise to the same excommunication. "Those excommunicate were some of the king's most familiar counsellors, and the number of them, some excommunicated by name, others by associating with those excommunicated, was so great that there was hardly one in the king's chapel who could offer his majesty the kiss of peace at the Mass."

Becket inhibited Roger, bishop of Worcester, when he entreated permission to communicate with his brethren. "What fellowship is there," he asked, "between Christ and Belial?" An emissary of Becket had the boldness to enter S. Paul's cathedral, in London, on Ascension Day, and thrust the sentence into the hands of the officiating priest at the offertory, and then to proclaim with a loud voice to the assembled congregation, "Know all men, that Gilbert, bishop of London, is excommunicated by Thomas, archbishop of Canterbury, and legate of the Pope."

He escaped with some difficulty from ill-usage by the people. Foliot immediately summoned his clergy. To them he declared the illegality, the injustice, the nullity of an excommunication without citation, hearing, or trial, and renewed his appeal to the Pope, during which the sentence of Becket must remain in abeyance. The dean of S. Paul's and all the clergy, except some monastic priests, joined in the appeal. The bishop of Exeter declined, nevertheless, to give to Foliot the kiss of peace.

Geoffrey Ridel, archdeacon of Canterbury, was excommunicated. The bishop of Hereford was cited to appear at Sens before his primate. He could not obtain permission to cross the water. The bishop of Winchester was dying. "I," he wrote, "sinking under disease and old age, have received a summons from the Almighty, and am incapacitated from appealing to an earthly tribunal." He sent money and necessaries to Becket, and published his sentence in his cathedral.

Henry at once sent Gilbert of London to Rome to prosecute his appeal in person, and the bishop of Seez to Louis to request the banishment from French soil of the troublesome primate.

Joscelin of Salisbury boasted that, if the Pope should die, Henry had the whole college of cardinals in his pay, and could name his Pope. Becket was alarmed at the influence of Henry's gold, and he wrote to Vivian, the new papal legate, to entreat him to beware of its insidious corruption.

But Alexander's affairs wore a more prosperous aspect now, and he was less dependent on Henry's largesses to his partisans. He began, yet cautiously, to show his real bias. He appointed as his new legates a lawyer named Gratian, nephew of Eugenius III., and Vivian, an advocate, as his associate. He wrote, however, to Becket to stay his shower of anathemas, and if he had really—as he could hardly believe—already cast them, then to suspend their powers till the appeals were heard.

The legates first visited King Henry, and Gratian spoke firmly and energetically in favour of the course Becket had pursued. Vivian, on the other hand, was prepared to see that there was reason in what the king urged. He took bribes to such an extent that his convoy of rich presents interfered with his travelling quickly. The interview took place at Damport on August 23. It lasted all day: as one legate blew hot, the other blew cold. At sunset the king burst out of the council chamber, swearing by the eyes of God that he would not submit to the terms imposed on him. Gratian firmly said, "Think not to threaten us; we come from a court which is accustomed to command emperors and kings." The king then rehearsed before his barons the offers he had made, so as to compromise the matter with the archbishop.

Another meeting was appointed to be held at Bayeux. The king came attended by the archbishops of Rouen and Bordeaux, the bishop of Le Mans, and all the Norman prelates. Only one English bishop appeared—Roger of Worcester. The king stated his grievances. The ex-chancellor would give no account of the money he had received whilst in office, and the king believed that he had squandered of it as much as 30,000 marks (£20,000). Next day the assembly met at Le Bar. The king requested the legates to absolve his chaplains without any oath; and, on their refusal, he sprang on his horse, and swore that he would never be friends with Becket, and never restore him to Canterbury, even if the Pope were to entreat him. The legates partially gave way, and the king returned to the hall of assembly. At length he consented to the return of Becket to Canterbury, if one of the legates would cross over with him, and absolve those labouring under the anathema of the archbishop. Vivian consented to do this, but Gratian refused. "Then I care not an egg for you or your excommunications," said the harassed monarch.

The envoys of the Pope were now thoroughly roused into hostility to Henry. There was no getting him to yield to Becket the point of unqualified submission. The archbishop now again felt himself at liberty to fling his anathemas. He wrote to the archbishop of Rouen, announcing that he had again proclaimed his excommunications, and threatening to lay the realm under an interdict, and excommunicate the king, unless the wrongs done to the see of Canterbury by those who had possessed themselves of its lands and benefices, without his consent, were fully righted.

But the Pope was still desirous of a reconciliation, and in January, 1170, he directed a fresh commission to Rotrou, archbishop of Rouen, and Bernard, bishop of Nevers, to endeavour to reconcile the king and the archbishop. The archbishop of Rouen had been favourably disposed towards Becket, till disgusted and alienated by his arrogance and violence;[1] the bishop of Nevers was a man of moderation, who had written a sensible letter to the Pope on the king's affairs.

Becket demanded of the king that 1,000 marks should be paid in compensation to those of his family who had been banished; that all those laymen who had taken advantage of his absence to possess themselves of lands belonging to the Church of Canterbury should be turned out, and that the king should give him the kiss of peace. The legates were to require the king to fulfil these conditions. The compensation was, indeed, not to be insisted on, and the kiss was to be given, if the king refused it, by his son Henry; but the surrender of all the lands of Canterbury was the point to which he was to be held fast. It was not that the king had himself appropriated these, but that various laymen had done so, and these laymen he was to eject. Curiously enough, Becket now demanded that which he had rejected with such vehemence before. If the ecclesiastical immunities were to be maintained, then these invaders of the property of the Church might only be tried in his diocesan court, and sentenced to be excommunicated. Excommunication had been tried, and had lost its force; and Becket

---

[1] "All his actions proceed from either pride or passion," was Rotrou's estimate of the character of Becket."—John of Salisbury.

was fain to abandon the principle for which he had battled, and appeal to the civil power to eject the usurpers. Consequently, nothing more was said about ecclesiastical immunities, that subject fell into the background. Thenceforth the contest was on other points.

Gilbert Foliot, bishop of London, had been to Rome and obtained his absolution from the Pope. He proclaimed it at Rouen on his way home, and was received to communion by the archbishop of Rouen in his cathedral on Easter Day.

The wrath of Becket broke all bounds. He wrote in angry remonstrance to Rotrou, but his fiercest expressions of disgust were crushed into a letter which he sent to one of the cardinals at Rome. The absolution of Foliot he characterized as an unbinding of Satan. " I know," he wrote, " that in the court of Rome the Lord's side is always sacrificed—that Barabbas escapes and Christ is put to death. . . . With you, the wretched, the exiles, the innocent are condemned, because they are the poor of Christ, and weak ; while, on the other hand, you absolve the sacrilegious, murderers, robbers, impenitent, whom Peter himself could not absolve in the sight of God. Let him dare (he is speaking of the Pope) to bind without regard to the sentence of the coming Judge. Let him absolve robbers, sacrilegious men, murderers, perjurers, men of blood, schismatics, without repentance. I will never remit to the impenitent the things they have taken from the Church. Is it not our spoils, or rather those of the Church, which the king's emissaries use for bribing the cardinals at Rome? . . . I will no longer trouble that court; let those resort thither who prevail in their iniquities ! "[1]

In the meantime Henry was busy with preparations for the coronation of his eldest son, who, in February, 1170, completed his fifteenth year. This was a new cause of alarm and anger for Becket. He, as archbishop of Canterbury and

[1] S. Thom. Ep. 31.

primate, claimed the right to crown, and, in his absence, that honour would fall to the share of his enemy, the archbishop of York. He appealed to the Pope to stay this interference with the privileges of his see, this audacious presumption of the archbishop of York to confer the crown and anoint. The Pope sent letters inhibiting the archbishop of York and the bishops of England from performing the ceremony. The letters arrived the day before the coronation, and the archbishop and bishops prudently forgot to open them till the ceremony was over. On Sunday, June 14, 1170, the young Henry was crowned in Westminster Abbey, by the archbishop of York, with the assistance of the bishops of London, Salisbury, Rochester, Seez, and others.

The archbishop of Rouen and his colleague now renewed their efforts at mediation, and found Henry inclined to peace, chiefly through fear of the interdict which he knew was prepared to be launched.

Becket was persuaded by the archbishop of Sens to meet the king of England at Freteval, between Tours and Chartres; and on July 22 he was admitted to an interview with Henry. Immediately on seeing the archbishop approach, the king hastened to meet him, and, uncovering his head, anticipated him in uttering a salutation. The old points of difference were avoided. Nothing was said of the Constitutions, or of the immunity of the clergy, the inconvenience of which Becket now himself experienced. It was promised that Becket should be allowed to return to England with all his kinsmen and attendants, without any oath being exacted from them; and harmony seemed restored. But the late coronation rankled in the heart of the primate, and he told the king that it was his purpose to inflict excommunication on those bishops who had taken part in it. The king said, in reply, that his son should be crowned anew by Becket along with the princess, his wife. On receiving this promise

Becket was delighted—to recrown him whom the northern primate had crowned would be the most notorious exhibition of contempt for the person who had dared to perform the ceremony. In his joy at the prospect of thus humbling his old enemy, he threw himself off his horse, and would have cast himself at the feet of the king. But Henry alighted, and held the stirrup for the archbishop, to assist him in mounting.

This was a service rendered by emperors to popes, and the performance of it by the king of England to a subject filled the heart of Becket with pride.

The king, in accordance with his promise to restore the property of the exiles, and of the Church of Canterbury, wrote to his son to see to this at once; but the execution of the order naturally met with delay, as the intruders raised every possible impediment to their ejection.

Not one jot of his claims would Becket abate. The castle of Rochester he still insisted was his. The castle of Salt-wood was less doubtfully the possession of the see ; from this Ranulf de Broc must be expelled.

Finding that the castles and lands were not vacated at once, Becket sent to the king to inquire the reason. "The king," says Herbert de Bosham, "as his manner was, put off, put off, and again put off."

As for the castle of Rochester, the king entirely disputed the right of the archbishop to hold it. The place was of importance, necessary for the defence of the Thames and the approach to London, and could not be left in the unarmed hands of a priest.

However, Becket determined to return to Canterbury. But, before doing so, he sent a boy across the channel with letters of suspension and excommunication pronounced against the archbishop of York and those bishops who had dared to assist him in his sacrilegious invasion of the prero-

gatives of the primacy of Canterbury, by crowning Prince
Henry in Westminster Abbey.[1] The king had hoped that
by consenting to have Henry crowned again by Becket, this
excommunication would have been obviated. But, no! Becket
never forgave an enemy. Before sailing, a rough sea-captain
remonstrated with Herbert de Bosham, "Are you mad? The
whole country is exasperated against the archbishop, especially the party of the king, who complain that he has thrown
everything into confusion by his anathemas and excommunications of the bishops, and that, too, at the period of Advent,
when he ought to be doing his utmost to preserve peace and
tranquillity."

After a favourable passage, Becket landed at Sandwich
(December 3) with the archiepiscopal banner flying, and with
the people shouting, "Blessed is he that cometh in the
name of the Lord!" He was met by Gervase de Cornhill,
sheriff of Kent, and others, in arms, asking him to absolve the
bishops. No! not in the moment of joy on returning, after
long exile, to his native land, would he extend forgiveness to
those who had infringed his prerogatives. After some high
words, the sheriff and his companions withdrew, at the instance of John of Oxford.

On the following day the archbishop proceeded to Canterbury. The news of his landing had spread, and the general
enthusiasm among those who had nothing to lose and much
to gain by his return, rendered his journey a scene of
triumph. Priests and people crowded to meet him. They
stripped off their clothes, and spread them in the way, and
sang, "Blessed is he that cometh in the name of the Lord!"

Strange resemblance, and yet strange contrast, to the
Palm Sunday procession. Thomas was on his way to
martyrdom; and the people, though ignorant of this, seemed
impelled to copy in detail the incidents of the ride into

[1] The archbishop of York was suspended, the other bishops were excommunicated.

Jerusalem. But what a contrast, when we look from the heart of the Son of David to that of Becket—from the former glowing with love, to the latter foaming with wrath and panting for the humiliation of his enemies!

As the archbishop entered the cathedral his face was flushed with exultation. He gave the monks the kiss of peace. De Bosham whispered to him, " My lord, now we need not care how soon you leave the world, for this day the Church has conquered in you ; " to which Becket replied only by a look.

Next morning the sheriff of Kent, with other officers of the king, appeared again, to urge the withdrawal of the sentence of excommunication launched against the bishops for having crowned Prince Henry. They were accompanied by some clerks from the prelates themselves, who remonstrated against the proceedings of the primate : when his suffragans were full of joy at his return, and ready to receive him with open arms and honour, they were met with a rebuff, with curse and denunciation : they complained that the archbishop should have returned after his long absence, not as the dove with the olive-leaf of peace, but with fire and sword, as a persecuting invader, trampling down his brethren, and making them his footstool. Becket was not to be moved. He would only absolve them if they would bind themselves by oath to obey the Pope's commands. It is said that the bishops of London and Salisbury were disposed to take this oath under protest of its being unconstitutionally exacted of them, but were dissuaded by Roger of York, who boasted that he had both the courts of the king and of the Pope in his pay, and that he was willing to empty his coffers, to spend eight, nay ten, thousand pounds, to put down Becket's insolence ; and the three prelates proceeded together to the king in Normandy.[1]

[1] Roger of York was notorious for his pride and avarice. The most notorious

The interval until Christmas was taken up in a visit to London, and in turning out clerks who had been intruded into livings.

It was noticed that persons of rank and wealth held aloof from him in cold indignation. He was isolated from all but the poor, whose love and devotion he bought by abundant alms.

In the meantime the archbishop of York and the other bishops under excommunication had reached the king at Bures, near Bayeux. " My lord," said the archbishop, " I alone of the three have the power of opening my mouth and speaking to your majesty; for my two colleagues (the bishops of London and Salisbury) are excommunicated, interdicted the use of fire and water. No one dares hold converse with them, for fear of being involved in the sentence which that ungrateful man has launched against all who were concerned in your son's coronation."

" By God's eyes," exclaimed the king, in a rage, " if all who were concerned in my son's coronation are to be excommunicated, I will be one of the number."

The popular demonstrations with which the archbishop had everywhere been received were represented as of a seditious tendency. The king was wrought up into one of his uncontrollable fits of fury. Gilbert Foliot of London is said to have endeavoured, with tears, to mitigate his wrath. " Have patience, sire," urged also Roger of York; "this storm cannot last long. Let him go on his own way for the present."

" What would you have me do ? " asked the king. " It is

display of his contentiousness was at a council held by a papal legate in 1176. Finding Richard of Canterbury seated in the place which he claimed for himself on the ground of his earlier consecration, he sat himself down in the southern archbishop's lap—" irreverenter natibus innitens," says Stephen of Birchington (Wharton, Angl. Sacr. i. 9), whereupon some of Richard's clerks dragged him down on the floor and tore his robes. The legate broke up the council in alarm.

not our duty to advise your majesty," answered the archbishop of York, "you must consult with your barons; it is
for them to say what ought to be done." One of the prelates unluckily said—probably Roger of York—"So long as
Thomas lives, there is no peace for the realm." "A fellow
who has eaten my bread has lifted up his heel against me!"
cried the king. "He insults over my favours, dishonours the
whole royal race, tramples down the whole kingdom. A
fellow who first broke into my court on a lame horse, with a
cloak for a saddle, swaggers on my throne, whilst you,
false varlets! look on, and have not attempted to rid me of
this insolent priest."

These hasty, unconsidered words were heard and caught
up by four knights, men of high connections, and officers of
the household—Reginald Fitzurse, Hugh de Morville,
William De Tracy, and Richard le Breton. Stung by the
king's reproaches, and thinking to gratify him by carrying
out his apparent wish, the four set out for England and hurried to the coast, whence, embarking at different ports, two
of them were conveyed to Winchelsea, and the others to a
harbour near Dover. "They landed," says Grim, "at
Dog's Haven—they who from that time deserved to be
called dogs and wretches, not knights and soldiers." On
Holy Innocents Day they reached Saltwood, and were
received by Ranulf de Broc.

While this was passing Becket had been subjected to fresh
annoyances. A shipload of wine sent him from France had
been seized by Ranulf de Broc, who, however, by order of
the young king Henry, was obliged to give it up. The
De Brocs hunted in his chase, killed his deer, carried off his
dogs, and Robert De Broc, the brother of Ranulf, cut off
the tail of one of the archiepiscopal sumpter-horses. Becket's
temper was exasperated to the highest pitch by these provo-
cations. On Christmas Day, at High Mass, after preaching

on the text, "On earth peace to men of goodwill," he passed from the uncongenial subject with flushed cheek and flashing eyes to the excommunication, in tones "fierce, indignant, fiery, and bold," of Nigel de Sackville, for obtaining the church of Harrow, into which he had been intruded during the exile; of another priest, the vicar of Thirlwood, guilty of a like offence; and of the brothers De Broc for cutting the tail off his horse, stopping the passage of his wines, and for other outrages against the property of the Church of Canterbury. The docking his horse's tail seemed specially to have rankled in his breast, for he spoke of it—the fact is recorded by all his biographers—from the pulpit, and made it one chief reason for pronouncing excommunication on the De Brocs. He recurred to it again with bitterness when face to face with his murderers. As for the three bishops who had not shrunk from encroaching on the rights of Canterbury by crowning the young king, their excommunication was emphatically renewed. "May they be cursed," he concluded, in a voice of thunder, "by Jesus Christ, and may their memory be blotted out of the assembly of the saints, whoever shall sow hatred and discord between me and the king!" An incongruous conclusion to a Christmas sermon on a text promising peace and goodwill.

After the meeting with the bishops at Bures, Henry, acting on their advice, took counsel with his barons what had better be done. The earl of Leicester said: "My lord, the archbishop was my father's intimate friend, but since he gave up your favour and left the kingdom, we have not been in communication." De Bohun, the uncle of the excommunicated bishop of Salisbury, then spoke: "The only way to deal with such a fellow is to plait some withes into a rope and haul him up on a gallows."

Finally it was decided that the tutors of the young king

Henry at Winchester should march privately with the house·
hold troops to Canterbury, and arrest the primate. The
absence of the four knights was noticed, and orders were
sent for their recall.

It is not clear on what day the fatal exclamation of the
king was made : Fitz-Stephen reports it as taking place on
Sunday, the 27th of December; others date it back to the 24th.
The knights were at Saltwood on December 28th, and there
they heard of the new excommunication hurled by Becket
against their host on Christmas Day. Early next morning
they issued orders in the king's name for a troop of soldiers
to be levied, and attended by Robert de Broc—Ranulf
was away—they rode into Canterbury and lodged with
Clarembald, abbot of S. Augustine's, who was a partisan of
the king and disliked Becket.

On Tuesday, the 29th of December,[1] as the day was
closing in, the knights rode to the archbishop's palace. It
was about three o'clock in the afternoon. The knights
wore their armour under the ordinary dress of civil life, but
without weapons. The archbishop's dinner was over, but
some of his retainers were still at table. Their presence
was announced. "Let them come in," said Becket; but
when they entered, with studied disrespect, he did not look
at them, but continued his conversation with the monk who
sat next him, and on whose shoulder he was leaning. There
were then with him John of Salisbury, Fitz-Stephen, and
Edward Grim, all three of whom have left us a minute
account of what followed.

The knights on entering seated themselves on the floor at
the feet of the archbishop. Becket then turned and gazed

[1] Tuesday was a significant day in Becket's life. On a Tuesday he had been
born, on a Tuesday he had been baptized, on a Tuesday he fled from Northampton,
on a Tuesday left the king's court in Normandy, on a Tuesday left England an exile,
on a Tuesday, at Pontigny, had by dream his forewarning of martyrdom, on a Tuesday
returned from exile, on a Tuesday died, and on a Tuesday his relics were translated.

steadfastly at them. After a few moments of silence he greeted De Tracy by name. The conspirators looked mutely at one another, till Fitzurse, who throughout took the lead, replied with a scornful expression, "God help you!" Becket's face grew crimson. "We have a message for you from the king," said Fitzurse. "Will you hear it in private or in public?" "As you wish," said the archbishop. "Nay, as *you* wish," said Fitzurse. "As you wish," repeated Becket, and signed to the monks to withdraw. They obeyed, but left the door ajar, that they might see and hear what went on. Fitzurse had hardly begun to speak before Becket, conscious of his danger, hastily recalled the monks, and in their presence Fitzurse resumed his statement of the complaints of the king. It is said that in the moment when they were alone with Becket, the thought entered the head of one of them to wrest his crozier from him and beat out his brains with it. When the clerks had returned, the knights remonstrated with the archbishop for having broken his agreement with the king, for having suspended and excommunicated the bishops who had taken part in the coronation, for excommunicating on Christmas Day some of the servants of the king, and for going about the country with formidable troops of followers and exciting the people to demonstrations which endangered the peace of the realm. "You have excited disturbances in the kingdom, and the king requires you to answer for them at his court." "Never," said the archbishop, "shall the sea come between me and my Church again, unless I am dragged hence by my feet." "You have excommunicated the bishops, and you must absolve them." "You must go to the Pope for that," answered Becket. He then appealed, in language which is variously reported, to the promises of the king at their interview in the preceding July, and intimated that these promises had not been kept.

"What is this you say?" Fitzurse exclaimed. "Do you dare to accuse the king of falsehood?" "Reginald, Reginald," answered Becket, "I do no such thing; but I appeal to those who were present, and you were one of them."

"I never saw or heard anything of the sort," said Fitzurse. "You were there," said Becket; "I saw you."

The knights, irritated by contradiction, swore, "by God's wounds," that they had borne with him long enough. Becket, in spite of the entreaty of John of Salisbury, continued the scene, by bringing forward his complaints. "My sumpter-horse's tail has been docked, my casks of wine have been carried off." Hugh de Morville answered, "Why have you not complained to the king of these outrages, instead of punishing them by your own authority?"

"Hugh," exclaimed the archbishop, "I wait no man's permission to avenge them. I will not give to the king the things that are God's. This is my business, and I alone will see to it."

At this haughty and defiant speech the knights sprang up, and their rage manifested itself in their infuriated gestures. "You threaten us!" exclaimed Fitzurse, wringing his long gloves in the excitement of his passion. "Are you about to excommunicate us also?" "He has excommunicated too many already," muttered one of the others.

"You threaten me in vain," said Becket, also springing up; "were all the swords in England drawn against me, you could not scare me from my obedience to God and the Pope."

"Who are on the king's side?" asked Fitzurse. "Let them stand off." No one withdrew. Fitzurse cried, "Guard him, lest he escape." "I shall not fly," said the archbishop. They went to the door. One said, "It is you who threaten us," and he muttered something in an undertone. The archbishop caught the words and ran after them to fling after them the last defiance: "I did not come here to run away, and I care nothing for your threats."

On entering the palace the knights had posted their followers opposite the gate. These were now called in, and the gate was fastened. The knights threw off their cloaks and gowns under a large sycamore in the garden, and girt on their swords. The servants of the archbishop fastened the door of the hall. In the meantime John of Salisbury was urging Becket to moderation. "It is wonderful, my lord," he said, "that you never take anyone's advice; it always was so, and always is your way, to do and say just what seems good to yourself alone." "What would you have me do?" asked Becket. "You ought to have consulted your friends, knowing that these men only seek occasion to kill you." "I am prepared to die," said the archbishop. "But we are not," added John; "so far as I can see no one cares to die without a cause, except yourself." The archbishop answered, "Let God's will be done." The dialogue was interrupted by one of the monks rushing in to announce that the knights were arming. "Let them arm," said Becket. Presently the blows of an axe were heard, as if the knights were trying to break down the door of the hall. Terrified by this noise, the monks and clergy fled in all directions. "All monks are cowards," said Becket, looking after them scornfully. A small band of intimate friends and faithful attendants remained by him. They dragged him along the cloister towards the cathedral. Two locked doors had to be passed, the first lock had to be wrenched off. Two cellarers, attracted by the noise, ran upon the other side and pulled off the second lock.[1] The archbishop struggled to get loose, his attendants pulled and pushed him. "Let me go, do not drag me!" he continued crying, and once he stubbornly refused to proceed till his crozier was

[1] Benedict of Peterb. 64.

brought and carried before him. At last they reached the door at the lower north transept of the cathedral, by the chapel of S. Benedict, from which a flight of steps led into the choir. As he entered, the knights were seen at the further end of the cloister, in pursuit. His attendants attempted to shut the door, and urged him to escape up the flight of steps in the wall to the chapel of S. Blaze, or hide in the triforium. But Becket was determined to be a martyr. He would not be saved from the death that threatened. He forced the attendants from the door and threw it open for the knights to enter, shouting to his clerks, "Away, you cowards! The church must not be turned into a castle."

Then the ecclesiastics who had clung to him fled in every direction, some to altars in the side chapels, some to the secret chambers in the roof and walls of the minster.

Vespers were in progress when the archbishop entered, but were interrupted by the scuffle.

Becket was ascending the steps into the choir, when Fitzurse rushed in from the cloister, shouting, "King's men! King's men!" Then stumbling in the dusk against a clerk, he asked, "Where is Thomas Becket, where is the traitor?" "Reginald," answered Becket, "here I am; no traitor, but a priest of God. What do you want?" And he descended the steps to meet him, and planted himself between the pillar that supports the chapel of S. Blaze and the wall that forms the south-west corner of the chapel of S. Benedict. Here the knights and their followers gathered round him, whilst De Morville kept back the crowd which poured in at the west doors of the minster.

"Absolve the bishops whom you have excommunicated," said the knights. "Never," answered Becket, "till they have made satisfaction." The knights tried to lift him on the shoulders of De Tracy, to carry him out of the church.

Becket struggled furiously, and flung De Tracy down on the pavement. Fitzurse held him by the collar of his long cloak, and said, " Come with us, you are our prisoner."

" Scoundrel ! "[1] exclaimed Becket, " I will not fly," and he wrenched the cloak from his grasp. Tracy had risen, Grim threw his arms round Becket and vainly endeavoured to draw him away. Fitzurse, brandishing his sword, stepped forward.

" Reginald ! " gasped the archbishop, " do not touch me ; you owe me fealty ! you pander." At this intolerable word the knight " glowed all over," and, striking with the point of his sword, dashed off his cap. The archbishop covered his eyes with his joined hands, bent his head, and committed his cause to God and the saints. Tracy then raised his sword, and Grim, wrapping his arm in a cloak, lifted it to ward off the stroke ; but the weapon almost severed the monk's arm, and descending on the archbishop's head, cut off the tonsured part of his crown. The next blow, whether struck by Tracy or Fitzurse, was with the flat of the sword. Becket recoiled, half stunned, and put his hands over his bleeding head. When the blood began to run over his face, he wiped it away with his arm, and said, " Into Thy hands, O Lord, I commend my spirit."

At the third blow he sank on his knees, with the hands clasped in prayer. " For the name of Jesus, and the defence of the Church, I am willing to die," he gasped, turning his face towards the altar of S. Benedict. Then, without moving hand or foot, he fell flat on his face with such dignity that his mantle which wrapped him was not disarranged. In this posture he received from Richard le Breton a tremendous blow which snapped the sword on the pavement. Then Hugh Mauclerc, a subdeacon of the household of De Broc, put his foot on the neck of the corpse, and with the point

[1] " Vir abominabilis."—Gervase of Canterbury.

of his sword drawing out the brains, scattered them over the pavement.

The murderers then rushed out of the church shouting, and, entering the palace, carried off all the papal bulls and letters they could lay hands on, and plundered it of gold and furniture to the value of 2,000 marks.

The crowd that flocked in from the town surrounded the body. There was a division of opinion then, as in his lifetime; some said that he had properly suffered for his obstinacy, some that "He wished to be king and more than a king; let him be a king now." Whatever horror was felt, was not at the murder, but at the desecration of the church with blood. At last the cathedral was cleared, and the gates shut.

The monks had long felt jealous at the elevation of the gay chancellor to the archbishopric. The primacy involved the abbacy of the cathedral monastery, and the primates had been, with scarcely any exceptions, chosen from among the monks. When they came to take off the clothes of the dead archbishop, they found to their delight that he wore under his ordinary dress the black habit of a monk; when they further found that beneath this habit was a hair-shirt and hair-cloth drawers, their delight became enthusiastic; and when they further discovered that this hair-cloth was "boiling over" with lice, their enthusiasm became hysterical transport.[1] His body was buried, the morning after the murder, by the Cistercian Abbot of Boxley, before the altars of SS. Augustine and John, in the crypt of the cathedral.

The Lambeth biographer says that some persons, however, argued that it was absurd to call Becket a saint and martyr, as his pretence of justice was merely a cloak for pride and vainglory; that he was lacking in charity, without which a

---

[1] They laughed and cried in wild excitement, say Roger of Hoveden and Garnier du Pont S. Maxence.

VESTMENTS OF S. THOMAS À BECKET.

man may give his body to martyrdom, and it will profit him nothing; that the cause for which he died was not a good one, and that even if it had been a good cause, his character and conduct in its defence had disqualified him from being regarded as a saint.   In defiance of Papal canonization and popular enthusiasm, it was mooted before the university of Paris whether the death of Becket was to be regarded as a just execution or a martyrdom.[1]

Not long after the murder, the archbishop of York ventured to declare that Becket had perished, like Pharaoh, in his pride.   But the multitude persisted in believing that miracles were wrought by his relics.   The papal court, vacillating, and often unfriendly in his lifetime, now took up his cause with vigour.   In 1172 legates were sent by Alexander III. to investigate the alleged miracles, and, in 1173, a council was called at Westminster to hear letters from the Pope, authorizing the invocation of the martyr as a saint. In the course of the same year he was regularly canonized.

His murderers were let off very easily.   Legend asserts that, struck with remorse, they went to Rome, to receive the sentence of Pope Alexander III., and by him were sent to expiate their sins in the Holy Land, where within three years they died.   De Tracy alone, it was said, was detained by contrary winds at Cosenza in Calabria, and died there, tearing his flesh off his bones with his teeth and nails, and shrieking, " Mercy, Thomas, mercy !"   But this is merely the fabrication of churchmen ill-satisfied with their real fate. The judgments of God are not as the judgments of men. Fitzurse went to Ireland, and became the ancestor of the

---

[1] Cæsar. Heisterbach. viii. 69.   " Beatus Thomas Episcopus Cantuariensis qui nostris temporibus pro ecclesiæ libertate usque ad mortem dimicavit, *nullis miraculis* in suis persecutionibus coruscavit, satisque de illo post occisionem disputatum est. Quidam dixerunt eum damnatum ut regni proditorem ; alii martyrem uti ecclesiæ defensorem.   Eadem quæstio Parisiis inter magistratus ventilata est.   Nam magister Rugerus juravit illum dignum fuisse morte, etsi non tali, beati viri constantiam ĳudicans contumaciam."

M'Mahon family. De Morville was dismissed from his office of justice itinerant of Northumberland and Cumberland, and in the first year of King John is recorded to have paid twenty-five marks and three good palfreys for holding his court. He procured a charter for a fair and market at Kirk Oswald, and died shortly afterwards, leaving two daughters. Within four years after the murder, De Tracy was justiciary of Normandy, and was present at Falaise in 1174, when William, king of Scotland, did homage to Henry II.; he was succeeded in his office, in 1176, by the bishop of Winchester. The present Lord Wemyss and Lord Sudeley are his lineal descendants. The pedigree, contrary to all received opinions on the subject of judgments on sacrilege, exhibits the very singular instance of an estate descending for upwards of seven hundred years in the male line of the same family.[1]

Henry II. hardly escaped excommunication and an interdict on his realm for his share in the murder. A reconciliation was at last effected with the Pope, on these terms. Henry stipulated to maintain two hundred knights at his own cost in the Holy Land, to abrogate the statutes of Clarendon, and reinvest the church of Canterbury in all the possessions and rights of which it had been deprived. He was reconciled in the porch of the cathedral of Avranches. But a further humiliation was in store for him. The crown of England was to have its Canossa, as well as that of Germany.

In 1174 Henry had to submit to open penance before the shrine of the martyr, to bare his back to the scourge willingly administered by the monks of Canterbury on his bare shoulders.

S. Thomas à Becket was not a martyr for any article of

[1] See full particulars about the fate of the murderers in Dean Stanley's " Memorials of Canterbury."

faith, or for the cause of pure morality. He was not a
martyr for the rights of the Catholic Church, not a martyr
even for the immunity of the clergy, but solely for the right
of the archbishop of Canterbury to crown a king of England ;
nay, hardly even for that, for Henry had consented to have
his son recrowned by Becket. He was a martyr for the
cause of his own resolution to punish with excommunication
those who had dared to infringe this right.

S. Thomas is represented in art, erroneously, as martyred
in full archiepiscopal canonicals before the high altar. A
sword transfixes his head.

Such of his relics as remain are—a chasuble at Sens, a
fragment of his tunic, and some portion of his brains at
S. Maria Maggiore in Rome.

Cæsarius of Heisterbach relates a miracle wrought by the
bridle of the saint's horse (viii. 70). There is a curious
account in the life of Erasmus of a visit paid by him and
Dean Colet to the shrine of S. Thomas.[1]

[1] For an elaborate account of the shrine and its fortunes and fate, see Dean Stanley's
"Memorials of Canterbury."

December 30.

S. Liberius I., *B. of Ravenna; circ.* A.D. 206.
SS. Sabinus, *B.M. of Assisi,* and Others, *MM. at Spoleto; circ.*
A.D. 303.
S. Anysia, *V.M. at Thessalonica;* A.D. 304.
S. Anysius, *B. of Thessalonica; circ.* A.D. 410.
S. Eugenius, *B. of Milan.*[1]
S. Jocundus II., *B. of Aosta;* A.D. 860.
B. Margaret Colonna, *V. at Rome;* A.D. 1284.
B. Sebastian Walfré, *C. at Verdun;* A.D. 1710.

S. LIBERIUS I., B. OF RAVENNA.

(ABOUT A.D. 206.)

[Roman Martyrology. Venerated at Ravenna on April 29 and Dec. 30.]

IBERIUS is one of the first bishops of Ravenna of whom we know anything, and that little is confined to his name. The church of Ravenna is said to have been founded by S. Apollinaris, disciple of S. Peter. He was succeeded by S. Adevitus, and both these first bishops are thought to have died as martyrs. The immediate predecessor of S. Liberius was S. Datus, who died in 185, when Liberius was elected in his room. There were afterwards two other bishops of Ravenna of the same name, Liberius II., who died in 351, and Liberius III., who sat between 374 and 379. All three are regarded as saints, and it is not easy to decide which receives veneration on the days on which the name of Liberius of Ravenna occurs in the Kalendars. But probably Liberius I. is commemorated on December 30, and either Liberius II. or Liberius III. on April 29.

[1] Unknown to history, not in any trustworthy lists of the bishops of Milan.

SS. SABINUS, B.M., AND OTHERS, MM.

(ABOUT A.D. 303.)

[Roman Martyrology and most Western Kalendars. Usuardus, Bede, Ado, &c. Authority :—The Acts in Surius, not trustworthy.]

SABINUS, bishop of Assisi, was arrested at Assisi by Venustianus, governor of Tuscany, and was cast into prison along with his deacons, Marcellus and Exuperantius. Venustianus produced a little statue of Jupiter which he kept in his bedroom, and which was habited in a gilded mantle, and required Sabinus to venerate it. The bishop took the image in his hands, flung it on the pavement, and broke it.

Venustianus was highly incensed, and ordered the hands of Sabinus to be cut off, and Marcellus and Exuperantius to be hung on the Little Horse before the eyes of their bishop, fire to be placed under them, and their sides to be torn with hooks and scrapers.

The deacons died under torment. Sabinus was then led back to prison. A fisherman-priest[1] took the bodies of the martyrs, and buried them on the third of the kalends of January (December 30). Then Serena, a Christian widow, who had the care of Bishop Sabinus in prison, led to him her son Priscianus, who was blind. The martyr raised his lopped arms towards the dark eyes, and scales fell from them, and Priscianus saw plainly. Then those who were the fellow prisoners of the saint cast themselves at his feet, and besought baptism. Nine or ten were regenerated in the prison.

What had taken place was reported to Venustianus, who himself suffered from inflamed eyes, which prevented him

[1] " Quidam piscator et presbyter."

from enjoying either food or sleep. He sent his wife to the prison to bring Sabinus to his house. And when Sabinus arrived, Venustianus and his wife and two sons prostrated themselves at his feet, and besought baptism, which Venustianus had now learned was good for sore eyes. On his issuing from the font his eyes were miraculously healed.

When the emperor Maximian heard that the prefect of Tuscany believed in Christ, he sent his tribune Lucius to execute Venustianus, Sabinus, and the wife and sons of the governor. When all were executed at Assisi, Serena took their bodies to Spoleto, and there buried them, on Dec. 7. But she put the hands of the bishop in a glass bottle with aromatic herbs.

Relics at Spoleto and Faenza; but as there are many saints of the name of Sabinus, some of those scattered about Italy may be incorrectly attributed to the martyr of Assisi.

S. ANYSIA, V.M.

(A.D. 304.)

[Roman Martyrology, introduced from the Greek Menæas and Menologies by Baronius. Authority :—The Greek Acts by Metaphrastes, in Latin in Surius. These have suffered from the mischievous rewriting by Metaphrastes, who has introduced long prayers and exhortations.]

ANYSIA was a maiden of Thessalonica, born of noble parents, brought up in the nurture and the admonition of the Lord. When her parents died, she was left with great wealth, a large house, and a crowd of slaves, male and female. She desired earnestly to be admitted to the full delights of Paradise, attained to only through stripes and celibacy.[1] She accordingly sold her goods, and distributed

---

[1] "Custodia et flagella in Christi nuptialem thalamum introducunt. . . . . Orabat, Domine Jesu Christe, præsta ne excludar thalamo."—Acta ap. Surium.

the proceeds to the poor.   One day, as she was going out
of a gate of Thessalonica, a heathen, struck by her beauty,
addressed her in tones of insolent familiarity.   The modest
girl in terror crossed herself.   He saw at once that she was
a Christian, and, drawing his sword, ran it into her side. She
sank and bled to death on the spot.

The church of Thessalonica raised an oratory over the
place of the martyrdom directly peace was established.
There is no reason to doubt that the main facts of this martyrdom are true.   No doubt Anysius, bishop of Thessalonica, received his baptismal name from the circumstance
of her martyrdom being fresh in men's memory when he
was born.

S. ANYSIUS, B. OF THESSALONICA.

(ABOUT A.D. 410.)

[Roman Martyrology and Greek Menæas.   Dec. 30 seems the day
of the election of S. Anysius.   Authorities :—The Epistles of Pope
Damasus and S. Ambrose.]

IN 383 S. Paulinus of Nola went with S. Epiphanius to
Thessalonica, where S. Anascholius had just died.   The
bishops of Macedonia and the clergy of Thessalonica wrote
to S. Ambrose thereupon, and stated that they had elected
Anysius, the disciple of the deceased prelate, to fill his
room.   S. Ambrose replied, eulogizing Anascholius, and
felicitating Anysius on his elevation, exhorting him to
follow the example of his predecessor.   Pope Damasus also
wrote to Anysius to recommend him to see after the well-
being of the Church in Eastern Illyria.   When Paulinus and
Epiphanius came to Thessalonica they were received by the
new bishop.   Anysius had the sad fortune to rule the Church
of Thessalonica when the horrible massacre was carried out

there in 389 by orders of the Emperor Theodosius. Botheric, who commanded the imperial troops in Illyria, and resided at Thessalonica, threw into prison a charioteer of the circus, who had been guilty of an attempt to commit an abominable crime. A great festival was coming on, and the people wanted the charioteer to drive in the circus, and begged that he might be set at liberty. Botheric refused, whereupon a riot of the people ensued, in which he and several of his officers were killed by the mob with stones and cudgels.

Theodosius was furious when he heard of the murder, and sent prompt orders that the people of Thessalonica should be assembled in the circus, and that 7,000 persons should be killed to atone for the riot. Rufinus, Master of the Offices, is said to have goaded Theodosius to this act of barbarity. When the circus was full, suddenly soldiers closed all passages of egress, and fell on the mob, and killed till they had made up the tale of 7,000. Some specially sad instances are mentioned as occurring. A merchant, who had taken his sons to see the sight, implored the soldiers to spare his children. They replied that they must make up the tale, and could only spare one. As the disconsolate father looked from one boy to the other, unable to resolve which to sacrifice, the impatient soldiers cut both down. A slave is said to have generously redeemed his master by offering his own breast to the sword. Several strangers who did not belong to Thessalonica were involved in the massacre.

In 391 a council at Capua had considered the errors of Bonosus, bishop of Sardica, who denied the perpetual virginity of B.V. Mary, and said that she was the mother of James and others. He also had disputed the divinity of our Lord. The council of Capua requested the bishops of Macedonia, with Anysius of Thessalonica at their head, to

consult on the heresy of Bonosus, and condemn him. The
Macedonian bishops wished to refer the case to the Italian
bishops; but the latter replied that, as the council of Capua
had appointed the Macedonians as judges, they must submit to the order of the council. Anysius and the other
bishops of Macedonia accordingly met and suspended
Bonosus.

In 404 S. Anysius and fifteen bishops of the party of S.
John Chrysostom wrote to Pope Innocent on the desolation
in which lay the Church of Constantinople, whilst its chief
pastor was languishing in exile at Cucusus, and referred the
matter in dispute, which had caused his banishment, to the
judgment of Innocent. Nothing further is heard of S.
Anysius.

B. MARGARET COLONNA, V.

(A.D. 1284.)

[Beatified by Pius IX. in 1847 ; and inserted in the Martyrology on
Dec. 30.]

THE Blessed Margaret was born a scion of the illustrious
and princely house of Colonna at Rome. She was left an
orphan when a child, and was brought up by her brothers,
who wanted to get her married when quite young, and so
rid themselves of their responsibility for her. But one of
them, James, who was studying at Bologna, and was destined
for the Church, opposed the others, and inspired in the
mind of the young girl an ardent desire to embrace the life of
celibacy. She escaped from her brothers' house, and having
cut off her long hair, took refuge in the house of the Poor
Clares, near Rome. She undertook the nursing of the sick,
and having overcome her natural repugnance to the sight of
their sores and the disagreeable nature of the unaccustomed

work to which she had devoted herself, passed through her profession, but was not admitted to take the veil on account of her being sickly. She accompanied her brother James, now a cardinal, on a visit of piety to the tombs of the Apostles. She suffered from a tumour during seven years, and died, whilst still young, in 1284.

December 31.

SS. Donatus, Paulinus, and Others, *MM. at Rome.*
S. Columba, *V.M. at Sens;* A.D. 274.
S. Sabinian, *B. of Sens; circ.* A.D. 300.
S. Sylvester, *Pope of Rome;* A.D. 335.
S. Barbatianus, *P. at Ravenna;* 5th cent.
S. Melania the Younger, *Mat. at Jerusalem;* A.D. 439.
S. Marius, *B. of Avenches in Switzerland; circ.* A.D. 593.
S. Leobart, *Ab. of Saverne in Elsass;* A.D. 607.
B. Warembert, *Ab. of Mont-Saint-Martin, near Cambrai;* A.D. 1141.
S. John Francis Regis, *S.J. at Louvesc in Dauphiné;* A.D. 1640 (*see* June 16).[1]

S. COLUMBA, V.M.

(A.D. 274.)

[Roman and Gallican Martyrologies. Usuardus, Ado, &c. Authority :—The Acts, late and untrustworthy.]

 COLUMBA, a native of Spain, of royal family still heathen, illumined by Divine grace, left her home at the age of sixteen, and came into Gaul along with S. Beatus, S. Sanctianus, and S. Augustine. She was baptized at Vienne, where a baptistery is shown in the church of the nunnery of S. Benedict, called after her, and where she is supposed to have received the sacrament of regeneration. It is much more probable that the baptistery had its dedication to the Holy Ghost in the form of a dove.

In the year 274 Aurelian was in Gaul and at Sens. He ordered the execution of S. Columba and her companions.

[1] He died on Dec. 31, but his commemoration was moved by Clement XI. to May 24, and by Clement XII. to June 16.

The church of S. Columba the Less in Sens is said to occupy the site of her prison. But previous to the execution Columba was sent to the amphitheatre, and lodged in one of the cells near where the wild beasts were confined. Aurelian offered a young man of his court to abandon the virgin to his passions. But when the youth approached Columba, a bear came upon him, and began to hug him with an ardour which threatened to break in his ribs. The young man struggled, and the virgin bade the bear let go. Bruin obeyed with a sulky growl, and retired; and the ravisher thought it best to follow the example of the bear, and disappear likewise.

Aurelian then ordered soldiers to enter the dungeon and draw Columba forth. The bear, however, threatened them with his paws, and they contented themselves with an attempt to smoke him out. A shower came on and extinguished the flames. The bear was allowed to depart, and Columba surrendered herself to the officers, who conducted her before Aurelian, and at his command her head was struck off outside the city, on the side of the road which now leads to Meaux; where afterwards was reared the abbey of S. Columba, which served as the asylum of Becket whilst in exile at Sens.

The relics of S. Columba are still shown in the cathedral of Sens.

S. SYLVESTER, POPE.

(A.D. 335.)

[Roman Martyrology and all Latin Martyrologies and Kalendars. Authority :—Anastasius Bibliothecarius.]

SYLVESTER was the son of a certain Rufinus, a Roman. He succeeded Melchiades in the chair of S. Peter, 314.

S. SYLVESTER. After Cahier.

His election took place on the 31st of January. When
Maxentius held Rome, Sylvester, not then Pope, had retired
for safety, or was driven, to Mount Soracte, and remained
there in concealment till Constantine defeated the tyrant at
Saxa Rubra, and Maxentius was drowned in attempting to
escape into Rome across the Milvian bridge (A.D. 312).
After the battle Sylvester returned to Rome, and two years
later succeeded Melchiades. Constantine is said to have
offered him a golden diadem set with jewels, but Sylvester
refused it, and wore instead a white Phrygian cap or mitre.

At the exhortation of Sylvester, Constantine built a
church near the Baths of Diocletian, and endowed it with a
farm. Sylvester issued several constitutions for the Church
of Rome. He ordered that chrism should be consecrated
by bishops only, but that priests might administer confirmation with it in emergency, as in that of approaching death. A
deacon was to wear a dalmatic when serving at the altar,
and his left shoulder should be covered with a linen napkin.[1]
A priest in celebrating was not to use silk or coloured cloth,
but linen, and that white, because the Lord's body was laid
in white linen.[2]

Constantine built the Lateran church and adorned the
pediment with a silver figure of Christ enthroned, with the
twelve apostles bearing silver crowns. He also placed in the
apse a figure of the Saviour, of silver, five feet high, and four
silver angels with " golden crowns and dolphins." He set up
a fountain of porphyry and silver near this basilica, on a
porphyry pillar stood a golden lamb, from which spouted the
water, and in the middle of the fountain was a phial containing balsam to be used for the lamps at night on the

---

[1] "Constituit ut Diaconi dalmatica uterentur in Ecclesia, et pallio linostimo læva
torum tegerentur."—Anast. in S. Silvest.

[2] Not apparently the vestments of the priest, but the napkins and corporals for the
Eucharist.

Paschal festival. On one side of the lamb stood a statue of
the Saviour, of silver ; on the other, one of the Baptist, bearing a scroll on which was engraved, " Behold the Lamb of
God, that taketh away the sins of the world." There were
also four silver stags which spouted water. Sylvester and
Constantine are the subjects of a forgery which was pro-
ductive of important results. In 728 Pope Gregory II.
made an attempt to form a confederation of States in Italy
which was to maintain itself against the Greek empire and
the Lombard kingdom. And, according to his scheme,
the papal chair was to be the head and centre of this confederation. The plan came to nothing. In Rome, however,
the idea ripened more and more, that the power of the Pope
might come forward in Italy and take the place of the
decaying power of the Greeks and the reluctantly tolerated
power of the Lombards. Accordingly between 752 and
777 a document was forged purporting to be a donation
made by Constantine, containing the following grants :—

1. Constantine desires to promote the chair of Peter over
the empire and its seat on earth, by bestowing on it imperial power and honour.

2. The chair of Peter shall have supreme authority over
the patriarchal chairs of Alexandria, Antioch, Jerusalem,
and Constantinople, and over all Churches in the world.

3. It shall be judge in all that concerns the service of
God and the Christian faith.

4. Instead of the diadem which the emperor wished to
place on the Pope's head, but which the Pope refused, Constantine gives him and his successors the phrygium (*i.e.* the
tiara) and the lorum which adorned the emperors' neck, as
well as the other gorgeous robes and insignia of the imperial
dignity.

5. The Roman clergy shall enjoy the high privileges of
the imperial senate, be eligible to the dignity of patrician or

consul, and have right to wear the decoration worn by the optimates or nobles in office under the empire.

6. The offices of cubicularii, ostiarii, and excubitores shall belong to the Roman Church.

7. The Roman clergy shall ride on horses decked with white coverings, and, like the senate, wear white sandals.

8. If a member of the senate shall wish to take orders, and the Pope consents, no one shall hinder him.

9. Constantine gives up the remaining sovereignty over Rome, the provinces, cities, and towns of the whole of Italy *or*[1] of the Western regions, to Pope Sylvester and his successors.

Pope Leo IX. recounted nearly the whole text of the donation to the patriarch Michael Cerularius in 1054, openly and confidently, without, apparently, the shadow of a suspicion that the document was forged.

He wished the patriarch to convince himself " of the earthly and heavenly imperial power, the royal priesthood, of the Roman chair," and to retain no suspicion " that this chair ' wished to usurp power by the help of foolish and old wives' fables. ' " On the strength of this document Urban II. claimed Corsica in 1091. On it also Hadrian IV. rested his claim to give Ireland to Henry II. in 1155.[2]

A story was fabricated, or grew up, to account for the donation. According to this tale, Constantine was afflicted with leprosy, and Sylvester baptized him in a porphyry basin. In gratitude for the cure which was the result of the baptism, Constantine made the donation. In a mosaic on the frieze of the Lateran basilica the scene of the baptism of Constantine by the Pope is represented. In reality, the emperor was baptized on his deathbed at Nicomedia, by

---

[1] Later the " aut," *or*, was changed into " et," *and;* for purposes which may be guessed.

[2] For a full account of the forged donation, see Dr. Döllinger's " Fables of the Popes in the Middle Ages."

the Arian Eusebius, bishop of that city. The Roman Martyrology and Breviary, however, still assert that "S. Sylvester baptized Constantine."

When the council of Nicæa met, Sylvester was very old, and unable to attend, and he sent in his place the two priests, who, according to the arrangement laid down by the emperor, would have accompanied him had he been able to make the journey. In this simple deputation later writers have seen the first germ of "legati a latere."

In order to supplement history and give Sylvester a more prominent place in the decision of the Arian controversy, a fable was invented, according to which, on the return of Victor and Vincent, the two priests who represented Sylvester at Nicæa, the aged pontiff summoned a council of 277 bishops, in which Sylvester reviewed the decrees of Nicæa, and formally ratified them. There was probably a synod in his reign in which the regulations were passed already mentioned, relative to the dress of deacons and the altar linen. But the story of a council of Western bishops held after Nicæa is a fable.[1]

Constantine is credited with the murder of his son Crispus, his wife Fausta, and his nephew Licinius. He, no doubt, felt great agony of remorse for his crimes, and his last visit to Rome, and the foundation of the churches there, already recorded, with their costly adornments, were probably the fruits of his penitence. According to one legend, Hosius of Cordova comforted the conscience-tortured monarch with promises of forgiveness in the Church. According to a story told by Sozomen, Constantine applied to a philosopher named Sosipater, who told him that there was no place of repentance for those guilty of such crimes. He

---

[1] Guerin and Giry assert it as history ! but then they also give at length the story of Constantine's leprosy and baptism by Sylvester, with only a faint qualification, and an attack on Eusebius, to discredit the statement of the historian, so as to substantiate the fable.

then applied to "some bishops, who told him that he would be cleansed from sin on repentance and the reception of baptism." But Sozomen rejects this story as "the invention of persons who desired to vilify the Christian religion." But it is easy to see how from this germ grew the legend of Constantine covered with leprosy (sin), seeking first cleansing in heathen rites and a bath of infants' blood, and then turning to Christianity and finding cleansing in baptism. When the forgery of the Donation was well established, this fable naturally attached itself to it, and the baptizer became Sylvester.[1]

S. Sylvester is represented trampling on a dragon,[2] the symbol of the paganism which received its death-stroke from Constantine in his reign.

S. MELANIA THE YOUNGER.

(ABOUT A.D. 439.)

[Roman Martyrology, introduced from the Greek Menæa. Authorities :—A Life by Metaphrastes ; and one in the "Lives of the Fathers of the Desert." She is mentioned also by S. Paulinus of Nola and S. Augustine.]

MELANIA, daughter of a consul, mother of a prætor, belonged to the illustrious family of Marcellinus, of Spanish origin. She was related to S. Paulinus of Nola, and was second to none in Aquitaine and Spain for wealth and nobility. She was born at Rome in 342 or 343, about two years after the consulate of Marcellinus, whose granddaughter she was.

Melania was married to a man in high office, whose name

---

[1] Metaphrastes gives a long story of Sylvester withstanding in argument a Jew named Zambres, and of his raising a dead bull to life, at sight of which miracle S. Helena asked for baptism.

[2] " Parce qu'il en fit mourir un à Rome, qui en corrompait l'air et causait la mort à beaucoup de monde par l'infection de son haleine."—Guerin et Giry.

is, however, not recorded ; and she bore him three children. He died and left her a widow when she was only twenty-three. She lost two of her children, and there remained to her only a son, Publicola. She then placed her child with guardians, and started on a pilgrimage to the East with Rufi-nus, priest of Aquileja. She arrived in Alexandria in 372, the last year of the life of S. Athanasius. She saw the great bishop of Alexandria, and received from his hands a relic of the Thebaid, a sheepskin which he had received from the holy abbot Macarius. She also met the priest Isidore the Hospitaller, who had attended S. Athanasius to Rome during the consulate of her grandfather, Marcellinus. She also visited the virgin Alexandra. This maiden was a slave girl, who, fearing her own beauty, and in pity for the poor soul of him who loved her, had buried herself alive in an empty tomb, and remained ten years without permitting any one to see her face.

Isidore had been brought up among the solitaries of Nitria, and as he spoke of their virtues to Melania, she resolved to visit the desert where they dwelt, and there she saw and conversed with S. Pambo and other illustrious anchorites.

On the death of S. Athanasius, the Arians, protected by the emperor Valens, persecuted the Catholics in Egypt. Many bishops, priests, and hermits were banished. Melania used her fortune to relieve their necessities. This S. Paulinus relates in a letter to Sulpicius Severus. He says that she fed during three days 5,000 solitaries who were in concealment, at great risk to herself. Melania followed 126 exiled bishops and hermits to Diocæsarea in Palestine, and supported them from her private fortune. As the guards were forbidden to allow their friends to visit them, Melania disguised herself as a slave, and carried them every evening their food. She was arrested by the governor, and put in prison.

She sent the consular magistrate this message: "I am the daughter of a consul. I have been the wife of a man illustrious in his generation; now I am the servant of Christ. Despise me not because of my mean dress, for I can attain a higher rank if I will; and I have sufficient credit to keep me from fearing you, and to hinder you from touching my goods. But lest you should do wrong by ignorance, I have thought fit to let you know who I am." And she added, "We must make head against fools, setting our pride against their insolence, as we loose a hound or a falcon against the deer."

When the magistrate heard who she was, and to what a powerful and wealthy family she belonged, he precipitately threw open the prison doors, showed her the most profound respect, and gave her full liberty to visit the exiles.

She founded a monastery at Jerusalem, in which she placed fifty virgins. For twenty-five years she devoted to the relief of the poor, and the entertainment of the bishops, monks, and pilgrims of every description, who came in swarms to the holy places, her own services, and the revenues drawn from her lands in Spain and Aquitaine, wrung from the hardworking labourers. She was guided and seconded by Rufinus, who inhabited a cell on the Mount of Olives, and who was at that period the old and tender friend of S. Jerome. A dispute afterwards took place between Rufinus and Jerome, as related in the life of the latter, occasioned by the doctrines of Origen. Their rupture long agitated the Church, and drew from them melancholy invectives against each other. Melania naturally sided with her guide Rufinus, and for having countenanced Origenist errors, has been excluded from the Martyrology of the Latin Church and the Menæas of the East. She is called Melania the Elder.

In the meantime her son Publicola had grown up, and

married Albina, daughter of Albinus and sister of Volusia-nus, præfect of Rome, whose family was one of the most illustrious in the empire.

From this marriage issued S. Melania the Younger. She was born about 382, and was brought up from infancy with the example of her grandmother held up to her as deserving of imitation. At the age of fourteen she was married to Pinianus, son of Severus, præfect of Italy and Africa; her husband was only seventeen. She became the mother of a daughter, whom she dedicated from her cradle to virginity. She had no taste for, or a religious prejudice against, conjugal union, and she besought her husband to let them separate. He refused till Melania was being confined a second time, when, in his alarm for her life, he vowed to yield. She gave birth to a child, which was baptized, and died immediately after. Her daughter also did not survive infancy. Accordingly, so soon as Melania was well, in 401, when she was aged twenty, and he twenty-four, it was arranged between them that they should separate. When Melania the Elder heard in Palestine of the determination of her granddaughter, nothing could exceed her enthusiasm and gratification. Although aged sixty, she at once started for Rome to encourage her granddaughter in her resolution, and by her presence prevent a foolish or sinful weakness from overcoming Melania, and drawing her back to the arms of the husband whom she had sworn to love and cherish so long as life should last. Albina, mother of the young Melania, disapproved of her conduct, but Melania the Elder was able to overcome this disapproval, and convert it into approval, and persuade her also to desert her husband, and join her in the exercises of the religious, as opposed to the family, life.

The brother of Pinianus, and his father Severus, were naturally incensed; and finding that Melania, without protest from her husband, was, as they thought, squandering his fortune on beggars and hermits, they seized on his estates and administered them for him. But Melania complained to the empress, her relative, and by her influence Honorius relieved Melania and her husband from all inconvenience from the relations of the latter. They sold their estates in Rome, Italy, Aquitaine, Spain, and Britain, and the result of this sale produced such a sum that it was thought that none but the emperor possessed more. The father and brother of Pinianus beheld this dispersion of the family estates with mingled emotions of rage and contempt ; but they were unable to oppose the emperor, who had sanctioned it. The only estates not disposed of were some in Campania, Sicily, and Africa, which belonged to Melania herself, and of which she could not dispose till her father's death.

The money obtained by the sales was spent in founding monasteries, feeding the idle and the indigent, and adorning churches with vessels of gold and silver. She emancipated her slaves, but many of them would not receive their freedom, and passed to the service of her brother Publicola. She sent messengers to Egypt, Antioch, and Jerusalem laden with money for the use of hermits and monks. The two Melanias and Albina, who now lived together almost inseparably, often visited S. Paulinus of Nola, their kinsman, and received from him warm encouragement.

Palladius, bishop of Helenopolis in Bithynia, like Rufinus, the panegyrist of the desert dwellers, came to Rome in 404 or 405, and remained there till the beginning of 406, and was received by the three ladies with much honour and affection. "When we were in Rome," he says, " they received us with every demonstration of respect, and made us the best cheer, rendering themselves worthy, by their hospitality and their holy manner of life, of participating in the eternal life of our Lord Jesus Christ."

Publicola, father of the younger Melania and son of the

elder of that name, would not allow his daughter and mother and wife to leave Rome, and give themselves up to all the extravagant asceticism of their highly enthusiastic desires. But on his death, in 407, Albina and Melania the Younger were free. The elder Melania was then in Africa, visiting and consoling the hermits in the desert. The younger Melania and Albina went to S. Paulinus for his advice, and Pinianus was consigned to cabbage-gardening with thirty solitaries.

Pinianus offered for sale his palace in Rome, but it was so splendid that no one could bid for it a worthy price till after 410, when Rome had been entered by the Goths, or the palace had been fired and plundered, by which its value was reduced. But before Alaric came to Rome at the head of his Goths, Melania, Albina, and Pinianus had taken refuge in Sicily with their treasures. Melania the Elder went on to Jerusalem, and there died, forty days after her arrival. Melania the Younger, drawing in her train her mother and husband, now left Sicily for Africa, that she might refresh her soul by a contemplation of the ascetic lives of the anchorites of the desert, of whom she had heard so much, and in the hope that their example would inspire Pinianus with ambition to settle in the wastes of Scete or Nitria among them, and disembarrass her of his somewhat burdensome society.

On their way they landed at Malta, and found the inhabitants suffering from a visit of barbarians, who threatened to pillage them and burn their houses unless they paid a heavy ransom. Melania and her husband gave large alms to the bishop, and he paid it to the Vandal freebooters, who thereupon left the island without further molestation.

Thence Melania and her party went to Africa and visited Tagaste, where Alypius, the friend of S. Augustine, was bishop. They gave costly ornaments to his church, and endowed and built two monasteries there : one for eighty monks, the other for 130 virgins. They were unable to see S. Augustine at Tagaste, for he was at Hippo ; they therefore visited him in his see, and gave liberal presents to the poor and to the Church. Pinianus was fearful of being chosen by the people to be priest at Hippo, for the sake of his wealth, and he extracted from S. Augustine a promise that he would not ordain him.

One day the people began to clamour for Pinianus as their priest, S. Augustine then told them of the promise he had made. The crowd thereupon broke into abuse of S. Alypius, who, they thought, wanted the wealthy man as priest for one of his churches ; and they would not be pacified till Pinianus swore solemnly that he would be ordained priest nowhere else but at Hippo.

Albina, who had remained behind at Tagaste, on hearing what had taken place wrote a letter full of feminine scolding to S. Augustine: "As for the people of Hippo," she said, "all they wanted was a man of fortune who could throw away money among them." Augustine wrote to pacify her and to give a better colour to the motives of his people. After seven years stay at Tagaste and Hippo, Melania carried her mother and husband with her to the Holy Land, A.D. 417, visiting S. Cyril on the way, at Alexandria.

In Palestine they met Pelagius, and were thrown into some doubt as to the soundness of his doctrines. They wrote to S. Augustine about them, and he sent to them in reply his two books on "The Grace of Jesus Christ" and on "Original Sin," which he addressed to them in 418.

From Palestine Melania took her husband into Egypt to visit the solitaries of Nitria, but they returned before 419 ; for S. Jerome in writing to S. Augustine in that year, saluted him on their part and that of Albina, whose age had prevented her accompanying Melania and Pinianus to Egypt. Whilst Melania was absent, S. Jerome prepared for her a

cell on the Mount of Olives, and on her return she shut
herself up in it, and saw no one but her mother, her husband, and a cousin, who were allowed to visit her once every
five days.

Melania passed fourteen years in this cell, and only left
it to pay her last duties to her mother, who died in 432.
Then she went into another cell, but left it after a year, to
place herself with a community of virgins in a convent she
built to receive them.

Pinianus died about the end of the year 435.

The brother of Albina was Volusianus, who was a heathen;
indeed the conduct of his sister and his niece had probably
seemed so foolish and offensive in his eyes, that he had
been hardened in his disgust at Christianity. But Volusianus may have seen that the days of the old religion of
Rome were ended past revival, and that it was in vain to
hope for its restoration. He therefore bowed to the inevitable, and prepared to give in his submission to the religion
of the emperors. He sent for Melania, and she hastened to
Constantinople, and found him prostrated by an accident.
She had the satisfaction of seeing him baptized before he
died.

She returned full of joy in the winter to Jerusalem. She
then built another monastery, and the Empress Eudoxia
visited Jerusalem whilst it was being built. Eudoxia put her
ankle out of joint on that visit; Melania replaced it with skill,
and, as the empress said with Oriental courtesy and exaggeration, without really hurting her at all.

Four years after the death of her husband, Melania made
a visit to Bethlehem at Christmas, and then hastened to
Jerusalem. She caught a chill whilst praying in the church
of S. Stephen, and died on the last day of the year, apparently that following the year 439, in which Eudoxia came to
Jerusalem.

S. MARIUS, B. OF AVENCHES.

(ABOUT A.D. 593.)

[Gallican Martyrology. Authority :—Acts of 2nd Council of Mâcon.]

MARIUS, bishop of Aventiacum, an old Roman city in Switzerland, now represented by Avenches, assisted with S. Palladius of Saintes, S. Prætextatus of Rouen, S. Evantius of Vienne, and other illustrious prelates of his age in the second council of Mâcon in 585.   S. Marius is the author of a continuation of the Chronicle of Prosper from the year 455, at which that of Prosper closes, to the year 581.   It contains chiefly events which occurred in Burgundy, and in the neighbourhood of the Lake of Geneva.

END OF VOL. XV.

Printed by BALLANTYNE, HANSON & Co.
at Paul's Work, Edinburgh